COOPERATION AND CONFLICT

Cooperation and Conflict

GDR Theatre Censorship, 1961–1989

LAURA BRADLEY

OXFORD

UNIVERSITY PRESS

OXFORD
UNIVERSITY PRESS

Great Clarendon Street, Oxford OX2 6DP

Oxford University Press is a department of the University of Oxford.
It furthers the University's objective of excellence in research, scholarship,
and education by publishing worldwide in

Oxford New York

Auckland Cape Town Dar es Salaam Hong Kong Karachi
Kuala Lumpur Madrid Melbourne Mexico City Nairobi
New Delhi Shanghai Taipei Toronto

With offices in

Argentina Austria Brazil Chile Czech Republic France Greece
Guatemala Hungary Italy Japan Poland Portugal Singapore
South Korea Switzerland Thailand Turkey Ukraine Vietnam

Oxford is a registered trade mark of Oxford University Press
in the UK and in certain other countries

Published in the United States
by Oxford University Press Inc., New York

© Laura Bradley 2010

The moral rights of the author have been asserted
Database right Oxford University Press (maker)

First published 2010

British Library Cataloguing in Publication Data

Data available

Library of Congress Cataloging in Publication Data

Data available

Typeset by SPI Publisher Services, Pondicherry, India
Printed in Great Britain
on acid-free paper by
MPG Books Group, Bodmin and King's Lynn

ISBN 978-0-19-958963-0

3 5 7 9 10 8 6 4 2

Acknowledgements

This monograph would not have been possible without the generous support of several institutions and funding bodies. I began the project during a Junior Research Fellowship at Merton College, Oxford, and completed it at the University of Edinburgh. I am grateful to both institutions for their support, and to the British Academy, Carnegie Trust, and the German Academic Exchange Service (DAAD) for providing additional funding for the archival work. A Research Leave Award from the Arts and Humanities Research Council provided me with the time needed to finish writing the book. I would like to thank my colleagues at Edinburgh for taking a lively interest in my research, and I particularly wish to thank Sabine Rolle, Frauke Matthes, and Corinna Häger for discussing linguistic nuances and details.

I am very grateful to all the archivists who helped me during the project, and to the people who kindly agreed to discuss their experiences of GDR theatre with me: Carmen-Maja Antoni, Uwe Behnisch, Josef Budek, Eveline Günther, Erika Hinckel, Arno Hochmuth, Petra Hübner, Bärbel Jaksch, Manfred Karge, Klaus Dieter Kirst, Karen Knittel, Michael Lorenz, Konstanze Mach-Meyerhofer, Grit Richter-Laugwitz, Kathrin Riedel, Monika Schmidt, Christoph Schroth, Barbara Schultz, Ernst Schumacher, Peter Ullrich, Siegfried Wilzopolski, Sabine Wolf, and Sabine Zolchow. Special thanks go to Raphaela Schröder for her untiring efforts in tracking down files at the BStU.

Finally, I wish to thank the following for kind permission to publish material in this book: Uwe Behnisch, the Berliner Ensemble, the Bertolt-Brecht-Archiv, Adelheid Beyer, Volker Braun, Barbara Brecht-Schall, Josef Budek, the Deutsches Theatermuseum München, Eveline Günther, Michael Hamburger, the Institut für Europäische Geschichte (Mainz), Lars Jung, Manfred Karge, Klaus Dieter Kirst, Irina Liebmann, Jörg Liljeberg, Sigrid Meixner, the MHRA and Maney Publishing, Miroslaw Nowotny, Christoph Schroth, the Staatsschauspiel Dresden, the Stadtmuseum Berlin, the Stiftung Archiv der Akademie der Künste, Peer-Uwe Teska, Peter Ullrich, the Volksbühne, John Wiley and Sons, and Siegfried Wilzopolski. All reasonable effort has been made to trace the holders of copyright in materials reproduced in this book, and any omissions will be rectified in future printings if notice is given to the publisher.

L.B.

Contents

List of Illustrations

List of Abbreviations

AdK	Stiftung Archiv der Akademie der Künste
AdSV	Archiv des Schriftstellerverbandes
BArch	Bundesarchiv
BB	'Büchners Briefe'
BBA	Bertolt-Brecht-Archiv
BE	Berliner Ensemble
BEA	Berliner Ensemble Archive
BStU	Archiv der Bundesbehörde für die Unterlagen des Sicherheitsdienstes der ehemaligen Deutschen Demokratischen Republik
CSA	Christoph-Schroth-Archiv
DDR	Deutsche Demokratische Republik
DEFA	Deutsche Film AG
DT	Deutsches Theater
DTA	Deutsches Theater Archive
DTO	Direktion für Theater und Orchester
FAZ	*Frankfurter Allgemeine Zeitung*
FDGB	Freie Deutsche Gewerkschaftsbund
FDJ	Freie Deutsche Jugend
GDR	German Democratic Republic
GLL	*German Life and Letters*
IM	Inoffizieller Mitarbeiter
IMB	Inoffizieller Mitarbeiter Bearbeitung
IME	Inoffizieller Mitarbeiter im besonderen Einsatz
IMK/KW	Inoffizieller Mitarbeiter Konspiration/konspirative Wohnung
LAB	Landesarchiv Berlin
LHAS	Landeshauptarchiv Schwerin
LHASA, Abt. MER	Landeshauptarchiv Sachsen-Anhalt, Abteilung Merseburg
LL	*Leonce und Lena*

MK	*Michael Kohlhaas*
MLN	*Modern Language Notes*
ND	*Neues Deutschland*
n.p.	no pagination
OV	Operativ-Vorgang
RDA	République démocratique allemande
RdB	Rat des Bezirks
RIAS	Radio in the American Sector
SächsStA-D	Sächsisches Hauptstaatsarchiv Dresden
SächsStA-L	Sächsisches Staatsarchiv Leipzig
SB	Stadtmuseum Berlin
SED	Sozialistische Einheitspartei Deutschlands
SED-BL	Bezirksleitung der Sozialistischen Einheitspartei Deutschlands
sen.	senior
SgT	*Sieben gegen Theben*
Stasi	Ministerium für Staatssicherheit
TdZ	*Theater der Zeit*
USSR	Union of Soviet Socialist Republics
VA	Volksbühne Archive
VdT	Verband der Theaterschaffenden
ZK	Zentralkomitee

Map. Administrative map of the GDR, showing regional capitals and theatres featured in case studies. Names of small towns are in italics. Basemap © IEG Mainz / A. Kunz

1

Introduction

1. THEATRE CENSORSHIP: PROBLEMS AND APPROACHES

Theatre poses distinctive challenges to any regime that seeks to control it. A script is only the starting point for a production, and much of the production's impact will depend on how the director has interpreted the script, using the acting, set design, and costumes. Actors recreate the production for each performance, communicating live with their audience, and they may introduce significant changes during the performance run. So censorship checks of the script or dress rehearsal can never offer the same level of security as pre-publication controls on literature, or as the final checks before a film is released. Censors can only attempt to predict how audiences will respond to performances, and spectators may subsequently find controversial allusions even where none were intended. If they do, laughter can spread quickly through an auditorium, allowing individual spectators to participate in an experience of collective subversion. This explains why the public nature of theatrical reception is a source of particular anxiety to censors.

In the German Democratic Republic, the media and arts were subject to a strict regime of censorship. Writers faced lengthy publication controls, and the state and Party authorities scrutinized their texts closely. Yet the fact that a play had been published in the GDR did not mean that any theatre was allowed to stage it, or even that it could be staged at all. The dramatist and novelist Christoph Hein experienced pre-publication and pre-performance censorship in the GDR, and he argues that the controls on theatre were more formidable. At the Tenth Writers' Congress in 1987, Hein asked those of his colleagues less familiar with theatre to imagine a printed, bound book being checked again by the authorities in every region, district, and town to see if its

2   *Introduction*

sale should be permitted in local bookshops.[1] This was, in effect, the situation that dramatists faced whenever a theatre decided to stage one of their plays. Directors and actors faced further challenges. Whilst a writer could keep a manuscript under wraps until the cultural climate thawed, a director could not do the same with a finished production. And as directors needed an institutional base, they relied on finding theatre managers and functionaries willing to employ them. It was not until the late 1980s that independent, non-legal theatre groups began to operate outside the official system.[2]

The considerable restrictions on performance in the GDR reflect the importance that the ruling Socialist Unity Party (SED) attached to theatre. SED cultural politicians subscribed to the Schillerian view of theatre as a 'moral institution' engaged in the education of society. In a famous lecture in 1784, Friedrich Schiller had argued that theatre had a vital civic role to play alongside the law: whilst laws served to restrict and proscribe certain forms of behaviour, theatre could encourage spectators to aspire to ideals, and it could promote social and national cohesion.[3] These ideas remained influential in the GDR, and policy-makers wanted theatre to play a positive role in shaping the identity of the new state and its citizens. Contemporary plays were given the task of reflecting society's progress towards socialism, helping to create socialist citizens, and even increasing industrial productivity. At the same time, Marxist-Leninist interpretations of canonical works were designed to demonstrate the GDR's historical roots and to present it as the true Germany, distinct from the Federal Republic. Theatre also emerged as a valuable source of prestige, capable of projecting a positive image of the GDR abroad. This was particularly important during the GDR's battle for diplomatic recognition in the 1950s and 1960s, when the Federal

---

[1] Christoph Hein, 'Literatur und Wirkung', in *X. Schriftstellerkongreß der Deutschen Demokratischen Republik*, ed. Schriftstellerverband der DDR, 2 vols. (East Berlin: Aufbau, 1988), ii. 225–47 at 240.

[2] The absence of legal loopholes distinguished GDR censorship from the systems in imperial Germany and the United Kingdom, where private performances for members' clubs were exempt from licensing regulations. UK theatre censorship was abolished in 1968. See Gary Stark, *Banned in Berlin: Literary Censorship in Imperial Germany, 1871–1918*, Monographs in German History, 25 (New York and Oxford: Berghahn, 2009), 18–19, 269; Steve Nicholson, *The Censorship of British Drama: 1900–1968*, 4 vols. (Exeter: University of Exeter Press, 2003–), i (2003): *1900–1932*, 31.

[3] Friedrich Schiller, 'Was kann eine gute stehende Schaubühne eigentlich wirken?', in Friedrich Schiller, *Sämtliche Werke*, 2nd rev. edn., 5 vols. (Munich: Carl Hanser, 1960), v. 818–31. On the use of Schiller's view of theatre to justify censorship in imperial Germany, see Stark, *Banned in Berlin*, 10–11.

Republic threatened to break off diplomatic relations with any state that officially recognized the GDR. The Berliner Ensemble—one of the leading East German theatres—acted as a cultural ambassador, representing the GDR on its tours to London and Paris at a time when the state's diplomats could not.

Conflicts over individual censorship decisions occurred from the 1950s through to the 1980s, but the need for theatre to be regulated was not widely questioned until 1987–9. Leninist doctrine gave the SED the right to control and influence cultural processes, and members were bound to follow Party decisions. At the same time, the creation of an anti-fascist, socialist order commanded a support from theatre practitioners that never entirely dissipated, even as disillusionment with the Party leadership increased. There was a widespread consensus among practitioners that theatre should intervene in society; disagreements with officials often focused on the purposes and nature of that intervention. Controversial productions tended to criticize the system from within, seeking to reform it and highlighting its distance from the ideal. This phenomenon led officials to criticize some theatre practitioners for harbouring 'abstract' and 'utopian' views of socialism.[4] Many practitioners did not see the West as a viable political alternative, and it was not uncommon for actors critical of individual policies at home to defend GDR socialism while on tours abroad.

Theatre censorship was sometimes articulated through production bans or the forced deletion of lines or scenes. Whilst these forms of intervention characterized the most public conflicts, production bans actually represented a breakdown in the system. From the authorities' viewpoint, they indicated that the producers had acted irresponsibly and that the usual political checks had failed. In order to understand censorship, we need to examine how the regulatory framework functioned; how theatre practitioners and officials negotiated the repertoire; and how directors and dramaturges framed production concepts, edited scripts, and approached politically sensitive aspects of texts in performance. Alongside production bans and textual or performance changes, we need to investigate other forms of intervention, such as closed previews, truncated performance runs, and staged press campaigns. In addition to sanctions, we need to consider the material and symbolic profits awarded to dramatists and theatre practitioners, such as prizes,

---

[4] 'Argumente und Meinungen von Schriftstellern und Künstlern', 7.2.1977, BArch DY 30 IV B 2/9.06/18.

scholarships, commissions, and permission to participate in tours to the West.

This inclusive approach is crucial because the system of controls and rewards helped to constitute how theatrical processes worked in the GDR. Censorship, particularly self-censorship, became embedded in theatre politics and the rehearsal process, influencing the ways in which practitioners interpreted texts and shaped productions. Individuals negotiated the system in different ways, but it was the only one available to those wanting to practise theatre in the GDR. The pressures towards internal and self-censorship were considerable, and it is not always possible to distinguish between self-censorship and the revisions that go on in any rehearsals. In fact, the point was precisely that it should not be.

My approach thus combines an understanding of censorship as a constitutive process with a more traditional emphasis on state regulation and intervention.[5] Constitutive or 'structural' censorship is particularly associated with the sociologist Pierre Bourdieu, who argues that any utterance involves 'a *compromise* between an *expressive interest* and a *censorship* constituted by the very structure of the field in which the discourse is produced and circulates' [italics in original].[6] In this statement, Bourdieu uses the term 'censorship' to describe the processes of selection and restriction that are at work in any speech act; in order to participate in a particular discourse, we adapt to the rules by which it operates. Judith Butler expands on this view, suggesting that censorship is 'a way of producing speech, constraining in advance what will and will not become acceptable speech'.[7] In the GDR, censorship influenced the kinds of subject matter dramatists chose and the ways in which theatre practitioners presented their plans to state and Party officials.

The need to retain a strong emphasis on state regulation and intervention is self-evident in the GDR context, given the restrictions on cultural life. Yet the term 'censorship' is now applied to a far wider range

[5] For an excellent discussion of censorship theory, see Beate Müller, 'Censorship and Cultural Regulation: Mapping the Territory', in Müller (ed.), *Censorship and Cultural Regulation in the Modern Age*, Critical Studies, 22 (Amsterdam and New York: Rodopi, 2004), 1–31.
[6] Pierre Bourdieu, 'Censorship and the Imposition of Form', in *Language and Symbolic Power*, ed. and introduced by John B. Thompson, trans. Gino Raymond and Matthew Adamson (London: Polity, 1991), 137–59 at 137.
[7] Judith Butler, 'Ruled Out: Vocabularies of the Censor', in Robert C. Post (ed.), *Censorship and Silencing: Practices of Cultural Regulation*, Issues and Debates, 4 (Los Angeles: Getty Research Institute, 1998), 247–59 at 248.

of restrictive practices, such as the decisions made by public funding bodies and the commercial decisions made by publishers. Proponents of the 'new censorship' have themselves expressed unease at this broad application of the term. Robert C. Post warns of a 'flatten[ing]' of distinctions between kinds of power; Richard Burt writes of the term 'censorship' becoming 'overwhelmed, even trivialized'; and Judith Butler questions 'whether "censorship" still works to describe this operation of power' as a productive, formative process.[8] It is worth noting that Bourdieu refers to the *metaphor* of censorship,[9] suggesting a willingness to distinguish between the 'censorship' of the imposition of form and more direct manifestations of power. Scholars are grappling with the fact that instances of discursive restriction exist on a continuum, yet the historical usage of the word 'censorship' suggests a severity that may not always seem appropriate. The challenge for researchers working on state censorship is how to use the insights of constitutive censorship to understand the mediated effects of state intervention and involvement in culture. This is particularly important in the GDR context, where the forms of direct intervention traditionally associated with state censorship—such as production or publication bans—were always a last resort.

Bourdieu's analysis of culture offers further useful perspectives on theatre production and reception in the GDR. It shifts the focus from individual artists to the networks of relations between cultural producers, treating culture as a site of struggles over the power to define what counts as legitimate art.[10] At any particular historical moment, cultural producers' perceptions of the 'space of possibles' will vary.[11] Individual GDR theatre practitioners—and state or Party officials—had different views of what it was possible to achieve, based partly on their previous

[8] Robert C. Post, 'Introduction', in Post (ed.), *Censorship and Silencing*, 1–12; Richard Burt, 'The "New" Censorship', in Burt (ed.), *The Administration of Aesthetics: Censorship, Political Criticism, and the Public Sphere*, Cultural Politics, 7 (Minneapolis and London: University of Minnesota Press, 1994), pp. xi–xxix at xiii; Butler, 'Ruled Out', 249. See also Richard Burt, *Licensed by Authority: Ben Jonson and the Discourses of Censorship* (Ithaca and London: Cornell University Press, 1993).
[9] Bourdieu, 'Censorship', 138.
[10] Pierre Bourdieu, 'The Field of Cultural Production, or: The Economic World Reversed', in Randal Johnson (ed.), *The Field of Cultural Production: Essays on Art and Literature* (Cambridge: Polity, 1993), 29–73 at 42. This chapter was translated by Richard Nice.
[11] Pierre Bourdieu, *The Rules of Art: Genesis and Structure of the Literary Field*, trans. Susan Emmanuel (London: Polity, 1996), 206.

experiences of censorship. What they were prepared to attempt depended also on their dispositions; Bourdieu uses the term 'habitus' to describe the sets of dispositions that incline individuals to react in particular ways. The status of individuals also affects their capacity for action.

Bourdieu uses the metaphor 'symbolic capital' to describe the recognition that artists receive from the authorities, their peers, and the public, suggesting that recognition serves as a currency that can be accumulated, exchanged, or forfeited. He cites the example of art dealers who stake their symbolic capital on new artists; they vouch for the artists' quality and promise, knowing that their professional reputation will suffer if the critics disagree.[12] We might equally cite the example of theatre managers who used their track record to convince the GDR authorities that they could be trusted with politically sensitive productions, at the risk of damaging their reputation if the productions were subsequently banned.

An emphasis on cultural networks facilitates a more nuanced analysis of GDR theatre than the binary division between loyalty and dissidence that has often dominated Western discussions of GDR culture. By paying close attention to the interaction among and between theatre practitioners and officials, we can avoid treating theatre practitioners as the passive objects of state power. Bourdieu argues that it is only through the interaction between individuals that the cultural heritage is maintained as a norm—or perhaps a standard—for practices in the present:

Through the criss-crossing constraints and controls which each person who is appropriated by it brings to bear on all the others, this *opus operatum*, otherwise fated to the insignificance of a dead letter, is continually asserted as a collective *modus operandi*, as the mode of cultural production whose norm is impressed, at each moment, on all producers.[13]

Jiřina Šmejkalová-Strickland makes a similar point in relation to literary censorship in Czechoslovakia during the Cold War. She argues that 'a structure of mutual anticipation...created the environment that controlled access to the text. By assuming a role within a network of performances, individual actors stabilized the institutional

[12] Pierre Bourdieu, 'The Production of Belief: Contribution to an Economy of Symbolic Goods', in *The Field of Cultural Production*, 74–111 at 76–7. This chapter was translated by Richard Nice.
[13] Bourdieu, *Rules of Art*, 271.

system.'[14] In 1988–9, as the number of individuals questioning and abandoning their roles grew, it became increasingly difficult to sustain collective belief in the restrictions on cultural production. This monograph has four interlocking objectives. The first is to investigate how theatre censorship worked in the GDR. For forty years, censorship was a fact of professional life for theatre practitioners and officials. As such, it encouraged and relied on practitioners' cooperation and cannot be viewed simply in terms of bilateral conflict.[15] Nor can theatre censorship be seen as a set of abstract mechanisms; it was a human process involving complex negotiations, sometimes with unpredictable outcomes. Conflicts certainly occurred, and their personal and professional consequences could be devastating. Careers were damaged and even destroyed, and theatre practitioners were harassed by the Ministry for State Security (Stasi) and placed under surveillance. But censorship conflicts ran along multiple lines, within as well as between institutions. Loyalties and modes of behaviour changed within individual careers, and we cannot explain either the system's longevity or its final collapse without understanding these behavioural patterns and changes, in the context in which they occurred.

The second objective is to explore the extent and nature of historical change and regional variations in theatre censorship. To this end, the monograph locates detailed case studies in a broad historical and geographical framework. It thus contrasts with accounts that focus on individual case studies, such as Matthias Braun's monograph on Heiner Müller's play *Die Umsiedlerin* (The Female Resettler) or the series of articles published in the theatre journal *Theater der Zeit* in 1990–1.[16] The monograph is conceived on a larger scale than Barrie Baker's study, which uses material from central archives to provide a survey of theatre

[14] Jiřina Šmejkalová-Strickland, 'Censoring Canons: Transitions and Prospects of Literary Institutions in Czechoslovakia', in Burt (ed.), *The Administration of Aesthetics*, 195–215 at 204–5.

[15] On censorship and cooperation in other contexts, see Burt, *Licensed by Authority*; Robert Darnton, 'Censorship, A Comparative View: France, 1789–East Germany, 1989', in Olwen Hufton (ed.), *Historical Change and Human Rights: The Amnesty Lectures 1994* (New York: Basic Books, 1995), 102–30; Sophia Rosenfeld, 'Writing the History of Censorship in the Age of Enlightenment', in Daniel Gordon (ed.), *Postmodernism and the Enlightenment: New Perspectives in Eighteenth-Century French Intellectual History* (London and New York: Routledge, 2001), 117–45.

[16] Matthias Braun, *Drama um eine Komödie: Das Ensemble von SED und Staatssicherheit, FDJ und Ministerium für Kultur gegen Heiner Müllers 'Die Umsiedlerin auf dem Lande' im Oktober 1961* (Berlin: Ch. Links, 1995); e.g. Martin Linzer, 'Weiße Flecken (2): *Fräulein Julie* von Strindberg', *TdZ* 45/7 (July 1990), 28–33.

censorship alongside discussions of GDR drama and cultural policy. Baker's case studies deal with productions at three theatres in the 1980s, focusing on contemporary drama and *Waiting for Godot*.[17] This monograph seeks instead to establish in detail how, and how far, censorship policy and practice changed between 1961 and 1989 under Walter Ulbricht and Erich Honecker. By comparing censorship disputes in six regions and seven theatres, it assesses the nature, timing, and extent of regional variations. As theatre is based in communities, it is well suited to reveal how power was exercised in local contexts in the GDR.

The third objective is to examine how theatres and officials negotiated political crisis points, such as the construction of the Berlin Wall, the Prague Spring, and the struggle over glasnost and perestroika. I consider how theatre practitioners responded to these developments, examining their interventions in political debates, discussions within individual institutions, and artistic responses on stage. I ask how theatre practitioners used the varying amounts of symbolic capital at their disposal, and how state censorship and self-censorship fluctuated in response to political events.

The final aim is to investigate how censorship affected different dramatic genres and modes of performance. By comparing the censorship of plays ranging from an Ancient Greek tragedy through to new GDR drama, I examine the problems, challenges, and opportunities associated with different genres. My case studies involve directors with a range of aesthetic styles and preferences, which allows me to examine how the authorities responded to different kinds of experimentation. I ask how, and how far, censorship helped to shape the choices open to directors and dramatists; this is crucial in understanding how GDR theatre developed within—and in reaction to—a system of state surveillance and intervention.

---

[17] Barrie Baker, *Theatre Censorship in Honecker's Germany: From Volker Braun to Samuel Beckett*, German Linguistic and Cultural Studies, 23 (Bern: Peter Lang, 2007). Baker's monograph focuses on *Die Übergangsgesellschaft* (Society in Transition) at East Berlin's Maxim Gorki Theater and *Waiting for Godot* at the Staatsschauspiel Dresden; it also examines Stasi infiltration of Potsdam's Hans-Otto-Theater. It is based on a doctoral thesis with additional chapters on *Der Georgsberg* (The Georgsberg Mountain, Maxim Gorki Theater), *Revisor oder Katze aus dem Sack* (Government Inspector or The Cat's out of the Bag, Hans-Otto-Theater), and *Die Ritter der Tafelrunde* (The Knights of the Round Table, Staatsschauspiel Dresden). See Barrie Baker, '"From Page to Stage": The State and the Theatre in the German Democratic Republic in the 1980s' (Ph.D. thesis, University of Reading, 2005).

Introduction

2. THE DENIAL OF CENSORSHIP

Censorship was palpably present in the GDR, whether on the state-run television, in the books and newspapers on sale in the shops, at the cinema, or at the theatre. And yet the SED always denied its existence. The word 'censorship' was taboo, and the GDR's first constitution professed its commitment to artistic freedom.[18] Critics have tended to note this denial in passing,[19] but this monograph examines its implications in detail. How and why did the authorities camouflage censorship? How did the need to conceal censorship affect its practice? And were dramatists and directors ever able to turn the regime's denial of censorship to their advantage?

The first reason for the SED's denial of censorship was historical. More than a century before the GDR was founded, the revolutions of 1848 had already dealt a fatal blow to the consensus that censorship was legitimate government practice. Whereas Frederick the Great had issued a General Edict on Censorship (*Allgemeines Zensuredikt*) in 1749 and the Prussian authorities had published a Censorship Decree (*Zensur-Verordnung*) in 1819, the liberal Frankfurt Parliament explicitly opposed censorship and asserted freedom of expression in its constitution of 1849.[20] Prior censorship of the press was abolished in 1874, and the censorship of literature and theatre became the subject of increasingly heated controversy.[21] When the Weimar Republic was founded in 1919, its constitution proclaimed that censorship did not take place.[22]

[18] *Die DDR-Verfassungen*, ed. Herwig Roggemann, 3rd rev. edn. (West Berlin: Berlin, 1980), 207. See Laura Bradley, 'GDR Theatre Censorship: A System in Denial', *GLL* 59 (2006), 151–62. I am grateful to John Wiley and Sons for permission to reproduce material from this article here.
[19] e.g. Siegfried Bräuer und Clemens Vollnhals (eds.), *'In der DDR gibt es keine Zensur': Die Evangelische Verlagsanstalt und die Praxis der Druckgenehmigung 1954–1989* (Leipzig: Evangelische Verlagsanstalt, 1995), 15; Manfred Jäger, 'Das Wechselspiel von Selbstzensur und Literaturlenkung in der DDR', in Ernest Wichner und Herbert Wiesner (eds.), *'Literaturentwicklungsprozesse': Die Zensur der Literatur in der DDR* (Frankfurt/M.: Suhrkamp, 1993), 18–49 at 18–21.
[20] *Dokumente zur deutschen Verfassungsgeschichte*, ed. Ernst Rudolf Huber, 3 vols. (Stuttgart: W. Kohlhammer, 1961), i. 95; *Deutsche Verfassungen: Dokumente zu Vergangenheit und Gegenwart*, ed. Hermann-Josef Blanke (Paderborn: F. Schöningh, 2003), 189.
[21] See Stark, *Banned in Berlin*, 261–2.
[22] *Deutsche Verfassungen*, ed. Blanke, 266.

Whilst the authorities still practised censorship, the act of censorship
had gone underground.

As the official 'Marxist' view of history posited the GDR as the heir of
the 1848 revolutions and the progressive legislation of the Weimar
Republic, East Germany's rulers were anxious to create the appearance
of democracy and civil rights. Accordingly, they incorporated the
Frankfurt constitution's commitment to freedom of opinion and artistic
expression into the GDR constitution of 1949, even though it contradicted the Leninist view that the Party should retain tight control of
information and the arts. The 1949 constitution also included a qualified form of the Weimar Republic's ban on censorship, stating that press
censorship did not take place.[23] These references to earlier constitutions
functioned as tokens of legitimacy, supplying evidence that the GDR
had inherited Germany's democratic traditions and was not simply
a Soviet import. Competition with the Federal Republic gave the
SED a strong incentive to conceal censorship from public view.

The denial of censorship served simultaneously to distance the GDR
from Germany's most recent past. From the outset, the SED defined the
GDR as an anti-fascist state that had broken with the practices of
National Socialism, including censorship of the arts and press. The
desire to draw a line under the past may explain why the SED did not
make a central institution officially responsible for the theatre repertoire
in 1949; any such institution would have been seen as a successor to
the Reichsdramaturgie, a department for theatre within Goebbels's
Ministry for Popular Enlightenment and Propaganda. It was through
this institution that Germany had acquired its first centralized system
of theatre censorship. In the GDR, decisions over productions and
appointments became the formal responsibility of the regional state
authorities, as they had been in the Weimar Republic.[24] The argument
that publicly funded theatre should be accountable to representatives of
the local community served to justify local 'consultations' over the
repertoire. Despite the official break with the practices of the Third
Reich, the East German files offer very occasional glimpses of
theatre practitioners comparing central GDR institutions with the

[23] *Die DDR-Verfassungen*, ed. Roggemann, 202. This clause was dropped from the
1968 constitution.
[24] Thomas Eicher, Barbara Panse, and Henning Rischbieter, *Theater im 'Dritten
Reich': Theaterpolitik, Spielplanstruktur, NS-Dramatik*, ed. Henning Rischbieter
(Seelze-Velber: Kallmeyer, 2000), 21.

Nazi Reichsdramaturgie.[25] These comparisons were made in outbursts directed against particular decisions by the Culture Ministry and affiliated organizations.

We can even date the SED's complete denial of censorship to a specific historical moment: the creation of the GDR in 1949. In the immediate post-war years, censorship had been presented as an integral part of de-Nazification. As David Pike comments, 'in 1945 neither the Soviets nor their wartime allies felt any need to apologize for instituting such controls'.[26] As late as 20 January 1949, an internal paper on theatre referred explicitly to questions of censorship (*Zensurfragen*) and argued that the GDR needed a department for artistic affairs that would ensure a standardized approach to censorship (*die Zensurangelegenheit*).[27] It was the imminent establishment of the German *Democratic* Republic that forced censorship underground, and theatre practitioners were initially slow to catch on. In August 1949, officials in Thuringia were alarmed when theatre managers referred to a ban on Goethe's *Egmont*, and they had to remind managers not to use the term.[28] Production bans belonged to the post-war state of emergency or—worse still—the Third Reich, not the new 'Democratic' Republic.

Once censorship was no longer publicly acknowledged, a euphemistic code evolved to describe it. The four distinct strands of the code reveal how officials presented, justified, and conceived of their activity. The first strand contained the vocabulary of the planned economy. Words like *Planung* (planning), *Leitung* (management), *Lenkung* (steering), *Spielplangestaltung* (shaping the repertoire), and *parteimäßige Führungstätigkeit* (leadership in accordance with Party principles) all denoted the SED's control of cultural processes, which officials were prepared to defend openly. In December 1965, Berlin's First Party Secretary Paul Verner declared that the Party had made it quite clear that it did not support a free market in culture.[29]

[25] e.g. 'Bericht über Vorbereitung und Durchführung von Vorgespräch und Bezirkskonsultation zur Erarbeitung der Theaterspielpläne im Bezirk Rostock', 25.4.1979, BArch DY 30 IV B 2/9.06/68. See Ch. 5, 168.
[26] David Pike, 'Censorship in Soviet-Occupied Germany', in Norman Naimark and Leonid Gibianskii (eds.), *The Establishment of Communist Regimes in Eastern Europe, 1944–1949* (Oxford: Westview, 1997), 217–41 at 218.
[27] 'Theaterplanwirtschaft', BArch DY 30 IV 2/9.06/186.
[28] 'Aufführung Goethe *Egmont*', 9.8.1949, BArch DY 30 IV 2/9.06/186. See Ch. 5, 176.
[29] Paul Verner, 'Wir haben die Kreissekretäre...', BArch NY 4281/63.

The second strand cloaked the control mechanisms in administrative language: officials called pre-performance censorship the *Genehmigungsverfahren* (approval procedures), censorship instructions *Weisungen* (instructions), and production bans *administrative Maßnahmen* (administrative measures). These euphemisms presented censorship as part of the normal, impersonal workings of bureaucratic government. However, 'administration' soon took on negative connotations, signifying a failure to convince and work with artists. In 1973, Ursula Ragwitz—an official in the Central Committee's Culture Department—warned that no one had the right to use administration instead of trying to convince colleagues in the arts.[30]

The third strand of the code portrayed officials as facilitators and protectors of culture. This view was enshrined in the 1949 constitution, which included a socialist get-out clause from the guarantee of artistic freedom, namely that the state would protect art and science from being abused for purposes contrary to the terms and spirit of the constitution.[31] This suitably elastic provision was reinforced in the new constitution of 1968:

Die Deutsche Demokratische Republik fördert und schützt die sozialistische Kultur, die dem Frieden, dem Humanismus und der Entwicklung der sozialistischen Gesellschaft dient. Sie bekämpft die imperialistische Unkultur, die der psychologischen Kriegsführung und der Herabwürdigung des Menschen dient.[32]

The German Democratic Republic promotes and protects socialist culture, which serves peace, humanism, and the development of socialist society. It opposes the degenerate culture of imperialism, which serves psychological warfare and the denigration of man.

According to this view, art stood in the front line of the GDR's national defences and had to be protected and strengthened as a weapon in the Cold War. Ideas about protecting culture resonated strongly with officials, even if some saw themselves as defending new literature against SED hardliners.[33]

---

[30] 'Information über die Beratung der Abteilung Kultur des ZK mit den Intendanten und Parteisekretären wichtiger Theater der Republik am 2.7.73', LHASA, Abt. MER, SED-BL Halle IV/C-2/9.02/0517.
[31] *Die DDR-Verfassungen*, ed. Roggemann, 207.
[32] Ibid. 146.
[33] See Darnton, 'Censorship, A Comparative View', 121.

Officials styled themselves as pedagogues in the fourth strand of the code, using terms such as *ideologische Klärungsprozesse* (processes of ideological clarification), *geduldige Überzeugung* (patient convincing), *Hilfe* (help), *Unterstützung* (support), and *Selbstkritik* (self-criticism). Konrad Franke points out that such terms were rarely meant cynically; officials genuinely viewed themselves as trying to bring artists back into the fold.[34] Their language characterized the Party as patient and omniscient, and presented dramatists and directors as troublesome teenagers who lacked sufficient wisdom and insight, needed careful tutoring, and had a good deal to learn. This attitude was neatly encapsulated in comments made by the Politbüro member Kurt Hager about the dramatist Peter Hacks. In 1963, after the authorities had forced the Deutsches Theater to withdraw its production of Hacks's play *Die Sorgen und die Macht* (Worries and Power), Hager declared that the Party had patiently conducted long discussions with the ensemble, that Hacks had not yet understood what life was really like in the GDR, and that the Party was criticizing the play for Hacks's own benefit, as it expected him to write better plays in future.[35] Jochen Genzel, from the Culture Ministry's Theatre Department, used similar language in 1968 when advising Minister Klaus Gysi on Volker Braun's *Hans Faust*:

Volker Braun soll gespielt werden, damit er an der konkreten Aufführung lernen kann. Im Falle des *Hans Faust* aber sollte man den Autor ermutigen, am Stoff weiterzuarbeiten, ihn philosophisch tiefer zu fassen und ihn formal zu verbessern.[36]

Volker Braun should have his work performed so that he can learn from an actual production. In the case of *Hans Faust*, however, the author should be encouraged to continue working on the material, grasp it in more philosophical depth, and improve its form.

These euphemistic descriptions of censorship were complemented by the discourse of responsibility, which promoted and described self-censorship. As several earlier productions of Braun's plays had been cancelled or caused controversy, the Theatre Department viewed the

[34] Konrad Franke, '"Deine Darstellung ist uns wesensfremd": Romane der 60er Jahre in den Mühlen der DDR-Zensur', in Wichner and Wiesner (eds.), 'Literaturentwicklungsprozesse', 101–26 at 102.
[35] 'Stenografische Niederschrift der Kulturberatung im Hause des Zentralkomitees, Kongreßsaal, am 25. und 26. März 1963', BArch DY 30 IV A 2/2.024/3.
[36] 'Bemerkungen zu *Hans Faust* von Volker Braun', 17.8.1968, BArch DR 1/8846.

uncontroversial premiere of *Großer Frieden* (The Great Peace) at the Berliner Ensemble (BE) as a major success. In April 1979, departmental head Gisela Holan wrote that this production showed how an ideologically and artistically challenging work could be staged with great political responsibility (*mit großer politischer Verantwortung*). She added that further productions must be restricted to theatres whose managers could be trusted to stage the play in a similarly responsible manner (*verantwortungsbewußt*).[37] The term 'responsibility' recurs in other discursive fields, and Siegfried Lokatis proposes it as a central tool in the study of GDR censorship.[38] As he argues, it conveys the ambivalence inherent in self-censorship. The notion of responsibility appealed positively to theatre practitioners' political convictions and their understanding of the constraints of a given situation.[39] It simultaneously functioned as a warning: managers remained personally responsible for their productions, even though state councils approved the repertoire.[40] This legal responsibility gave those staging new drama an incentive to consult the authorities during rehearsals in order to limit their own exposure to risk.

In the day-to-day dealings and correspondence between the Party, Culture Ministry, and theatres, a clear scale of coded censorship instructions developed. It ranged from polite requests (*wir bitten zu bedenken*), via recommendations and urgent recommendations (*wir empfehlen, wir empfehlen dringend*), to instructions (*Weisungen*), which directors and managers were obliged to follow. Arno Hochmuth, who headed the Central Committee's Culture Department from 1966 until 1972, confirms that officials rarely deviated from their euphemistic code, even behind closed doors.[41] A rare exception occurred in a heated

---

[37] 'Zur Uraufführung des Stückes *Großer Frieden* von Volker Braun', 23.4.1979, BArch DY 30 IV B 2/2.024/86.

[38] Siegfried Lokatis, *Der rote Faden: Kommunistische Parteigeschichte und Zensur unter Walter Ulbricht*, Zeithistorische Studien, 25 (Cologne: Böhlau, 2003), 19–23.

[39] At this point I intended to cite the example of a director who agreed to postpone a production at a time of heightened political tension, but the director refused permission for publication.

[40] e.g. 'Versuch zur Entwicklung einer Prognose des Theaterschaffens in der DDR', BArch DR 1/8846.

[41] Interview with Arno Hochmuth, 7.10.2004. There is some evidence of similarities between censorship discourse in the Third Reich and GDR, showing how functionaries in both systems tried to encourage self-censorship and to resist the perception that they were laying down the law. Eicher argues that it was usually enough for officials in the Reichsdramaturgie to make 'requests', as theatre managers were almost certain to comply with them. See Eicher, Rischbieter, and Panse, *Theater im 'Dritten Reich'*, 292.

discussion in 1972, when the official responsible for culture in East Berlin's Party administration, Roland Bauer, used the forbidden word *verboten*: 'Wenn nötig, sagt die Partei auch: So geht es überhaupt nicht!—Dann wird das Kunstwerk verboten.'[42] (If necessary, then the Party will also say: 'That is completely out of the question!' Then the work of art will be banned.)

It was equally rare for the authorities to acknowledge the euphemistic nature of their code. In 1965, when Verner told his colleagues that the Maxim Gorki Theater had 'withdrawn' a play after an eleven-day performance run, his addition of the word *sozusagen* (in a manner of speaking) acknowledged that the play had effectively been banned.[43] But the fact that the Maxim Gorki Theater had nominally withdrawn its own production illustrates the lack of transparency surrounding theatre censorship. As production bans did not officially exist, theatre practitioners had no formal means of appealing against them. Indeed, the GDR's leaders consistently opted for denial as the best form of defence where censorship was concerned. When Alexander Dubček abolished press censorship in Czechoslovakia in 1968, Ulbricht claimed that the GDR had no censorship to abolish. Honecker took the same line in 1990, when he argued that the GDR had not practised censorship, unlike other socialist states.[44]

3. THE REGULATORY FRAMEWORK

As theatre censorship was not acknowledged to exist in the GDR, it was practised through surrogate organizations: parallel Party and state institutions at central, regional, and district levels, supported by the Stasi, professional bodies like the Writers' Union and Union of Theatre Practitioners, and mass organizations like the Free German Youth (FDJ). Theatre was initially the responsibility of the Education Ministry, which transmitted its directives through the Office for Theatre Affairs between 1948 and 1958. But in the period under consideration here, the leading central institutions in charge of theatre were the SED

---

[42] 'Stenografische Niederschrift der Beratung des Genossen Kurt Hager mit den Sekretären für Wissenschaft, Bildung und Kultur der Bezirksleitungen', 17.4.1972, BArch DY 30 IV B 2/2.024/29.
[43] Paul Verner, speech to Berlin's SED-*Bezirksleitung*, [Dec. 1965], BArch NY 4281/63.
[44] Jäger, 'Das Wechselspiel', 18.

Central Committee's Culture Department and the Culture Ministry, which had been created in 1954.

The Culture Department was primarily responsible for supervising the Culture Ministry, the specialist theatre periodical *Theater der Zeit*, and cultural officials in the regional Party authorities (*Bezirksleitungen*).[45] It answered to Alfred Kurella—who headed the Politbüro's Culture Commission until 1963—and then to Kurt Hager, who remained in charge until 1989. In practice, there was a bilateral cooperation between the Culture Department and Ministry. Klaus Gysi, who served as Culture Minister from 1966 to 1973, told the Culture Department which theatres needed stronger 'assistance' from the local Party authorities.[46] The Ministry itself was responsible for managing state institutions, planning central investments, and dealing with the publication of drama. Within the Ministry, the Theatre Department planned policy, kept statistics, managed training, approved appointments, and provided ideological guidance for commissioned plays.[47] Several theatres in East Berlin—including the BE and Deutsches Theater—were directly responsible to the Ministry, which also dealt with problem cases elsewhere.

In 1989–90, the GDR had sixty-eight theatres. Of these, fifty staged drama, either on their own (fourteen theatres), in performances for children or young people (four theatres), or alongside opera, musicals, or ballet (thirty-two theatres). In addition, there were nine marionette theatres and nine musical theatres or opera houses.[48] The theatres were classed in three main groups, and their status affected the amount of funding they received and the wages that their actors earned. Theatres in Category A were deemed internationally significant; those in Category B were considered nationally significant; and those in Category C were seen as locally significant. The most prestigious ensembles in East Berlin, including the Deutsches Theater and the BE, were accorded special 'S' status.

---

[45] '1. Entwurf–Arbeitsplan der Abt. Kultur für das 2. Halbjahr 1965', 1.7.1965, BArch DY 30 IV A 2/9.06/33.

[46] Gysi to Hochmuth, 23.5.1969, BArch DY 30 IV A 2/9.06/116.

[47] 'Versuch zur Entwicklung'.

[48] Knut Lennartz (ed.), *Vom Aufbruch zur Wende: Theater in der DDR* (Velber: Erhard Friedrich, 1992), 68–9. See also Ralph Hammerthaler, 'Die Position des Theaters in der DDR', in Christa Hasche, Traute Schölling, and Joachim Fiebach, *Theater in der DDR: Chronik und Positionen. Mit einem Essay von Ralph Hammerthaler* (Berlin: Henschel, 1994), 151–273 at 187.

The sheer number of theatres meant that the central authorities had to delegate day-to-day controls to local state and Party bodies. In East Berlin, this meant the *Magistrat* (City Council) and the Party's *Bezirksleitung* and *Kreisleitungen* (District Authorities). The Party's influence also pervaded state institutions, as officials in most key positions were Party members and each administrative body had its own Party group or organization, just like any other workplace. Some officials moved between the Party and state administration; Hans-Joachim Hoffmann worked in Leipzig's SED-*Bezirksleitung* and briefly headed the Central Committee's Culture Department before succeeding Gysi as Culture Minister in 1973. There was also a two-way traffic between the Ministry and theatres. Werner Rackwitz, for example, worked as Deputy Culture Minister before becoming the manager of the Komische Oper in Berlin, and Siegfried Böttger worked at ten theatres and lectured at the Acting School in Rostock before heading the Theatre Department and then becoming Deputy Culture Minister.[49] It was not uncommon for prominent theatre practitioners to serve in the Party bureaucracy. The dramaturge Bärbel Jaksch was a candidate of the SED-*Bezirksleitung* in Schwerin, while the director Horst Schönemann was a member of the SED-*Stadtleitung* (Municipal Authority) in Dresden. The directors Karl Kayser and Manfred Wekwerth were members of the Central Committee, along with the actor Hans-Peter Minetti.

The management structure of GDR theatre encouraged and institutionalized cooperation with the authorities. Theatre managers were appointed by the state and were expected to meet regularly with Stasi officers. Each theatre had its own Party organization (*Grundorganisation*), management team (*Parteileitung*), and Secretary, although Party members formed a relatively low percentage of the total staff in ensembles.[50] Party Secretaries were sometimes drafted in from outside, particularly if a theatre gave cause for concern. Christine Ostrowski, for example, was sent from her existing position as Party Secretary in the VEB Schleifkörperunion Dresden—a factory producing bonded abrasives—to the Staatsschauspiel Dresden in 1988, after the theatre

[49] Herbert Arlt and Ulrike Bischof (eds.), ... *mir ist in den 80er Jahren kein DDR-Theater bekannt... Dokumentationsgespräche, Materialien, Anmerkungen* (Frankfurt/ M.: Peter Lang, 1993), 214.
[50] 9.1% of members of the Mecklenburgisches Staatstheater belonged to the SED in 1984, and Baker reports an average of 9.4% in the Karl-Marx-Stadt region in 1976–9. See 'Bericht der Leitung der Grundorganisation des Mecklenburgischen Staatstheaters Schwerin', LHAS BPA IV/7/242/008; Baker, *Theatre Censorship*, 63.

had protested about the regime's resistance to perestroika. But some internationally renowned artists also served as Party Secretaries, including the singer and actress Gisela May and the director Ruth Berghaus at the BE. This evidence of cooperation and involvement supports Mary Fulbrook's view of the GDR as a 'participatory dictatorship'.[51]

Theatre managers and Party Secretaries are prime examples of what Bourdieu calls 'double personages': individuals representing the interests of both the authorities and cultural producers.[52] Controversial productions could potentially cost them their jobs, as manager Hans-Diether Meves discovered when he staged Heiner Müller's *Mauser* in Magdeburg in 1973. But political loyalty alone did not guarantee success, and managers and Party Secretaries needed to establish their professional credibility with their colleagues. Two hard-line managers, Hanns Anselm Perten and Karl Kayser, used their political capital to stage new East and West German plays, and they are defended by actors who worked with them in Rostock and Leipzig.[53] But Perten was unable to function effectively as manager of the Deutsches Theater when he moved to East Berlin because the authorities had appointed him against the will of the majority of the ensemble. A report claimed that some members were even talking of the need to unite against the 'occupying forces' from Rostock.[54]

Each theatre in the GDR had at least one dramaturge who read new plays, helped to draw up the repertoire and production concepts, and worked closely with directors. In theory, dramaturges functioned as part of a system of checks and balances designed to guard against political 'irresponsibility'; Ragwitz noted in 1976 that Ruth Berghaus, now the BE's manager, needed a politically reliable dramaturge.[55] But directors could also help to keep dramaturges in check: the Stasi viewed Volker Braun's appointment as a dramaturge at the BE as a means of enabling Manfred Wekwerth to influence his dramatic works while they were

---

[51] Mary Fulbrook, *The People's State: East German Society from Hitler to Honecker* (New Haven and London: Yale University Press, 2005), esp. 12–16.

[52] Bourdieu, *Rules of Art*, 216.

[53] See e.g. Erika Stephan, 'Himmel, strahlender Azur? Eine Unterhaltung mit Wolfgang Pampel', in Wolfgang Engel and Erika Stephan (eds.), *Theater in der Übergangsgesellschaft: Schauspiel Leipzig 1957–2007* (Berlin: TdZ, 2007), 98–100 at 98.

[54] 'Information über die Situation am Deutschen Theater', 28.9.1971, LAB C Rep. 902 2861.

[55] Ursula Ragwitz, 'Einige Gedanken für das Gespräch mit Ruth Berghaus', 19.1.1976, BArch DY 30 IV B 2/2.024/102.

still in progress.[56] This was part of a wider strategy of containment: the authorities sought to ensure that talented but potentially 'irresponsible' practitioners were embedded in a secure context.

The ambivalence of these individual functions was reflected at institutional level in the Union of Theatre Practitioners, an organization that functioned as a double personage. Until 1966, theatre practitioners were represented only by the Academy of Arts and the Trade Union for the Arts, whereas dramatists were also represented by the Writers' Union. The authorities' declared aim in creating the Union of Theatre Practitioners was to prevent the need for production bans.[57] The Union encountered suspicion and resistance in some quarters; the actor Ekkehard Schall declared at its founding congress that he was not aware of any demand for it.[58] Kayser subsequently warned that the Union could not perform the function that Schall allegedly desired: of telling the Party and state how to create theatre.[59] This limited debate points to different views on what the Union should become, a matter that could be settled only through its subsequent practice.

Underneath this open system, the Stasi cultivated a network of informers, designed to provide advance warning of subversion so that officers might 'paralyse' its effectiveness.[60] In 1964 the Stasi created Linie XX, a department with responsibility for culture, art, the state apparatus, the church, and the political underground. Joachim Walther notes that the Stasi had previously targeted artists as recruits only in exceptional circumstances, in connection with specific operations.[61] The next structural change came in 1969 in reaction to the Prague Spring, when the Stasi created a new sub-department, XX/7, responsible specifically for culture. By October 1972, XX/7 had 221 informers, known as *Inoffizielle Mitarbeiter* (Unofficial Collaborators) or IM.[62] Each potential informer was carefully vetted in a preliminary investigation

[56] BStU AOP 15582, i, fos. 132–3.
[57] 'Vorlage an das Politbüro des Zentralkomitees der SED', 7.11.1966, BArch DR 1/8749.
[58] 'Information über den Gründungskongreß des Verbands der Theaterschaffenden am 10./11. Dezember 1966', BArch DY 30 J IV 2/2 J 1849.
[59] 'Protokoll über die Berichtswahlversammlung der PO Städtische Theater Leipzig am 12.12.66', 15.12.1966, SächsStA-L 21123 SED-BL Lpz. IV/A-2/9/2/366.
[60] BStU BV Gera Abt. XX SA 19, fo. 59.
[61] Joachim Walther, *Sicherungsbereich Literatur: Schriftsteller und Staatssicherheit in der Deutschen Demokratischen Republik*, rev. edn. (Berlin: Ullstein, 1999), 180.
[62] Ibid. 193.

known as an *IM-Vorlauf*, and after a series of contact meetings the
informer would usually be asked to write and sign an oath committing
him- or herself to working covertly for the Stasi.

The Stasi divided informers into different categories denoting their
role and status. From 1979, for example, the abbreviation IMB (*IM
Bearbeitung*) designated informers who were in direct contact with the
'enemy' and were given more complex tasks. In contrast, informers
known as IME (*IM im besonderen Einsatz*) occupied positions of professional authority, and their roles included serving as mentors to artists.
The abbreviation IMK/KW (*IM Konspiration/Konspirative Wohnung*)
designated an informer whose home was used for meetings between
officers and other informers, usually in return for payment. Informers
from the theatre profession included directors, actors, dramaturges,
technical staff, and archivists—the latter having direct access to internal
documents, correspondence, and production concepts. Stasi officers
often encouraged informers to strengthen their relationships with colleagues who were of particular interest. At the Deutsches Theater,
for instance, 'Hölderlin' was instructed to adopt a maternal attitude
towards one of the company's dramaturges, in the hope that he might
confide in her, and to supply him with any books he wanted.[63] Those
under close investigation could also expect their post to be intercepted,
their telephones tapped, and their offices and homes bugged.

Individual motives for collaborating with the Stasi varied from case to
case, as did the duration and nature of the relationship. Some informers
were motivated by political conviction, seeing cooperation with the
Stasi as entirely consistent with the morality of the class struggle. This
motive was implied by one theatre director's choice or acceptance of the
codename 'Saint Just', an outspoken advocate of the Jacobin Reign of
Terror, familiar from Georg Büchner's play *Dantons Tod* (Danton's
Death).[64] Some individuals collaborated with the Stasi in an attempt to
gain influence, advance their careers, or secure permission to participate
in tours abroad. The technician 'Dario Fo', for instance, was said to
harbour ambitions of becoming an actor.[65] It was not uncommon for
actors to become informers early on in their careers, only for their
relationships with the Stasi to sour after they had gained appointments

[63] BStU BV Bln. AIM 2382/91, ii.i, fo. 77.
[64] BStU BV Bln. AIM 6049/91; Georg Büchner, *Dantons Tod* (Stuttgart: Reclam,
1973), esp. 43–5 (II. vii).
[65] BStU BV Nbg. III 1620/88.

at prestigious theatres in East Berlin.[66] Personal profit was another possible motive: while some informers received nothing, others received birthday and wedding anniversary presents, one-off rewards, and favours for themselves or family members, and some received substantial sums on a regular basis. But theatre practitioners were sometimes blackmailed into collaborating with the Stasi, a process euphemistically termed *Wiedergutmachung* (making amends). On learning that one actress had had an illegal abortion, Stasi officers threatened her with criminal proceedings unless she agreed to 'cooperate' as an informer.[67]

Whilst the structure of GDR theatre encouraged collaboration with the authorities, the partnership between theatre practitioners and officials was clearly an unequal one. Verdicts were passed down from above, and theatre practitioners were under pressure to reach predetermined conclusions in discussions of censored productions. But we still need to be careful about viewing this structural inequality as an absolute rule, given the existence of director-managers with high Party offices, or of internationally renowned managers like Brecht's widow Helene Weigel. Hager and Gysi were terrified in 1969 that Weigel might close the BE or defect to the West.[68] At least to some extent, the regime needed the legitimacy that high-profile artists like Weigel could provide. These artists were clearly in a stronger bargaining position than their less-established colleagues, and some did use their status to their advantage. The regime's need for legitimacy varied over time; in 1989, this need was sufficiently high for Hoffmann to use Christoph Hein's public denunciation of censorship at the Tenth Writers' Congress as a reason why the premiere of his play *Die Ritter der Tafelrunde* (The Knights of the Round Table) should be allowed to proceed.[69]

4. THE REPERTOIRE AND ITS RECEPTION

The two key ingredients of the theatre repertoire were contemporary drama and those classics that the regime deemed part of the GDR's cultural heritage. Theatres were also expected to mark political and

---

[66] e.g. BStU AIM 1401/83.
[67] File reference not cited to preserve the actress's anonymity.
[68] 'Ergänzendes Protokoll zur Beratung über die Berliner Theatersituation am 23.10.1969 beim Genossen Kurt Hager', BArch DY 30 IV A 2/2.024/30.
[69] BStU HA XX 10282, fo. 5.

historical anniversaries, such as the Russian Revolution of 1917, the establishment of the GDR, or dates associated with leading historical and cultural figures such as Luther, Beethoven, or Brecht. But there was still some room in the repertoire for 'progressive' Western drama, particularly plays by writers such as Rolf Hochhuth, Peter Weiss, and Friedrich Dürrenmatt, who were critical of fascism and/or developments in the Federal Republic. However, the GDR's perennial shortage of foreign currency acted as a practical constraint on performances of Western plays.

Theatre repertoires also featured plays from other socialist countries, although such plays could present problems. Officials in Halle noted in 1975 that preparations for a festival of socialist drama had sparked discussions on what dramatists in other states were allowed to publish.[70] In the 1970s, the provenance of Soviet plays could still help to reassure nervous theatre managers and officials. Deputy Culture Minister Klaus Höpcke even criticized theatres for leaving sensitive topics to Soviet dramatists, asking which theatres would be prepared to perform Alexander Gelman's works if they had been written by a German called Hellmann.[71] But critical drama from the Soviet Union did not always have an easy passage in the GDR, and in 1982 Ragwitz said that a series of contemporary Soviet plays could not be staged at present.[72] The obstacles to performing new Soviet drama increased in the second half of the 1980s, as the SED leadership opposed Mikhail Gorbachev's programme of perestroika.

Scripts were published for the use of GDR theatres by the Henschel Bühnenvertrieb, an agency with a monopoly on the distribution of performance rights. In 1975, it split into henschel SCHAUSPIEL (theatre) and henschel MUSIKBÜHNE (musical theatre), but remained under SED ownership.[73] Ralph Hammerthaler notes that whilst authors were free to send their scripts straight to theatres, dramaturges would

[70] 'Bemerkungen zum Gespräch mit Theaterschaffenden unseres Bezirkes am 28. Februar 1975', LHASA, Abt. MER, SED-BL Halle IV/C-2/9.02/0517.

[71] 'Bericht vom Chefdramaturgenseminar in Berlin vom 11. bis 14. September 1978', 25.9.1978, BArch DY 30 IV B 2/9.06/67.

[72] 'Mitschrift von der Beratung der Kulturabteilung des ZK der SED mit den Abteilungsleitern für Kultur der SED-Bezirksleitungen', 7.6.1982, SächsStA-D 11857 (SED-BL Dresden) IV E-2/9/02/544.

[73] Susanne Misterek, *Polnische Dramatik in Bühnen- und Buchverlagen der Bundesrepublik Deutschland und der DDR* (Wiesbaden: Harrassowitz, 2002), 70. For an excellent, detailed discussion of controls on drama publication, see ibid. 43–80.

usually contact Henschel to discover why it had rejected them.[74] Some scripts were developed in house by dramaturges, and plays were also published in the periodicals *Theater der Zeit* and *Sinn und Form*. The premature publication of a play in a journal could cause a public row, and this was certainly the case when *Sinn und Form* published Heiner Müller's play *Der Bau* (The Construction Site) in April 1965.[75] From 1974, *Theater der Zeit* was permitted to publish plays only after their premiere had been approved, a move that was clearly designed to prevent embarrassment.[76] Even though newly published texts had already passed a series of controls, further political changes would often have to be negotiated before they could be staged. After the premiere of *Großer Frieden* in 1979, Gisela Holan stipulated that future productions should use the BE's text, not the published version.[77]

Some taboos persisted through most of the GDR's history. Samuel Beckett's plays were outlawed until 1987, when *Waiting for Godot* was staged in Dresden; Heiner Müller's *Germania Tod in Berlin* (Germania Death in Berlin) was not staged until 1989; and Volker Braun's *T.*—a play about Trotsky—was published only in 1989 and never staged in the GDR. But officials worked mainly inductively, reading Party pronouncements, listening to guidelines at training events, and learning from production bans. When assessing proposals for productions, they paid attention to the theatres and directors involved, as well as the play and the production concept. Officials even wanted to ensure that theatres connoted the level of prestige appropriate to individual authors and their work. Hence one official was concerned that a production of *In der Sache Robert J. Oppenheimer* (In the Matter of Robert J. Oppenheimer) at the BE might enhance the standing of its author Heinar Kipphardt, who had left the GDR in 1960.[78] Officials and theatre practitioners also paid attention to the overall configuration of the repertoire. In 1989, for example, the Party Secretary of the Mecklenburgisches Staatstheater said that the timing of a performance of socialist songs would depend partly on when *Die Ritter der Tafelrunde* was

---

[74] Hammerthaler, 'Die Position des Theaters in der DDR', 195.

[75] See Heiner Müller, *Geschichten aus der Produktion 1* (West Berlin: Rotbuch, 1988), 137–46.

[76] Knut Lennartz, 'Klaus Höpcke und das Drama von Drama', *Deutschland Archiv*, 21 (1988), 12–14 at 13.

[77] 'Zur Uraufführung'.

[78] 'Heinar Kipphardts Schauspiel *In der Sache Robert J. Oppenheimer*', 10.12.1964, BArch DY 30 IV A 2/9.06/113.

staged. In her view, it would not be politically viable to stage the two productions in succession.[79]

Pre-performance control of the repertoire was followed by post-performance control of the press, as officials attempted to steer reception processes. Some productions were not reviewed at all, or only after long delays, a phenomenon that Brecht had complained of in 1953.[80] In 1972, Hoffmann wrote to Hager about the Volksbühne's forthcoming production of Ulrich Plenzdorf's *Die neuen Leiden des jungen W.* (The New Sorrows of Young W.), saying that the premiere should not receive extensive press coverage.[81] In 1976, officials attempted to distract public attention from the premiere of Volker Braun's *Tinka* in Karl-Marx-Stadt by scheduling it on the same day as the GDR dance championships, to be held in the same building. The premiere was to be announced only in the district press, not in other newspapers, on the radio, or on television.[82] In 1978, East Berlin's First Party Secretary Konrad Naumann ordered three of his colleagues to help him secretly buy up tickets for the first two performances of Rudi Strahl's *Flüsterparty* (Secret Party) at the Volksbühne.[83] In other cases, officials mobilized opposition from spectators and critics in order to pressurize theatres into cancelling productions. But press campaigns could easily backfire, creating the subversive effect that they had been designed to prevent, or convincing audiences to steer clear of conformist productions.

5. SOURCE MATERIALS AND METHODS

My methodological approach is guided by three considerations: the dispersal of censorship powers in the GDR, the complexity of theatre as a social and artistic practice, and the problems inherent in the source material. The dispersal of censorship powers means that we need to cast

[79] 'Parteiinformation', 4.9.1989, LHAS 10.34-3 4706.
[80] Bertolt Brecht, *Große kommentierte Berliner und Frankfurter Ausgabe*, ed. Werner Hecht and others, 30 vols. (Frankfurt/M. and Berlin: Suhrkamp and Aufbau, 1988–2000), xxvii (1995), 346.
[81] Hoffmann to Hager, 7.12.1972, BArch DY 30 IV B 2/9.06/66.
[82] Ragwitz to Hager, 17.5.1976, BArch DY 30/vorl. SED/18541.
[83] Naumann, 'Zur Information der Abteilung Kultur der Bezirksleitung vom 21.9.78 über die geplante Premiere des Stückes *Flüsterparty*', LAB C Rep. 902 4550. The production was subsequently cancelled.

the net widely. This study is based on extensive research in federal and regional state archives, the Stasi archive (BStU), and theatre archives. I have examined files in the federal archive (Bundesarchiv) and five regional archives (Landesarchive or Staatsarchive), systematically checking files on culture and theatre from 1961 to 1989, and drawing additionally on some earlier material. By consulting regional archives in Berlin, Halle (Merseburg), Dresden, Leipzig, and Schwerin, and local archives in Anklam and Bautzen, I have covered a broad range of regions and theatres. These archives contain the files of state and Party administrative bodies, and the contents of the files range from policy documents, correspondence, and records of Party meetings in theatres to assessments of theatres, scripts, and productions. The archive in Schwerin holds the files for both the Schwerin and Neubrandenburg regions.

Substantial records of theatre censorship have survived in central and regional archives, even some documents instructing the addressee to destroy them.[84] The files also include reports on telephone conversations, and officials may well have wanted to protect themselves by keeping a written record of what they had agreed over the telephone with colleagues in other institutions. But as Helen Freshwater points out, the holdings of any archive are contingent on 'the duality of random inclusion and considered exclusion'.[85] In the GDR's case, significant amounts of material were destroyed in 1989, and the files from the Central Committee's Culture Department are far thinner for the 1980s than for the preceding decades. Some surviving reports gloss over problems. A theatre manager in Görlitz, for example, explained that if he admitted certain difficulties he would never win the Hans Otto Competition.[86] These different problems underline the need for a broad empirical base when investigating theatre censorship. My research in regional archives has filled in some of the gaps in central archives, e.g. concerning the Culture Department's activities in the 1980s, or Ministry briefings with local officials. As day-to-day control of theatre was delegated to regional and local authorities, it is surprising

[84] e.g. Harich to Hager, 14.5.1971, BArch DY 30 IV A 2/2.023/74.
[85] Helen Freshwater, 'The Allure of the Archive', in *Poetics Today*, 24 (2003), 729–58 at 740.
[86] 'Auszug aus dem Bericht über die Beratung des Aktivs "Parteiarbeit an den Theatern" vom 19.12.68', 13.2.1969, SächsStA-D 11857 IV B-2/9/02/487. Theatres competed each year to win the Hans Otto Prize, named after a communist actor murdered by Nazi storm troopers in 1933.

that Baker's study ignores regional state archives, except for one file from Berlin's regional archive.

Research in the Stasi archive is complicated by the fact that most files relate to individuals, although Stasi officers did highlight cross-references between cases. As it would have been impracticable to investigate the files on every theatre practitioner involved in the productions considered in this monograph, I focused initially on the directors, key theatre managers, dramaturges, and actors, and the authors of new plays. I then followed up links to the main informers in each case, consulting their files. The destruction of material in 1989 had an uneven impact on the files consulted in this study; many were preserved intact, but some were partly or even largely destroyed. The surviving file on 'Saint Just', for instance, contains only two pages in the first volume and an envelope with four receipts in the second.[87] The first volume of the file on 'Hölderlin'—which would originally have contained information concerning the informer's identity—is empty except for a blank contents page, yet 1,771 pages of reports survive in another four volumes.[88] But even when informers' files have been destroyed, it is still possible to collate evidence of their activity from copies of reports deposited in other files. These copies provide a rough guide to the length and intensity of the informers' collaboration with the Stasi. I reveal informers' identities only where clear evidence exists and where the information is relevant to the understanding of the censorship cases under investigation.

The material in these files is inevitably filtered through the political perspective of the Stasi. Its definition of opposition did not necessarily coincide with the intentions and self-perceptions of the individuals under investigation; in the 1950s and early 1960s, arguing for minimal changes in cultural policy was enough for even an SED member to be considered an opponent of the regime. Officers often wrote up informers' reports for the files, translating their testimony into the Stasi's terminology and—in some cases—constructing the informer as an authoritative witness and ideological judge. The original, unfiltered reports may therefore come as a surprise, particularly when they are couched in simple, unsophisticated language and are littered with spelling and punctuation errors. But the Stasi's own documents also contain misspellings, which reveal that those compiling reports and

---

[87] BStU BV Bln. AIM 6049/91.　　　　[88] BStU BV Bln. AIM 6282/91.

transcribing conversations sometimes had only a patchy knowledge of the subject matter in question. The French director Guy de Chambure presented the Stasi with particular challenges; reports refer to him variously as 'Gy', 'Gie', 'G.', and 'Gi'.[89] Officers also had difficulty with the Volksbühne's manager Karl Holàn, referring to him as 'Herr Holland', 'Hohlan', and 'Hollan'.[90]

Eyewitness accounts of GDR theatre have proliferated since 1990, whether in the form of interviews, collections of essays, or autobiographies.[91] I use these sources and have conducted my own interviews with theatre practitioners, critics, and former officials. Their testimony is valuable, but it is important to remember that censorship processes were at least partly concealed from theatre practitioners and dramatists. After Hans Modrow, Dresden's First Party Secretary, had sent Ragwitz two plays to assess, she informed him that the Culture Department would send him its views in confidence, without contacting the authors concerned.[92] Since reading the Stasi files, Walther has reflected on how little concrete knowledge he previously had of how the GDR functioned, despite living there for forty years.[93] And theatre practitioners are sometimes surprised by evidence of productions that they staged decades earlier: when I interviewed him in 2004, Manfred Karge was astonished to discover how outspoken he and his co-director Matthias Langhoff had been when staging Aeschylus' *Seven against Thebes* in 1968–9.[94]

I supplement censorship evidence from the state and Stasi archives with performance-related material from theatre archives and the Academy of Arts. This material includes prompt books, rehearsal notes, photographs, audiovisual recordings, and transcripts of post-show discussions with spectators. Matthias Braun places less emphasis on this material in his study of *Die Umsiedlerin*, and Barrie Baker relies

[89] BStU AOP 1958/71, viii and ix.
[90] BStU AOP 1958/71, xi and xii.
[91] e.g. Thomas Irmer and Matthias Schmidt, *Die Bühnenrepublik: Theater in der DDR*, ed. Wolfgang Bergmann (Berlin: Alexander Verlag, 2003); J. Lawrence Guntner and Andrew M. McLean (eds.), *Redefining Shakespeare: Literary Theory and Theatre Practice in the German Democratic Republic* (London: Associated University Presses, 1998); Angelica Domröse, *Ich fang mich selbst ein: Mein Leben* (Bergisch Gladbach: Lübbe, 2003).
[92] 'Niederschrift über ein Gespräch, das Genosse Hans Modrow...mit Genossin Ragwitz...am 12.7.1978 in Berlin zu folgenden Fragen führte', 20.7.1978, SächsStA-D 11857 IV D-2/9/02/556.
[93] Walther, *Sicherungsbereich Literatur*, 17.
[94] Interview with Manfred Karge, 19.3.2004.

primarily on newspaper reviews for evidence of performance. I analyse the choices that theatre practitioners made concerning scripts, costumes, set designs, acting, and publicity material; track how theatre practitioners responded to official instructions and recommendations; and identify politically significant textual and aesthetic changes. Audience response is notoriously difficult for theatre historians to gauge, but I examine evidence of reactions on audio recordings, in records of post-show discussions, in Stasi reports, and in memoirs. I also investigate how audience response played into censorship, given that productions always remained malleable.

6. STRUCTURE AND SCOPE

This monograph is structured chronologically as a series of comparative case studies, combining microhistorical depth with a broad analytical framework. It focuses on 1961–89, the period between the construction and the fall of the Berlin Wall. The decision to start in 1961 was partly pragmatic; covering the entire period of the GDR would have exceeded the scope of this monograph. There is already a significant body of work on censorship in the Soviet-occupied zone and on the censorship cases involving Brecht and Eisler in the early GDR, and Petra Stuber has investigated the late 1940s and the 1950s in detail.[95] I emphasize in Chapter 2 that the construction of the Wall did not mark a caesura, but that it did bring qualitatively new aspects to the conditions in which theatre productions were staged.

Part I (Chapters 2–4) focuses on East Berlin during the 1960s and 1970s. This allows me to explore how theatre was censored in the capital, how different dramatic genres were affected, and how far censorship varied between theatres in the same city. I examine how theatre practitioners responded to the construction of the Wall, the Prague Spring, and Wolf Biermann's expatriation. Four of the eight productions in Part I involve the Deutsches Theater; this enables me to trace the impact of censorship disputes on the company over two decades.

---

[95] Andrea Schiller, *Die Theaterentwicklung in der sowjetischen Besatzungszone (SBZ) 1945 bis 1949* (Frankfurt/M.: Peter Lang, 1998); *Die Debatte um Hanns Eislers Johann Faustus: Eine Dokumentation*, ed. Hans Bunge (Berlin: BasisDruck, 1991); *Das Verhör in der Oper: Die Debatte um die Aufführung 'Das Verhör von Lukullus' von Bertolt Brecht und Paul Dessau*, ed. Joachim Lucchesi (Berlin: BasisDruck, 1993); Petra Stuber, *Spielräume und Grenzen: Studien zum DDR-Theater* (Berlin: Ch. Links, 1998), 12–197, 257–376.

In Part II, I broaden the focus to Dresden, Leipzig, Halle, Schwerin, and Neubrandenburg. These regions include theatres which served as centres of experimentation at different times (e.g. Halle, Schwerin, Dresden), theatres seen as more conservative (e.g. Leipzig), a range of target audiences (more cosmopolitan in Leipzig and Dresden, more rural in Schwerin and Neubrandenburg, more industrial in Halle), and different-sized theatres (major companies, e.g. the Mecklenburgisches Staatstheater and Staatsschauspiel Dresden; small ensembles, e.g. Anklam and Bautzen). This range extends to the political views of directors in these regions, their relationships with officials, and their theatrical styles. Chapter 5 functions as a bridge between Parts I and II, and it investigates regional differences in censorship provision and practice in the 1960s and 1970s. I then examine two contrasting pairs of case studies from the 1980s. Chapter 6 focuses on productions in Schwerin and Anklam in 1984, and Chapter 7 examines stagings in Dresden and Bautzen in 1989. Part II focuses clearly on regional comparisons but provides continuity with Part I through cross-references to East Berlin and insights into different genres and political developments. The conclusion brings together developments in East Berlin and the regions, and it explores the political role that theatre practitioners across the GDR played in the 1989 protests.

The overriding factor in my selection of case studies was their interest in terms of theatre censorship. I examine cases with different outcomes, ranging from production bans, through uneasy compromises, to official approval. The case studies cover a range of authors and genres, indicating how censorship affected a broad cross-section of the repertoire, not just the inevitably sensitive area of contemporary drama. As the monograph focuses clearly on theatre censorship, it does not investigate the procedures behind the publication of new plays, nor does it aim to provide a history of the development of GDR drama. Both issues have been dealt with effectively elsewhere.[96] The historical scope of this analysis allows us to compare theatre practitioners' roles in different disputes and to trace individual paths through a complex system. By placing high-profile disputes back into a comparative context, we can begin to assess the relative importance of cooperation and conflict in GDR theatre censorship.

---

[96] e.g. Misterek, *Polnische Dramatik*; Ulrich Profitlich, *Dramatik der DDR* (Frankfurt/M.: Suhrkamp, 1987).

PART I

THEATRE CENSORSHIP
IN EAST BERLIN

2

Contemporary Drama in the 1960s: A Contested Space

Es geht eben nicht mit Realismus.
(Realism just doesn't work.)
Heiner Müller, *Krieg ohne Schlacht*, 422

1. INTRODUCTION

Contemporary drama was a matter of national prestige for the SED: a means of proving the vitality of GDR culture and showing that it was developing along distinctively socialist lines. In the late 1950s and early 1960s, Peter Hacks and Heiner Müller wrote for and about the GDR, undertook research in factories and on building sites, and solicited feedback from workers. Whilst they remained sceptical about the Party's campaign to turn factory workers into writers, their plays did respond to other aspects of the *Bitterfelder Weg*, namely the call for artists to address contemporary socio-economic issues. Werner Mittenzwei argues that the reception of their drama therefore presents us with a paradox: when writers were following the Party's slogans most closely, the authorities brusquely rejected their work.[1] But it was precisely because Hacks and Müller were attempting to represent GDR industry and agriculture on stage that their work was so vulnerable to criticism.

Such criticism came from fellow artists as well as functionaries. Orthodox Socialist Realism had staunch defenders in writers like Helmut Sakowski and directors like Karl Kayser, who believed that drama should uplift spectators and provide them with positive role

---

[1] Werner Mittenzwei, *Die Intellektuellen: Literatur und Politik in Ostdeutschland von 1945 bis 2000* (Leipzig: Faber & Faber, 2001), 187.

models. For this, they were rewarded with prizes: the financial carrot to censorship's stick. But Hacks and Müller insisted on exposing more challenging social conflicts and replacing stock working-class heroes with more differentiated characters. In their view, this approach made dramatic and political sense. Theatre thrives on conflict and critical drama could confront spectators with uncomfortable facts, involving them in the search for solutions to social and industrial problems. Hacks found an ally in the eminent director and theatre manager Wolfgang Langhoff, who had declared in 1958 that plays needed to argue and prove their case, and that he had no desire to return to texts like *Golden fließt der Stahl* (The Golden Flow of Steel), a 1950 propaganda play by Karl Grünberg.[2]

Contemporary drama thus operated within a contested space whose parameters were continually being redefined, partly as scripts and productions were deemed to have transgressed them. Using Party pronouncements as their guidelines, functionaries had the unenviable task of deciding how much and what kinds of criticism to allow, what compromises to make, and where to draw the line. To make matters harder still, Culture Ministry officials were charged with promoting as well as controlling new drama. The tensions between these tasks, and the different shades of opinion within the administration, explain why decision-making sometimes seems schizophrenic. The Ministry supported all of the most controversial productions of the decade at some stage, awarding Müller grants to work on *Die Umsiedlerin* (The Female Resettler), urging the Deutsches Theater to perform Hacks's *Die Sorgen und die Macht* (Worries and Power), and pressing the director Benno Besson to ensure that Hacks's *Moritz Tassow* could be staged at the Volksbühne.[3]

The question, then, is how and where the political pressure for post-premiere bans originated. Whilst the regime always strove to present a united front, Monika Kaiser and Peter Grieder have identified significant tensions within the SED leadership in the 1960s.[4] They argue that

[2] 'Bericht über die Wahlberichtsversammlung im Deutschen Theater', 14.4.1958, BArch DY 30 IV 2/2.026/68.

[3] Heiner Müller, *Krieg ohne Schlacht: Leben in zwei Diktaturen*, rev. edn. (Cologne: Kiepenheuer & Witsch, 1994), 161; Bork to Bentzien, 16.3.1962, Besson, 26.2.1965, and Heinz, 26.2.1965, BArch DR 1/8688.

[4] Monika Kaiser, *Machtwechsel von Ulbricht zu Honecker: Funktionsmechanismen der SED-Diktatur in Konfliktsituationen 1962 bis 1972*, Zeithistorische Studien, 10 (Berlin: Akademie, 1997); Peter Grieder, *The East German Leadership 1946–73: Conflict and Crisis* (Manchester and New York: Manchester University Press, 1999).

from 1962–3 Walter Ulbricht moved away from his earlier dogmatism as he sought to make the regime more effective, modern, and attractive through economic reforms and a more liberal youth policy, and that these reforms increasingly faced opposition from conservatives in the Politbüro and Central Committee, including Erich Honecker, Paul Verner, and Kurt Hager. We need to be careful in relating these tensions to cultural policy: Ulbricht himself had conservative views on art and was in no doubt that the Party should remain in control of cultural processes. However, some officials and theatre practitioners did perceive scope for more critical approaches in drama and film as Ulbricht's other reforms took shape. Thus, the theatre critic and academic Ernst Schumacher sees genuine new openings in the early 1960s alongside warning shots, such as the ban on *Die Sorgen und die Macht*, that point towards the triumph of the dogmatic line at the Central Committee's Eleventh Plenary Session in 1965.[5]

This chapter investigates negotiations over this contested cultural space, and the parts played by theatre practitioners and different groups within the authorities. I start by examining the impact of the construction of the Berlin Wall on GDR theatres, particularly in East Berlin. This event posed major logistical challenges to theatres and tested their loyalty to the regime, but their reactions have hitherto received little attention.[6] In the following sections, I investigate the three most important contemporary drama controversies of the decade: Müller's *Die Umsiedlerin* (1961) and Hacks's *Die Sorgen und die Macht* (1962–3) and *Moritz Tassow* (1965–6). These texts dealt directly with events in the GDR and were banned only after their respective premieres, when sections of the administration campaigned against them. As Matthias Braun has published an excellent monograph on *Die Umsiedlerin*, I focus primarily on *Die Sorgen und die Macht* and *Moritz Tassow*.[7] Whilst Müller and Hacks were under surveillance in the same Stasi operation at this time, there were significant political and aesthetic differences in their approaches to drama, which influenced the authorities' responses to their work.

[5] Ernst Schumacher, 'DDR-Dramatik und 11. Plenum', in Günter Agde (ed.), *Kahlschlag: Das 11. Plenum des ZK der SED 1965: Studien und Dokumente* (Berlin: Aufbau, 1991), 93–105 at 94, 97.
[6] See Laura Bradley, 'A Different Political Forum: East German Theatre and the Construction of the Berlin Wall', *Journal of European Studies*, 36 (2006), 139–56.
[7] Braun, *Drama*.

2. THEATRE AND THE CONSTRUCTION
OF THE BERLIN WALL

The construction of the Berlin Wall did not mark a complete break in the GDR's cultural life, for the plays of the 1960s continued to explore themes set out at the First Bitterfeld Conference in 1959.[8] Both *Die Umsiedlerin* and *Die Sorgen und die Macht* had been drafted before the Wall was built, just as the productions that opened in autumn 1961 had been planned months beforehand. Even so, productions from 1962 onwards were rehearsed and performed under significantly different circumstances, as the closure of the GDR's borders had sealed the state off from the West and made it far harder for directors to follow developments in Western theatre. There was also an immediate and substantial shift in audience structure, as Western spectators stayed away, and the loss of revenue dismayed the Deputy Finance Minister.[9]

The construction of the Wall began on 13 August 1961, during the summer break. Although most theatres had begun rehearsals for the new season, only the Friedrichstadtpalast, a variety theatre, was putting on performances.[10] This gave theatre managers much-needed time to deal with the formidable logistical difficulties that the Wall caused. In August 1961, over 600 employees in East Berlin's theatres and opera houses still lived in the West, and few were prepared to move permanently to the East. So managers urgently needed to recruit new staff and recast productions in time for the new season and the high-profile autumn festival, which ran concurrently with its West Berlin rival. Maintaining the appearance of 'business as usual' was essential if the GDR was not to lose face.

Whilst East Berlin's theatres were less severely affected than its orchestras and opera houses, the BE and Deutsches Theater both lost members and the Volksbühne lost nearly one quarter of its staff. Those BE members who opted for the West included Peter Palitzsch, who had co-directed the internationally acclaimed production of Brecht's *Arturo Ui*, and the actors Harry Gillmann and Heinz Schubert. Given these

---

[8] See Manfred Jäger, *Kultur und Politik in der DDR 1945–1990* (Cologne: Nottbeck, 1995), 87–117.

[9] Sandig to Bentzien, 13.10.1961, BArch DY 30 IV 2/2.026/19.

[10] Kurt Schwarz, 'Wie ich als Sekretär für Kultur der Bezirksleitung Berlin den 13. August erlebte', 23.1.1989, LAB C Rep. 902 6826.

pressures, Culture Minister Hans Bentzien had to write to East Berlin's theatre managers, reminding them not to poach each other's actors.[11] Most gaps were filled at the expense of ensembles elsewhere in the Republic, creating new opportunities for talented actors who remained in the GDR. Eberhard Esche, for example, was offered work at both the BE and the Deutsches Theater, and Manfred Karge suddenly inherited several good roles at the BE.[12] Theatre practitioners had stronger incentives to stay in the East than many professionals, for its theatres boasted generous state funding, established stars like Ernst Busch, Helene Weigel, and Wolfgang Langhoff, and rising young directors like Besson. Indeed, the actress Angelica Domröse explains that the idea of moving to the West never occurred to her in the summer of 1961; after all, the BE was in the East.[13]

The SED closely monitored reactions to the Wall in the GDR's cultural institutions, including theatres. In East Berlin, Culture Secretary Kurt Schwarz had been summoned hastily to a secret meeting at midnight on 13 August, at which the city's First Secretary and Politbüro member Paul Verner had outlined the security measures. Schwarz and his colleagues mobilized the Party units in each area and institution, so that the SED's core members could canvass support and warn of resistance.[14] Politicians visited the worst-affected institutions: on 31 August, Deputy Culture Minister Hans Rodenberg explained the reasons for the Wall's construction to the Volksbühne.[15] During this period, Party Secretaries submitted regular reports on theatres to the SED-*Bezirksleitung*, which forwarded summaries to the Central Committee.[16]

The Wall forced artists and intellectuals to decide where their loyalties lay. Many rallied in a patriotic show of support for the regime. Officials in the Politbüro's Culture Commission informed Ulbricht that it had received far more direct expressions of support than in the past.[17] The SED-*Bezirksleitung* in Suhl reported that actors in Meiningen had

[11] Bentzien to Kurella, 29.11.1961, BArch DY 30 IV 2/2.026/71.
[12] Eberhard Esche, *Der Hase im Rausch* (Berlin: Eulenspiegel, 2000), 95; Dramaturgen des Berliner Ensemble, 'Theater zur Zeit der Mauer: Ein Gespräch mit dem Schauspieler Manfred Karge', *Berliner Zeitung*, 27.12.2002.
[13] Domröse, *Ich fang mich selbst ein*, 100.
[14] Schwarz, 23.1.1989.
[15] Report dated 1.9.1961, LAB C Rep. 902 1002.
[16] e.g. BArch DR 1/8619; LAB C Rep. 902 1002 and C Rep. 902 995.
[17] Kurella's office to Ulbricht, 5.10.1961, BArch DY 30 IV 2/2.026/72.

welcomed the security measures and that instances of heckling—a regular feature of previous theatre meetings—had ceased.[18] The authorities did note that several past dissenters seemed to have been silenced rather than won over, as they hesitated to back a resolution supporting Ulbricht. Even so, only one actor actually protested against the Wall, saying: 'Wenn sich die Arbeiter und die Bevölkerung der DDR das gefallen lassen, dann sind sie dumm. Man muß sehen, daß man nach dem Westen kommt.'[19] (If the workers and the people of the GDR put up with that, then they're fools. We've got to get out to the West.) One price of remaining in the GDR, of course, was censorship.

However, at least some dramatists and theatre practitioners, including Hacks and Müller, hoped that the containment of refugees and the disappearance of most Western spectators might increase their room for artistic manoeuvre.[20] Some theatre practitioners regarded as ideologically reliable also shared this view. At the BE, Manfred Wekwerth staged Brecht's *Tage der Commune* (Days of the Commune) in order both to justify the Wall, by showing that the Revolution should be defended with force, and to call for transparency in government. The Communard Langevin declares:

Erheben wir keinen Anspruch auf Unfehlbarkeit, wie es alle alten Regierungen ohne Ausnahme tun. Veröffentlichen wir alle Reden und Handlungen, weihen wir das Publikum ein in unsere Unvollkommenheit, denn wir haben nichts zu fürchten außer uns selbst.[21]

Let us lay no claim to infallibility, as all old-style governments never fail to do. Let us publish all our speeches and actions, let us share the secret of our imperfection with the public, for we have nothing to fear but ourselves.

Whilst the SED leadership was formally committed to de-Stalinization, which Khrushchev had launched in the USSR in 1956, the scope of this policy remained strictly limited. Reform-minded socialists hoped that the SED would now go further and examine the trials and arrests of the 1950s. Wolfgang Langhoff, for instance, had been falsely charged as a

---

[18] 'Einschätzung der Stimmung und politischen Haltung der Intelligenz zu den Maßnahmen der Regierung', 23.8.1961, BArch DR 1/8619.

[19] Ibid.

[20] *Du tust mir wirklich fehlen: Der Briefwechsel zwischen Peter Hacks und Heinar Kipphardt*, ed. Uwe Naumann (Berlin: Eulenspiegel, 2004), 44; H. Müller, *Krieg*, 487.

[21] Manfred Wekwerth, *Erinnern ist Leben: Eine dramatische Autobiographie* (Leipzig: Faber & Faber, 2000), 182–3; Brecht, *BFA*, viii (1992), 291–2.

spy and stripped of his Party offices in connection with the Noel Field Affair in 1950. He had since been exonerated but never publicly rehabilitated. Knowing that the Deutsches Theater had a vested interest in initiating a frank examination of both the Party and GDR society, officials watched it particularly closely.

Müller and Hacks were under Stasi surveillance as part of the same operational investigation (*Operativ-Vorgang* or OV), owing to their known sympathy for a more thorough process of de-Stalinization. Müller had been under surveillance since 1957 in the OV 'Donnerstagskreis' (Thursday Circle), together with other writers such as Manfred Bieler and Günter Kunert, and Hacks was subsequently added to the investigation. It was reorganized into a new OV 'Zersetzer' (Subversive Elements) in October 1962, and the Stasi continued to intercept the suspects' post and to recruit informers, so that Hacks and Müller were subjected to a far greater level of surveillance than most other dramatists and theatre practitioners in this period. Officers claimed that the suspects formed a camouflaged opposition, directed primarily against the government and its cultural policy.[22] Although the Stasi concluded that the suspects no longer formed a tight-knit group, officers argued that they continued to pose a risk.

For all the Stasi's attempts to identify common ground between these writers, there were substantive differences in their attitudes towards the GDR and its representation. Whereas Bieler was already considering leaving the GDR and had adopted a sharply critical stance towards the regime, Hacks had only recently moved to the GDR and conceived his criticism as constructive. He remained a lifelong supporter of Ulbricht and backed his economic reforms, and he was able to conceive of a harmonious resolution to the industrial and personal conflict in *Die Sorgen und die Macht*.[23] Whilst Müller's production plays affirm that socialism is making progress, he depicts this progress as highly contradictory and painful. Even in his comedy *Die Umsiedlerin*, Soviet tractors arrive too late to prevent a farmer from committing suicide, and a tractor driver is injured when a landmine explodes in the field that he is ploughing.[24] Müller's support for socialism was accompanied by a

[22] BStU AOP 1958/71, iv, fo. 7.
[23] See e.g. André Müller sen., *Gespräche mit Hacks 1963–2003* (Berlin: Eulenspiegel, 2008), 37, 66.
[24] Heiner Müller, *Werke*, ed. Frank Hörnigk, 12 vols. (Frankfurt/M.: Suhrkamp, 1998–2008), iii (2000): *Die Stücke 1*, 194, 244.

hard-hitting realism that made officials more resistant to his drama than they were to that of Hacks.

3. *DIE UMSIEDLERIN* (1961)

Just six weeks after the construction of the Wall, the ban on B. K. Tragelehn's production of *Die Umsiedlerin* dealt a blow to theatre practitioners hoping to examine society more critically. Heiner Müller's uncompromising depiction of the conflicts in an agricultural community during collectivization was banned straight after its premiere on 30 September 1961, during a GDR student theatre festival. Even though the performance had been seen by only three hundred spectators, many of them cultural functionaries, the authorities came down heavily on those responsible at the student theatre of the Hochschule für Ökonomie (University for Economics) in Berlin-Karlshorst. The SED issued more than twenty reprimands, expelled Müller from the Writers' Union, and sent Tragelehn to work in a coal mine. Müller's plays were not performed again in the GDR until 1971, and Tragelehn would not direct again in Berlin until Ruth Berghaus hired him at the BE in 1972.

Matthias Braun's detailed analysis of the archival evidence highlights the retrospective stylization in reports, as those in the firing line sought to defend themselves.[25] This is evident, for instance, in a letter sent to the SED-*Bezirksleitung* on behalf of the Deutsches Theater, whose members were alarmed at their association with the production; the theatre had helped Müller gain a scholarship to write the play and Langhoff had been the festival's patron. The theatre's representative distanced the company from the production, admitted to the SED-*Bezirksleitung* that they had been too trusting, and adeptly sought to shift the blame:

Niemand bei uns hatte es auch nur entfernt für möglich gehalten, daß ausgerechnet im Bereich der Aufsichtspflicht der Genossen von der Hochschule (deren Unterrichtsgegenstand unmittelbar der Marxismus-Leninismus ist!) ein Stück republikfeindlichen Charakters aufgeführt werden könnte.[26]

None of us had considered it even remotely possible that a play hostile to the Republic might be performed in—of all places—a theatre under the supervision of comrades from the University (who actually teach Marxism-Leninism!).

[25] Braun, *Drama*, 31.
[26] BStU AOP 1958/71, v, fo. 65. Quoted in Braun, *Drama*, 59.

Braun infers the motivations of different sections of the state and Party apparatus from their reports: whilst the FDJ authorities carried the main responsibility and compensated for their earlier failure by making particularly harsh demands, the Culture Ministry's representatives wanted to avoid draconian measures against a writer whom they considered talented, and the Central Committee's Culture Department was in favour of clarifying points of principle but without aggravating the cultural climate unnecessarily.[27] This explains why the FDJ's demands for the arrests of Müller, Tragelehn, and the head of the theatre were not met.

Whilst the authorities' response to *Die Umsiedlerin* dominated discussions in the theatre community for a time, it did not halt productions of critical contemporary drama. Many theatre practitioners actually shared the SED's concerns about the play's open structure, critical presentation of functionaries, and references to the former internment camp and current Stasi prison in Bautzen. Several theatre practitioners reportedly left the premiere early in protest, including the actress Mathilde Danegger and the dramatist Helmut Baierl.[28] Since *Die Umsiedlerin* aroused controversy amongst theatre practitioners themselves, rejection of it did not amount to a renunciation of critical drama per se. Indeed, one official was irritated that theatre practitioners had not appreciated the production's wider significance, complaining that many simply argued that something like this could never happen in their theatres.[29] If the Culture Department and FDJ had belatedly sought to set an example with *Die Umsiedlerin*, the text's experimental nature and the theatre's amateur status made the production ill-suited to such a task.

4. *DIE SORGEN UND DIE MACHT* (1962–1963)

Peter Hacks was the one dramatist in the Writers' Union who consistently refused to denounce *Die Umsiedlerin* and abstained from the vote on Müller's exclusion.[30] Two of his plays, *Die Sorgen und die Macht* and

---

[27] Braun, *Drama*, 37.
[28] Ibid. 30.
[29] 'Wie wurde die Aussprache der Parteileitungen der Theater im ZK von den Institutionen ausgewertet?', 20.8.1961, LAB C Rep. 902 995.
[30] 'Information über Tendenzen des Revisionismus auf dem Gebiet der Kultur', 9.11.1961, LAB C Rep. 902 995.

Moritz Tassow, sparked the other major contemporary drama controversies of the decade, even though they had passed far more stringent
pre-performance controls than *Die Umsiedlerin.* The authorities had
been more alert, partly because they had failed to prevent the earlier
controversy and partly because more prominent theatres were involved:
the Deutsches Theater and the Volksbühne. The fall-out over *Die
Umsiedlerin* had actually prompted Bentzien to write to regional
administrations across the GDR, warning Culture Secretaries to read
and assess new plays before they entered rehearsals, and to forward the
scripts and assessments to the Ministry.[31] Hacks's plays provoked
genuine disagreements amongst officials, and even some of his staunchest critics conceded that the plays had positive points.

The censorship of *Die Sorgen und die Macht* had a greater impact on
the theatre community than that of *Die Umsiedlerin.* Whereas Müller
and Tragelehn were setting out on their careers and experimenting with
a student theatre, 61-year-old Langhoff was a respected director, concentration camp survivor, and loyal Party member. Langhoff and the
Deutsches Theater had not set out to court controversy, and many
spectators reacted positively to the twenty-two performances of *Die
Sorgen und die Macht.* The company would never forget what it perceived to be a gross injustice: an anonymous letter-writer criticized an
actress for her part in it in 1976, the company revisited the case at public
matinees in 1986 and 1991, and its dramaturge Alexander Weigel
published a collection of newly released documents on it in 1991.[32]

Industrial Conflicts and Constructive Criticism

Hacks had moved from Munich to East Berlin in 1955, prompting
SED officials to argue in the early 1960s that he needed more time to
understand life under socialism.[33] The Deutsches Theater had already
staged three of his historical dramas, but *Die Sorgen und die Macht* was
his first play set in the GDR. It took its title from Ulbricht's comment
'wer die Macht hat, hat auch bestimmte Sorgen' (those who hold power

---

[31] Bentzien to Sieber, 25.11.1961, SächsStA-D 11430 (RdB Dresden) 6539.
[32] Anonymous letter postmarked 8.12.1976, LAB C Rep. 902 3614; 'Im Rahmen der
traditionellen Sonntags-Matineen...', LAB C Rep. 902 5908; Alexander Weigel (ed.),
'Der Fall *Die Sorgen und die Macht* 1962/63: Dokumente', *Blätter des Deutschen
Theaters,* 19 (1991), 609–52.
[33] e.g. 'Information', 9.5.1962, LAB C Rep. 902 1001.

also have certain worries), and it shows how a supposedly model coal factory has sacrificed quality in order to win competitions predicated only on quantity. As the inadequate briquettes do not provide enough heat, they prevent the workers in the neighbouring glass factory from meeting their own production targets. The glass workers lose out as the briquette workers grow rich.

The regime had already acknowledged the difficulties of balancing quality and quantity in industrial production. Hacks's play had been inspired by a complaint published by three steelworkers in the SED newspaper *Neues Deutschland*, and it complemented the State Planning Commission's campaign to improve the quality of briquettes. As Langhoff's team explained at length in the programme, Hacks showed how workers could solve their problems and enable both factories to meet their targets. These factors indicate why officials responded more positively to the play than they had done to *Die Umsiedlerin*. The problem, though, was that Hacks needed to achieve a more realistic presentation of workers and Party functionaries if his constructive criticism was to work in dramatic terms. Accordingly, he attributed the poor quality of the briquettes to the workers' self-interest and the Party's internal rivalry and poor leadership. The briquette factory's problems are solved by a non-Party member, Max Fidorra, who acts not out of socialist conviction but out of love for Hede Stoll, a worker in the glass factory. As a result, romantic cliché wins out over the conflicts inherent in the production process. Even though Hacks had not intended to court controversy, these aspects of the plot and characterization were bound to cause offence among Party functionaries. Deputy Culture Minister Kurt Bork later argued that the play might leave spectators with the impression that socialism was unstoppable, despite the SED.[34]

Divided Reactions and the Senftenberg Premiere

After Hacks had completed the first draft of *Die Sorgen und die Macht* in 1959, Kurella's office commissioned a private performance from the Deutsches Theater, directed by Fritz Bennewitz. There was no shortage of spectators, for Kurella had invited representatives of the Culture

---

[34] 'Gedächtnisprotokoll über eine Aussprache mit Schauspielern des Deutschen Theaters am 29.10.1962', 5.11.1962, BArch DY 30 IV 2/2.026/68.

Ministry, Culture Department, SED-*Bezirksleitung*, Writers' Union, and FDJ, along with students and coal workers.[35] Kurella also sent the script to leading Party members, and it provoked a particularly strong reaction from the 66-year-old director and playwright Gustav von Wangenheim. After reading the play, Wangenheim informed Kurella of his horror and disgust: the play offended the working class and showed Hacks's arrogance towards the Party.[36] When spectators also criticized the private performance, Hacks was sent to rework the script.

The revised version was premiered in the mining town of Senftenberg, at a theatre sponsored by the Deutsches Theater, on 17 May 1960. Rather like the earlier private performance, this low-key production tested reactions before the play was showcased at one of the Republic's major theatres. Local Party members and factory workers reacted positively to the initial reading. They agreed that the play should definitely be staged, and one worker commented that Hacks's characters were true to life.[37] But the director Klaus Gendries reports that the SED-*Bezirksleitung* banned the production two days before rehearsals were due to start, and the ban was only overturned after an appeal to Rodenberg. After the premiere, a representative of the Central Committee informed Gendries that performances could continue, but that the production could not be shown at the forthcoming Workers' Festival. He also objected to certain aspects of the staging: the Party Secretary's trousers needed ironing, and a sign to the toilets was displayed next to Lenin's portrait in one scene. These aspects were duly changed, and the production was performed more than thirty times.[38]

Pre-performance Controls at the Deutsches Theater

After the Senftenberg premiere, the Deutsches Theater examined the latest draft of Hacks's script. With the exception of one actress,

[35] Kurella to Apel, Ebert, Hager, Kaschel, 5.9.1959, BArch DY 30 IV 2/2.026/68. See also A. Müller sen., *Gespräche mit Hacks*, 7.
[36] Wangenheim to Kurella, no date, BArch DY 30 IV 2/2.026/68.
[37] 'Protokoll über die Diskussion am 9. November 1959 über *Die Sorgen und die Macht* von Peter Hacks', DTA file 'Hacks Programmheft'.
[38] Klaus Gendries, 'Konterrevolutionäre Plattformbildung', in Sewan Latchinian and Harald Müller (eds.), *Glück auf! 60 Jahre Theater Senftenberg* (Berlin: TdZ, 2006), 40–2 at 41–2.

the theatre's Party members agreed to perform the play, even though they believed that it would not appeal to their regular audience.[39] In the Culture Commission, Erhard Scherner argued that the play had improved and would be useful if it was staged carefully and discussed appropriately.[40] The Ministry agreed, and Bork allowed the theatre to start rehearsals on condition that further cuts were made and the production team remained in close contact with the Ministry and the SED-*Bezirksleitung* or the Culture Department.[41]

Whilst Bork had not endorsed the play unreservedly, the central state and Party authorities had approved the production at every phase before the premiere. The Deutsches Theater stressed this when it subsequently came under fire. On 29 October, Langhoff declared that Rodenberg had not expressed any reservations, while Hermann Axen—the chief editor of *Neues Deutschland*—had even said that the play had to be staged.[42] The theatre's Party members reiterated these arguments on 14 December, pointing out that the Culture Ministry had wanted the play staged in time for the Workers' Festival in Erfurt and that the Culture Department had checked the new script and approved the plan to perform it.[43] Similarly, Bork's notes from a meeting on 30 December indicate that Mathilde Danegger and the Party Secretary Jürgen Schmidt still blamed the Culture Department and Ministry, arguing that they had made the same mistakes as the theatre.[44] In January 1963, the dramaturge Lily Leder asked why Culture Department officials had allowed the staging to go ahead, when it was now deemed hostile to the Party.[45] The theatre's members were justifiably indignant that they alone had been blamed for a production that the authorities had monitored closely. (See Fig. 2.1 for a photograph of the staging.)

There is no evidence that the Deutsches Theater intended to mount a subversive production. According to Bork, Langhoff emphasized

[39] 'Zusammenfassendes Protokoll der *Sorgen und die Macht*-Diskussion in der Parteiversammlung vom 13.3.', AdK ID 884.

[40] 'Zusammenfassung', BArch DY 30 IV 2/2.026/68.

[41] Bork to Bentzien, 16.3.1962.

[42] 'Gedächtnisprotokoll', 5.11.1962.

[43] 'Analyse der Betriebsparteiorganisation Deutsches Theater zu Stück und Inszenierung', 14.12.1962, LAB C Rep. 904–94 Nr. 4.

[44] Bork, handwritten notes on a meeting at the DT, 30.12.1962, BArch DR 1/8850.

[45] 'Bericht über die Auseinandersetzung im Deutschen Theater', 5.1.1963, BArch DY 30 IV 2/2.026/68.

Fig. 2.1. The glass factory in *Die Sorgen und die Macht* at the Deutsches Theater, 1962 (Willy Saeger, Deutsches Theatermuseum München)

on 29 October that the play had been staged to promote socialism and was not intended as an attack on SED cultural policy.[46] During rehearsals, Langhoff had cut details that might have caused offence, such as a line blaming the theft of Hede's bicycle on construction workers.[47] He also suggested cutting lines that were implicitly critical of Paul Kunze, the Party Secretary in the briquette factory. Kunze has failed to notice that his wife has cancelled their subscription to *Neues Deutsch-land* to save money, even though he was the best local campaigner for the paper.[48] So although Petra Stuber claims that Langhoff was attempting to use the production to assert his theatre's autonomy against the Culture Department, the rehearsal notes suggest that he directed the play in good faith.[49] Even Bork acknowledged that he was entirely convinced of the theatre's honourable intentions.[50]

Although the central authorities had approved the production, officials from the SED-*Bezirksleitung* had raised doubts during rehearsals. East Berlin's Culture Secretary reportedly criticized a scene set in the Party office of the briquette factory. However, he admitted that he had not learned how to read plays and might see the scene differently if it were explained to him.[51] More serious doubts were raised in an assessment of 9 May 1962, which argued that the entire concept of the original version had been wrong, and that Hacks could not have made far-reaching changes in the time available. Surprisingly, the assessor had not actually read the revised script. He or she simply referred to the 1959 version, saying that Hacks's critical characterization of the Party Secretary—presumably Kunze—could not be allowed as a typical representation of holders of this office.[52] Writers attempting to introduce more critical forms of characterization repeatedly found that criticism of individual functionaries was read metonymically and related to the Party as a whole, including its leadership.

[46] Bork, 30.12.1962.
[47] 'Einige Notizen zur ersten Besprechung *Die Sorgen und die Macht*', 22.3.1962, AdK Ulrich-Thein-Archiv 77.
[48] '2. Besprechung zur Inszenierung *Die Sorgen und die Macht*', 26.3.1962, AdK Ulrich-Thein-Archiv 77.
[49] Stuber, *Spielräume und Grenzen*, 191.
[50] 'Gedächtnisprotokoll', 5.11.1962.
[51] '2. Besprechung'.
[52] 'Information', 9.5.1962.

48   *Part I. Theatre Censorship in East Berlin*

From Endorsement to Opprobrium

Despite the concerns voiced by the SED-*Bezirksleitung*, workers and even some Party functionaries responded enthusiastically to the previews, quite in contrast to the reactions elicited by the test performance in 1959. Workers repeatedly praised Hacks's realism and lack of rose-tinted spectacles, and employees from a local radio station observed that the characters resembled their colleagues.[53] The production even seemed to have won official approval, when the first brief review in *Neues Deutschland* described it as impressive, exciting, and true to the Party, and reported that three high-ranking Party members, Kurella, Rodenberg, and Foreign Secretary Lothar Bolz, had applauded heartily.[54] The Culture Department's initial assessment, written after the previews, stated that Hacks had understood the Party's role and that the play could be performed in important industrial towns across the GDR.[55] The writer made short work of functionaries who claimed that the play misrepresented workers and the Party:

Solche Funktionäre glauben offensichtlich, daß eine realistische Darstellung von Widersprüchen des Lebens der Politik der Partei schade. Wir halten solche Auffassungen für unbegründet und für unsere Politik schädlich.[56]

Such functionaries obviously believe that a realistic portrayal of life's contradictions causes political damage to the Party. We consider such views unfounded and politically damaging for us.

So although Stuber claims that the production was under permanent fire from the Culture Department,[57] the Department actually approved the production, both during the rehearsals and immediately after the previews. As Langhoff explained, the theatre was therefore genuinely shocked by the sudden change in the Department's attitude.[58]

[53] 'Probeneindrücke von Kollegen der Braunkohlenbrikettfabrik Senftenberg und der Securawerke Berlin'; Achim Dyballa, '*Die Sorgen und die Macht*'. Both in AdK ID 884.
[54] H. Keisch, 'Zu einer eindrucksvollen und anregenden Darbietung...', *ND*, 3.10.1962.
[55] 'Information über die Premiere von *Die Sorgen und die Macht* von Peter Hacks im Deutschen Theater am Dienstag, dem 2. Oktober 1962', 25.9.1962, BArch DY 30 IV 2/2.026/68.
[56] Ibid.
[57] Stuber, *Spielräume und Grenzen*, 191.
[58] 'Gedächtnisprotokoll', 5.11.1962.

Evidence of more hostile early reactions can be found in the Stasi files. The informer 'Jenny' had seen the premiere on 2 October with her husband and discussed it afterwards with other Party members in East Berlin's Press Club. She and her companions considered it counter-revolutionary in the extreme, failed to understand how the production had come about, and wished they had interrupted the performance. 'Jenny' reported that the production had been praised prematurely before the premiere, claiming that a member of the Culture Department had visited the offices of the weekly newspaper *Sonntag* and spoken in favour of the play.[59]

The tide began to turn on 4 October, when Walther Pollatschek published a controversial review in the *Berliner Zeitung*. Whilst the Culture Department had praised Langhoff for overcoming the play's political infelicities, Pollatschek blamed Langhoff and Hacks for the production's political flaws.[60] Since the *Berliner Zeitung* was the organ of the SED-*Bezirksleitung*, the review suggested that local Party officials endorsed Pollatschek's criticisms. Indeed, when Bork analysed the situation on 4 December, he identified the *Bezirksleitung* as the play's prime opponent and distinguished clearly between the response of the Ministry and that of Verner and his officials, whom he described as almost hostile.[61]

East Berlin's theatre practitioners rallied immediately to Langhoff's defence, no doubt mindful of the earlier attacks on his reputation. Sixty-two members of the Deutsches Theater and Volksbühne signed a letter of protest to the head of the Berliner Verlag, which published the *Berliner Zeitung*.[62] Yet this well-intentioned gesture of support backfired, for Verner forwarded the letter to Ulbricht, and the authorities quickly united to avoid all appearance of internal dissent. Hans Grümmer—the member of the Culture Department responsible for theatre—distanced himself frantically from the production:

Ich hatte sehr viele Einwände gegen das Stück und wir haben diskutiert, ob man es absetzen oder laufen lassen soll. Wir haben uns entschieden, das Stück laufen zu lassen und zu diskutieren, weil sich an Hand dieser Inszenierung... viele

[59] BStU AOP 1958/71, viii, fo. 53.
[60] Walther Pollatschek, '*Die Sorgen und die Macht*', *Berliner Zeitung* (East Berlin), 4.10.1962.
[61] Bork, handwritten notes, 4.12.1962, BArch DR 1/8850.
[62] Actors to Hermann Leupold, 8.10.1962, BArch DY 30 IV 2/2.026/68.

Grundprobleme der Entwicklung unserer sozialistischen Dramatik und der Theaterkunst herausarbeiten lassen.[63]

I had a great many objections to the play and we discussed whether to cancel it or let it continue. We decided to let the play continue and discuss it, as this production...can be used to identify many basic problems concerning the development of our socialist drama and theatre.

The shift in pronouns was significant: Grümmer singled out himself as an opponent of the production and then claimed that the Department was collectively responsible for the decision to proceed. As officials rushed to conceal their earlier support, the campaign against the production gained momentum, and Willi Köhler officially retracted the earlier report in *Neues Deutschland.*[64]

The Causes of the Controversy

Why was this production so much more controversial than the Senftenberg premiere? For a start, the Deutsches Theater had a higher profile and more senior Party officials saw its productions. These officials included Verner, whose assessment carried weight: he was a member of the Politbüro and the production took place in his region, even though the Deutsches Theater was directly responsible to the Culture Ministry. The international context strengthened Verner's argument that the regime could not afford to make ideological concessions. Even though the subject matter of *Die Sorgen und die Macht* had no direct bearing on the Cuban Missile Crisis of October 1962, allusions to it recur in the files.[65] Alexander Weigel rightly locates the attack on the production within a broader cultural offensive in the months following the crisis: in December 1962, Peter Huchel was sacked as editor of *Sinn und Form* and Stephan Hermlin was attacked after organizing an evening of readings by young poets at the Academy of Arts.[66]

[63] Grümmer, draft statement, 13.10.1962, BArch DY 30 IV 2/2.026/68.

[64] Willi Köhler, 'Die Sorge um den Schriftsteller', *ND*, 16.10.1962.

[65] 'Gedächtnisprotokoll über die Sitzung der Zentralen Parteileitung des Deutschen Schriftstellerverbandes', 4.1.1963; cf. 'Entschließung', 30.12.1962; 'Einschätzung der Leitungssitzung der Berliner Parteiorganisation des Deutschen Schriftstellerverbandes vom 3. Januar 1963', 4.1.1963. All in BArch DY 30 IV 2/2.026/68.

[66] Weigel, 'Der Fall *Die Sorgen und die Macht* 1962/63', 610.

The latest version of Hacks's script contained new material that proved controversial under this heightened scrutiny. The most contentious sections compared the present negatively with the future communist Utopia. The young, naive Party worker Emma Holdefleiß argues that the present is simply a painful route to a glorious end:

HOLDEFLEISS   Kollegen, Kommunismus, wenn ihr euch
    Den vorstelln wollt, dann richtet eure Augen
    Auf, was jetzt ist, und nehmt das Gegenteil;
    Denn wenig ähnlich ist dem Ziel der Weg.
    Nehmt so viel Freuden, wie ihr Sorgen kennt,
    Nehmt so viel Überfluß wie Mangel jetzt
    Und malt euch also mit den grauen Tinten
    Der Gegenwart der Zukunft buntes Bild.[67]

    Colleagues, if you want to imagine
    Communism, then train your eyes
    On what we have now and take the opposite;
    For the path bears little resemblance to the goal.
    Take as many joys as you know sorrows
    Take as much excess as you know scarcity
    And use the grey hues of the present
    To paint the bright image of the future.

In attempting to convince the workers that present-day sacrifices were worthwhile, Holdefleiß had suggested that the GDR's contemporary reality was the opposite of communism. When one Party member declares that nothing is improving, the Party Secretary in charge of the coal plant immediately disputes this view. Yet even he acknowledges that it is difficult to judge how much progress has been made and how long it will take to reach the goal:

TWARDOWSKI   Ein Mann, der durch den Wald zum Fluß herabsteigt,
    Zweifelt, wie weit er kam, und spürt's aus nichts.
    Nämlich ob ihn ein Tag vom Ziel trennt, oder
    Eine Sekunde, stets in gleichem Dämmer
    Hält ihn derselbe laubichte Kamin
    Von Büschen und Gestrüppen. Während dauernd
    Sein Ort sich ändert, scheint sich nichts zu ändern

[67] Peter Hacks, 'Die Sorgen und die Macht' (Inspizientenbuch), 57, DTA. Holdefleiß's name comments on her character: 'hold' means 'fair' or 'lovely', and 'Fleiß' means 'diligence'.

Und vorwärtsschreitend scheint er stillzustehn
Bis zu dem Nu, wo er ansetzt und schleunig
Vom Dunkel ins Licht tritt und ans breite Wasser.[68]

A man descending through the forest to the river
Doubts how far he has come and has no way of telling.
For whether a day separates him from his goal or
A second, the same leafy shaft
Of bushes and undergrowth holds him trapped
In the same twilight. While his location
Changes constantly, nothing seems to change
And while moving forwards he seems to stand still
Until the moment when he sets forth and steps
Quickly from darkness into light and to the open water.

Neither of these speeches questioned the regime's ability to succeed in the long term, as Holdefleiß and Twardowski are confident that they will eventually reach the communist Utopia. This explains why, even though the Culture Department had identified the passages as problematic, it approved them for performance. But conservative Party officials wanted to be congratulated on their achievements since 1945, not reminded of how far short of their ideals they fell. This problem grew as time went on: in the second decade of socialist rule, the SED found it increasingly hard to blame contemporary problems on the legacy of capitalism.

Hacks's constructive criticism of the government and Party proved equally controversial. His new prologue declared:

Und viel, viel, viel, schreit die Regierung, der's
Um Katarakte geht von Energie;
Sie murmelt auch von Qualität was, aber
Lobt dich für Menge. Gute Gründe pflastern
Den Weg des Irrtums.[69]

And lots, lots, lots, shouts the government, which
Wants an unlimited flow of energy;
It also murmurs something about quality but
Praises you for quantity. The road to error
Is paved with good intentions.

---

[68] Hacks, Inspizientenbuch, 19.
[69] Ibid. 2.

These lines addressed a serious industrial problem: by bribing workers to increase production, the government was giving them a financial incentive to disregard quality. In fact, Ulbricht was grappling with this very problem as he developed what would become his New Economic System. In speeches in October and November 1962, he acknowledged that the current system of rewards was flawed and argued that bonuses needed to be carefully targeted and calibrated.[70] But instead of showing that the Party was taking steps to resolve the problem, Hacks indicates that its representatives in the coal plant and briquette factory have wilfully ignored it:

TWARDOWSKI Wer hält denn das aus, alles sehen, alle Übel? . . . Also, Genosse, hätte ich tausend Augen, ich schlösse sie alle bis auf eins, mit dem würde ich vorsichtig blinzeln.[71]

Who can stand seeing everything, everything that's wrong? . . . Well, comrade, if I had a thousand eyes, I would close them all except for one, which I would use cautiously to steal a look.

Twardowski admits his failings here in the spirit of self-criticism, a point that was lost as soon as the earlier part of his speech was quoted out of context in internal reports. Yet the production's critics did not object publicly to such lines, as doing so would have drawn attention to the very arguments that they wanted to suppress. Instead, they criticized Hacks for distorting the Party's image and offending workers by suggesting that they were motivated only by material greed and sex.[72] Hacks's wife reportedly disputed this view, claiming that workers liked the play and only functionaries did not, as it criticized them.[73]

---

[70] See Walter Ulbricht, *Zum neuen ökonomischen System der Planung und Leitung* (East Berlin: Dietz, 1966), 65. Müller sen. argues that as Ulbricht's reforms were controversial within the Party, *Sorgen und die Macht* attracted criticism from both opponents and supporters of the reforms; Ulbricht had no interest in alarming his opponents before the reforms had been implemented. A. Müller sen., *Gespräche mit Hacks*, 29 n. 2.

[71] Hacks, Inspizientenbuch, 16.

[72] Köhler, 16.10.1962; 'Einschätzung der Aufführung *Sorgen und die Macht*', 26.10.1962, BArch DY 30 IV 2/2.026/68.

[73] Schwarz to Scherner, no date, BArch DY 30 IV 2/2.026/68.

Staged Debates and Public Retractions

As Langhoff's production was already in the public arena and had been reviewed positively in *Neues Deutschland*, it could not be withdrawn quietly like the test performance in 1959. Instead, officials staged a debate in the press and behind the scenes. Although several statements supporting the production were published, there was also some misrepresentation. Pollatschek and the Culture Department presented the debate as a clash between enthusiastic intellectuals and outraged workers, but surveys carried out by the Deutsches Theater suggest almost the opposite. Workers reacted enthusiastically to the production, whereas theatre students expressed their indignation in terms suspiciously similar to Pollatschek's review.[74]

Bork subsequently criticized the press discussion as a tactical error.[75] By denouncing the production, the Party inadvertently encouraged people to see it, on the grounds that it deviated from the official line and might soon be banned. Indeed, the Party's disapproval created a vicious circle: it heightened spectators' sensitivity to criticisms and ambiguities in the text, so that spectators' reactions confirmed the authorities' suspicions. Contrary to the intentions of the Deutsches Theater, the production began to elicit a subversive effect. Otto Mellies, who played Fidorra, is said to have protested on 29 October that the production was attracting the wrong kind of spectators and that the West Berlin radio station RIAS (Radio in the American Sector) had been encouraging people to attend.[76] In their final statement, the theatre's Party members distanced themselves from any suggestion that the high attendance figures marked a victory over official cultural policy.[77]

The Writers' Union played an ambivalent role in the debate, as it was both an instrument of control and a union whose members expected mutual support. The fact that the control function dominated did not

---

[74] 'Weitere Stimmen zu *Die Sorgen und die Macht*' and 'Einige Äußerungen von Studenten der Theaterwissenschaft (2. und 4. Studienjahr) während eines Seminars zu *Die Sorgen und die Macht*'. Both in AdK ID 884.

[75] Bork, handwritten notes for a discussion in the Culture Commission, 10.2.1962 [*sic*], BArch DR 1/8850.

[76] 'Gedächtnisprotokoll', 5.11.1962.

[77] 'Entschließung der SED-Betriebsparteiorganisation Deutsches Theater', 22.3.1963, BArch DY 30 IV A 2/2.024/32.

surprise Hacks, for the Union had strongly criticized the first draft of
Die Sorgen und die Macht. Indeed, when its managers had 'invited' him
to defend his play in 1959, he had acerbically reminded them of the
distinction between agreeing a date for a conversation and issuing a
summons to a tribunal.[78] In 1962–3, the Union sided collectively and
publicly with the authorities by issuing a statement that reproduced
the Party's criticisms and blamed the production on the theatre's
Party Organization, particularly Langhoff.[79]

Individually, however, several writers did support Hacks. At a
meeting of the Union's Central Party Leadership, attended by representatives of the Culture Department and the SED-*Bezirksleitung*, Günter
Görlich reportedly warned Party members against expressing opinions
on plays that they did not know.[80] Some members criticized the
Culture Department and suggested that it had misinformed Ulbricht.[81]
The novelist Anna Seghers even supported Hacks publicly by sending a
favourable review to *Neues Deutschland*. After consulting with the Politbüro and failing—despite the assistance of Köhler and Kurella—to
persuade Seghers to withdraw her article, Axen eventually published
it.[82] Some public debate was possible, in this case because of the symbolic capital that Seghers possessed as an internationally renowned anti-
fascist writer.

The most intensive discussions occurred behind the scenes at the
Deutsches Theater in regular meetings between late October and
March. Although the Ministry and Culture Department had initially
approved *Die Sorgen und die Macht*, they now closed ranks with the
SED-*Bezirksleitung*, attempting to persuade the theatre to withdraw
the production and admit its mistakes.[83] This public and 'voluntary'
recantation was essential to maintain the charade of censorship as
pedagogy and avoid the appearance of state intervention.

The authorities applied the greatest pressure to Party members,
assuming that the rest of the theatre would follow their lead. This
pressure reached a climax in the first two weeks of January in the run-
up to the Sixth Party Conference, at a time when Langhoff was out of

---

[78] Hacks to Erwin Strittmatter (1960), AdK AdSV 156.
[79] 'Stellungnahme des Sekretariats des Deutschen Schriftstellerverbandes zum
Theaterstück *Die Sorgen und die Macht* von Peter Hacks', AdSV 156.
[80] 'Gedächtnisprotokoll', 4.1.1963.
[81] 'Einschätzung', 4.1.1963.
[82] See correspondence in BArch DY 30 IV 2/2.026/68.
[83] 'Einschätzung', 26.10.1962.

action due to illness.[84] What is surprising is not that Party members at the Deutsches Theater eventually succumbed, but that they held out so long. It was not until Grümmer questioned them individually on 3 January that most accepted the SED's criticisms. Even so, the Culture Department had to concede another failure on 5 January, when the proposed recantation was rejected.[85] The partial breakthrough came a week later, when—after ten hours of thorough discussions, in which Wagner and Grümmer repeatedly intervened—twenty-three members accepted most of the criticisms and advised Langhoff to halt performances.[86] Even this represented only a partial victory, as five members—Kilger, Leder, Hiemer, Esche, and Höchst—voted against the resolution and four—Stolper, Kupke, Christoph, and Henny Müller—abstained.[87] Moreover, the Department reported that those who voted in favour had sacrificed the play in order to save Langhoff as their manager, a report that Jürgen Schmidt confirmed in 1991.[88]

On the eve of the Sixth Party Conference, the Party Organization of the Hans-Otto-Theater in Potsdam advised its manager to withdraw its own production of *Die Sorgen und die Macht*.[89] This decision was timely, for Verner and Kurella criticized the play in their conference speeches. Verner argued that the case was particularly serious because the Deutsches Theater—unlike the student theatre in Karlshorst—was one of the GDR's leading theatres.[90] He made it clear that the production had crossed the boundaries of any legitimate process of de-Stalinization:

einige wenige [Künstler] meinten, daß es jetzt nach der Sicherung der Staatsgrenze möglich sei, ideologische Zugeständnisse zu machen...

---

[84] Jürgen Schmidt, *Ich möchte Ich bleiben: Lebenslauf eines mittleren Kultur-Kaders geschrieben nach 40 Jahren DDR (gekürzte Fassung)* (Schkeuditz: GNN, 1996), 203.

[85] 'Bericht über die Auseinandersetzung'.

[86] 'Erste Information über die Parteiversammlungen im Deutschen Theater am 8. und 11.1.1963', 12.1.1963, BArch DY 30 IV 2/2.026/68.

[87] Bork to Bentzien, 25.1.1963, BArch DR 1/8688. See Esche, *Der Hase im Rausch*, 144–8.

[88] 'Erste Information'; Jürgen Schmidt, 'Beilage', *Blätter des Deutschen Theaters*, 19 (1991), [n.p.].

[89] 'Stellungnahme der Parteiorganisation des Hans-Otto-Theaters Potsdam zum Stück *Die Sorgen und die Macht*', 16.1.1963, AdK Gerhard-Meyer-Archiv W/R 16.

[90] Weigel, 'Der Fall *Die Sorgen und die Macht* 1962/63', 639–40. For Kurella's speech, see *Dokumente zur Kunst-, Literatur- und Kulturpolitik der SED*, ed. Elimar Schubbe (Stuttgart: Seewald, 1972), 820–2.

Niemand soll glauben, daß der Kampf unserer Partei gegen alle Erscheinungen des Dogmatismus und Sektierertums sowie gegen revisionistische Auffassungen grünes Licht für den Formalismus in der Kunst und für die Verbreitung
uns feindlicher Ideologien bedeutet...![91]

a few [artists] thought that it would be possible, now that the state border has
been secured, to make ideological concessions...

No one should believe that our Party's struggle against all manifestations of
dogmatism and sectarianism as well as against revisionist views gives the green
light to Formalism in art and to the spread of ideologies hostile to us...!

Verner was using *Die Sorgen und die Macht*, like *Die Umsiedlerin*, to
prove that cultural policy would not be relaxed following the construction of the Wall. His personal denunciation of the production supports
Bork's claim that Verner played a leading role in this censorship
campaign.

Both in the reviews and at the Conference, the SED's language
showed that there was no room for compromise. By calling the underlying ideas and attitudes of the play 'falsch' (wrong), Verner staked the
Party's exclusive claim to cultural hegemony.[92] In *Neues Deutschland*,
Wagner and Bork—representing the united forces of the Culture
Department and Ministry—denounced Hacks's dramaturgy in equally
uncompromising terms, criticizing him for foregrounding what was
wrong and for relegating positive examples to the margins.[93] By refusing
to allow constructive criticism to dominate a play, Wagner and Bork
reasserted the conservative interpretation of Socialist Realism. Bork
seemed conveniently to have forgotten that he had originally urged
Langhoff to perform the play at the Workers' Festival in Erfurt.

The regime's understanding of censorship as pedagogy demanded
that Langhoff and the Deutsches Theater should admit their
mistakes. At a meeting on 22 March, Langhoff, Leder, Christoph,
Esche, Hiemer, and Lucke expressed their contrition, and the theatre's
Party Organization described the SED's intervention as a great help.[94]
Yet when Langhoff came to criticize his failings, probably before
the SED-*Bezirksleitung*, he qualified his admissions. Instead of stating

[91] Weigel, 'Der Fall *Die Sorgen und die Macht* 1962/63', 640.
[92] Ibid. 639.
[93] Siegfried Wagner and Kurt Bork, 'Über den Standpunkt des Künstlers zu unserem
Kampf: Bemerkungen zu einer Diskussion', *ND*, 16.12.1962.
[94] 'Kurzbericht über die Mitgliederversammlung im Deutschen Theater am
22.3.1963'; Schröder to Hager, 23.3.1963; 'Entschließung', 22.3.1963. All in BArch
DY 30 IV A 2/2.024/32.

unequivocally that the play was as damaging as the SED had claimed, Langhoff conceded only that the theatre's Party members had been right to say so and to withdraw the production.[95] He also indicated that he was obeying Party discipline out of principle, not out of the conviction that the Party was right:

Es gibt eine Reihe von Fragen, besonders auf dem Gebiet der Ästhetik und der Kunst, mit denen ich nicht klar komme, aber in einem komme ich ganz klar: Es ist diskutiert worden, es ist ein Beschluß gefaßt worden, und nach dem Beschluß wird gehandelt.[96]

There are a series of questions, particularly in the area of aesthetics and art, with which I have not got to grips. But I have got to grips with one thing: the matter has been discussed, a resolution has been passed, and we do what the resolution says.

According to a Stasi report, the Volksbühne's dramaturge Gerhard Wolfram believed that Langhoff's self-criticism was not to be taken seriously and that the Deutsches Theater would not change its approach.[97] Langhoff's private remarks corroborate both his public comments and Wolfram's alleged suspicions. On 7 February, Langhoff reportedly told Wagner and Grümmer that he disagreed with the Party's cultural policy, including its conflict-free, rose-tinted depiction of the GDR; he is said to have reiterated this view in a conversation with Bork and Grümmer five days later.[98]

Bork's files provide a rare insight into the Ministry's own post-mortem. At a meeting on 4 February, an unnamed spokesperson—possibly Bork himself—defended the decision to approve the script, arguing that it had positive features and dealt with new subject matter, and that the Ministry had always intended to provoke a debate. He or she criticized the Ministry only for failing to make its reservations sufficiently clear and to take broader developments in the arts into account—a reference to the crackdown in cultural policy. Matters had escalated only because the Deutsches Theater had ignored Party discipline and turned the play into a platform against official cultural policy. The spokesperson blamed this development partly on the press

[95] Weigel, 'Der Fall *Die Sorgen und die Macht* 1962/63', 645. For Langhoff's recantation before the Politbüro, Präsidium of the Council of Ministers, writers, and artists, see *Dokumente*, ed. Schubbe, 883.
[96] Weigel, 'Der Fall *Die Sorgen und die Macht* 1962/63', 645.
[97] BStU AIM 2268/77, ii.i, fo. 16.
[98] Weigel, 'Der Fall *Die Sorgen und die Macht* 1962/63', 641, 643–4.

Contemporary Drama in the 1960s

discussion, which had given the theatre the impression that it was under concerted attack.[99]

Whilst Bork and his officials escaped any reprisals, *Die Sorgen und die Macht* illustrates the personal and professional consequences of censorship for theatre practitioners. Langhoff was already ill, and the controversy brought his distinguished career to an abrupt halt. Wagner and Grümmer reported:

In einem anderen Zusammenhang äußerte Langhoff, daß er eigentlich nicht mehr leben möchte. Er werde periodisch kritisiert. Er fragte, ob es nicht besser sei, wenn er demissioniere.[100]

In another context Langhoff said that he did not really want to carry on living. He said that he was criticized on a regular basis. He asked if it would not be better if he resigned.

The despair in these comments explains why critics have cast Langhoff in the role of tragic hero, betrayed by his own Party; Linzer likens Langhoff's 'friends' to the cancer that killed him in 1966.[101] Langhoff's son Thomas reports that the fire in him burned out in 1963. However, he also writes that his father came to enjoy being relieved from his responsibilities, and Esche informed the Stasi in October 1963 that everyone at the theatre agreed that Langhoff had recovered from his resignation and now preferred his new role.[102] This does not alter the fact that Langhoff and his colleagues had had to agree to the censorship of their own production, withdraw it voluntarily, and thank the authorities for their assistance. The regime kept its repressive mechanisms from public view: after denouncing the production at a meeting between the Politbüro, leading members of the Council of Ministers, writers, and artists on 26 March, Ulbricht assured his listeners that there had been no 'administrative' intervention.[103]

---

[99] 'Zentrale Mitgliederversammlung' [typescript with corrections in Bork's handwriting], 4.2.1963, BArch DR 1/8851.
[100] Weigel, 'Der Fall *Die Sorgen und die Macht* 1962/63', 641.
[101] Martin Linzer, *'Ich war immer ein Opportunist...': 12 Gespräche über Theater und das Leben in der DDR, über geliebte und ungeliebte Zeitgenossen*, ed. Nikolaus Merck, TdZ Recherchen, 7 (Eggersdorf: TdZ und Literaturforum im Brecht-Haus, 2001), 61.
[102] Hans-Dieter Schütt, *Spielzeit Lebenszeit: Thomas Langhoff* (Berlin: Das Neue Berlin, 2008), 121; BStU AIM 1401/83, FK, fo. 87.
[103] 'Stenografische Niederschrift der Kulturberatung', BArch DY 30 IV A 2/2.024/3. André Müller sen. argues that cultural functionaries had misinformed Ulbricht about workers' reactions to the production, raising the possibility that Ulbricht was not aware of the full details of discussions at the Deutsches Theater. However, the point remains that the production's withdrawal was to be presented as voluntary. See Müller sen., *Gespräche mit Hacks*, 9–10.

5. *MORITZ TASSOW* (1965–1966)

Pre-performance Controls

The Ministry's initial approval of *Moritz Tassow* contrasted with the uncertain and occasionally vehement early reactions that *Die Sorgen und die Macht* had provoked. Peter Hacks's new play returned to the subject of *Die Umsiedlerin*, the post-war agricultural reforms. Hacks turned this historical material into a comedy about the unsuccessful attempts of a pig-keeper, Moritz Tassow, to carry out a revolution in his village. As suggested by his name, a combination of a Prussified variant of Goethe's idealistic Tasso and Wilhelm Busch's roguish Moritz, Tassow is an impractical utopian and a mischievous anarchist rolled into one.[104] His commune descends into chaos, none of the crops are harvested, and he offends the smallholders so much that they join forces with the dispossessed Junker. From the perspective of 1965, five years after the collectivization of agriculture had been completed, the play suggested that the authorities had been right to moderate the pace of change.

A more conventional revolutionary enters the play in the form of Mattukat, a Party member and concentration camp survivor whose tact, pragmatism, and humour win over the local inhabitants and save the revolution. Mattukat is portrayed far more positively than the Party members in *Die Sorgen und die Macht*, and Karl-Heinz Hafranke praised him when he assessed the script for the Ministry. Indeed, Hafranke regarded the entire play as proof that Party policy was correct and that the GDR's socialist revolution was being guided and managed with scientific precision.[105] Heinz Schröder, the head of the Ministry's Theatre Department, agreed that the play was performable and argued that it represented a step forwards.[106] The Ministry backed *Moritz Tassow* and arranged for the Deutsches Theater to grant Benno Besson leave to direct the play at the Volksbühne.[107] Besson, a Swiss national who had trained under Brecht at the BE, had recently won international acclaim with his productions of Aristophanes' *Der Frieden* (Peace,

---

[104] The play was also inspired by August Kotzebue's *Bruder Moritz*. See Müller sen., *Gespräche mit Hacks*, 169.

[105] 'Kurzanalyse zu *Moritz Tassow* von Peter Hacks', LAB C Rep. 902 2012.

[106] 'Betr.: *Moritz Tassow*, Komödie von Peter Hacks', 28.6.1965, BArch DY 30 IV A 2/9.06/112.

[107] Bork to Wolfgang Heinz, 26.2.1965, BArch DR 1/8688.

1962), in an adaptation by Hacks, and Jewgeni Schwarz's *Der Drache* (The Dragon, 1965).

Whilst the Ministry had no doubt that *Tassow* should be performed, it argued that Besson would have to overcome problems in the script. Its chief objection was that Mattukat, who has yet to recover from his imprisonment in a concentration camp, is replaced by his deputy Blasche, a pen-pushing bureaucrat who lacks Tassow's energetic enthusiasm and Mattukat's quiet humour and common sense. The Ministry warned:

Das Stück läßt, zugespitzt gesagt, die Lesart zu, nach der die wirklichen Revolutionäre in den Widernissen der Gegenwart zugrunde gehen (Mattukat), die Tassows weiter ihre Zeit abwarten und die schönfärbenden und bürokratischen Blasches das Heft in die Hand bekommen.[108]

Put bluntly, the play can be read as suggesting that the real revolutionaries perish in the trials and tribulations of the present (Mattukat), the Tassows carry on waiting for their time to come, and the bureaucratic Blasches take charge, glossing over problems.

Even so, it saw no indication that the Volksbühne was planning to interpret the play along these lines.[109]

The Culture Department had stronger reservations and commissioned the theatre academic Wilfried Adling to assess the play. Adling argued that Mattukat grossly underestimated the masses' creative energies and criticized Blasche as a narrow-minded petit-bourgeois bureaucrat. In his view, the play suggested that the socialist state harboured an inevitable tendency towards mediocrity and bureaucratic stagnation. Adling argued that these views had been endemic in particular intellectual circles in the GDR since Khrushchev's denunciation of Stalinism in 1956.[110] Even so, Adling did not recommend that rehearsals should stop, only that Blasche should not replace Mattukat.

Officials from the Ministry and Culture Department observed the rehearsals closely because they were suspicious of the artists involved. Even though the Ministry had arranged for Besson to direct the play, its officials warned that the combination of Besson as director, Fritz Cremer as set designer, and Rudolf Wagner-Régeny as composer carried

[108] 'Betr.: *Moritz Tassow*'.
[109] Ibid.
[110] 'Zu der Komödie *Moritz Tassow* von Peter Hacks', 25.8.1965, BArch DY 30 IV A 2/9.06/112.

aesthetic and ideological risks.[111] This ambivalence points again to
the tension between the Ministry's functions: the Ministry wanted
the best theatre practitioners to produce the play but feared the
consequences. The SED-*Bezirksleitung* instructed the theatre's Party
members to monitor the production, and Verner warned that the
Ministry and Volksbühne would need to make certain corrections
during rehearsals.[112]

On 3 October, the Culture Department's officials reported that the
run-throughs had reassured them: even if several scenes in the text
allowed audiences to see Tassow as ahead of his time, the production
presented him as a man who did not appreciate the possibilities in a
concrete situation and therefore acted incorrectly.[113] These comments
indicate that the officials distinguished clearly between the text and the
theatre's interpretation of it. But as the reception of *Die Sorgen und die
Macht* had already shown, not everyone would watch the production
before criticizing the play. The danger was that politicians would judge
only the text published in *Sinn und Form* or, worse still, quotations
taken out of context in reviews.

Critical Responses and the Cultural Crackdown

The premiere of *Moritz Tassow* took place on 5 October. In the month
that followed, the Culture Department considered the production a
qualified success. Its draft assessment of 12 October even argued that
Hacks had tried to learn from criticisms of *Die Sorgen und die Macht*.[114]
But whilst officials praised Hacks's depiction of Mattukat and criticism
of Tassow, they were concerned about his presentation of Blasche and
the agricultural workers, and about the audience's composition. In their
opinion, the production had not attracted the Volksbühne's usual
audience, and spectators' responses to individual punchlines or literary
and political references showed that they were expecting a sensation.[115]

[111] 'Betr.: *Moritz Tassow*'.
[112] Verner to Wagner, 27.8.1965, BArch DY 30 IV A 2/9.06/112.
[113] 'Information über die Inszenierung der Komödie *Moritz Tassow* von Peter Hacks
in der Volksbühne', 3.10.1965, BArch DY 30 IV A 2/9.06/112.
[114] 'Entwurf einer Stellungnahme zur Inszenierung der Komödie *Moritz Tassow* von
Peter Hacks in der Volksbühne und zum Schauspiel *Der Bau* von Heiner Müller',
12.10.1965, BArch DY 30 IV A 2/9.06/112.
[115] Ibid.

Believing that the production needed to be managed carefully, the
Department arranged for *Theater der Zeit* to publish a critical assess-
ment of the press reviews, for the Ministry to conduct a discussion, for
the Volksbühne's Party members to issue a statement, and for the SED-
Bezirksleitung and the *Magistrat* to monitor spectators' responses.[116]
Thus the Department's role was to coordinate the efforts of the other
Party and state institutions.

This time, the reviews were overwhelmingly positive. Christoph
Funke, Ernst Schumacher, and Wolfgang Gersch agreed that it was
the Volksbühne's best staging for years.[117] Even Rainer Kerndl, who
criticized aspects of the production in *Neues Deutschland*, welcomed
Mattukat and Hacks's criticism of Tassow.[118] In the *BZ am Abend*, Kurt
Wandel—a reader from Prenzlauer Berg—praised Hacks for writing a
comedy that made people laugh as well as think, adding that the same
could not be said of every new play.[119] The production played to
packed houses, and Schumacher reported the audience's enthusiastic
and interested reactions in the *Berliner Zeitung*.[120] But neither these
reactions nor the initial support of the Culture Department and Ministry were enough to save the production. Arno Wyzniewski, who played
Mattukat, explains that this was the first time he experienced how a
highly successful, critically acclaimed production could be destroyed
overnight.[121]

This sudden change in the production's fortunes was part of a much
broader crackdown on culture at the Eleventh Plenary Session of the
Central Committee, which Kaiser relates to growing internal opposition
to Ulbricht's economic and youth policy reforms.[122] The Youth
Communiqué of September 1963 had certainly represented a personal
blow for Verner, who lost his position as head of the Politbüro's Youth
Commission to Ulbricht's protégé Kurt Turba. Since Khrushchev's fall
from power in October 1964, the political line in the USSR had

[116] Ibid.

[117] Christoph Funke, 'Der Narr von Gargentin', *Der Morgen* (East Berlin),
7.10.1965; Ernst Schumacher, 'Göttlicher Sauhirt und irdisches Paradies', *Berliner
Zeitung* (East Berlin), 7.10.1965; Wolfgang Gersch, 'Utopist oder Narr?', *Tribüne*
(East Berlin), 8.10.1965.

[118] Rainer Kerndl, 'Tassows Gaben und Getöse', *ND*, 9.10.1965.

[119] Anon., 'Tassow—Vorbild oder Provokation?', *BZ am Abend*, 29.10.1965.

[120] Schumacher, 7.10.1965.

[121] Birgid Gysi, 'Weiße Flecken (3): *Moritz Tassow* von Peter Hacks an der Volksbühne Berlin, 1965', *TdZ* 45/10 (Oct. 1990), 31–6 at 35.

[122] See Kaiser, *Machtwechsel von Ulbricht zu Honecker*, 182–231.

hardened, clearing the way for a retreat from de-Stalinization in the GDR. On 12 November 1965, the Culture Department forwarded analyses of a series of films and plays to the Politbüro as evidence of the urgent need to tighten control of cultural processes.[123] The Eleventh Plenary Session met from 16 to 18 December 1965, and Honecker took the lead in attacking developments in culture.[124] Hager agreed, arguing that officials in the Culture Ministry, DEFA, and Writers' Union had harboured reservations about Party cultural policy. In Hager's view, these officials had in fact been pursuing their own line—a point that Bentzien chooses to accept in his autobiography, written after reunification.[125] A speech in Verner's archive, delivered before an audience including Party Secretaries from East Berlin's cultural organizations and artistic institutions in the week leading up to Christmas 1965, accused Ministry officials of capitulating to artists out of anxiety not to be accused of dogmatism.[126] Bentzien's days as Culture Minister were clearly numbered, and Klaus Gysi replaced him early in 1966.

Conference speeches suggest that *Moritz Tassow* played a relatively minor part in this cultural crackdown, and that it may well have been a victim of collateral damage from the more sustained attacks on Müller's *Der Bau* (The Construction Site) and Bieler's *ZAZA*, plays that the Ministry had actually rejected. *Tassow* was mentioned only briefly in the speeches published in *Neues Deutschland*, where Sakowski argued that it contained 'Pornographie von europäischem Rang' (European-class pornography).[127] This was because Hacks had packed the play with sexual allusions and puns and included a nude scene in which a smallholder discovers his daughter in bed with Tassow. The depiction of Red Rosa was undeniably provocative, for although her name served as a reminder of Rosa Luxemburg, the similarity ended there. Hacks's Rosa is a

[123] Günter Agde (ed.), *Kahlschlag: Das 11. Plenum des ZK der SED 1965: Studien und Dokumente* (Berlin: Aufbau, 1991), 132.
[124] *Dokumente*, ed. Schubbe, 1076–81.
[125] Ibid. 1114–17 at 1114, 1115; Hans Bentzien, *Meine Sekretäre und ich* (Berlin: Neues Leben, 1995), 228.
[126] 'Wir haben die Kreissekretäre für Agitation und Propaganda und Kultur . . .', BArch NY 4281/63.
[127] *Dokumente*, ed. Schubbe, 1108–11 at 1109. According to a Stasi report, Hacks claimed that this was an insult, as his pornography was world-class. See BStU AOPK 2666/77, fo. 26.

Fig. 2.2. Ursula Karusseit as Red Rosa and Jürgen Holtz as Moritz Tassow
(Abraham Pisarek, Stadtmuseum Berlin / Reproduktion Friedhelm Hoffmann)

self-confessed thief, who has difficulty making a good political speech or constructing a clean sentence (Fig. 2.2).[128]

One spectator wrote to the Volksbühne, saying that dirty jokes were no basis for socialist drama, and two more spectators complained to *Neues Deutschland*:

> *Moritz Tassow* ist keine Komödie, über die man sich gelassen amüsieren könnte, sondern eine mit intellektuellen Geistreicheleien und platten Zoten und Obszönitäten verzierte Verunglimpfung und Beleidigung jener einfachen, mutigen und aufopferungsvollen Menschen, die unmittelbar nach 1945 mit revolutionärem Elan die Voraussetzungen dafür schufen, daß aus den Trümmern des faschistischen Reiches und den Überresten des Feudalismus ein sozialistischer Staat entstehen konnte.[129]

> *Moritz Tassow* is not a comedy which you can sit back and enjoy; on the contrary, it is full of intellectual quips and tedious dirty jokes and obscenities, and it disparages and insults those unassuming, courageous, and self-sacrificing people who set to work with revolutionary vigour straight after 1945, creating the preconditions for a socialist state to emerge from the rubble of the fascist Reich and the remnants of feudalism.

Given that these are the only two complaints in the Volksbühne's files, Sakowski probably exaggerated public outrage. In the press, the production provoked nothing like the debate that had followed *Die Sorgen und die Macht*—perhaps because the authorities had learned from Bork's criticisms. But the play's colourful language and action allowed conservatives to play the moral card and identify the production as a danger to young people, supporting their argument that the youth policy reforms had gone too far.

As with *Die Sorgen und die Macht*, several of the conservatives' key objections to the play probably went unspoken. Fritz Rödel—the Volksbühne's Party Secretary in 1965—believes that the play was seen to criticize Ulbricht. He told Birgid Gysi in 1990:

> unsere Interpretation der Äußerungen verschiedener Funktionäre... lautete: Das Stück ist schädlich, weil es einen Angriff auf Walter Ulbricht enthält... Mattukat ist Thälmann, sozusagen der alte Klassenkämpfer, der mit großem Verständnis für die Menschen an die Lösung seiner Aufgaben geht. Und dann kommt sein Stellvertreter Blasche, der das letzte Wort im Stück hat[,] und setzt

---

[128] Peter Hacks, 'Moritz Tassow' (unpublished Volksbühne script), 16, 19, VA.
[129] W. G. to Holàn, 6.10.1965, and H. and R. B. to the *ND* Kultur-Redaktion, 11.10.1965, VA yellow *Tassow* file.

die These in die Welt: die Welt braucht Lenkung und nicht Bewegung. Und das wurde eine Verunglimpfung der Leitungskräfte der damaligen Zeit.[130]

our interpretation of the statements of various functionaries ... went as follows: the play is damaging because it contains an attack on Walter Ulbricht... Mattukat is Thälmann, as it were the old class warrior, who goes about solving his tasks with great understanding for the people. And then his deputy Blasche comes along; he has the last word in the play and delivers the thesis: the world needs management and not movement. And that disparaged those in authority at the time.

However, Hacks's well-known respect for Ulbricht casts doubt on whether this analogy was ever intended. A Stasi report of discussions among students at the State Acting School suggests an alternative interpretation:

Im Zentralkomitee der SED gibt es zwei Gruppen. Auf der einen Seite steht Walter Ulbricht, der übrigens der einzigste [*sic*] vernünftige Mann im ZK ist, und auf der anderen Seite steht Paul Verner[,] ein Dogmatiker, der mit der Figur des Blasche aus dem Tasso [*sic*] zu vergleichen ist.[131]

In the Central Committee of the SED there are two groups. On the one hand there is Walter Ulbricht, who is incidentally the only sensible man in the Central Committee, and on the other there is Paul Verner, a dogmatic politician who can be likened to the character of Blasche from *Tassow*.

Whilst there is no evidence to suggest that either Hacks or the Volks-bühne intended to identify Blasche with any specific member of the SED leadership, the programme did quote from a parable by Henri de Saint-Simon, saying that incompetent men were appointed as leaders over competent ones in every walk of life.[132]

There was enough other evidence of the critical thrust of the script, programme, and staging to confirm conservatives' suspicions. Whilst the play demonstrated that Tassow's spontaneous idealism was imprac-ticable, it also suggested that the GDR had marginalized innovative, enthusiastic men instead of harnessing their idealism and energy. The programme supported this interpretation, for it located Tassow

[130] Gysi, 'Weiße Flecken (3)', 35. Rödel had previously worked at the Culture Ministry and had helped to censor *Die Umsiedlerin* in 1961.
[131] BStU AOPK 2666/77, fo. 25a.
[132] *Moritz Tassow* programme insert, VA; Gottfried Salomon (ed.), *Saint-Simon und der Sozialismus*, trans. Hanna Hertz (Berlin: Paul Cassirer, 1919), 44.

in a line of utopian thinkers forcibly restrained by society.[133] Further-more, by abandoning politics at the end of the play and becoming a writer, Tassow mischievously suggested that the GDR's unwelcome idealists had been relegated to the artistic sphere. On stage, Cremer's set depicted the bureaucratization of the GDR; the production opened with a set of improvised offices on stage, and these offices were joined by a great many more during the play.[134] Together, the script, programme, and staging suggested that the revolutionary impulses of 1945 had stagnated, idealism had been replaced by pragmatism, and the GDR lay in the hands of well-meaning but mediocre bureaucrats.

Procrastination and Uncertainty

Moritz Tassow was treated differently from *Die Sorgen und die Macht*: instead of launching a sustained campaign to break the theatre's resis-tance, the authorities procrastinated. By early January, after the Elev-enth Plenary, there were rumours that the production had been banned. The BE's manager and lead actress Helene Weigel argued that the play was not hostile and called for a compromise: 'wenn man schon bei Torquato einen Bleistift zum Streichen benutzt, dann kann man das, denke ich, auch bei Moritz'.[135] (If we cut lines from Torquato, then I think we can do the same with Moritz.) According to one of the Stasi's informers, a woman told Hacks on 23 December that Verner had visited the Volksbühne and that performances would probably be suspended until changes had been discussed with Hacks.[136] In a meeting with Rödel, the Volksbühne's manager Karl Holàn, and the Ministry official Gero Hammer on 6 January, Hacks reportedly agreed to four changes but warned that he would take legal action if further cuts were made without his agreement.[137]

A new edited performance was scheduled for 15 January, and City Councillor Ernst Hoffmann asked the Ministry to cover his back by providing written details of the cuts and confirming that the

---

[133] *Moritz Tassow* programme insert.
[134] '5. Probe 1. Bild (Büro)', 15.7.1965, VA beige *Tassow* file.
[135] Copy of a letter from Weigel to Hager, 4.1.1966, VA yellow *Tassow* file.
[136] BStU AOP 1958/71, viii, fo. 159.
[137] Hammer, 'Information über ein Gespräch mit Dr. Peter Hacks', 8.1.1966, BArch DR 1/8849.

performance could take place.[138] In an internal memorandum, Schröder informed Bork and Hammer that the Ministry supported the edited production and that the *Magistrat* should therefore take the decision it regarded as appropriate.[139] A Stasi report dated 14 January claimed that Hacks had discussed the changes with the Culture Minister and had agreed to cut one 'obscene' line after the demands had been reduced.[140] This suggests a two-way process of negotiation, and a separate report notes that Hacks received the impression that Bork was trying to save the production.[141] Yet on the eve of the performance, after all the tickets had been sold, the *Magistrat* ordered its cancellation.[142] The local state authorities thus took a harder line than the Ministry, a fact that Hacks repeatedly blamed on Verner and the SED-*Bezirksleitung*.[143] His interpretation is supported by a speech in Verner's archive attacking *Tassow*, *ZAZA*, and *Der Bau*.[144]

Although the *Magistrat* had effectively banned *Moritz Tassow*, the Volksbühne's manager officially withdrew the production, maintaining the appearance of self-regulation. Holàn issued a statement presenting the withdrawal as a temporary move while the play was revised in response to 'justified' criticism.[145] His cooperation enabled Bork to entrust him with the ensuing negotiations with Hacks, so that the matter could be presented as a dispute between the theatre and the author, thereby isolating Hacks.

The withdrawal of *Moritz Tassow*, the Volksbühne's most successful production in years, was a serious blow for a theatre that was only just beginning to recover from its brief, failed fusion with the Maxim Gorki Theater. Ironically, Holàn had reported after the premiere that there were signs that the situation at the Volksbühne was beginning to improve and the company might be able to develop into an

[138] Hammer to Bork, 7.1.1966, BArch DR 1/8849.
[139] Memorandum by Schröder, 13.1.1966, BArch DR 1/8849.
[140] BStU AOPK 2666/77, fo. 31. According to this report, Hacks said that Besson could be relied on to reincorporate the cuts one by one at a later date. The report did not reveal the source of this information.
[141] Ibid. 33.
[142] Ernst Hoffmann to Gysi, 6.2.1967, BArch DR 1/8849.
[143] BStU AOP 1958/71, viii, fo. 174.
[144] 'Wir haben die Kreissekretäre'.
[145] Birgid Gysi, '*Moritz Tassow* von Peter Hacks an der Volksbühne Berlin: Eine Dokumentation', in Christa Neubert-Herwig (ed.), *Benno Besson: Theater spielen in acht Ländern: Texte, Dokumente, Gespräche* (Berlin: Alexander, 1998), 275–86 at 275.

ensemble.[146] His cancellation of the performance generated massive resentment within the theatre, particularly because the cuts had already been agreed. In a confidential letter to the *Magistrat,* Holàn expressed sympathy for his colleagues' frustration:

Innerhalb des Theaters wird dieser Entschluß nur von wenigen Mitgliedern der Theaterleitung verstanden. Alle übrigen Mitarbeiter sind zutiefst bestürzt und verständnislos. Dies ist auch nicht verwunderlich, da nach mehrfachen Diskussionen in den leitenden Gremien des Theaters, an denen sowohl Mitarbeiter des Ministeriums für Kultur, der Bezirksleitung der SED und des Magistrats von Gross-Berlin teilnahmen, ausführlich über die Problematik dieser Aufführung beraten wurde.[147]

Within the theatre only a few members of the management team understand this decision. All the other colleagues are extremely upset and unable to understand it. This is not surprising either, as we had talked at length about the problems associated with this production, following repeated discussions in the theatre's management meetings, in which colleagues from the Culture Ministry, SED-*Bezirksleitung*, and the *Magistrat* of Greater Berlin participated.

Holàn went on to criticize the Ministry's inconsistency:

Schwankungen der Meinungen und der Beschlüsse eines übergeordneten Organs [haben] so ausserordentliche Komplikationen hervorgerufen..., dass ich um eine dringende Klärung des exakten Sachverhalts auch vor dem Ensemble bitte, da ich mich sonst ausserstande sehe, das völlig zerrüttete Vertrauen in absehbarer Zeit wieder zu gewinnen.[148]

The fluctuating opinions and decisions of a supervisory body have caused such extraordinary complications... that I must ask for the exact facts of the matter to be clarified urgently before the ensemble too, as otherwise I see myself as unable to win back its trust—which has been completely ruined—in the foreseeable future.

Having directed the play on the Ministry's request, Besson was indignant at the cancellation of his production. He protested to Bork and demanded an immediate explanation.[149] However, it appears that Besson was not directing his objections to the production's main opponents: whilst the Culture Department had supplied the material

---

146 Holàn to Ernst Hoffmann, 18.10.1965, BArch DY 30 IV A 2/9.06/112.
147 Holàn to Ernst Hoffmann, 17.1.1966, VA yellow *Tassow* file.
148 Ibid.
149 Besson to Bork, 15.1.1966, VA yellow *Tassow* file.

for the denunciation at the Eleventh Plenary and the *Magistrat* had instructed Holàn to drop the production, the Ministry had actually attempted to secure a compromise. Whereas the authorities had been determined to remove *Die Sorgen und die Macht* permanently, they presented the withdrawal of *Moritz Tassow* as temporary. There were repeated reports that performances would soon be resumed; the Stasi claimed in February 1966 that Hacks believed he had reached an agreement with the Volksbühne, allowing it to cut the final eleven lines of the text if the performance run was allowed to reach a natural conclusion.[150] His apparent optimism proved premature: on 24 August, Holàn informed Hacks that performances would not be resumed.[151] The internalization of the dispute within the Volksbühne ensured that no heads rolled there: Holàn remained in post, having defended the authorities' interests to their satisfaction, and Besson continued to direct to acclaim.

The Search for Legal Redress

The unforeseen consequence of the authorities' approach was that Hacks sued the Volksbühne for breach of contract. He found an unlikely ally in the publishing house Henschel, which played an ambiguous role. As Henschel exercised a monopoly over the distribution of performance rights, it oversaw the process of screening and editing most new plays; but it was also charged with representing its authors' interests. In this case, the curtailed performance run had significantly reduced the income that Hacks had expected to gain from the production, in addition to discouraging other theatres from taking on his plays. His reported aim was to secure either financial redress or an official statement that the play had been banned, not to question the principle and practice of censorship itself.[152]

On 4 May 1966, Henschel demanded that Holàn should either set a date for performances to be resumed or compensate Hacks.[153] The Ministry's legal adviser conceded that the Volksbühne had violated Henschel's contract because the play could no longer be performed

---

[150] BStU AOP 1958/71, viii, fo. 388.
[151] Holàn to Hacks, 24.8.1966, BArch DR 1/8849.
[152] BStU AOP 1958/71, viii, fo. 182.
[153] Henschel to Holàn, 4.5.1966, VA yellow *Tassow* file.

for 'objective' political reasons, but stated that the case would be new legal territory and the court's decision could not be predicted.[154] In his view, the political risks outweighed the legal benefits of creating a precedent: the Volksbühne would need to prove that it was objectively impossible to perform the play in the GDR, which would open up a whole raft of questions concerning cultural policy.[155] Consequently, he recommended paying Hacks a financial settlement so that censorship would not be subjected to public scrutiny.

Although Bork was willing to settle, Hacks and the *Magistrat* both refused, for different reasons.[156] The *Magistrat* blamed Hacks for the production's cancellation because he had refused to make all the changes it considered necessary.[157] Once again, the local authorities took a stricter line than the Ministry. Hacks, for his part, considered the amount offered an insult, and the matter was referred to the Writers' Union for arbitration.[158] A report dated 12 September 1968 noted that although the Union had ruled that Hacks should receive compensation, none of the parties involved—the Ministry, Volksbühne, and Henschel—was prepared to make any payments.[159] In July 1970, the case went before a local court in East Berlin, and the Volksbühne disputed Hacks's claim on the grounds that its original contract with him had been superseded by a subsequent contract with Henschel, and that even the original contract did not specify a minimum number of performances.[160] The court ruled against Hacks, and his ingenious attempt at securing redress failed.[161]

6. CONCLUSION

Theatre censorship was unpredictable in the 1960s, despite the high priority accorded to planning and prognosis. There were real differences of opinion within the cultural bureaucracy; Verner consistently took a

[154] 'Stellungnahme zu dem Rechtsstreit Dr. Hacks ./. Volksbühne', BArch DR 1/8849.
[155] Ibid.
[156] Bork to Kaul, 29.12.1966, and Ernst Hoffmann, 29.12.1966. Both in BArch DR 1/8849.
[157] Hoffmann to Gysi, 6.2.1967.
[158] Hacks to Kaul, 6.1.1967, BArch DR 1/8849; BStU AOPK 2666/77, fo. 50.
[159] BStU AOPK 2666/77, fo. 63.
[160] Ibid. 77–9.
[161] Klausch to Holàn, 10.12.1970, VA yellow *Tassow* file.

much harder line than Ministry officials such as Bork. Whilst the Ministry did try hard to mediate in the case of *Moritz Tassow*, *Die Sorgen und die Macht* shows that officials would switch sides if they had approved a play that was subsequently deemed hostile to the Party. This unpredictability was related not just to opportunism or self-preservation, but to the contradictory tasks of censoring and promoting contemporary drama. The Ministry both wanted and feared contemporary drama, and this ambivalence sometimes persisted even after productions had been withdrawn. As late as May 1966, the Ministry was seeking to arrange a production of *Tassow* in Leipzig, one of the GDR's 'safest' theatres.[162]

Banned productions like *Die Sorgen und die Macht* represented a failure of censorship, for officials had misjudged the political climate and the offence that a play would cause. At the same time, they were an essential part of the system because they reminded theatre practitioners that the Party was in charge, its unwritten contract with artists had not changed, and self-censorship was advisable. But highly public confrontations promoted more self-censorship than the Culture Department and Ministry wanted, for they discouraged critical dramatists from addressing contemporary subjects and gave them an incentive to migrate to the safer ground of history and classical myth—as Hacks and Müller subsequently did. This points to the difficulties of writing contemporary drama—which relies on conflict—under a regime that resists the public examination of serious social problems. Each genre posed additional challenges: tragedy was too pessimistic, satire was too critical, and comedy contained too many jokes at the Party's expense. Even if a production did not intend to generate dissent, there was always the risk that lines would be taken out of context and used as evidence against the playwright and theatre.

So although cultural officials had hoped that *Die Sorgen und die Macht* would encourage the creation of new socialist plays, its public ban had the opposite effect. From the mid-1960s onwards, the Culture Department and Ministry complained regularly about the dearth of good contemporary GDR drama.[163] Conferences like the biennial Forum for Socialist Drama and contests like the Hans Otto

---

[162] 'Aktenvermerk', 11.5.1966, BArch DR 1/8849.

[163] e.g. 'Vorlage über Probleme der sozialistischen Entwicklung des Theaterschaffens' and 'Gestalterische Probleme in der Dramatik der DDR'. Both in BArch DY 30 IV A 2/9.06/109.

Competition could not compensate adequately for the fact that censorship discouraged dramatists from tackling contemporary subjects. Believing that vibrant socialist drama was needed to prove that the GDR was the true home of German culture, the Party perceived such difficulties, both in the genre and in the state's leading theatres, as harmful to its reputation. On 19 March 1966, Schröder warned Gysi that the situation at the Volksbühne endangered not only the ensemble itself, but also the authority of the Party and state leadership.[164] As the SED's officials fell victim to their rhetoric, censorship began to create its own problems.

[164] Schröder to Gysi, 19.3.1966, BArch DR 1/8849.

3

The Prague Spring: Allegories
and Allusions

> Und eh der Feind kam, warum schwieg ich da?
> Kam er nicht, weil ich schwieg?
> (And before the enemy came, why was I silent then?
> Did he not come because I was silent?)
>
> Adaptation of Aeschylus, *Seven against Thebes*, by
> Manfred Karge and Matthias Langhoff (1968)

1. INTRODUCTION

During the few months that became known as the Prague Spring, Alexander Dubček pursued an ambitious programme of economic modernization and democratization in Czechoslovakia. Attempting to create 'socialism with a human face', he began to relax the Party's Soviet-style grip on culture and politics, and promised to legislate for freedom of assembly, travel, and the press. By February 1968, the country's newspapers were openly debating these reforms.

Across the border, many of the GDR's citizens followed Dubček's policies closely through Western television, Radio Prague's German broadcasts, and the Czechoslovak newspaper *Der Volkswille*. The essayist Friedrich Dieckmann remembers young people in particular investing their own hopes in events in Prague.[1] So the disappointment was correspondingly great on 21 August 1968, when the Warsaw Pact invaded Czechoslovakia and forcibly halted Dubček's experiment.

---

[1] Friedrich Dieckmann and others, 'Das pazifistische Programm ist abgestürzt—25 Jahre '68', *TdZ* 49/3 (Mar. 1994), 60–5.

76 Part I. Theatre Censorship in East Berlin

The apparent involvement of GDR troops increased the shock, as the invasion came almost exactly thirty years after Germany's annexation of the Sudetenland.[2] As at the Munich Conference in 1938, foreign powers were dictating Czechoslovakia's future.

The SED leadership saw the crackdown as a vindication of its long-standing criticisms of cultural and intellectual life in Czechoslovakia. On 18 October, Ulbricht told the Council of State that Czech and Slovak artists and scholars had paved the way for the crisis through their calls for ideological coexistence and their isolation from the working class.[3] A few days later, Karl Kayser reminded the Ninth Plenary Session of the Central Committee that the 'so-called' Prague Spring had had its forerunners in the theatres, which had systematically abandoned Socialist Realism.[4]

In the days and weeks after the invasion, the GDR authorities monitored their own theatres, changed existing productions to pre-empt unwelcome reactions, and cajoled prominent actors and directors into declaring their support for the Warsaw Pact's actions. Whereas very few theatre practitioners had criticized the construction of the Wall openly in 1961, several actors spoke out against the invasion of Czechoslovakia; they are said to have included Marianne Wünscher at the Volksbühne, Rolf Ludwig at the Deutsches Theater, and Helmar Stöß at the Theater Anklam.[5] Werner Piontek brought a funeral wreath to rehearsals in Annaberg, just a few miles from the Czech border, and the opera director Horst Bonnet was sentenced to two-and-a-half years' imprisonment for copying and distributing leaflets critical of the invasion.[6] Several prominent theatre practitioners, including Helene Weigel, refrained from making public statements of support. Meanwhile, East Berlin's SED-*Bezirksleitung* reported that more ideological work

---

[2] Although we now know that the East German army did not leave GDR soil, SED propaganda gave the impression that it participated in the invasion. See Rüdiger Wenzke, *Die NVA und der Prager Frühling 1968: Die Rolle Ulbrichts und der DDR-Streitkräfte bei der Niederschlagung der tschechoslowakischen Reformbewegung*, Forschungen zur DDR-Geschichte, 5 (Berlin: Ch. Links, 1995).

[3] *Dokumente*, ed. Schubbe, 1395.

[4] Ibid. 1413.

[5] 'Künstler, die sich gegen die Maßnahmen der Verbündeten der ČSSR geäußert haben oder die einer Stellungnahme ausgewichen sind', 27.9.1968, BArch DY 30 IV A 2/9.06/28.

[6] Ibid.; anon., 'Ost-Berliner Regisseur verurteilt', *FAZ*, 12.10.1968.

was needed at the Berliner Ensemble, as its members had many questions regarding the legality of the intervention.[7]

The suppression of the Prague Spring heightened the SED's sensitivity to possible subversion in theatre productions. This chapter focuses on two stagings that were premiered after the invasion and elicited contrasting responses from officials. At the Deutsches Theater, *Faust I* evaded all pre-performance controls, only for its iconoclasm and allusions to censorship to spark a scandal at the premiere on 30 September 1968. Even though the directors Adolf Dresen and Wolfgang Heinz had not included any explicit references to the Prague Spring, both the authorities and the audience interpreted their theatrical rebellion in political terms. While the authorities rushed to limit the damage, the Berliner Ensemble's young directors Manfred Karge and Matthias Langhoff—Wolfgang Langhoff's son—were transforming Aeschylus' *Sieben gegen Theben* (Seven against Thebes) into a powerful allegory of the invasion of Prague. But because the BE's Party members alerted the authorities before the premiere, pre-performance censorship averted a scandal. Comparison of these productions shows how the reliance on internal controls caused censorship practices to diverge, even in the same city.

As these stagings were of classic texts, they received far less scrutiny in the initial stages than productions of contemporary drama. Although the translation and adaptation of a foreign classic like *Sieben gegen Theben* offered opportunities for political subversion, the authorities examined the script only after it had been denounced. The text of *Faust I* was beyond question, even though the audience interpreted some lines in the light of recent events. But if the texts of the German classics were fixed, then so were the regime's expectations, particularly when it came to *Faust*, the supreme national cultural icon. Staging the classics was not an easy option in the 1960s; such productions brought their own problems and challenges.

Whereas Karge and Langhoff's production of *Sieben gegen Theben* has attracted little academic attention, the Dresen/Heinz *Faust I* features prominently in surveys of East German theatre and specialized studies of *Faust* in the GDR. Deborah Vietor-Engländer's account identifies the main trends in the production and its official reception; however, as it was published in 1987, it inevitably excludes documents now

---

[7] 'Information zur Situation im kulturellen Bereich', 23.8.1968, LAB C Rep. 902 2567.

available in the Bundesarchiv and Stasi files.[8] Since 1990, interviews and
memoirs have provided more privileged insights into the production
process, particularly through Dresen's own essays and the theatre critic
Martin Linzer's interview with the dramaturges Alexander Weigel and
Klaus Wischnewski.[9] Whilst Lothar Ehrlich and Bernd Mahl published
useful surveys of GDR productions of *Faust* in 1995 and 1998, they do
not refer to this testimony or the archive material that is now available.[10]
This chapter is therefore the first to draw on the primary sources
now available from the Bundesarchiv, BStU, Academy of Arts, and
Deutsches Theater. The most important new sources include unpublished analyses of the production and its censorship carried out by the
dramaturges Frieder Kratochwil and Michael Hamburger during the
performance run.[11]

2. *FAUST I* AT THE DEUTSCHES THEATER

Speaking in Weimar on 28 August, the anniversary of Goethe's birth,
Culture Minister Klaus Gysi held up the character Faust as a symbol of
all that was positive about the GDR. By way of contrast, he identified
Gregor Samsa, the protagonist of Kafka's *Die Verwandlung* (Metamorphosis), with the counter-revolutionary forces that had until so recently
been at work in Prague.[12] This focus on Kafka was significant, not only
because Samsa's metamorphosis into a bug served as a symbol of the
supposed anti-humanist tendencies of modernist art, but also because in
1963 the first Kafka Conference in Liblice had heralded a major

[8] Deborah Vietor-Engländer, *Faust in der DDR* (Frankfurt/M.: Peter Lang, 1987).
[9] Adolf Dresen, *Wieviel Freiheit braucht die Kunst? Reden Briefe Verse Spiele 1964 bis 1999*, ed. Maik Hamburger, TdZ Recherchen, 3 (Eggersdorf: TdZ and Literaturforum im Brecht-Haus, 2000), 75–102; Dresen, 'Opposition mit Klassikern: Meine Arbeiten am Deutschen Theater', in Henning Rischbieter (ed.), *Theater im geteilten Deutschland 1945 bis 1990* (Berlin: Propyläen, 1999), 98–104; Martin Linzer, 'Weiße Flecken (4): *Faust* von Goethe, Deutsches Theater, 1968', *TdZ* 46/1 (Jan. 1991), 18–23.
[10] Lothar Ehrlich, '*Faust* im DDR-Sozialismus', in Frank Möbus, Friederike Schmidt-Möbus, and Gerd Unverfehrt (eds.), *Faust: Annäherung an einen Mythos* (Göttingen: Wallstein, 1995), 332–42; Bernd Mahl, *Goethes 'Faust' auf der Bühne (1806–1998): Fragment—Ideologiestück—Spieltext* (Stuttgart and Weimar: Metzler, 1998), 192–236.
[11] Frieder Kratochwil, 'Aufführung und Wirkung von *Faust I* im Deutschen Theater', 30.11.1968; Michael [Maik] Hamburger, '*Faust* im DT als "Soziologisches Experiment" (Diskussionsbeitrag zu Ks Untersuchung)'. Both in AdK D 52 c.
[12] Anon., 'Die alte, neue Frage: Wie soll man leben?', *ND*, 30.8.1968.

relaxation in the cultural policy of the ruling Party in Czechoslovakia. The participants at this conference, including the Western critical communist intellectuals Ernst Fischer and Roger Garaudy, had challenged Kafka's exclusion from the socialist literary canon and asserted the relevance of his work to contemporary signs of alienation in the Eastern bloc. This was bound to provoke resistance from the SED, which insisted that alienation occurred only under capitalism.[13] So when—just one month after Gysi's speech—Dresen and Heinz challenged the dominant GDR interpretation of *Faust*, Ministry officials saw the production both as an affront to Gysi and as evidence of an ideological affinity between the production team and those who had sought to revise the canon in Czechoslovakia.[14]

Until the premiere, it had not even occurred to the authorities that *Faust I* might cause a scandal. The status of the text, the performance location, and the involvement of the politically loyal Heinz all seemed to guarantee a safe production.[15] The SED had anticipated the production's success by issuing positive press statements on the eve of the premiere, and Heinz was due to receive a National Prize one week later.[16] Officials would probably have been less sanguine had they realized that Heinz had allowed Dresen to lead rehearsals on his own, particularly since Dresen's production of *Hamlet* had been banned in Greifswald in 1964 on the grounds that it had defaced the cultural heritage.[17] In the case of *Faust*, pre-performance censorship failed partly because the controls for classic texts were far less strict than those for contemporary drama, and partly because the Deutsches Theater guarded its production concept with such secrecy. Linzer remembers that the dramaturges prevaricated whenever he asked to see the rehearsal notes.[18] Although the Culture Department subsequently claimed that officials

[13] Martina Langermann, '"Faust oder Gregor Samsa?" Kulturelle Tradierung im Zeichen der Sieger', in Birgit Dahlke, Martina Langermann, and Thomas Taterka (eds.), *LiteraturGesellschaft DDR: Kanonenkämpfe und ihre Geschichte(n)* (Stuttgart and Weimar: J. B. Metzler, 2000), 173–213 at 203–4; Wenzke, *Die NVA und der Prager Frühling 1968*, 44.

[14] 'Vorschläge für die Diskussion der *Faust*-Aufführung im Deutschen Theater', 15.10.1968, BArch DR 1/8846.

[15] Hamburger, 'Faust im DT', fo. 1.

[16] 'Notiz zur Inszenierung *Faust I* im Deutschen Theater', 3.10.1968, BArch DY 30 IV A 2/2.024/32.

[17] Adolf Dresen, *Siegfrieds Vergessen: Kultur zwischen Konsens und Konflikt* (Berlin: Ch. Links, 1992), 17, 238.

[18] Linzer, '*Ich war immer...*', 99.

from the Ministry's Theatre Department had attended rehearsals without raising the alarm, Hamburger and Dresen both state that there were no controls before the premiere.[19] After the first performance, Stasi Lieutenant Klemer resolved to cultivate new contacts within the theatre, in the hope that his officers might discover the ideological implications of future productions before they were premiered.[20]

Faust and the GDR's Cultural Heritage

The German classics were central to the SED's image of the GDR. Although West Germany had inherited the Ruhr and its heavy industry, the East could boast Weimar, the cultural centre and home of Goethe and Schiller. After the Second World War, returning exiles like Ulbricht, Rodenberg, and Alexander Abusch styled first the Soviet-occupied zone and then the GDR as the protector and preserver of German national culture, in contrast to the 'decadent' Federal Republic.[21] Their argument that the GDR had inherited Germany's humanist traditions served to bolster the nascent state's claims to legitimacy. Through this selectively teleological view of German history, politicians could present the GDR as the heir and executor (*Vollstrecker*) of the hopes of the progressive thinkers of the past.

Faust took pride of place in the GDR's cultural heritage. It was an obvious choice to mark the reopening of the National Theatre in Weimar in 1948, and it became central to Ulbricht's attempt to create a new national myth. In a speech delivered in March 1962, he even presented the GDR as *Faust III*: the realization of Faust's utopian vision of standing on free soil with a free people ('auf freiem Grund mit freiem Volke stehn', l. 11580).[22] In *Faust II*, this vision is undercut by the context of its delivery: the blind, aged Faust mistakes the sound of the

---

[19] 'Aktennotiz über eine Beratung mit der Leitung des Ministeriums für Kultur am 3. Dezember 1968', 4.12.1968, BArch DY 30 IV A 2/9.06/51; Dresen, *Wieviel Freiheit*, 80; Hamburger, '*Faust* im DT', fo. 1.

[20] BStU BV Bln. AKK 3476/89, i, fo. 126.

[21] e.g. *Dokumente*, ed. Schubbe, 140–4; See also Linzer, '*Ich war immer*…', 22.

[22] Vietor-Engländer, *Faust in der DDR*, 27. For a critique of the Marxist view, see Hans Rudolf Vaget, 'Act IV Revisited: A "Post-Wall" Reading of Goethe's Faust', in Jane K. Brown, Meredith Lee, and Thomas P. Saine (eds.), *Interpreting Goethe's Faust Today* (Columbia, SC: Camden House, 1994), 43–58. For a measured critique of both Vaget and the Marxist position, see Frank Lamport, 'Goethe's *Faust*: A Cautionary Tale?', *Forum for Modern Language Studies*, 35 (1999), 193–206.

lemures—spirits of the restless or malignant dead—digging his grave as the sound of workers toiling away at his land reclamation project. However, for Georg Lukács this disjunction demonstrated only the impossibility of achieving Faust's vision in a capitalist society, and Ulbricht argued that Goethe had not been able to write *Faust III* because the time had not yet been ripe:

> Erst weit über hundert Jahre, nachdem Goethe die Feder für immer aus der Hand legen mußte, haben... alle Werktätigen der Deutschen Demokratischen Republik begonnen, diesen dritten Teil des *Faust* mit ihrer Arbeit, mit ihrem Kampf für Frieden und Sozialismus zu schreiben.[23]

> It is not until now, well over a hundred years after Goethe had to lay down his pen forever, that... all the working people of the German Democratic Republic have begun to write this third part of *Faust* through their work, through their fight for peace and socialism.

Such overt ideological manipulation of *Faust* meant that any break with the authorized GDR interpretation would be perceived as a challenge to Ulbricht himself.

In the early 1950s, the SED suppressed two significant alternative readings of *Faust*. In 1952, a production of *Urfaust* by Egon Monk and Bertolt Brecht was dropped after a handful of performances in Potsdam and East Berlin, and Hanns Eisler's libretto *Johann Faustus* was strongly criticized the following year.[24] The SED's detailed complaints centred on the fact that Eisler—like Brecht and Monk—had presented Faust pessimistically as a petty-bourgeois renegade, not as a bold Renaissance hero.[25] This fifteen-year-old controversy acquired a new relevance in 1968 because the staunchest defender of *Johann Faustus* was none other than Ernst Fischer, now a prominent opponent of the invasion of Czechoslovakia.[26] In *Neues Deutschland*, Klaus Höpcke argued that no

---

[23] Georg Lukács, *Faust und Faustus: Vom Drama der Menschengattung zur Tragödie der modernen Kunst* (Reinbek bei Hamburg: Rowohlt, 1967), 159; Klaus Höpcke, 'Faust in faustischer Landschaft: Zwischenbemerkungen zur Diskussion um die Inszenierung am Deutschen Theater', *ND*, 16.10.1968.

[24] See *Dramaturgie in der DDR (1945–1990)*, ed. Helmut Kreuzer and Karl-Wilhelm Schmidt, 2 vols. (Heidelberg: Universitätsverlag Winter, 1998), i. 96–110; Mahl, *Goethes 'Faust' auf der Bühne*, 192–7; Vietor-Engländer, *Faust in der DDR*, 139–55.

[25] e.g. Alexander Abusch, 'Faust—Held oder Renegat in der deutschen Nationalliteratur', *Sonntag* (East Berlin), 17.5.1953.

[26] Ernst Fischer, 'Doktor Faustus und der deutsche Bauernkrieg: Auszüge aus dem Essay zu Hanns Eislers Faust-Dichtung', *Sinn und Form*, 4 (1952), 59–73.

engagement with *Faust* could disregard the tension between Fischer's revisionism and GDR socialism. He concluded that staging *Faust* today was a matter of the highest political and aesthetic importance.[27]

A Wholesale Break with Tradition

The orthodox GDR interpretation set Goethe's text in the Renaissance, following Faust as he casts off the superstition of the Middle Ages and sets out to discover and conquer the world. Höpcke argued that it was precisely this identification of Faust with the Renaissance that invited comparison with the GDR's programme of change and renewal.[28] The exemplary productions of the 1960s, by Karl Kayser in Leipzig (1965) and Fritz Bennewitz in Weimar (1967), presented Faust as a proto-revolutionary, reading the oft-quoted vision from the end of Part II back into Part I.[29] Cultural politicians expected to find the same confidence in progress in *Faust* as in contemporary Socialist Realist literature.

Dresen and Heinz broke entirely with this setting and view of Faust, creating a production that was insufficiently optimistic and insufficiently reverent. Like Brecht and Monk, they set the play in the *Sturm und Drang* (Storm and Stress) of the 1770s, without suggesting any of the idealism and revolutionary energy associated with the movement. Instead, the actor Fred Düren took Faust's suicidal tendencies at the start of the play seriously, foregrounding his despair and self-obsession. In the opening scenes, he was hunched of, literally turned in on himself, fidgeting nervously and rushing through his lines instead of declaiming them in the time-honoured tradition (Fig. 3.1).[30] In Faust's walk on Easter morning, Dresen and Heinz rejected the Marxist interpretation of the line 'hier bin ich Mensch, hier darf ichs sein' ('Here I am Man, am free to be!') as an expression of Faust's sense of liberation amongst ordinary people. Instead, Düren delivered the line as a description of the

[27] Höpcke, 16.10.1968. Höpcke was on the *ND* editorial team from 1964 to 1973; in 1973 he would become Deputy Culture Minister responsible for publishing and the book trade.
[28] Ibid.
[29] See Mahl, *Goethes 'Faust' auf der Bühne*, 197–204; Vietor-Engländer, *Faust in der DDR*, 135–8, 157.
[30] e.g. Christoph Funke, 'Sinnlicher Faust im Halbdunkel', *Der Morgen* (East Berlin), 3.10.1968; Wolfgang Gersch, 'Die Größe und der Zwiespalt', *Tribüne* (East Berlin), 4.10.1968; Rainer Kerndl, 'Faust gegen Faust?', *ND*, 3.10.1968; Helmut Ullrich, 'Mehr Leidenschaft als Weisheit', *Neue Zeit* (East Berlin), 3.10.1968.

Fig. 3.1. Fred Düren as Faust (Gisela Brandt, Deutsches Theater)

people's joy, in which Faust was unable to share. The punctuation justified this interpretation:

> Zufrieden jauchzet groß und klein:
> Hier bin ich Mensch, hier darf ichs sein! (ll. 939–40)
>
> And young and old exult in glee:
> 'Here I am Man, am free to be!'[31]

In keeping with this interpretation, Düren's Faust closed the bet with Mephisto because he had ceased to value life, not because he was thirsting for knowledge or seeking to serve mankind.[32] The Culture Department noted with dismay:

> In dieser Inszenierung erscheint Faust nicht so sehr als der nach Wissen drängende, nach Erkenntnis suchende Mensch, sondern vielmehr als ein Mensch, der—angeekelt von seinem bisherigen Leben als Wissenschaftler, unzufrieden mit sich und seiner Umwelt, an ihr fast verzweifelnd—den Pakt mit Mephisto schließt, um aus dieser 'engen, kleinen' Welt aufzubrechen.[33]
>
> In this production Faust appears not so much as a man thirsting for knowledge, searching for insight, but rather as a man who—repulsed by his previous life as a scholar, dissatisfied with himself and those around him, almost despairing at them—seals the pact with Mephisto in order to break out of this 'narrow, small' world.

After Faust's rejuvenation, Dresen and Heinz continued to thwart any perception of him as a revolutionary figure by dressing him in an eighteenth-century blue coat that identified him with the self-indulgent sentimentality of Goethe's Werther.[34]

The Deutsches Theater offset its pessimistic presentation of Faust through vibrant visual and theatrical comedy. The costume designers Christine Stromberg and Andreas Reinhardt presented Mephisto in the tradition of the popular legend, with a jester's hat. Played by Dieter Franke, this stocky plebeian devil gave the audience the thumbs-up while Faust leaned on his back to sign the bet.[35] Whereas

---

[31] Johann Wolfgang von Goethe, *Faust*, trans. Walter Arndt, ed. Cyrus Hamlin, 2nd edn. (New York and London: Norton, 2001), 27.
[32] DT, 'Diskussionsgrundlage zur *Faust*-Konzeption des Deutschen Theaters', Dec. 1967, fos. 2–3, AdK D 52 c.
[33] 'Notiz zur Inszenierung'.
[34] C. U. Wiesner, 'Theater-Eule', *Eulenspiegel*, 45/68, AdK D 52 c.
[35] Dresen, *Wieviel Freiheit*, 84–5, 87.

later productions would entertain and shock their audiences by adding references at odds with the text, Dresen and Heinz built much of the humour out of the text itself. Aware that in the Prelude in the Theatre the director tells his players not to scrimp on stage machinery (ll. 233–4), Dresen commissioned the mask-maker Eddie Fischer to contrive an ingenious poodle that swelled up into a huge monstrosity, complete with flashing eyes.[36] But the authorities interpreted such comedy as disrespect for the play's philosophical content, and conservative spectators agreed that the audience was having too much fun. Karla and Peter Thiele, for instance, claimed that the poodle provided inappropriate entertainment, missing the point that the visual gag was grounded in Goethe's text (ll. 1252–5, 1310–13).[37] So the theatrical comedy fuelled the controversy sparked by the production's departure from the orthodox interpretation. As the West German critic Rolf Michaelis put it, Faust had been removed from his pedestal and brought firmly down to earth.[38]

The provocation through comedy reached its climax in an updated version of the Walpurgis Night's Dream, the only scene in which the Deutsches Theater departed significantly from Goethe's text. It was the first time that this scene had been performed in the GDR, as an extensive commentary would have been needed to explain Goethe's satirical allusions to poetry, philosophy, and politics in the late eighteenth-century German states. In the original, guests present these satirical verses as golden wedding anniversary gifts to Oberon and Titania, characters from *A Midsummer Night's Dream*. But at the Deutsches Theater, the actors Peter Aust and Hans Lucke presented the couple with a series of apologies from the absent guests, contemporary figures from the GDR cultural scene (Fig. 3.2). This in itself was risqué, for it could be interpreted either as an indication that the GDR establishment would steer clear of the production, or as an allusion to the euphemisms with which theatres so frequently camouflaged instances of censorship.

The stanzas themselves poked fun at the contemporary cultural scene, much in the spirit of Goethe's original lines. One stanza punned on the names of three theatre critics: Günther Bellmann, Christoph Funke,

[36] Ibid. 87–8.
[37] Anon., 'Für und Wider zum *Faust*', *Berliner Zeitung*, 16.10.1968.
[38] Rolf Michaelis, 'Theater heute—in Ostberlin', *Theater heute*, 9/12 (Dec. 1968), 30–6 at 30.

Fig. 3.2. The Walpurgis Night's Dream (Eva Stokowy, Stiftung Archiv Akademie der Künste)

and Ernst Schumacher, also referring to the loyalist playwright and reviewer for *Neues Deutschland,* Rainer Kerndl:

> Ein Bellmann hebt an uns das Bein,
> Ein Funke will nicht zünden,
> Ein Schuster bleibt bei seinem Leim,
> Kein Kerndl ist zu finden.[39]

> A barker cocks his leg at us,
> A spark just won't ignite.

---

[39] Adolf Dresen, 'Zensur oder nicht Zensur?', *TdZ* 45/6 (June 1990), 5–8 at 6.

> A cobbler sticks to what he knows,
> And Kerndl's out of sight.

Another made fun of the GDR activist Kast and Ulbricht's wife Lotte, weaving their names into the titles of popular musicals at East Berlin's variety theatre:

> Auch im Friedrichstadt-Palast [*sic*]
> Entsagt man der Klamotte,
> Heute gibt es Kiss Me Kast,
> Morgen My Fair Lotte.[40]

> In the Friedrichstadtpalast
> They go without their clobber.
> Today they're playing Kiss Me Kast
> Tomorrow My Fair Lotte.

These apparently harmless jokes confirmed that the Deutsches Theater was intent on pulling the GDR's cultural and political icons down to earth.

The Deutsches Theater moved onto more precarious ground in stanzas alluding to theatre censorship. Aust and Lucke announced that 'illness' prevented Heiner Müller from attending the celebrations, as his play had been premiered only the previous evening.[41] On asking where they might see the play, Oberon and Titania were informed that it had already been dropped for technical reasons, clear code for a ban.[42] When Titania asked after Peter Hacks, she was told that he could not attend either, as he had failed to reconcile Marx with Moritz. This was an obvious allusion to the ban on *Moritz Tassow*, couched in a pun about Wilhelm Busch's troublesome duo Max and Moritz.[43]

The most provocative stanza proved too daring even for Dresen, as it suggested that the SED's ageing elite had taken it upon itself to defend socialism against the heretical ideas emanating from China and Czechoslovakia:

> Leer ist auch der Staatsverschlag,
> Wo sind sie denn, die Alten?
> Ab nach Peking und nach Prag
> Und die Chose halten.[44]

---

[40] Dresen, *Wieviel Freiheit*, 93.
[41] Ibid. 92.
[42] Ibid.
[43] Ibid. 93.
[44] Ibid. 94.

The box where statesmen lurk is empty too,
Where have they gone, the oldies?
Off to Peking and to Prague
To keep the show in order.

But instead of just cutting the stanza, Dresen highlighted its omission, turning this instance of self-censorship into the most provocative part of the evening. He explains that the actors hummed the tune and Aust stepped forward, bowed, and announced that the management had cut the stanza—whereupon the audience burst into laughter.[45] So although the production team had censored the only direct reference to Prague, they gave free rein to the spectators' imagination and allowed them to imagine even more subversive lines.

   These topical stanzas were provocative, particularly so soon after the suppression of the Prague Spring. Dresen explains that a worried Heinz prevented the actors from performing many of the stanzas, but that they kept others from him, only performing them in full at the premiere.[46] So Dresen and his colleagues were sufficiently aware of the risks to hide the full extent of their subversion from Heinz and to cut the most directly political comments, but they were insufficiently intimidated to abandon their plans entirely. The stanzas that they did perform reflected their irreverent approach towards GDR cultural policy more than serious political criticism of the kind that Karge and Langhoff would attempt to voice through *Sieben gegen Theben*.

Censorship: Constraints and Compromises

Cultural politicians were in no doubt that the Deutsches Theater had defaced the GDR's national icon. At a meeting of the Council of State, Gysi argued that this portrayal of Faust contradicted both Goethe's interpretation and Marxist readings of the play.[47] In *Neues Deutschland*, Höpcke attacked the theatre's interpretation of Faust's walk on Easter morning, and in the FDJ newspaper *Junge Welt* Werner Pfelling concluded that this anti-heroic presentation of Faust would not make the

[45] Dresen, 'Zensur', 6.
[46] 'Dieter Kranz im Gespräch mit Adolf Dresen', Berliner Rundfunk, 26.3.1990, AdK AV 32.8572.
[47] *Dokumente*, ed. Schubbe, 1406.

play accessible to young people.[48] Stasi Lieutenant Klemer agreed, claiming that Faust had been turned into any old average character and that Goethe's profound philosophical intentions had been 'sträflich vergewaltigt', a phrase that translates literally as 'criminally raped'.[49] Yet even though the authorities disapproved wholeheartedly of the production, they could not afford to ban such a classic text at such a prominent theatre, particularly since they had only just awarded Heinz a National Prize. Hamburger argues that the regime would have found it hard to recover from such a ban, both at home and abroad.[50] By the late 1960s, the regime's concern to avoid negative publicity had begun to act as a pragmatic constraint on censorship.

On the morning after the premiere, representatives from the Ministry arrived at the Deutsches Theater and ordered the first cuts, which included the entire Walpurgis Night's Dream.[51] One day later, performances were suspended for nineteen days so that further changes could be made: only eight of the twenty-six scenes escaped unscathed.[52] Brighter lighting was used in the scenes set in Faust's study, to counter complaints that the portrayal was pessimistic, and in Marthe's garden blossoming trees replaced the original bare saplings, which had been covered in brown sacks to protect them from the frost.[53] This second change was designed to avoid unwelcome analogies with the recent chill in the political climate. The authorities then attempted to stage a public debate, even though this strategy had backfired in the case of *Die Sorgen und die Macht*. Newspapers carried reviews and comments from spectators, and speakers addressed the production before the Council of State and the Central Committee.[54] The authorities sought to keep this debate under control: the Ministry asked the Deutsches Theater to desist with its own post-performance discussions and forbade its members from discussing the production with Western spectators.[55]

[48] Höpcke, 16.10.1968; Werner Pfelling, 'Von der Lust des Begreifens', *Junge Welt* (East Berlin), 7.10.1968.
[49] BStU BV Bln. AKK 3476/89, i, fo. 124.
[50] Hamburger, 'Faust im DT', fo. 1.
[51] 'Dieter Kranz im Gespräch'.
[52] Kratochwil, 'Aufführung und Wirkung', fo. 8.
[53] Ibid.; Rolf Michaelis, 'Faust im Nacken', *FAZ*, 9.11.1968.
[54] e.g. *Dokumente*, ed. Schubbe, 1406.
[55] Kratochwil, 'Notate zu Vorgängen', AdK D 52 c.

Given the level of state interference in this production, it is surprising that the Stasi files seem to contain few references to it, other than Klemer's report dated 16 October. Whilst some documents may have been destroyed and others may yet come to light, the Stasi does seem to have lacked sufficiently well-placed, cooperative informers at the Deutsches Theater in 1968. At the end of October, the Stasi was still trying to obtain an up-to-date version of the script from its long-standing informer 'Gustav Adolf'. Whilst 'Gustav Adolf' promised to borrow the prompter's copy, he explained that he would need to wait until a break in performances in mid-November.[56] 'Gustav Adolf' was in fact a member of the theatre's technical staff, and the Stasi's reliance on him suggests that it could not draw on informers more closely involved in the artistic decision-making process, with easier access to the revised script. Whilst 'Gustav Adolf' described Dresen's contributions to Party meetings as those of a troublemaker and as 'a little oppositional', he said that he could not follow the political discussions well enough to assess their ideological significance.[57] His main information concerned the technicians' negative reactions to the production, which he attributed partly to its complex technical demands and partly to positive memories of stagings of *Faust* by Wolfgang Langhoff and even Max Reinhardt.[58]

Soon after the premiere, Kratochwil and Hamburger each analysed the censorship measures and the theatre's response. The very existence and explicitness of these analyses testify to the unusual degree of trust amongst the dramaturges who read and annotated them. Both Kratochwil and Hamburger highlighted the official denial of censorship. Kratochwil pointed out that neither the Ministry's instruction to cut the Walpurgis Night's Dream nor the heated discussions between the theatre and the SED-*Bezirksleitung* was made public.[59] Hamburger went further:

Die Repression muß sich selbst mitvertilgen, das Faktum Zensur muß mitzen-suriert werden. Die Repression darf weder nachweisbar noch widerlegbar sein, und zwar grundsätzlich nicht.[60]

---

[56] BStU BV Bln. AIM 8002/91, ii.ii, fo. 26.
[57] Ibid. 26.
[58] Ibid. 26–7.
[59] Kratochwil, '*Faust* im DT als "soziologisches Experiment"', fo. 1, AdK D 52 c.
[60] Hamburger, '*Faust* im DT', fo. 3.

Repression must eradicate every trace of itself; the fact of censorship must itself be censored. Repression must be neither provable nor refutable, and that is a matter of principle.

Hamburger acknowledged that the production team had become complicit in covering up the Ministry's censorship of the Walpurgis Night's Dream. He argued that this 'gentleman's agreement' was acceptable in the circumstances but that the theatre needed to be careful not to enter into greater compromises.[61]

Publicly, the debate culminated on 12 November when the Union of Theatre Practitioners held a colloquium that attracted some 180 participants from theatres across the GDR.[62] The Union had been founded in 1967, in the wake of the Eleventh Plenary Session, and *Faust I* was its first major test. Although the hard-line theatre directors Hans-Dieter Mäde and Karl Kayser had already criticized the production at the Ninth Plenary Session, they did not control the Union. Heinz was himself the President, and more debate was possible than at the Writers' Union in 1962. Even those sent to represent the orthodox view of *Faust* were not in full agreement: Abusch interrupted the opening speech by Edith Braemer, professor at the Karl Marx University in Leipzig, and disagreed with her very first sentence.[63] In fact, some of the theatre practitioners present demonstrated considerable solidarity with the Deutsches Theater. Bennewitz supported the production, undermining the authorities' attempts to use his recent staging as a positive counter-example.[64] And when the director Gert Jurgons voiced similar support for the Deutsches Theater, his speech was interrupted five times by unusually lively reactions indicating the agreement of those present.[65] In its concern to encourage theatre practitioners to regulate each other's work, the regime had created a forum in which circumscribed debate was possible.

The Culture Department was alert to signs of revisionism at the colloquium, showing that it associated the production with recent events in Prague. It criticized Ernst Schumacher for arguing that theatre should be interpreted more in terms of its theatrical than its political

[61] Ibid. 2.
[62] 'Kurzinformation über das Kolloquium zur *Faust*-Inszenierung des Deutschen Theaters', 15.11.1968, BArch DR 1/8846.
[63] 'Dieter Kranz im Gespräch'.
[64] Dresen, *Wieviel Freiheit*, 97.
[65] 'Kolloquium des Theaterverbandes über *Faust I* am 12.11.68', AdK D 52 c.

significance.[66] According to the Culture Department, this argument stood in dangerous proximity to the views of the Czech director Otomar Krejca, the founder of Prague's Divadlo za branou (Theatre behind the Gate). Noting the links between Schumacher's views and those that Fischer had expressed in 1953, the Department concluded that the Party Group in the Humboldt University's Institute for Theatre Studies should clarify the matter with Professor Schumacher.[67]

Whereas the Deutsches Theater had vehemently resisted the censorship of *Die Sorgen und die Macht* in 1962, this time it adopted a conciliatory approach. The directors and dramaturges listened carefully at the colloquium, mostly letting others like Bennewitz argue for them.[68] The team presented itself as flexible and willing to learn, complying publicly and voluntarily with the rhetoric of pedagogy. Together with the dramaturges Alexander Weigel and Klaus Wischnewski, Heinz and Dresen issued a statement:

Gemeinsam mit dem Zuschauer beobachtend und lernend, arbeiten wir an der Aufführung weiter, suchen für befriedigende Lösungen gute, für unvollkommene bessere, für falsche richtige.[69]

Observing and learning together with the spectator, we are continuing to work on the production, looking to replace satisfactory solutions with good ones, imperfect ones with better ones, and wrong ones with correct ones.

After the colloquium, the Ministry was able to report that the Deutsches Theater had reacted positively to a whole series of detailed criticisms and was busy revising the production.[70] The following month, the theatre's Party organization even thanked the SED-*Bezirksleitung* for its help, claiming that Culture Secretary Roland Bauer had been particularly supportive.[71]

These conciliatory tactics substantiate the participants' testimony that they had learned from their past experiences of censorship. Whilst older members of the Deutsches Theater recalled *Die Sorgen und die*

[66] 'Information über den gegenwärtigen Stand der Diskussion zur *Faust*-Inszenierung des Deutschen Theaters', 18.11.1968, BArch DY 30 IV A 2/2.024/32.

[67] Ibid.

[68] Ibid.

[69] Adolf Dresen, Wolfgang Heinz, Alexander Weigel, and Klaus Wischnewski, 'Probleme einer *Faust*-Inszenierung', BArch DY 30 IV A 2/2.024/32.

[70] 'Kurzinformation', 15.11.1968.

[71] DT *Betriebsparteiorganisation* to Hen[t]schel, 2.12.1968, BArch DY 30 IV A 2/9.06/114.

Macht, Dresen had experienced censorship in Greifswald, and Wisch-newski had been criticized at the Eleventh Plenary Session in connection with the banned DEFA films. According to Hamburger, veterans of *Die Sorgen und die Macht* argued that Hacks had won a polemical victory that killed off the production. Instead of trying to pull off a victory, Hamburger claims that the team responsible for staging *Faust* sought to be accommodating without surrendering its principles.[72] But he argues that this show of flexibility was possible only because the production had been unfinished at the premiere, unlike the stagings in Chapter 2:

Die Regie konnte ehrlichen Muts die Aufführung verbessern, und die Vertreter des Systems konnten die Verbesserung als Reaktion auf ihre Kritik auffassen ... Eine relativ fertige Premiere hätte vermutlich sofortige Konfrontation und beiderseitige Verhärtung zur Folge gehabt, in der die Regie nur sehr begrenzt zu Konzessionen bereit gewesen wäre, mit vermutlich schlimmen Folgen.[73]

The directors could improve the production with a clear conscience, and the representatives of the system could interpret the improvement as a reaction to their criticism ... A relatively polished premiere would probably have resulted in an immediate confrontation and a hardening of the attitudes on both sides; the directors would have been prepared to make only very limited concessions, probably with severe consequences.

Equally significantly, the Deutsches Theater knew that *Faust I* had taken the authorities by surprise, whereas much of its indignation in 1962 had come from seeing officials denounce *Die Sorgen und die Macht* after they had previously approved it. Members of the theatre never claimed that Ministry officials had approved of *Faust I*, even though the Culture Department stated that they had attended some rehearsals. Finally, Dresen explains that he and his colleagues still felt enough loyalty towards the GDR to mitigate the political fall-out from the production: as committed, albeit critical, Marxists, they did not want to force the state into the embarrassing position of having to ban *Faust* at the Deutsches Theater.[74]

---

[72] Hamburger, '*Faust* im DT', fo. 3.
[73] Ibid. 2.
[74] 'Dieter Kranz im Gespräch'.

Reception and Impact

As the authorities discovered after *Die Sorgen und die Macht* and *Moritz Tassow*, their public disapproval encouraged spectators to read political messages into *Faust I* even where none had been intended. In the *FAZ*, Rolf Michaelis listed a series of lines that had acquired controversial meanings, such as Mephisto's comment that the wrong path is hard to avoid (l. 1985), or Faust's claim that people often dismiss what they do not understand (ll. 1205–6).[75] Similarly, Karoll Stein reported in *Die Zeit* that spectators giggled and laughed when, in the Prelude in the Theatre, the director bemoaned the fact that some audience members would have come fresh from reading the press (l. 116).[76] Whilst the Deutsches Theater might have been entitled to a certain *Schadenfreude* on hearing the authorities' worst fears realized, such wholesale politicization changed the production's impact. Dresen recalls that spectators applauded at Faust's line 'O ja, bis an die Sterne weit!' (Oh yes, right up to the stars!, l. 574), taking it as a reference to the Soviet space programme. He argues that reactions like this began to disrupt performances.[77]

In the longer term, however, the production opened the way for more innovative and iconoclastic interpretations of the classics. Eleven years later in Schwerin, Christoph Schroth would stage the Witch's Kitchen as a transvestite show, and in Weimar—of all places—Mephisto would give Faust's student a porn magazine to accompany his Reclam text.[78] Even though these productions went much further than the 1968 staging, they did not arouse similar controversy. By celebrating the Schwerin *Faust* as a sign of theatrical pluralism, the SED avoided a public clash between its own expectations and the production, the factor which had contributed most to the subversive impact of the 1968 *Faust*. As this shift in official attitudes suggests, the 1968 *Faust* was a highwater mark of GDR theatre censorship. It was the last time that the SED's collective forces would publicly confront a production head-on and mobilize a pseudo-democratic debate in the press. To conclude with Dresen: the GDR leadership realized that it would ultimately lose

[75] Michaelis, 9.11.1968.
[76] Karoll Stein, 'Faust war kein Sozialist', *Die Zeit*, 16.11.1968.
[77] 'Dieter Kranz im Gespräch'.
[78] Mahl, *Goethes 'Faust' auf der Bühne*, 215, 219.

out from wars of this kind; later productions benefited from this, his own included.[79]

3. *JOHANN FAUSTUS* AT THE BERLINER ENSEMBLE

Just days before the premiere of *Faust I* shocked the guests of honour at the Deutsches Theater, the Culture Ministry banned a far less controversial public reading of Eisler's *Johann Faustus* at the Berliner Ensemble, a theatre with a better political track record in the 1960s. Deputy Culture Minister Bork feared partly that listeners would recall the fact that Fischer had defended Eisler's libretto in 1953, and partly that the reading would be seen as an affront to Gysi following his speech in Weimar. But after the controversy at the Deutsches Theater, it seemed as if the authorities had banned the 'wrong' *Faust*, as Western critics like Karoll Stein noted with glee.[80]

The Ministry's intervention outraged the BE's members: not only was it the first time that one of their productions had been banned, but they did not even agree that the reading posed a political risk. In no uncertain terms, Helene Weigel informed Gysi:

Ich sehe mich außerstande, den Mitgliedern unseres Hauses diese Sache mit gewichtigen politischen Gründen zu erklären. Die in dem gestrigen Brief... genannten Gründe sind bei Gott nicht zureichend.[81]

I find myself unable to explain this matter to the members of our ensemble using weighty political reasons. God knows, the reasons given in yesterday's letter...are not sufficient.

Although Weigel agreed to follow the Ministry's instructions, she warned Abusch that the ensemble was not satisfied and did not regard the matter as closed.[82] Weigel refused to offer the usual public excuses for the cancellation, leaving this task to the Ministry's press office—a move that contrasted with Holàn's cooperation over the cancellation of *Tassow* in 1966.[83]

---

[79] Dresen, 'Opposition mit Klassikern', 101.
[80] Stein, 16.11.1968.
[81] Weigel to Gysi, 25.9.1968, BEA file 104.
[82] Weigel to Abusch, 26.9.1968, BEA file 104.
[83] Report sent from the BE to Abusch, Gysi, and Hentschel, BEA file 104.

Manfred Karge and Matthias Langhoff had planned and co-directed the reading of *Johann Faustus*. When it was banned, Langhoff sent Gysi a letter of protest, signed by fifteen colleagues.[84] As in the case of *Die Sorgen und die Macht*, such direct, organized defiance hardened the authorities' resolve: although they were prepared to tolerate Weigel's private, individual protests, they were determined to crush any sign of organized opposition. The manner of Langhoff's protest appalled the *Parteileitung*, destroying the company's solidarity regarding the issue.[85]

This episode is important because Karge and Langhoff, the set designer Pieter Hein, and five of the actors involved in *Johann Faustus* went on to mount a devastating critique of the Warsaw Pact's invasion of Prague through their production of *Sieben gegen Theben*. The early rehearsals for Aeschylus' play actually overlapped with the internal disciplinary procedures that Langhoff faced over his letter of protest. Moreover, the *Parteileitung*, which Langhoff had just accused of bigotry, was responsible for the theatre's ideological output.[86] Neither side was in any mood to compromise.

4. *SIEBEN GEGEN THEBEN* AT THE BERLINER ENSEMBLE

Like *Faust I*, *Sieben gegen Theben* initially seems worlds away from the tumultuous events of 1968. The action forms the link between the myths of Oedipus and Antigone: before the play starts, Oedipus has cursed his twin sons, Eteokles and Polyneikes, to divide their inheritance, the city-state of Thebes, with the sword. On his death, they agree to rule in turn, but when Eteokles refuses to relinquish the throne, Polyneikes bribes the city's enemies to invade. Although Eteokles saves Thebes, the brothers die in mutual combat, fulfilling Oedipus' curse.

The BE actually chose the play in 1967, before the Prague Spring, at the suggestion of its chief director Manfred Wekwerth, who had an impeccable political track record; they intended the play to contribute to the reception of classical drama, a burgeoning area in GDR theatre since Besson's internationally acclaimed production of *Der Frieden* at

[84] See BArch DY 30 IV A 2/2.024/74 and DY 30 IV A 2/9.06/113.
[85] Report of a *Parteileitung* meeting in the BE, 10.10.1968, BArch DR 1/8849.
[86] Langhoff to the *Parteileitung*, 2.10.1968, BArch DR 1/8849.

the Deutsches Theater in 1962.[87] Karge and Langhoff used the existing German translations to produce an adaptation which the BE's management approved.

In interviews since German reunification, Karge and Langhoff have explained that the theme of fraternal conflict partly attracted them to Aeschylus' play.[88] This had the potential for topical political parallels even before the invasion of Prague, because Soviet and East German propaganda presented the USSR as the GDR's brother. But the events of 1968 made the text far more subversive than Karge and Langhoff could ever have foreseen, as striking new parallels emerged between Prague and Thebes, Eteokles and Dubček, and Polyneikes and the USSR. In the play, Thebes is besieged by foreign armies raised by Eteokles' brother Polyneikes, while Prague was invaded by its 'brother', the USSR, together with the foreign armies of the Warsaw Pact. Polyneikes' behaviour also invited comparison with the Czech and Slovak hardliners who had backed the Warsaw Pact's invasion of their own country; the script warns:

> voller Recht ist heimatliche Erde
> Die den Verblendeten verflucht, der sie betritt
> Um eigenes Volk in Feindesflammen einzuhüllen. (*SgT* 1–4, 21)[89]

> The soil of our homeland is rich in justice.
> It curses the man who blindly sets foot on it
> To engulf his own people in hostile flames.

The text's warnings against the consequences of invasion and occupation would have had a strong contemporary resonance in the autumn of 1968: members of the chorus beg the gods to save them from slavery and paint an apocalyptic picture of their beloved homeland burnt to

---

[87] 'Protokoll von der Beratung der Parteileitung vom 18.12.1968 mit Frau Weigel und Joachim Tenschert', LAB C. Rep. 902 2860; 'Arbeitsbesprechung der Regie und Dramaturgie', 15.9.1967, BEA file 'Protokolle 50er'.

[88] Barbara Villiger Heilig, 'Im Dickicht der Theaterstätten: Ein Gespräch mit dem Regisseur Matthias Langhoff', *Neue Zürcher Zeitung*, 3.5.1995; interview with Karge, 19.3.2004. See Laura Bradley, '*Prager Luft* at the Berliner Ensemble: The Censorship of *Sieben gegen Theben*, 1968–9', *GLL* 58 (2005), 41–54.

[89] Aeschylus, 'Sieben gegen Theben', unpublished adaptation by Manfred Karge and Matthias Langhoff. Four versions of the adaptation are held in the BEA, box file 48, and the extract quoted above appears on fo. 27 of each version. Further references appear in the text in the form *SgT* 1 (1967 typescript), *SgT* 2 (1968 typescript with amendments to 23.1.1969), *SgT* 3 (spring 1969 typescript), and *SgT* 4 (1968 prompt book with amendments to 25.10.1969).

ashes, the women dragged away, the children drowned in blood (*SgT* 2: 5, 11).

The most telling commentary on recent events came in a controversial new ending, written by Karge and Langhoff. Here the chorus, the women of Thebes, debates the brothers' responsibility for the war and comes down harshly against the invader Polyneikes. One speaker argues that, even though Polyneikes was legally in the right, he must still be held to account for the suffering he has caused:

> Sein Recht erzwingend, brachte uns doch
> Leid Polyneikes. Es fehlen im Haus
> Die, die sein Tun mit dem Leben bezahlten. (*SgT* 2: 27)

> Claiming his rights by force, Polyneikes brought
> Suffering upon us. At home we miss those
> Who paid for his actions with their lives.

Another argues that Eteokles acted in the city's best interests by driving Polyneikes away:

> Recht wars, als er verjagte den Bruder
> Denkend an Theben, behielt er die Herrschaft
> Zeigte der Angriff des Feinds Polyneikes
> Uns doch, wie er zu herrschen gedachte. (*SgT* 2: 27)

> He was right to drive away his brother;
> Thinking of Thebes, he held on to power.
> After all, the attack of our enemy Polyneikes
> Showed us how he planned to rule.

The very fact that the chorus debates these matters is significant: previously, the chorus had tended to react as a unit, yet here its members voice different opinions and reach a consensus through democratic debate—another example for the GDR audience.

The consensus was political dynamite. The chorus castigates itself for having shirked its civic responsibility by failing to speak out earlier, when it might have helped to avert the invasion and save Eteokles:

> So hätt ich reden sollen, als der Feind
> Mit Pferd und Wagen, Eisen und Geschrei
> Verwüstung schwor der Stadt und Tod ...
> Schamvoll entdeck ich die eigene Schuld
> Lüge wurd Wahrheit, ich folgte ihr schweigend
> Nährte durch Schweigen die rechtlose Herrschaft
> Bis daß mein Schweigen sich gegen mich kehrte. (*SgT* 2: 28–9)

This is how I should have spoken when the enemy,
With his horses and chariots, arms and battle-cries,
Swore devastation and death upon the city...

Full of shame, I discover my own guilt.
The lie became truth, I went along with it silently,
Nurtured the unlawful regime through silence
Until my silence turned against me.

The chorus resolves to speak now, regardless of the consequences:

Reden nun will ich, entsteht auch Bedrängnis
Den Schatten beschwören, der über uns lastet
Suchen nur nach der verschütteten Wahrheit
Die Antwort verlangen, wie immer sie ausfällt. (*SgT* 2: 29)

Now I wish to talk, even if it causes distress,
To banish the shadow that hangs over us
To search for the truth that lies buried
To demand the answer, whatever it may be.

In this purpose-built ending, the chorus spoke for the silent majority of
the GDR's citizens who had failed to oppose the Warsaw Pact's military
action, for Czechs and Slovaks who had not encouraged Dubček to
organize the successful civil defence seen in Aeschylus' play, and for the
production team whose members had spoken out about *Faustus* but not
about the underlying political issues. The lines were simultaneously
outspoken and reticent, providing a clear allegory of the Prague Spring
without commenting on it directly. These associations were accentuated
in the production concept, an eighteen-page document that was circulated initially just to the actors but eventually reached the authorities. In
it, Karge and Langhoff argued that Eteokles embodies a contradiction
between democracy and autocracy, between progress and tradition:
although his methods of governing demand the people's trust, his
government did not come to power through the people; as a result, his
government faces one obstacle: Eteokles himself.[90] These comments
applied equally to Dubček, who had risen to power through the ranks
of the ruling Party in Czechoslovakia, with the support of its Soviet
backers. Yet there were important differences: whilst Eteokles had used
his popularity to inspire his citizens to save their city, Dubček had
reluctantly acquiesced in the Soviet invasion.

Even more provocative was the view that the production concept
took of the function of theatre in general and this play in particular.

---

[90] Production concept, fo. 27, BArch DY 30 IV A 2/2.024/74.

Karge and Langhoff argued that GDR theatre should emulate its Ancient Greek forebear by providing a forum for the discussion of political, social, and ethical issues.[91] They emphasized that Greek theatre, although basically loyal to the state, never replicated its ideology. They also quoted Brecht's statement that, rather than arousing Aristotelian fear and pity, theatre should seek to remove the conditions where people have to fear and pity each other.[92] Just in case their actors had missed the point, Karge and Langhoff explained that they intended to stage *Sieben gegen Theben* as a model—a clear indication that the action would have allegorical significance.[93]

This political and theatrical rebellion extended to the artistic aspects of the production, which were inspired by the stylized acting and costumes of Japanese Noh theatre, introduced to the production team by a visiting Japanese director, Hideo Kanze. Karge explained to me that he and his colleagues were fascinated by the fact that Noh theatre had retained its ancient theatrical forms, as they were not familiar with the original form of Greek tragedy.[94] In addition, the Oriental aesthetic promised a breath of fresh air and exoticism and offered a means of releasing Aeschylus' play from its historical confines so that it could function as a parable.

The BE's dramaturge Joachim Tenschert was in no doubt that the production constituted a wholesale rebellion against the political and aesthetic norms of GDR theatre. Fearing that the elaborate masks and hair designs (Fig. 3.3) might re-ignite the old debate about Formalism, he warned the directors against using the project to launch a political and stylistic attempt at theatrical revolution. In Tenschert's view, this intention—conscious or otherwise—would undermine the project to such an extent that its successful completion could not be guaranteed.[95]

The Censorship Process

Even though this production came to the authorities' attention before the premiere, both they and the BE's management were surprisingly

[91] Production concept, fo. 27, BArch DY 30 IV A 2/2.024/74. 11–12, 16.
[92] Ibid. 1, 11; Brecht, *BFA*, xxii.ii (1993), 710.
[93] Production concept, fo. 16, BArch DY 30 IV A 2/2.024/74.
[94] Interview with Karge, 19.3.2004.
[95] Tenschert to Karge and Langhoff, 7.12.1968, BEA file 48.

Fig. 3.3. Eteokles and the chorus in *Sieben gegen Theben* (Vera Tenschert, Bertolt-Brecht-Archiv)

slow to perceive it as subversive. This was because of the weakness and informality of the external and internal controls. Whilst the Ministry claimed that it had repeatedly asked the BE for the production concept, it failed to act when this information was not provided, even though most of the production team had only just protested against Ministry policy.[96] Meanwhile, on 10 October, a committee of the BE's managers, directors, and dramaturges approved the updated script without discussing the possible new parallels with the Prague Spring.[97] Tenschert, the only senior figure involved in the rehearsals, was not a Party member and was subsequently described as politically unreliable by the BE's Party Secretary, Ruth Berghaus.[98] Otherwise, the rehearsals were not monitored at all by the theatre's management, let alone by the authorities.

These omissions were strongly criticized by Elisabeth Hauptmann, one of Brecht's key collaborators and now an unofficial adviser to the BE:

Dabei wäre es ganz gleich gewesen, von wem eine solche Vorführung des bis dahin Inszenierten gefordert worden wäre, von der Intendanz, vom Oberspielleiter, von der Dramaturgie, den beiden Regisseuren usw. Eine Forderung der Parteileitung nach einer solchen Vorführung wäre durchaus angemessen gewesen... Diese Vorführung hätte vor allem deshalb längst angesetzt werden müssen, weil die politischen Ereignisse seit dem Sommer 68 immer dringender mit der Konzeption des Stückes zu tun haben.[99]

It would have made no difference who had demanded a run-through of what had been rehearsed so far: the management, the chief director, the dramaturges, the two directors, etc. It would have been entirely appropriate for the *Parteileitung* to call for such a performance... This performance should have been arranged long ago, above all because the political events since the summer of '68 have become ever more urgently bound up with the concept of the play.

Her comments highlight the ad hoc nature of the internal controls. As there were no standard procedures for monitoring productions before

---

[96] Bork to Weigel, 3.12.1968, BArch DY 30 IV A 2/2.024/74.

[97] Weigel to Bork, 10.12.1968; 'Gespräch über *Sieben gegen Theben* am 10. Oktober 1968'. Both in BEA file 48.

[98] 'Kurzinformation über ein Gespräch mit Genossin Ruth Berghaus, Parteisekretär, über die Situation im Berliner Ensemble', 12.3.1969, BArch DY 30 IV A 2/2.024/74. On Berghaus's role in the dispute, see Corinne Holtz, *Ruth Berghaus: Ein Porträt* (Hamburg: Europäische Verlagsanstalt, 2005), 154–6.

[99] Elisabeth Hauptmann, 'Einige Punkte zu *Sieben gegen Theben*', Feb. 1969, BEA file 48.

the dress rehearsals, Karge and Langhoff were left entirely to their own devices for six weeks.

When the *Parteileitung* and the authorities finally read the production concept, they were horrified. Arno Hochmuth, the head of the Central Committee's Culture Department, warned Gysi that the entire concept obviously amounted to a lecture on the need to unite socialism and 'democracy', adding an exclamation mark.[100] Wekwerth subsequently outlined the concerns of the *Parteileitung* in a letter to Verner, reporting that the play's ending and the production concept were revisionist, and that they provided a platform for oppositional behaviour by the directors and Hilmar Thate, the actor playing Eteokles.[101] In the SED-*Bezirksleitung*, Bauer reminded Verner that Karge and Langhoff were known for their rejection of the Warsaw Pact's intervention in Czechoslovakia and had been prevented from staging *Johann Faustus*.[102] But it was the Central Committee's Culture Department that first spurred the Ministry into action. On 3 December, Hochmuth held a meeting with Gysi and his deputies, criticizing the Ministry and citing *Sieben gegen Theben*, *Faust I*, and *Johann Faustus* as signs that theatre needed tighter ideological controls.[103] On the very same day, Bork informed Weigel that the authorities could not agree to the current version or concept.[104]

More than the productions discussed so far, the negotiations over *Sieben gegen Theben* show how theatre censorship could combine the personal and the bureaucratic. While Culture Minister Gysi was negotiating with Weigel and corresponding with the Party authorities, his daughter Gabriele was rehearsing her part in the chorus. Gysi's deputy, meanwhile, was married to Weigel's secretary Elfriede Bork and had known Weigel and Brecht since the Weimar Republic. It is sometimes difficult to ascertain exactly how such links worked, because they extended to parties on both sides of the conflict: although Wekwerth was not actually related to the authorities, he was on first-name terms with many officials, and although Bork's wife provided Weigel with a direct link to the Ministry, she was also the Ministry's link to Weigel. However, Linzer argues that Bork did treat Weigel with greater leniency than other equally prominent theatre practitioners, such as Wolfgang

[100] Hochmuth to Gysi, 29.11.1968, BArch DY 30 IV A 2/2.024/74.
[101] Wekwerth to Verner, 26.12.1968, BArch DY 30 IV A 2/2.024/74.
[102] Bauer to Verner, 4.12.1968, BArch DY 30 IV A 2/2.024/74.
[103] 'Aktennotiz', 4.12.1968.
[104] Bork to Weigel, 3.12.1968.

Langhoff, and Stuber has shown that Bork protected Brecht and Weigel in the 1950s.[105] The relatively small size of the GDR's cultural elite created the potential for theatre practitioners and censors to exploit their personal influence and connections, and this is precisely how Weigel defended the production.

Sieben gegen Theben reveals that the regime had infiltrated the BE to a far greater extent than some of its members realized. When I interviewed him, Karge confirmed that he had viewed censorship as external and assumed, however naively, that Party members would place their loyalty to their colleagues above their loyalty to the SED.[106] Even though Langhoff was hardly on good terms with the *Parteileitung*, he was still shocked when it denounced his production to the authorities.[107] In fact, the *Parteileitung* was in regular contact with the SED-*Bezirksleitung*, to which it forwarded details of its discussions. Bauer noted on the confidential minutes of a meeting between Weigel and the *Parteileitung* that there was no need for Weigel to know that the *Bezirksleitung* had them.[108] Unbeknown to Karge and Langhoff, Wekwerth was in regular contact with the *Bezirksleitung* and Ministry, about both the production and Weigel's management.[109] Meanwhile, the dramatist Helmut Baierl briefed the Stasi about developments, as five reports written between 17 October and 11 March indicate.[110] The sheer volume of this behind-the-scenes activity shows that a substantial section of the BE was actively involved in censorship.

A corollary of this internal involvement was that theatre censorship became closely bound up with professional rivalries and disputes. Weigel and Wekwerth had been at loggerheads over artistic and organizational issues for over a year, and Wekwerth argued that *Sieben gegen Theben* exemplified the problems caused by Weigel's failure to observe socialist management norms and her tendency to shield politically

---

[105] Linzer, '*Ich war immer...*', 57; Stuber, *Spielräume und Grenzen*, 168.

[106] Interview with Karge, 19.3.2004.

[107] Brähmer to Verner, 16.12.1968, LAB C. Rep. 902 2860.

[108] 'Protokoll von der Beratung'.

[109] e.g. Wekwerth to Verner, 26.12.1968, BArch DY 30 IV A 2/2.024/74. Brähmer to Verner, 25.4.1969; Wekwerth to Gysi, 14.1.1969. Both in LAB C. Rep. 902 2860.

[110] BStU BV Bln. Abt. XX A-576/1, fos. 20, 25, 27–9, 30–1, 37. Baierl was a contact (*Kontaktperson*) of the Stasi between 1968 and 1970; his codename 'Flinz' alludes to his play *Frau Flinz*. See BStU ZA AP 3788/73, fo. 155; Walther, *Sicherungsbereich Literatur*, 756–7.

wayward directors like Karge and Langhoff.[111] The *Parteileitung* endorsed these criticisms: Weigel had reportedly rejected its concerns as unjustified interventions in artistic processes and argued that Karge and Langhoff should be allowed to work in peace as they were so talented.[112] Wekwerth cited his concerns over *Sieben gegen Theben* when urging the authorities to limit Weigel's power and strengthen his own position.[113]

One reason why these complaints encountered little success was that theatre censorship operated through a range of institutions, whose different priorities and responsibilities affected their approaches to the conflict. As the recipient of almost daily complaints from the *Parteileitung*, the *Bezirksleitung* was primarily concerned with the SED's credibility within the BE. So Bauer joined Hochmuth in urging the Ministry to intervene, supplying a point-by-point analysis of the ideological dangers in the script and production concept.[114] The Ministry, in contrast, had to work with the BE's non-Party members, including Weigel, and feared antagonizing her in case she went to the Western press or, worse still, defected to her native Austria; and so a further two months passed before Bork ordered her to stop the rehearsals.[115] There is evidence of tensions between the Party's representatives and the Ministry: whilst Brähmer warned that the Ministry's failure to act strengthened Weigel's 'incorrect' position, Bork reportedly criticized the BE's *Parteileitung* for being anarchistic.[116] But the Ministry and *Bezirksleitung* did agree about the need to avoid another outright ban, euphemistically known as 'administrative measures'.[117] Such action would have further damaged the authorities' relations with the BE's members and, as in the case of *Faust I* and *Faustus*, added grist to the mill of Western journalists.

[111] Wekwerth to Giersch and Häntzsche, 20.12.1968, BArch DY 30 IV A 2/2.024/74; Wekwerth to Gysi, 14.1.1969.

[112] Bauer to Verner, 4.12.1968, and Brähmer to Verner, 5.12.1968. Both in BArch DY 30 IV A 2/2.024/74.

[113] See e.g. Wekwerth to Gysi, 14.1.1969.

[114] Bauer to Verner, 4.12.1968. Bauer sent Hager a copy of this letter.

[115] 'Gespräch mit Gen. Klaus Gysi über die Situation am Berliner Ensemble und Maßnahmen des Ministeriums', 13.3.1969, BArch DY 30 IV A 2/2.024/74; '*Sieben gegen Theben* im Berliner Ensemble', 7.2.1969, BArch DY 30 IV A 2/9.06/113; Wekwerth to Bauer, 12.1.1970, LAB C. Rep. 902 2860.

[116] Brähmer to Verner, 25.4.1969 and 16.12.1968, LAB C. Rep. 902 2860.

[117] Bork to Weigel, 3.12.1968; Brähmer to Verner, 16.12.1968.

The problem with using the *Parteileitung* to broker a deal in the BE was that neither it nor the directors were in any mood to compromise. On 7 December, Tenschert warned Karge and Langhoff that only tactical concessions could save their production. He explained that they needed to accept certain criticisms and respond to the political concerns that had been raised, so that members of the BE could defend the production with a clear conscience.[118] Yet far from trying to appease the *Parteileitung*, Langhoff continued to attack it in what he mistook for private conversations with his colleagues. He reportedly accused the *Parteileitung* of issuing one-sided judgements instead of having a critical relationship to the Party line, like Brecht, and he criticized the *Parteileitung* for having turned to the Ministry and the Party authorities.[119]

When Langhoff was summoned before the *Parteileitung*, he reportedly failed to hide his support for Dubček's reforms. He is also said to have expressed his disagreement with the authorities' unilateral decision to cancel *Johann Faustus*:

Die nicht geführte Diskussion und das Absetzen der *Faustus*-Lesung wäre ein Fehlverhalten, das nur Widerstand hervorrufen kann. Es sei sein Grundanliegen, die damit verbundenen theoretischen Fragen zu diskutieren. Dem diene seine Arbeit an *Sieben gegen Theben*.[120]

The lack of discussion and the cancellation of the *Faustus* reading was a mistake that was bound to provoke resistance. His overriding concern was to discuss the theoretical questions associated with this matter. This was what his work on *Seven against Thebes* was designed to achieve.

Such unguarded comments indicate how Langhoff's ignorance of the extent of his colleagues' collusion with the authorities, together with his frustration, gave the *Parteileitung* the advantage and enabled its members initially to present the stronger case to the authorities.

Matters changed only when Weigel took charge of the fight to save *Sieben gegen Theben*, giving Karge and Langhoff her personal assurance that the production would go ahead.[121] Her approach clearly marks the difference between the experienced manager, who had helped to steer the BE through the battles of the 1950s and had substantial symbolic

---

[118] Tenschert to Karge and Langhoff, 7.12.1968.

[119] Report of a 'private' conversation between Langhoff, Giersch, Häntzsche, Kilian, and Thalmer, 12.12.1968, LAB C. Rep. 902 2860.

[120] Brähmer to Verner, 16.12.1968.

[121] Interview with Karge, 19.3.2004.

capital, and her young, politically inexperienced directors. By exploiting her personal contacts, including the philosopher Wolfgang Heise and the critic Werner Mittenzwei, Weigel forged an alliance to counter Wekwerth and the *Parteileitung*. She even courted her long-standing acquaintance Alfred Kurella, who had been one of Brecht's main opponents during the Expressionism debate in the 1930s. Whilst Kurella was no longer in charge of cultural matters, he still wielded political clout as a hard-line member of the Politbüro's Ideological Commission. By exercising her unique blend of personal charm and home-made lemon cake, Weigel convinced Kurella that Karge and Langhoff had been entirely misjudged.[122] He informed the Ministry that they were genuinely trying to adapt the play well and stage it correctly, and he even accused the *Bezirksleitung* of deliberately misinterpreting the production's political thrust.[123] By sacrificing sections of the script, including the provocative ending, Weigel saved the production. Even now, Karge is full of admiration for her negotiating skills.[124]

From Text to Performance

When the rehearsals resumed in April, the new script still contained potentially controversial material, simply because it was so integral to the action. This material included Eteokles' calls for civil defence, his appeals to his citizens' love of their homeland, and the chorus's warnings against invasion and occupation (*SgT* 4: 3, 11a). Its survival explains why, in the final rehearsals, Weigel focused on the actors' line delivery and their relationship with the audience. Having only just managed to save the production, Weigel was anxious to avoid giving any impression that it was intended as an allegory. She warned Thate not to invest so much significance in a line referring to the dead and injured, and she noted that she still found his eye contact with the audience dangerous.[125] Instead, Weigel attempted to confine the

---

[122] Weigel to Sonja Kurella, 25.2.1969, BEA file 'HW Allg. Briefwechsel '69'. In this letter, Weigel explained that Kurella had enjoyed her lemon cake so much that he had asked for the recipe.

[123] 'Ergänzung zur Notiz über Berliner Ensemble', 21.3.1969, BArch DY 30 IV A 2/ 2.024/74.

[124] Interview with Karge, 19.3.2004.

[125] Weigel, 'Zur Generalprobe *Sieben gegen Theben* am 27. Mai 1969', BEA file 48.

relevance of potentially subversive lines to the action, telling Thate to deliver one such passage to the chorus, not to the audience.[126]

Whilst it is difficult to establish exactly how audiences reacted to the premiere on 28 May, there is no evidence that the early performances had any subversive effect. Western theatre critics had taken great pleasure in noting signs of politically motivated laughter in spectators' reactions to *Faust I*, but reviewers in East and West were unenthusiastic about *Sieben gegen Theben* and even criticized its lack of contemporary relevance.[127] One of the BE's assistants, who watched the audience's reactions to the early performances, reported signs of surprise, displeasure, and even boredom, which may have been partly attributable to the unusual performance aesthetic.[128] Ironically, one Stasi officer claimed that the production team had not succeeded in linking the problems in the play to the present and did not even seem to have tried to do so.[129] There is no evidence that the Party and state authorities—whose representatives attended the final rehearsals and the premiere—raised any political objections. The only such criticisms came from Klemer, who argued:

Allein die x-fache Ausdeutbarkeit der eben so nahezu kodefizierten [*sic*] Aussagen dieser Inszenierung sind ein deutliches Indiz dafür, daß hier...eine unserer sozialistischen Kunstpolitik zuwiderlaufende Absicht...zugrunde liegt.[130]

Given that the production's messages were virtually explicit until recently, the infinite number of ways in which they can now be interpreted is itself a clear sign that...the production's underlying intention runs counter to our socialist artistic policy.

Even this argument was based on Klemer's knowledge of the earlier production concept and the production team's failure to produce a clear declaration of support for GDR socialism, not on any concrete evidence of subversion.

---

[126] Weigel, 'Zur Generalprobe *Sieben gegen Theben* am 27. Mai 1969', BEA file 48.

[127] e.g. Jürgen Beckelmann, 'Wie aufgescheuchte Hühner', *Süddeutsche Zeitung* (Munich), 4.6.1969; Günther Bellmann, 'Kein Schlüssel zu Aischylos', *BZ am Abend* (East Berlin), 3.6.1969; Günther Cwojdrak, 'Aischylos im Berliner Ensemble', *Die Weltbühne* (East Berlin), 10.6.1969; Wolfgang Gersch, 'Versuche mit der Kunst der Größe', *Tribüne* (East Berlin), 6.6.1969; R. M., 'Griechenland in Ost-Berlin', *FAZ*, 4.6.1969.

[128] 'Abendbericht', 11.9.1969, BEA file 'Abendberichte'.

[129] BStU BV Bln. Abt. XX A-477–4, fo. 31.

[130] Ibid. 33.

The apparent lack of any political response from the audience, Ministry, Culture Department, or SED-*Bezirksleitung* suggests that classical myth offered no easy means of smuggling subversive material into performance. Karge and Langhoff were attempting a more difficult balancing act than they initially realized: when their allegory was transparent, it was censored; yet when the actors played down its contemporary relevance, it lost much of its political force, even though potentially controversial lines remained. Since most spectators would have been unaware of the production's original thrust or its censorship, they were not hypersensitive to the text's contemporary connotations, as they had been with *Faust*. The five-month delay helped to soften the production's impact; by May 1969, Dubček had been replaced as Party leader and the Czechoslovak Central Committee had been purged, indicating that the political changes were permanent.[131]

Nevertheless, there are some signs that Karge and Langhoff may, once the premiere had passed without incident, have strengthened the production's impact. The internal reports show that the audience's response improved as the run—of just ten performances, spread over six months—continued, particularly after additional changes were made in August.[132] The brief records of these rehearsals tantalizingly reveal that Karge and Langhoff tried to bridge the distance between the actors and the audience and to involve the audience in the play's intellectual debates, in line with the earlier production concept.[133] This evidence suggests that they sought to reverse Weigel's efforts to seal off the action and thereby encouraged the audience to interpret it as an allegory. Furthermore, handwritten changes in the prompt script indicate that several controversial lines were re-incorporated at some point between April and October, possibly during these additional rehearsals. These lines included a coded reference to Dubček's Soviet-backed successor, Gustav Husák:

> keiner will
> Zum Herrscher den, der eignes Volk
> Anfällt mit fremdem Heer (*SgT* 4: 20)

---

[131] See Lutz Prieß, Václav Kural, and Manfred Wilke, *Die SED und der 'Prager Frühling' 1968: Politik gegen 'Sozialismus mit menschlichem Antlitz'* (Berlin: Akademie, 1996), 270.

[132] 'Abendberichte' dated 3.9.1969, 11.9.1969, and 25.10.1969, BEA file 'Abendberichte'.

[133] 'Änderungen an der Inszenierung *Sieben gegen Theben*', 27.6.1969, BEA file 'Dramaturgie '65–'69'.

no one wants
As their ruler a man who attacks
His own people with a foreign army.

5. CONCLUSION

The autumn after the Prague Spring was felt not only in Czechoslovakia, but in the theatres of East Berlin. The Ministry's decision to ban *Johann Faustus* signalled its determination to suppress any appearance of dissent, even though only a fifteen-year-old controversy linked the production with an opponent of the Prague Spring. *Faust I* proved far more controversial, not because it alluded to events in Prague but because its theatrical rebellion and topical cabaret betrayed a complete disrespect for authority. *Sieben gegen Theben* was the only production of the three to respond directly to the suppression of the Prague Spring, through a bold reworking of Aeschylus' text. Accordingly, whereas all the BE's members had supported *Johann Faustus*, only those who sympathized with the Prague Spring defended the controversial adaptation.

The status, timing, and censorship of *Faust I* and *Sieben gegen Theben* explain their contrasting reception by the audience. *Faust I* made a strong political impact because it challenged Ulbricht's instrumentalization of the text and was premiered only six weeks after the invasion of Prague. It was a high-profile production, and the contrast between the press build-up and the authorities' horrified reactions could hardly have been more striking. Whilst even the censored version of *Sieben gegen Theben* responded far more directly to the Prague Spring, it was not performed in public until nine months after the invasion. By ensuring that the strongest political criticisms were removed, delaying the premiere, and keeping the performances low-key, officials softened the production's impact. In this, they were aided by the fact that a play by Aeschylus was never likely to draw as much interest, either from GDR theatregoers or from Western reporters, as Goethe's classic text. So even though the script remained provocative on paper, it exerted a less subversive effect than *Faust I* and represented a more successful outcome for the authorities.

Faust I and *Sieben gegen Theben* were surprisingly daring productions, the former in its references to censorship and the latter in its allusions to the invasion of Prague. They show that censorship was unable to silence inner-Marxist criticism of the regime; indeed, the links between *Johann Faustus* and *Sieben gegen Theben* suggest that censorship provoked subversion. The BE's theatre practitioners were remarkably assertive in defending their interests: whilst Weigel was prepared to accept censorship if she agreed that it was politically necessary, she refused to cover up for the ban on *Faustus* because she perceived it as unreasonable. She viewed Ministry officials as her colleagues and equals, and did not hesitate to disagree with them. But as Weigel was essentially loyal to the regime, she voiced such disagreement privately and challenged specific decisions, not the controls themselves. When Langhoff—a far less senior figure—organized a protest against the ban on *Faustus* and made no secret of his sympathy with the Prague Spring, he overstepped the boundaries of tolerated private protest. As the Deutsches Theater had learned from *Die Sorgen und die Macht*, such assertiveness was not the best tactic in a censorship dispute: both Weigel and the Deutsches Theater achieved far more through compromise.

Comparison of *Faust I* and *Sieben gegen Theben* suggests that internal solidarity was the key to bringing controversial productions of the classics as far as the premiere, but that only compromise and negotiation could ensure the continuation of a performance run. Whereas the Deutsches Theater kept its theatrical rebellion a closely guarded secret, whistleblowers at the BE prevented Karge and Langhoff from forcing their original concept through to the premiere. As political differences over the Prague Spring exacerbated pre-existing personal and professional conflicts at the BE, *Sieben gegen Theben* became a tool in the dispute over the theatre's management and future. Leading members of the BE sought to use officials as allies, turning censorship to their advantage. By May 1969, it became clear that internal relations in the company had broken down irretrievably. Weigel accepted the resignation that Wekwerth had offered a year earlier, and Karge and Langhoff decided to join the Volksbühne. Change was under way at the Ministry too; following Hochmuth's calls for tighter ideological controls, Bork lost his portfolio for theatre.[134]

The reliance on internal controls was essential to GDR theatre censorship, but it was also its Achilles heel. The authorities relied on theatre managers and Party members to monitor productions and warn of any concerns; this devolution of day-to-day control was vital given

[134] Helmut Müller-Enbergs, Jan Wielgohs, and Dieter Hoffmann (eds.), *Wer war wer in der DDR? Ein biographisches Lexikon* (Berlin: Ch. Links, 2000), 96.

the sheer number of theatres and other artistic institutions in any one region. But there was no automatic external scrutiny of productions; it was the exception rather than the rule for officials to attend dress rehearsals, unless a new contemporary drama was being premiered or a text was known to be controversial. The BE's internal controls did eventually meet with some success in the case of *Sieben gegen Theben*, but such checks failed to prevent or even predict the scandal that *Faust I* unleashed two streets away at the Deutsches Theater. Such local variation was a major difference from the censorship of literature, where texts were submitted to publishing houses under the supervision of a central state authority, and most writers faced publishers and officials alone. As the premiere of *Faust I* showed so clearly, theatre was far more difficult to control.

4

Heine, Kleist, and Büchner
in the 1970s

Ich bin mir der Ironie bewußt, ... daß wir in jedem Dezember
einen Heinrich-Heine-Preis verleihen und dabei mancher die
Empfänger furchtsam anschaut, ob sie nicht etwa ernst mit diesem
Erbe machen.
(I am aware of the irony ... that every December, when we award
a Heinrich Heine Prize, quite a few people look fearfully at the
recipients in case they act upon his legacy.)

Volker Braun, 'Die ausgelassenen Antworten', 108–9

1. INTRODUCTION

As Volker Braun's comments on Heine indicate, the SED's rhetorical
homage to its so-called literary forefathers belied an anxiety regarding
their enduring relevance. This chapter explores productions of nineteenth-century texts which the SED included in the cultural heritage
but still found problematic: Eberhard Esche's readings of Heinrich
Heine's *Deutschland: Ein Wintermärchen* (Germany: A Winter's Tale,
1974); Adolf Dresen's production of Heinrich von Kleist's *Michael
Kohlhaas* (1977); and Jürgen Gosch's staging of Georg Büchner's *Leonce
und Lena* (1978). Whilst the SED endorsed the critique of the nineteenth-century German states in these texts, their subject matter also
resonated with the views of Marxist dissidents, particularly Wolf Biermann, Rudolf Bahro, and Robert Havemann. The texts could be used
to imply socio-political criticisms that would not be tolerated in contemporary drama, and their enduring relevance suggested that the SED
had fallen short of its ancestors' ideals.

Only one of the three texts, *Leonce und Lena*, had originally been
written for the stage. In the 1970s it became increasingly common for

theatres to perform adaptations and readings of non-dramatic texts. This trend was not restricted to the classics; in fact, the most popular productions included dramatizations of recent prose texts, such as Ulrich Plenzdorf's *Die neuen Leiden des jungen W.* (The New Sorrows of Young W.) and Brigitte Reimann's *Franziska Linkerhand.* Like the classics, these texts had the advantage that they had already been sanctioned for public dissemination. Their prominent position in the repertoire reflected the difficulties of writing and staging new drama, which had been so clearly demonstrated in the 1960s.

Deutschland: Ein Wintermärchen and *Michael Kohlhaas* were both staged at the Deutsches Theater, whose production of *Faust I* had established the pattern of dusting down the classics. The Central Committee's Culture Department and the Culture Ministry did not share Dresen's enthusiasm for this approach, and even the manager Gerhard Wolfram reportedly said that his theatre had had a botched relationship with the classics for years.[1] The Deutsches Theater continued to come into conflict with officials in the 1970s. After Heinz had resigned as manager in 1969, sections of the ensemble mounted concerted resistance to his successor Hanns Anselm Perten, who had won a reputation for staging contemporary drama in Rostock but lasted just two years in Berlin. Wolfram argued that after Perten's departure the actors were demoralized, felt that their interests were not even being considered, and just derived satisfaction at having defeated Perten. He added that most of the actors felt as if the state did not need them, indeed that it regarded them as an irritant.[2] Wolfram himself experienced difficulties at the Deutsches Theater, particularly in the initial period, and is said to have complained that some actors were refusing to work with his director Horst Schönemann.[3] Wolfram's relationship with East Berlin's SED-*Bezirksleitung* was tense, contrasting with the productive relationship that he had established with Halle's First Secretary Horst Sindermann during his time at the Landestheater. The Volksbühne also embarked on a period of transition in 1978, when it staged *Leonce und Lena.* Its manager Benno Besson had just left to direct in France, and Karge and Langhoff had obtained visas to work abroad. They had been responsible for many of the Volksbühne's successes earlier in the decade.

---

[1] 'Information für Gen. Minister Hoffmann', 22.3.1973, BArch DY 30 IV B 2/9.06/65.
[2] 'Material zur Erarbeitung einer Analyse der Entwicklung und des Standes der Arbeit im DEUTSCHEN THEATER BERLIN', BArch DR 1/7232.
[3] 'Information', 22.3.1973.

The expatriation of Wolf Biermann and its repercussions in East Berlin's theatre community will be central to this chapter. Biermann was a relentlessly subversive singer and writer, who hoped that the GDR might yet experience its own Prague Spring. His expatriation in November 1976 triggered an unprecedented protest from artists and intellectuals, which affected performances of *Wintermärchen* and rehearsals for *Kohlhaas*. It would be wrong, however, to see theatre practitioners as polarized into supporters and opponents of Biermann, and this chapter aims to establish a differentiated picture of the political positions and ties within the theatre community, particularly at the Deutsches Theater.

The Cultural Heritage in the 1970s

In 1971, Erich Honecker achieved his long-standing aim of replacing Walter Ulbricht as leader of the SED. In his inaugural speech to the Eighth Party Conference in June, Honecker seemed to signal an important shift in cultural policy towards the encouragement of breadth and diversity. Several months later, he confirmed this impression by telling the Central Committee that there would be no taboos on artistic experimentation.[4] But this speech also stipulated that artists needed the authorities' advice and must proceed from socialist principles, and the Party continued to define what this meant. The fact that Honecker had launched the crackdown against culture at the Eleventh Plenary Session, only now to offer an olive branch to artists, indicates how culture was being instrumentalized in larger political battles and intrigues. In 1971, it suited Honecker to present himself as an advocate of limited liberalization in culture, both to win domestic support and to project a more tolerant image of the GDR abroad, at a time when he was seeking international recognition for it. In 1972, these efforts were rewarded when the Federal Republic finally recognized the GDR.

Even so, Honecker's pronouncements did change artists' and officials' perceptions of the parameters for action in the arts. This was evident as early as 1971–2 in the reception of innovative literary and theatrical treatments of the cultural heritage, such as the Karge/Langhoff staging

---

[4] *Dokumente zur Kunst-, Literatur- und Kulturpolitik der SED 1971–1974*, ed. Gisela Rüß (Stuttgart: Seewald, 1976), 287.

of *Die Räuber* (The Robbers) at the Volksbühne (1971), Müller's *Macbeth* (1971), and Plenzdorf's *Neue Leiden* (1972). These productions and adaptations found vocal defenders in the literary periodical *Weimarer Beiträge*, where few critics now insisted that theatres should preserve the classics like museum exhibits.[5] Whilst Hager sought to rein in these developments, he did not suggest a return to the reverence of earlier decades. When addressing the Central Committee's Sixth Congress in July 1972, he opposed not only 'nihilistic' treatments of the cultural heritage but also the false idealization of it.[6] The Ministry also tried to curb artists' expectations, arguing in 1973 that directors must stop updating works superficially and must free the cultural heritage from all attempts at distortion and falsification.[7] Notions of historicization and fidelity to the original work remained tools for controlling theatrical interpretation, but in the early 1970s they did not result in production bans.

Although all three texts in this chapter were included in the canon, their authors' status and reception in the GDR differed. From the start, Ulbricht and cultural politicians like Alexander Abusch embraced Heine as one of Germany's four greatest writers, alongside Goethe, Schiller, and Lessing.[8] Literary critics cited Heine's friendship with Marx as evidence of his socialist credentials, even though his attitude towards communism was ambivalent and he was highly critical of Ludwig Börne.[9] In 1956, GDR cultural organizations marked the centenary of his death and an international Heine congress met in Weimar.[10] In contrast, the SED's homage to Büchner was chiefly rhetorical, and his works were rarely performed.[11] Many of the SED's

---

[5] See e.g. Hans Kaufmann, 'Zehn Anmerkungen über das Erbe, die Kunst und die Kunst des Erbens', *Weimarer Beiträge*, 19/10 (Oct. 1973), 34–53 (esp. 47–8).

[6] Kurt Hager, *Zu Fragen der Kulturpolitik der SED* (East Berlin: Dietz, 1972), 57.

[7] 'Zur Theatersituation nach dem VIII. Parteitag', BArch DY 30 IV B 2/9.06/67.

[8] Jost Hermand, *Streitobjekt Heine: Ein Forschungsbericht 1945–1975* (Frankfurt/M.: Athenäum Fischer, 1975), 23.

[9] Ronald H. D. Nabrotzky, 'Die DDR: Heinrich Heines verwirklichter Lebenstraum', *MLN* 92 (1977), 535–48; Hans Boldt, 'Heine im Zusammenhang der politischen Ideen seiner Zeit', in Wilhelm Gössmann and Manfred Windfuhr (eds.), *Heinrich Heine im Spannungsfeld von Literatur und Wissenschaft: Symposium anläßlich der Benennung der Universität Düsseldorf nach Heinrich Heine*, Kultur und Erkenntnis, 7 (Bonn: Reimar Hobbing, 1990), 65–80.

[10] Hermand, *Streitobjekt Heine*, 24.

[11] Otto F. Riewoldt, '"…der Größten einer als Politiker und Poet, Dichter und Revolutionär": Der beiseitegelobte Georg Büchner in der DDR', in Heinz Ludwig Arnold (ed.), *Georg Büchner III* (Munich: text + kritik, 1981), 218–35. See Laura

hesitations stemmed from Büchner's pessimistic presentation of the French Revolution in *Dantons Tod*, but they were also a reaction against his frank depiction of sexuality and his preference for episodic forms. Kleist received different treatment again, as the SED—following Franz Mehring and Georg Lukács—excluded most of his works from the canon, claiming that Kleist was a bigoted Prussian Junker and a forerunner of most of the decadent trends of later bourgeois literature.[12] Like Lukács and Mehring, the SED made an exception for *Michael Kohlhaas*, praising Kohlhaas's rebellion but arguing that the absence of a Party apparatus made its failure inevitable.[13]

There were early signs of change in the literary reception of Büchner and Heine in the 1960s, when Müller and Braun started to engage with Büchner's techniques and ideas, and when Biermann began a topical adaptation of *Wintermärchen*, published in West Germany in 1972.[14] In 1977, the reception of Büchner took on a similarly topical, subversive edge, when Braun used an essay on his letters to attack censorship, police oppression, and the SED's failure to live up to his ideals.[15] In the same year, the SED took Kleist's bicentenary as an opportunity to argue for the critical appropriation of his entire oeuvre, and Christa Wolf used a fictional meeting between Kleist and Karoline von Günderrode to explore the conflict between individual subjectivity and social constraints in *Kein Ort. Nirgends* (No Place. Nowhere).[16] The productions in this chapter reveal theatrical parallels with this literary reception. I look first at Stasi surveillance of theatre in the 1970s, then at the productions and their political resonances, before considering what the authorities' responses reveal about censorship of the classics.

Bradley, 'Stealing Büchner's Characters? *Leonce und Lena* in East Berlin', *Oxford German Studies*, 35 (2006), 66–78. I am grateful to *Oxford German Studies*, the MHRA, and Maney Publishing for permission to republish material from my article here.

[12] Georg Lukács, 'Die Tragödie Kleists', in *Heinrich von Kleists Nachruhm: Eine Wirkungsgeschichte in Dokumenten*, ed. Helmut Sembdner (Munich: dtv, 1977), 459–60 at 459.

[13] Ibid.

[14] Wolf Biermann, *Deutschland: Ein Wintermärchen* (West Berlin: Klaus Wagenbach, 1972).

[15] Volker Braun, 'Büchners Briefe', in *Verheerende Folgen mangelnden Anscheins innerbetrieblicher Demokratie* (Leipzig: Reclam, 1988), 83–94. The essay was first published in *Connaissance de la RDA*, 7 (1978), 8–17.

[16] Hans-Georg Werner, 'Dichtung im Namen menschlicher Würde', *ND*, 18.10.1977; Christa Wolf, *Kein Ort. Nirgends* (East Berlin and Weimar: Aufbau, 1979).

2. THEATRE AND THE STASI IN THE 1970S

In 1969, the SED leadership had already decided to strengthen the Stasi's scrutiny of culture because of the role it believed artists had played during the Prague Spring. But Joachim Walther argues that it was not until 1975 that surveillance increased significantly. It was then that the number of operational investigations (OV) into authors soared, from eight in 1974 to thirty-one in 1976–7.[17] The experiences of Gosch and Dresen point to a parallel intensification of the Stasi's activities against theatre practitioners: OV 'Revisionist' was opened against Gosch and a number of his colleagues in November 1975; OV 'Schnittpunkt' (Intersection) was opened against Dresen, Friedrich Dieckmann, and Michael Hamburger in March 1976; and Gosch was also investigated in OV 'Chef' (Boss) from 1976.[18] By this time, the Stasi feared that an underground opposition was developing at the Deutsches Theater around Dresen, who was moving consciously towards an oppositional position within Marxism. Dresen asked unsuccessfully to be released from his Party membership in May 1975, and he produced a paper in which he engaged critically with Bahro's ideas and argued that the best Marxists were being driven into the arms of the opposition.[19] Believing that there were links between the theatre practitioners in OV 'Chef' and 'Revisionist', officers working on the investigations liaised with each other.[20]

The Stasi heightened its surveillance of theatre practitioners by extending its network of informers. According to Walther, the Stasi department now responsible for culture (HA XX/7) had 379 informers in December 1975, compared with 221 in October 1972.[21] By 1976, the Stasi's informers at the Deutsches Theater included 'Hölderlin' (*1974–89), 'Robert Hinz' (1968–82), 'Dorfrichter' (*1974–*88), and 'Gustav Adolf' (1955–87).[22] Other theatre practitioners also

---

[17] Walther, *Sicherungsbereich Literatur*, 203.
[18] BStU BV Schwerin AP 1753/76, i; HA XX 2256, i; BV Pts. AOP 1325/77, i.
[19] Dresen, *Wieviel Freiheit*, 142; BStU AOP 6418/87, i, fo. 6.
[20] BStU BV Pts. AOP 1325/77, i, fos. 119–24.
[21] Walther, *Sicherungsbereich Literatur*, 193.
[22] 'Hölderlin' worked at the DT and should not be confused with the poet Gabriele Eckart, who was briefly registered under the same codename. The dates in brackets indicate the duration of an informer's collaboration with the Stasi; asterisked dates indicate the first/last surviving evidence of activity, where the records are incomplete. The IM listed above were not necessarily at the DT for the entire period of their collaboration; 'Robert Hinz', for example, was recruited in Rostock and moved to the DT in 1970.

supplied information on the company. They included the actress 'Galina Mark', who happened to be one of Dresen's neighbours, and the directors 'Sumatic' (1971–*1980s) and 'Saint Just' (*1976–*86). 'Saint Just' went out of his way to gain information for the Stasi; on 3 November 1976, for example, he took advantage of a chance meeting with Dresen on Alexanderplatz to discuss Dresen's critique of Bahro. On being invited back to Dresen's flat, 'Saint Just' gave the pretext of suffering from a personal crisis concerning contradictions between Marxist-Leninist theory and socialist praxis to persuade Dresen to speak more freely.[23]

The title 'IM' and its subcategories encompassed a broad range of collaborative relationships varying in duration, intensity, and motive. Whilst 'Saint Just', 'Hölderlin', 'Sumatic', 'Gustav Adolf', and 'Dorf-richter' all worked as informers for periods of between one and three decades, the dramaturge Ilse Galfert ('Charlotte Brauns') seems to have started trying to distance herself from the Stasi after three years. She was recruited in October 1970 while working at the Volksbühne and returned to the Deutsches Theater in 1971; in June 1973, Wilhelm Girod—the officer now responsible for the Deutsches Theater and BE—noted that she was reluctant to report on her colleagues, continually postponed meetings, and had claimed that she was afraid of mentioning her Stasi connections during a forthcoming operation, as she had a tendency to talk under anaesthetic.[24] Galfert finally succeeded in ending her collaboration in May 1974.[25]

Eberhard Esche's files also indicate a process of disengagement, in his case followed by prolonged surveillance. He was recruited as an IM in Erfurt in 1959, early on in his acting career, and adopted the codename 'Baum' (tree), an allusion to his surname (ash). The Stasi's initial assessments of Esche's efforts were generally positive, but the relationship changed after he moved to the Deutsches Theater in August 1961. This is reflected in the dramatic fall in the number of reported meetings: from thirty-one between 1959 and 30 June 1961 to two in 1962, two in 1963, and one in 1965. By 1963, the Stasi believed that Esche held oppositional views and solicited reports on him from other informers. In December 1979, Major Reinhardt noted that the Stasi had had no continuous contact with Esche during the 1970s and that meetings had

[23] BStU AOP 6418/87, ii, fo. 7.
[24] BStU AIM 8586/74, i.i, fo. 116.
[25] Ibid. 144–5.

taken place only at considerable intervals.²⁶ The nature of these alleged
meetings is unclear. Reinhardt claimed that Esche did not contact the
Stasi of his own accord, but that he did not refuse to give information
when asked.²⁷ Whilst 'Sumatic' and 'Dorfrichter' received substantial
sums of money from the Stasi, the latter for allowing the Stasi to use his
flat for meetings, Esche received only what he regarded as a one-off loan
of 100 East German marks in 1960.²⁸ He was still insisting on repaying
it in 1965, saying that he did not want the Stasi to buy his services or
gain a financial hold over him.²⁹ The active phase of his collaboration
was restricted primarily to 1959–61 and was far exceeded by the decades
in which he was under surveillance. No records of individual meetings
after 1965 survive in Esche's files, which the Stasi finally archived
in 1983.

3. *DEUTSCHLAND: EIN WINTERMÄRCHEN*

The first of Esche's readings of *Deutschland: Ein Wintermärchen* took
place on 18 October 1974, and they continued until his death in 2006.
The production was Dresen's idea, and the premiere was originally
scheduled for 7 October 1974, the GDR's twenty-fifth anniversary.³⁰
Both the SED-*Bezirksleitung* and -*Kreisleitung* had warned the
Deutsches Theater that the planned performance was ill considered
and potentially politically insensitive.³¹ This did not amount to an
instruction to desist, and the production went ahead. Esche emphasized
the text's contemporary parallels, only to tone down his performance
after Biermann's expatriation.

Heine's criticism of Germany's territorial fragmentation was a gift to
Esche in 1974, as he played to the gallery. Even if Germany was now
divided into two states instead of thirty-six, Heine's comments on
hearing German at the border were immediately relevant to the present
situation.³² His criticisms of the restrictions caused by the Carlsbad

---

²⁶ BStU AIM 1401/83, FK, final [unnumbered] fo.
²⁷ Ibid.
²⁸ BStU AIM 1401/83, i.i, fo. 61.
²⁹ 'Treffbericht', 29.9.1965, BStU AIM 1401/83, FK.
³⁰ Esche, *Der Hase im Rausch*, 340–1.
³¹ 'Information betr. Interpretation von Heinrich Heine *Deutschland ein Winter-märchen*, am 16.11.1974', LAB C Rep. 902 3621.
³² Ibid.

Decrees of 1819 enabled Esche to refer to censorship, a word that remained taboo in the GDR:

> Da kommt der Hoffmann
> Auch mit seiner Zensorschere!
> Die Schere klirrt in seiner Hand,
> Es rückt der wilde Geselle
> Dir auf den Zeile [*sic*]—er schneidet ins Fleisch —
> Es war die beste Stelle.[33]

> Oh dear! here's Censor Hoffmann too,
> and he's brought his official scissors!
> The scissors are clicking in his hand—
> he's wild, he's foaming, he's hissing—
> he rushes up to you—there's a snip—
> alack! Now your best piece is missing.[34]

Heine's reference to his publisher, Hoffmann, was wonderfully fortuitous, given that the GDR's Culture Minister was now Hans-Joachim Hoffmann. Esche also retained Heine's dismissive comments on writers who were subservient to the state, describing them as swine decorated with laurel leaves.[35] These criticisms came close to the satire of the Walpurgis Night's Dream, with the crucial difference that the historical context and origin of *Wintermärchen* provided Esche with an alibi.

Esche's subversive performance did not escape the authorities' attention. A representative of the SED-*Bezirksleitung* argued that Esche related the attack on Prussian ideology directly to aspects of the GDR.[36] According to Hanns Kießig, head of the Culture Department in the *Bezirksleitung*, Esche provoked laughter and applause by gesturing towards the former royal box, now reserved for senior Party officials.[37] But when the theatre's Party Secretary objected to the performance, Kießig reported that most members of the *Parteileitung* thought that he was worrying excessively, and some even suggested that his concerns were motivated by hostility towards Esche.[38]

[33] Ibid. 'Auch' (1.2) should have appeared at the end of the previous line, and 'Zeile' (1.5) should have read 'Leib'.
[34] Heinrich Heine, *Deutschland: A Winter's Tale*, trans. and introduced by T. J. Reed, 2nd edn. (London: Angel, 1997), 159.
[35] 'Information betr. Interpretation'.
[36] 'Information: Eberhard Esche spricht H. Heine', [Oct. 1974], LAB C Rep. 902 3621.
[37] Kießig to Naumann, 29.11.1974, LAB C Rep. 902 3621.
[38] Ibid.

The Party Secretary was hardly helped by the fact that Wolfram had praised the performance.[39]

The result was that the production remained in the repertoire. It was discussed again at Party meetings at the theatre in February 1975 and January 1976. At the first meeting, Dresen took issue with local officials' complaints and invited Esche to perform the reading to 'prove' that there was nothing controversial about his delivery. Three months later, the writer Harald Hauser indicated to the Stasi that Esche had performed a balancing act in *Wintermärchen*, emphasizing topical allusions and then compensating later for the offence caused.[40] At the second meeting, Esche professed himself pleased with his colleagues' assessment and claimed that an invitation to perform *Wintermärchen* in Moscow had secured the performance run in Berlin, even though the Ministry had cancelled the Soviet invitation.[41] However, rumours had reached Esche that Sakowski had attacked his performance in the Central Committee as a thinly veiled act of homage to Biermann.[42] Roland Bauer from the *Bezirksleitung* sought to calm the situation, saying that Esche had been warned after the premiere but that he personally had nothing against Esche or Heine.[43] This should not be taken as a sign that the attitude of the *Bezirksleitung* towards the Deutsches Theater had softened; on the contrary, it was repeatedly critical of Wolfram's management and backed the cancellation of productions of Volker Braun's *Tinka* (1974) and *Che Guevara* (1977).[44] But the authorities were striking a balance by focusing their attention on contemporary drama. For pragmatic reasons, they resisted individual calls for a stricter response to subversion through the classics.

4. THE EXPATRIATION OF WOLF BIERMANN

Some ten months after this discussion, Wolf Biermann was expatriated from the GDR while on a concert tour in the Federal Republic.

---

[39] Kießig to Naumann, 29.11.1974, LAB C Rep. 902 3621.
[40] BStU BV Bln. Abt. XX A-465-3, fo. 52.
[41] 'Bericht der Wahlberichtsversammlung vom 10.1.1976', LAB C Rep. 904-054 Nr. 13.
[42] Ibid.
[43] Ibid.
[44] See Matthias Braun, '*Che Guevara—oder der Sonnenstaat*—Bedenken hatten nicht nur die kubanischen Genossen', in Frank Hörnigk (ed.), *Volker Braun*, TdZ Arbeitsbuch (Berlin: TdZ, 1999), 123–7.

This event came as a major shock to the East German intelligentsia. This was partly because expatriation was associated above all with the Third Reich, when countless artists and left-wing intellectuals had been deprived of German citizenship. But it was also because Biermann was still committed to socialism and the GDR, despite his criticisms of the SED. On 13 November, only three days before the Politbüro announced his expatriation, he told an audience in Cologne that the GDR was a major achievement for the German working class and that the state was making progress towards socialism, albeit with difficulty.[45] At the suggestion of the writer Stephan Hermlin, Biermann's supporters formulated a resolution asking the regime to reconsider its decision, and by 21 November this resolution had 106 signatures.[46] The public, collective nature of this protest contrasted sharply with the reactions to the invasion of Czechoslovakia and particularly to the construction of the Wall.

Theatre practitioners played an important part in the protest, along with writers and other artists. After all, Biermann had been a familiar figure in East Berlin's theatres; during the eleven years when he had been forbidden to perform in public, he had given impromptu performances in the Deutsches Theater canteen.[47] Those who signed the protest included the dramatists Braun and Müller; the directors Dresen, Tragelehn, and Matthias Langhoff; the set designer Horst Sagert; and the actors Domröse, Esche, and Hiemer. Some of these names are familiar from earlier controversies, but the signatories also included Langhoff's brother Thomas, Brecht's son-in-law Ekkehard Schall, and the actresses Katharina Thalbach, Jutta Wachowiak, and Käthe Reichel.[48] The signatories' motives included friendship with Biermann, concern that his expatriation handed a propaganda victory to the West, and anxiety that the measure might be applied to other artists.[49] Some who did not sign still did not support the expatriation, and whilst Wekwerth did back the

---

[45] *Biermann und kein Ende: Eine Dokumentation zur DDR-Kulturpolitik*, ed. Dietmar Keller and Matthias Kirchner (Berlin: Dietz, 1991), 123.

[46] Ibid. 138.

[47] Linzer, '*Ich war immer...*', 109; Irmer and Schmidt, *Die Bühnenrepublik*, 175.

[48] 'Liste von Personen, die einen sogenannten Protestbrief gegen die Aberkennung der Staatsbürgerschaft der DDR BIERMANNS unterschrieben haben', LAB C Rep. 902 3614.

[49] Oliver Schwarzkopf and Beate Rusch (eds.), *Wolf Biermann: Ausgebürgert. Fotografien von Roger Melis* (Berlin: Schwarzkopf & Schwarzkopf, [1996?]), 13.

government's decision, he asked whether it might not have involuntarily
strengthened Biermann's image as a martyr.[50]

Such a public show of solidarity against a Politbüro decision was
unprecedented in the GDR theatre community, but it would be wrong
to interpret it as a sign of united opposition to the regime, far less to
socialism itself. Some theatre practitioners issued statements supporting
Biermann's expatriation. They included communist veterans from the
Weimar Republic, such as Ernst Busch; Biermann's former colleagues at
the Distel cabaret theatre; Albert Hetterle from the Maxim Gorki
Theater; and Wolfram and Heinz from the Deutsches Theater.[51]
Peter Hacks published a controversial article denouncing Biermann in
Die Weltbühne.[52] Signatories of the original protest disagreed over the
decision to send it to the Western press, and they were splintered further
when they came under pressure to retract their signatures. At the
Deutsches Theater, an anonymous letter was sent to an actress who
supported Biermann's expatriation:

Mit besonderer Dummheit und beharrlicher Kritiklosigkeit unterstützt Du
seit Jahren alles, was von Partei und Regierung kommt, auch die eingestan-
denen Fehler. Du hast Dich auch damals gegen unseren Intendanten, Herrn
Langhoff, ausgesprochen, irregeführt durch inhumane Taktlosigkeiten unserer Parteileitung.[53]

With particular stupidity and a persistent lack of critical judgement, you have
supported everything emanating from the Party and government for years, even
the mistakes they have admitted. You also spoke out against our manager,
Mr Langhoff, years ago, misled by the inhuman insensitivity of our *Parteileitung*.

This accusation offers an intriguing insight into the long-term impact of
censorship disputes, showing how they continued to affect internal
theatre politics, even in subsequent decades. This can be attributed
partly to the stability in personnel: an engagement at the Deutsches
Theater was usually a job for life, and theatre practitioners had few
incentives to move from such a prestigious company.

Representatives of East Berlin's SED-*Bezirksleitung*, -*Kreisleitung
Mitte*, and *Magistrat* visited performances on 19 and 20 November,

---

[50] Wekwerth, 'Mich hat es eigentlich nicht so überrascht...', [no date], LAB C Rep.
902 3614.
[51] 'Bisher gaben ihre Stellungnahmen zu den Maßnahmen gegen Biermann ab...',
22.11.1976, LAB C Rep. 902 3614.
[52] Peter Hacks, 'Neues von Biermann', *Die Weltbühne*, 7.12.1976.
[53] Anonymous letter postmarked 8.12.1976, LAB C Rep. 902 3614.

checked that there were no untoward occurrences, and spoke to theatre practitioners.[54] Esche's *Wintermärchen* came under renewed scrutiny. He reportedly told the actor Manfred Krug that he found trembling Party officials waiting for him at the theatre, along with an equally nervous Wolfram.[55] The officials, Wolfram, and Esche himself needed the audience not to respond to the text's contemporary resonances. When a spectator applauded a line referring to publishing restrictions, Esche gave him a sharp look and declared that he was speaking the words of Heinrich Heine.[56] This silenced the spectator, allowing Grote to report that Esche had done all he could to prevent the audience from reacting out of turn.[57] So although Esche had signed the public protest, he worked actively to suppress inopportune reactions to his performance—the very reactions that he had solicited in 1974. On stage, Esche operated within the boundaries of permitted dissent, observing shifts in these boundaries as the political climate changed. His former wife, the actress and director Cox Habemma, recalls that on other occasions the technicians switched the house lights on if the laughter got out of hand.[58] This again discouraged transgression by destroying the spectators' sense of anonymity. What we are seeing here is an agreement involving three partners: an explicit agreement between officials and theatre practitioners, and an implicit agreement between theatre practitioners and spectators. Theatre practitioners used the skills of their trade to police the implicit agreement with spectators and ensure that performances could continue.

The Culture Department and *Bezirksleitung* organized individual meetings with signatories of the resolution. One director claimed that he had been unaware that it would be sent to the Western media, and that he simply wanted to discuss the expatriation with Party and government organizations, as he disagreed with it.[59] Heiner Müller distanced himself from the involvement of the Western media but did

---

[54] 'Bericht der Bezirksleitung Berlin der SED über politisch-ideologische Erscheinungen...', 6.12.1976, LAB C Rep. 902 3886; 'Information zur Diskussion...', 22.11.1976, LAB C Rep. 902 3614.

[55] Manfred Krug, *Abgehauen: Ein Mitschnitt und ein Tagebuch* (Munich: Ullstein, 2003), 186.

[56] Ibid. 186–7.

[57] 'Referat der PL auf der Mitgliederversammlung vom 6.12.1976', LAB C Rep. 904-094 Nr. 14.

[58] Cox Habemma, *Mein Koffer in Berlin oder das Märchen von der Wende*, trans. Ira Wilhelm (Leipzig: Militzke, 2004), 104.

[59] 'Die verschärfte und wütende Kampagne...', 22.11.1976, LAB C Rep. 902 3614.

not explicitly retract his signature; according to Biermann, he did so only two years later, on the condition that the retraction would not be made public.[60] By 29 November, the records of the *Bezirksleitung* show that most meetings with theatre practitioners had produced no result, qualified in some cases by expressions of loyalty to the state or disagreement with the decision to involve the Western media.[61] Refusal to back down brought consequences of varying severity: job offers dried up for Domröse, more than half of Krug's concerts were cancelled, and Havemann was placed under house arrest.

Esche and Dresen were the only two SED members of the Deutsches Theater who had signed the protest and therefore faced Party disciplinary proceedings. Esche maintained that he had signed out of friendship with Biermann and that his loyalty to the Party remained intact.[62] Although we might be tempted to view Esche's comments as a convenient defence, he continued to deny having mounted resistance to the regime after the GDR's demise. Writing of his support for Wolfgang Langhoff in 1962–3, he claimed that protesting was a whim that he occasionally indulged, not a political statement.[63] Any protest had political implications in the GDR, but Esche's ambivalence helps to explain why he clamped down on spectators' reactions to *Wintermärchen* after the protest. Viewing Esche's case as the less serious of the two, the *Parteileitung* issued him with a severe reprimand but allowed him to remain in the SED.[64]

In contrast to Esche, Dresen made it clear that serious political principles were at stake and that he could no longer remain in the SED. In his letter of resignation, Dresen emphasized that he still considered himself a communist and believed that there had been progress in cultural policy. But he explained that he was no longer able to tolerate the lack of democracy and frank discussion in the Party and its press.[65] Dresen traced this decision back to his experience over *Faust*, which had destroyed his faith in the authorities' openness to

---

[60] Heiner Müller, 'Ich habe die Anfrage zu Wolf Biermanns Ausbürgerung mit unterzeichnet...', LAB C Rep. 902 3614; Schwarzkopf and Rusch, *Wolf Biermann*, 11.

[61] 'Information über den Stand der Gespräche mit Schriftstellern und Künstlern', LAB C Rep. 902 3614.

[62] 'Aktennotiz', 24.11.1976, LAB C Rep. 902 3614.

[63] Esche, *Der Hase im Rausch*, 146.

[64] 'Protokoll-Teil Diskussion der Mitgliederversammlung vom 28.12.1976', LAB C Rep. 904-094 Nr. 14.

[65] Dresen to the DT *Parteileitung*, 23.11.1976, LAB C Rep. 902 3614.

reasoned argument and distanced him from the theatre's *Parteileitung*.
Dresen emphasized the lasting impact of the dispute, saying that he had
neither forgotten nor come to terms with it.[66]

Dresen went on to draw a parallel between his situation and a scene
that he was currently rehearsing:

Der historische Luther rät dem historischen Kohlhaas, und wenn er Unrecht
und Unrecht litte, er müsse es nehmen. Wir haben gewiß viele brave Luther-
aner, ich gehöre ja selbst dazu.[67]

The historical Luther advises the historical Kohlhaas: even if he suffers injustice
after injustice, he must accept it. We certainly have many good Lutherans;
indeed, I myself am one of them.

Outwardly at least, Dresen had accepted the SED's decision on *Faust*,
just as he had accepted its verdict on his production of *Hamlet* in
Greifswald. But he regarded Biermann's expatriation as a point too
far: the point at which he seemed to switch his identification from
Luther to Kohlhaas, in refusing to accept what he viewed as injustice.

Where Dresen differed from Kohlhaas was in the nature of his
rebellion and his line of argument. His rebellion remained backstage,
confined to the rehearsal room and Party meetings. And where Kohlhaas proceeded from an unswerving commitment to the abstract notion
of justice, Dresen pursued the pragmatic line of argument that the
regime's measures were damaging the cause that they were designed to
protect:

Was oft persönliches Unrecht war, war oft zugleich Beschädigung der *Sache*, die
ich für eine gemeinsame hielt. Im Fall *Faust*, dessen bin ich sicher, hat nicht die
Aufführung, sondern der anschließende Umgang mit ihr, dem Klassenfeind
genützt und uns geschadet.[68]

What was often injustice against individuals often simultaneously damaged the
cause, which I considered to be a common one. In the case of *Faust*, I am sure, it
was not the production but the way it was dealt with afterwards that benefited
the class enemy and damaged us.

Dresen's language shows that he still identified with the GDR's socialists
('us') against their opponents at home and abroad ('the class enemy')
and that he still subscribed to the Marxist-Leninist view that the Party's
interests were paramount. Accordingly, he strove to minimize the

---

[66] Dresen to the DT *Parteileitung*, 23.11.1976, LAB C Rep. 902 3614.
[67] Ibid.   [68] Ibid.

impact of his resignation, saying that he did not want to supply ammunition to people with whom he had nothing in common. This decision was prefigured earlier in the letter when he used the present tense to identify himself as one of the GDR's 'good Lutherans'. So although Dresen seemed to have switched his identification from Luther to Kohlhaas, he actually identified simultaneously with both roles. This dual identity points to the complexities and inherent limitations of inner-Marxist dissent in the GDR, which left its mark on Dresen's production of *Kohlhaas*.

5. *MICHAEL KOHLHAAS*

Michael Kohlhaas was premiered on 20 January 1977, after a tense period of rehearsals that had run concurrently with the disciplinary proceedings against Dresen and Esche. Dresen had adapted the text and planned the staging as the last of a trilogy of Kleist productions, after *Prinz Friedrich von Homburg* (Prince Frederick of Homburg) and *Der zerbrochne Krug* (The Broken Jug). One of his intentions had been to investigate the relationship between the state and the individual: the relationship between the Elector and the Prince in *Prinz Friedrich*, the abuse of state power by judge Adam in *Der zerbrochne Krug*, and Kohlhaas's attempts to achieve the redress denied to him by the state. Another intention had been to explore the local roots of the historical Hans Kohlhase, who had lived on the Fischerinsel and been executed on Strausberger Platz, both in East Berlin.[69] But as Dresen explains, after Biermann's expatriation everyone read the text differently.[70] The connections between Kohlhaas's rebellion and Biermann's expatriation eclipsed the second aspect of the production concept and made the first much more topical. This left Wolfram in a quandary: according to Dresen, he could ill afford either to allow the play or—given the mood in the ensemble—to drop it.[71]

Michael Kohlhaas attracted far more interest from the Stasi than the productions in Chapter 3. Stasi officers commissioned IM 'Maxim' to prevent Dresen from holding rehearsals in a studio owned by the Maxim Gorki Theater. This studio was in Weißensee, a northern suburb of East

---

[69] Anon. 'Michael Kohlhaas auf der Bühne', *Berliner Zeitung*, 20.1.1977.
[70] Dresen, *Wieviel Freiheit*, 170.
[71] Ibid. 170.

Berlin, and officers hoped to force Dresen to relocate to the Deutsches Theater, where he could be kept under closer scrutiny. Although 'Maxim' eventually succeeded, Dresen moved rehearsals to the television studios instead, and 'Hölderlin' warned the Stasi that no representatives of the theatre management or *Parteileitung* were attending rehearsals.[72] The Stasi obtained a draft of the script, which 'Saint Just' and 'Verlag' analysed, identifying topical material.[73] Officers warned Konrad Naumann—Verner's successor—about the production on 17 December, and they proposed tipping off Bauer and monitoring spectators' reactions to the first three performances.[74]

Textual Resonances

Recalling the rehearsals for *Kohlhaas*, Dresen writes that almost all of Kleist's sentences seemed directed against the GDR.[75] Shortly before the premiere, Wischnewski drew Dresen's attention to the contemporary relevance of Kohlhaas's confrontation with Luther.[76] In lines taken word-for-word from Kleist's text, Luther dismisses Kohlhaas's claim that he has been cast out by the state:

LUTHER Verstoßen? Welch eine Raserei der Gedanken ergriff dich? Wer hätte dich aus der Gemeinschaft des Staats, in welchem du lebtest, verstoßen? Ja, wo ist, solange Staaten bestehen, ein Fall, daß jemand, wer er auch sei, daraus verstoßen wäre?

KOHLHAAS (ruhig): Verstoßen nenne ich den, dem der Schutz der Gesetze versagt ist![77]

LUTHER Cast out? What flight of madness has seized your thoughts? Who could possibly have cast you out of the community of the state in which you live? Indeed, in the history of all states, where is there a case in which someone—whoever he might be—was cast out of the state community?

KOHLHAAS (calmly): An outcast is what I call a man denied the protection of the law.

---

[72] BStU BV Bln. AKK 3476/89, ii, fo. 175; BV Bln. AIM 6282/91, ii.ii, fo. 177.
[73] BStU BV Bln. AKK 3476/89, ii, fos. 218, 221.
[74] Ibid. 221.
[75] Dresen, *Wieviel Freiheit*, 171.
[76] Wischnewski to Dresen, [Jan. 1977], DTA orange file 'Michael Kohlhaas'.
[77] Adolf Dresen, 'Michael Kohlhaas nach Heinrich von Kleist' (typescript), fo. 32 of 71, DTA. Further references appear in the text as (*MK*, page number).

Despite Wischnewski's concerns, the lines survived: after the premiere, a West German critic quoted Luther's words in his review.[78] However, Dresen and his colleagues may well have cut the clearest textual parallel with Biermann's expatriation, for no Western reviewers commented on it. This was the line where, buoyed up by the support for Kohlhaas's rebellion, his servant calls for someone to draw up a list, adding that they will need a large sheet of paper (*MK*, 25). As this line is not in Kleist's text, we can assume it was added in response to the resolution against Biermann's expatriation. But this made it particularly vulnerable to self-censorship, as Dresen knew that he would not be able to cite Kleist's authorship in his defence.

Dresen acknowledges that self-censorship played a role during rehearsals, but he argues that his textual changes made little difference.[79] As the action of *Michael Kohlhaas* takes place in Brandenburg-Prussia and Saxony, the text included frequent references to cities and towns in the GDR, such as Berlin, Schwerin, Wittenberg, Leipzig, and Dresden. The authorities' disagreements over Kohlhaas's rebellion provided opportunities for comparison with recent events. Geusau, a hardliner, quotes a resolution calling Kohlhaas a useless troublemaker (*MK*, 15), recalling the Politbüro's view of Biermann. The Elector's key concern is that Kohlhaas has attracted substantial public support (*MK*, 36), but Kunz dismisses the supporters as dubious riff-raff (*MK*, 36); this was the only line in the debate not taken from the original text. Whilst Wrede argues that only an immediate rectification of the government's mistake can bring a positive conclusion to the whole sorry business (*MK*, 38), he is in a minority. Kohlhaas's lawyer reports the view that it would be better to commit a clear act of injustice against him than to reward his violent rebellion with justice (*MK*, 53).

These resonances with Biermann's expatriation, the protest, and the Politbüro's refusal to retract its decision were striking. Even so, the parallels between Kohlhaas and Biermann only worked up to a point. Kohlhaas starts out as a model citizen and is a reluctant rebel, whereas Biermann had a track record of subversion. In fact, Kohlhaas's case had a broader relevance for the dilemma of critical Marxist intellectuals in the GDR, as Dresen's identification with Kohlhaas suggests. This relevance was strongly implied in an essay published in a programme for all three Kleist productions. Its author argues that Kohlhaas, Prinz

---

[78] Heinz Ritter, 'Held unserer Zeit?', *Der Abend* (West Berlin), 24.1.1977.
[79] Dresen, *Wieviel Freiheit*, 171.

Friedrich, and Eve all find themselves in serious conflicts with the state, through no intention of their own.[80] After assuring readers that the state concerned was Brandenburg-Prussia, the writer proceeds to explore the contradictions between loyalty to, and conflict with, the state:

Kohlhaas, Adam und Homburg sind . . . eng mit ihrem Staat verbunden, anerkennen ihn, besorgen seine Geschäfte, kämpfen für ihn. Trotzdem verstoßen sie, ohne es selbst ursächlich zu wollen, gegen seine Ansprüche und Gesetze . . . Jedesmal erscheint dieser Konflikt nicht subjektiv gewollt; . . . ja, er entsteht gerade durch ihr Bemühen, dem Staat und seinen Rechtsnormen zu dienen und nachzuleben.[81]

Kohlhaas, Adam, and Homburg have . . . close ties to their state, acknowledge its authority, carry out its work, and fight for it. Even so, they offend against its claims and laws, without setting out to do so . . . Each time this conflict does not appear consciously intended; . . . indeed, it arises precisely through their efforts to serve the state and live in accordance with its legal norms.

This hinted at the dilemma that theatre practitioners repeatedly faced at the Deutsches Theater: they viewed themselves as committed GDR socialists but came into conflict with officials, whether over *Die Sorgen und die Macht*, *Faust*, or Biermann. This dilemma is central to understanding Dresen's staging of *Kohlhaas*.

Restraint and Solidarity

Dresen's production concept was characterized by restraint. The set design was neutral and understated, with just black velvet curtains marking the sides of the acting space.[82] One reviewer even commented that there was no set in the traditional sense of the word.[83] As the costumes included details from the medieval period to the nineteenth century, they neither tied the conflict down to the sixteenth century nor related it to the present (Fig. 4.1).[84] The acting was similarly restrained,

---

[80] DT, 'Heinrich von Kleist: Prinz Friedrich von Homburg und Der zerbrochne Krug, Michael Kohlhaas' [theatre programme], Berlin 1977, [n. p.].

[81] Ibid.

[82] Ernst Schumacher, 'In der Art des epischen Theaters', *Berliner Zeitung*, 25.1.1977.

[83] Michael Stone, 'Sein Zorn bleibt blind', *Deutsche Zeitung Christ und Welt* (Stuttgart), 28.1.1977.

[84] Karl-Heinz Müller, 'Michael Kohlhaas—Erzählung und Szene', *TdZ* 32/3 (Mar. 1977), 4–6 at 5.

Fig. 4.1. Kurt Böwe as Michael Kohlhaas (Eva Kemlein, Stadtmuseum Berlin)

and the GDR critic Erika Stephan argued that the actors seemed to exclude the audience from their communicative circuit:

Das Ensemble, wie befangen im Gestus des Sich-miteinander-Verständigens, bestimmt durch eine Haltung solidarischer Intimität, scheint auf Öffentlichkeit geradezu verzichten zu wollen.[85]

The ensemble almost seems to want to forgo public attention, seeming caught in the *Gestus* of communicating with each other, characterized by an attitude of solidarity and intimacy.

---

[85] Erika Stephan, 'Michael Kohlhaas', *Sonntag* (East Berlin), 13.2.1977.

This suggests that the actors' engagement with the text in rehearsals was a private matter, not to be shared with the audience. The performance foregrounded this internal solidarity: the actors brought the minimalist props on and off stage as needed, and the cast list did not credit their individual roles.[86] These details brought the performance into proximity with a central feature of Brecht's *Lehrstücke* (learning plays): the idea that the primary purpose of a production is to engage its actors in a learning process, and that performance before an audience is optional but not essential.[87]

Stephan proceeded to relate the apparent internalization of the production concept to the actors' line delivery and diction, arguing that spectators would find the text hard to understand unless they had just read the original.[88] Four other critics made similar observations, and Schumacher claimed that even spectators in the first third of the stalls could not understand a word.[89] The Stasi informer 'René' agreed that the delivery was poor, claiming that some actors had forgotten or mispronounced lines.[90] Whilst the pressure of the situation and the frequent changes to the text probably explain some of these problems, it is also possible that the actors were swallowing potentially controversial lines—particularly when we consider that the cast included some of the GDR's most talented and experienced actors, who knew the acoustics of the Deutsches Theater well. Even leaving aside the problem of audibility, the neutral set points to a production that was predicated partly on non-communication, or on leaving the lines that reached the audience to communicate for themselves. The theatre's debates on Biermann, Dresen, and the production were not hinted at in front of the spectators.

Reception

Far from creating the expected scandal, the premiere of *Kohlhaas* made little discernible impact on spectators. In the SED-*Bezirksleitung*, Kießig noted that the performance had passed without incident and that

[86] Günther Cwojdrak, 'Bühnenheld Kohlhaas', *Die Weltbühne*, 1.2.1977; Schumacher, 25.1.1977.
[87] Bertolt Brecht, 'Zur Theorie des Lehrstücks', in *BFA*, xxii.i. 351–2.
[88] Stephan, 13.2.1977.
[89] Wolfgang Gersch, 'Kleistsche Novelle im Theater', *Tribüne* (East Berlin), 25.2.1977; Cwojdrak, 1.2.1977; Christoph Funke, 'Die Erzählung auf der Bühne', *Der Morgen* (East Berlin), 26.1.1977; Schumacher, 25.1.1977.
[90] BStU BV Bln. AKK 3476/89, ii, fo. 225.

spectators had not applauded at the 'wrong' moments.[91] At the Stasi regional headquarters, Klemer reported that there had not been any spontaneous applause during the scenes, adding an exclamation mark.[92] As the Stasi had been convinced that Dresen would use the production to justify the protest against Biermann's expatriation, officers were at something of a loss to explain its apparent lack of impact. Klemer thought that spectators did not know what to make of the production, adding that the staging might have been designed to provoke political reflection after the curtain had fallen.[93]

Whilst Klemer based most of his report on the actual performance and its apparent reception, Girod concentrated instead on the ways in which the text could potentially be interpreted. Girod believed that the text's relevance to the GDR became clear in the first few lines. In his view, it suggested that individuals who experience injustice at the hands of the state have the right to seek redress by anarchistic means, without paying any heed to social norms.[94] Whilst Girod conceded that the performance contained no specific topical allusions, he argued that the lack of period detail itself amounted to criticism of the GDR.[95] His conclusions were diametrically opposed to those of Kießig, who maintained that Dresen had presented Kohlhaas and his rebellion in a critical light.[96]

These contrasting reactions suggest that the restrained acting and set enabled the production to function as a blank canvas onto which spectators could project their own interpretations—a process that was also evident in the West German reviews. Whilst Heinz Ritter hailed Kohlhaas as a precursor of the modern civil rights activist,[97] Michael Stone criticized Dresen precisely for failing to make this link. Stone interpreted the lack of audience reaction as a sign that the production team had failed to communicate the text's contemporary relevance.[98] In contrast, Marianne Eichholz assumed that the parallels must have been obvious to the audience. She concluded that the spectators had been 'sitting on their hands', 'paralysed' by the divisions over Biermann's

---

[91] 'Information für Genossen Konrad NAUMANN', 21.1.1977, LAB C Rep. 902 4570.
[92] BStU BV Bln. AKK 3476/89, ii, fo. 222.
[93] Ibid. 222.
[94] Ibid. 223.
[95] Ibid. 224.
[96] 'Information', 21.1.1977.
[97] Ritter, 24.1.1977.
[98] Stone, 28.1.1977.

expatriation.[99] Peter Iden was more reluctant to speak for East German spectators. Instead, he drew a parallel between Kohlhaas's border dispute and his own difficulties crossing the border to West Berlin after the performance. Iden argued that if anyone were to try to see the production as a protest against the authorities, the protest would be evident only in the total lack of topical allusions, as if the actors were biting their lips.[100] He concluded: 'Ausdrücke der tiefsten Resignation, ersterbende Mitteilungen aus einem Trauerhaus—mehr scheint auf einer Bühne der DDR momentan nicht möglich.'[101] (Expressions of the deepest resignation, dying news from a house in mourning—more than that does not seem possible on stage in the GDR at the moment.)

After the first two performances, the actors seem to have modified their restrained approach. According to Stasi reports, they began to emphasize topical allusions, addressing controversial lines to the audience. The informer 'Ewald' reported that a section of the audience responded by applauding or laughing when they heard politically charged phrases, such as references to international law, extradition, or visits to relatives on the Elbe.[102] In March, another informer reported a conversation with a Party member who had just seen *Kohlhaas*. The Party member was allegedly indignant at the text's contemporary resonances, claiming that spectators had shown signs of unrest on hearing Luther's words to Kohlhaas, and that the actress playing Kohlhaas's wife had emphasized the word 'border' when expressing her horror at his plans to send their children across it to Schwerin.[103]

It is tempting to conclude from this that Dresen and his cast had acted with Schweykian cunning, playing down topical allusions at the premiere with the intention of emphasizing them later on, once the risk of a ban had passed. But reports suggest that Dresen and his colleagues were disappointed by the premiere's apparent lack of impact. Klemer noted that the opening night party seemed to have been cancelled or to have broken up early, and Wolfram reportedly claimed that the 'failed' premiere was one of the reasons why Dresen did not attend an appointment at the Culture Ministry the following day.[104] On 27 January, a Ministry

[99] Marianne Eichholz, 'Kohlhaasens Kinder', *Süddeutsche Zeitung* (Munich), 25.1.1977.
[100] Peter Iden, 'Aus einem Trauerhaus', *Die Zeit* (Hamburg), 28.1.1977.
[101] Ibid.
[102] BStU BV Bln. AKK 3476/89, ii, fo. 227.
[103] Ibid. 243.
[104] BStU HA IX 3600, fo. 156.

official reported that Dresen seemed under immense nervous strain and was dissatisfied with the staging.[105] If these reports are to be believed, then the production team may well have used the ten days between the second and third performances to work on the staging and line delivery, in response to criticisms in the GDR press. Dresen did voice his dissatisfaction with the production publicly in July 1978, after he had moved to the Federal Republic. In an interview with the West German journal *Theater heute*, he argued that the text's overwhelming topicality had placed an intolerable strain on the production. He explained that the staging had lost its impact due to the production team's excessive caution, even though the authorities had not intervened directly.[106]

6. *LEONCE UND LENA*

The overall restraint of the acting and set design of *Michael Kohlhaas* contrasted with a far cheekier production of *Leonce und Lena* at the Volksbühne in 1978. This production was directed by 35-year-old Jürgen Gosch, who had trained at the State Acting School, acted in Parchim, and directed in Potsdam and Erfurt. His planned production of Goethe's *Stella* (1975) had been dropped after twenty-eight rehearsals in Schwerin, and the fallout had led to his departure from the theatre.[107] Gosch was then employed as a guest director in Brandenburg, where his production of *Die Ausgezeichneten* (The Award Winners) by Regina Weicker was cancelled for political reasons before the premiere.[108]

Gosch's alleged interest in the literature and politics of Czechoslovakia had attracted the Stasi's attention while he was working at the Hans-Otto-Theater in Potsdam, and he had been investigated in the *Vorlaufakte operativ* 'Konzert' (Concert), the preliminary stage before an OV.[109] After Gosch's arrival in Schwerin, he and his closest colleagues were subjected to intense Stasi surveillance in OV 'Revisionist' from November 1975. The Stasi suspected the theatre practitioners of

[105] BStU HA IX 3600, fo. 157.
[106] Christoph Müller, 'Adolf Dresen: "Meine Situation ist experimentell"', *Theater heute*, 19/6 (June 1978), 27–9 at 28.
[107] 'Information zur Absetzung *Stella*', LHAS 7.11-1 Z31/1981 19112; open letter from Gosch to sections of the Mecklenburgisches Staatstheater Schwerin, 9.11.1975, LHAS 10.34-3 2809.
[108] BStU BV Pts. AOP 1325/77, ii, fo. 96.
[109] BStU AP 12010/72.

forming a hostile group within the Mecklenburgisches Staatstheater, of writing and staging anti-socialist drama, and of falsifying 'progressive' plays.[110] Stasi officers arranged for Gosch's apartment to be bugged and boasted that its informers had guaranteed almost total control of the suspects.[111] In February 1976, officers were planning to set Gosch up to prepare a controversial staging of *Wie es euch gefällt* (As You Like It), with a view to banning it before the premiere and using it as grounds for his dismissal.[112] The fallout from *Stella* rendered this plan unnecessary. Once Gosch had taken up his next position, he was soon added to OV 'Chef', an investigation into members of the Brandenburger Theater.

There were important political and artistic differences between Gosch and Dresen. Gosch never joined the SED, and Stasi reports suggest that he was reticent about his political views in public, except for one occasion in 1970, when he tore up his ballot paper in a polling station.[113] Stasi reports state that the suspects of OV 'Chef' expressed solidarity with Biermann only in private and did not make any public statements of support after his expatriation.[114] Aesthetically, Gosch was more radical than Dresen, experimenting with stylized approaches to performance and elements of the Theatre of the Absurd. His production of *Leonce und Lena* actively exploited the text's resonances with the GDR, created new contemporary allusions through the acting, set, and props, and broke further taboos by referring to homosexuality. It was more explicitly subversive and amounted to a more radical treatment of the cultural heritage than either of the productions at the Deutsches Theater. The premiere was originally scheduled for 8 June 1978, but Michael Gwisdek—the actor playing Leonce—had an accident in a rehearsal only days beforehand. The premiere finally went ahead on 5 September, at the start of the new season.

Büchner, Braun, and Gosch

In 1977, Volker Braun had already used Büchner's criticisms of nineteenth-century Hesse to launch a savage attack on conditions in the

---

[110] BStU BV Schwerin AP 1753/76, i, fo. 27.
[111] Ibid. 32.
[112] Ibid. 153–5, 231.
[113] BStU BV Bln. Abt. XX 4109, i.i, fos. 71, 121.
[114] BStU BV Pts. AOP 1325/77, ii, fo. 104.

GDR. In his essay 'Büchners Briefe' (Büchner's Letters), Braun declared
that modern readers sometimes had to force themselves to remember
that Büchner was not their contemporary.[115] Braun argued that the
GDR had suppressed Büchner's relevance, celebrating him as a relic
from a bygone era (BB, 83). Whereas politicians claimed that the GDR
had overtaken the forefathers of socialism, Braun argued that the state
had made a detour around them (BB, 83). Their continuing relevance
was distressing (BB, 83), a cause for shame because it exposed present-
day failures. According to Braun, Büchner's questions about post-revolutionary France applied equally to the GDR: 'HAT DIE REVOLU-
TION GELOHNT? WAS IST NUN DIESE NEUE EPOCHE? Die
Frage immer, die eine kühle, illusionslose Antwort fordert' (BB, 84).[116]
(WAS THE REVOLUTION WORTHWHILE? WHAT IS THIS
NEW EPOCH? The question that always demands a sober, realistic
answer.)

   Whilst Braun's essay was not published in the GDR until 1988, the
programme for Gosch's production contained many of the same quotations from Büchner's letters, along with others that were equally provocative. On discovering that the police had searched his papers,
Büchner declared that he felt ill whenever he thought of his most sacred
secrets lying in their hands—a statement that invited comparison
with the Stasi.[117] But unlike Braun, Gosch printed Büchner's letters
intact, without accompanying comment. This created the misleading
impression that the Volksbühne wanted to share its historical research
with the audience and offer an accurate picture of German society in the
1830s. However, the production encouraged spectators to relate the text
and the programme to the present, particularly as the set and costumes
were free from historical detail.

Satire, Claustrophobia, and Transgression

After the premiere of *Leonce und Lena*, Gisela Holan from the Ministry's Theatre Department concluded that Büchner's critique of

[115] Braun, 'Büchners Briefe', 83. Further references appear in the text as (BB, page
number).
[116] Braun uses capitals to denote quotations from Büchner's letters.
[117] Georg Büchner, 'An die Familie', 5.8.1834. Quoted in the Volksbühne's
programme for *Leonce und Lena*, 1978, AdK ID 323.

Fig. 4.2. King Peter and his Council of State (Adelheid Beyer, Stiftung Archiv Akademie der Künste)

feudalism seemed to have been transposed directly to the GDR.[118] The costumes immediately set the younger generation apart from the ageing authorities. Leonce, Lena, and Valerio wore white clothes that connoted innocence and contrasted with the long brown plastic coats of the state councillors and the grey suit of the corpulent, balding King Peter, whose thick-rimmed glasses were suspiciously reminiscent of Honecker's own (see Fig. 4.2).[119] Büchner's satire against Peter's ineffectual leadership immediately made the audience laugh, especially when Peter-Honecker finally remembered why he had tied a knot in his handkerchief: to remind himself of his people.[120] This production contained all the performance allusions that *Kohlhaas* had lacked.

[118] 'Information', 6.9.1978, BArch DY 30 IV B 2/9.06/66.
[119] Album of photographs of *Leonce und Lena*, taken by Adelheid Beyer, AdK ID 323a. Further comments on the visual aspects of the production are based on these photographs.
[120] Audio recording of *Leonce und Lena* (1978), AdK D 323/I and /II.

Gosch mocked King Peter's Council of State by portraying its members as lame, blind geriatrics. The GDR's highest state authority rejoiced in the same name (Staatsrat), and an audio recording reveals that the audience erupted into laughter when a courtier announced that the Council of State had arrived.[121] Holan described how Leonce and Valerio chased the councillors offstage as if they were vermin:

Die Mitglieder des Staatsrates, blinde, senile Greise mit weißem Stock, langen Regenmänteln und Baskenmützen, zu jeder Aktion unfähige Parasiten, werden durch Leonce und Valerio wie eine Herde erschrockener, hilfloser Tiere kriechend, stolpernd, fallend, erbärmlich von der Bühne getrieben.[122]

The members of the Council of State, blind, senile old men with white sticks, long raincoats, and berets, parasites incapable of any activity, are driven from the stage by Leonce and Valerio like a herd of startled, helpless animals, crawling, stumbling, and falling down pathetically.

Valerio paused after telling Leonce that he was a book without letters, with nothing but dashes, allowing the audience to make the link with censorship in the GDR.[123] More audaciously, Gosch introduced a new reference to the Stasi in the form of two policewomen, who do not feature in Büchner's play. Valerio and Leonce conduct this dialogue from Büchner's text in their presence:

VALERIO Ja!
LEONCE Richtig!
VALERIO Haben Sie mich begriffen?
LEONCE Vollkommen.
VALERIO Nun, so wollen wir von etwas anderem reden. (*LL*, 3)

VALERIO Yes!
LEONCE Right!
VALERIO Did you understand me?
LEONCE Completely.
VALERIO Then let's talk about something different.

The dialogue asserts that an act of communication has taken place, but in the policewomen's presence communication can only occur safely between the lines. The audience immediately grasped the point: on the audio recording, spectators applauded for six seconds.

[121] Audio recording of *Leonce und Lena* (1978), AdK D 323/I and /II.
[122] 'Information', 6.9.1978.
[123] '*Leonce und Lena* Textbuch', fo. 9, VA. Further references appear in the text as (*LL*, fo. number).

Gosch continued his topical interpretation by relating the claustrophobia of Büchner's characters to the GDR's travel restrictions. Both Leonce and Lena complain of claustrophobia: Lena, for example, declares she cannot remain inside, as the walls are collapsing in on her (*LL*, 25). Gero Troike's grey and brown set suggested a prison: although he stencilled doors and windows on the back walls, the outlines merely emphasized the lack of any view onto the outside world.[124] Many of the allusions to borders derived from Büchner's satirical treatment of Germany's territorial fragmentation. Valerio exclaims in annoyance on arriving at yet another border (*LL*, 16). Meanwhile, Lena expresses her desire to travel around the world, born from reading behind her garden wall (*LL*, 23).

The references to rebellion, travel restrictions, and the Wall reached their climax in Leonce's decision—rooted in Büchner's text—to escape with Valerio to Italy. The dramaturge Otto Fritz Hayner explains how the characters forced their way out of the only (closed) exit: 'Die Tür wird durchgesägt, eingetreten, zerstört. Dann öffnet man die Tür, geht durch und ist draußen—in Italien?'[125] (The door is sawn through, kicked in, destroyed. Then they open the door, go through, and are outside—in Italy?) Leonce and Valerio returned carrying the forbidden fruits of their escape: bananas, oranges, and apples. While the bananas and oranges symbolized Western luxuries, the fruit also provided a bright splash of colour against the monotonous greys and browns of Troike's set. Gosch reinforced the contemporary parallels at the end of the scene, when the policewomen returned to restore order: they replaced the door and announced that it looked respectable again (*LL*, 15). Again, the spectators appreciated the joke, laughing for eighteen seconds and applauding for six.

For all the humour and provocative allusions, Gosch's treatment of boundaries and transgression was ambivalent. He undercut the characters' rebellion: after sawing down the door, Leonce and Valerio discovered that it was unlocked.[126] Both literally and metaphorically, they had rebelled against open doors; their entrapment was an illusion and their claustrophobia was an existential more than a physical condi-

[124] Martin Linzer, 'Volksbühne Berlin: *Leonce und Lena*', *TdZ* 33/11 (Nov. 1978), 2.
[125] Otto Fritz Hayner, 'Notierungen zur *Leonce und Lena*: Aufführung an der Volksbühne', AdK ID 323a.
[126] Elke Tasche, '*Leonce und Lena*: Öffentliche Generalprobe am 4. September 1978', AdK ID 323a.

tion. The characters' escape was just another temporary diversion from their ennui, not the solution to it. Leonce and Valerio returned disillusioned, with only a few consumer luxuries to show for their rebellion. Indeed, Hayner's question 'in Italy?' suggests that the Italy of their imagination was an unattainable paradise, distinct from the real place. The production may have mocked the authorities, but it also cast doubt on the possibility of escape for the younger generation, just like Büchner's text.

Unlike the two stagings at the Deutsches Theater, the Volksbühne's production broke theatrical and sexual taboos. Leonce and Valerio found an outlet for their boredom in clowning, which invited critics to compare them with Samuel Beckett's Vladimir and Estragon. This explains why reviewers perceived the production as a substitute for *Waiting for Godot*, which was not staged in the GDR until 1987.[127] Leonce's clowning became increasingly aggressive and sexually charged:

Zwei Herren in Unterhosen: Prinz Leonce schnipst auf Valerio, bis es wehtut: zieht das Gummi immer länger, schnipst und schnipst, bis Valerio vor Schmerz 'tot' schreit. Erwartet man von Valerio die Gegenlist, bleibt sie aus: er unterwirft sich, da gibt's nichts zu lachen.[128]

Two men in underpants: Prince Leonce snaps at Valerio's elastic until it hurts; he stretches the elastic further and further, letting it snap back again and again until the pain makes Valerio scream 'dead'. We expect Valerio to take his revenge, but he does not: he surrenders; this is no laughing matter.

This abrupt refusal to satisfy the spectators' expectations recalled Beckett's subversion of clowning in *Godot*. The aggression soon resurfaced: when Valerio slapped quark on Leonce's face, Leonce drove Valerio into a corner and imprisoned him.[129] Gosch made the homosexual undercurrents of this performance explicit by allocating Rosetta's lines to Valerio. This resulted initially in humour, when Leonce told a simpering Valerio that he was a clever girl (*LL*, 10). Ultimately, however, the characters could interact only through violence, and Hayner explains that their horseplay ended in violent despair and total exhaustion.[130] The result was an unsettling mix of sexual aggression, existential angst, and political satire.

---

[127] e.g. Günther Cwojdrak, 'Warten auf Büchner', *Die Weltbühne*, 19.9.1978; Heinz Klunker, 'Leonce und Valerio warten auf Godot', *Frankfurter Rundschau*, 13.1.1979.
[128] Hayner.
[129] Ibid.
[130] Ibid.

Reception

Censorship reports suggest that East Berlin's theatre community had eagerly awaited the premiere of *Leonce und Lena*. Significant numbers of actors attended, particularly from the Deutsches Theater and the Volksbühne, together with Heiner Müller and the permanent representative of the Federal Republic, Günter Gaus.[131] They almost certainly belonged to the section of the audience that, as Holan reported, reacted enthusiastically to every allusion and gag.[132] These spectators were responding to explicitly provocative signals in the performance, just as spectators had done at the premiere of *Wintermärchen*. Such signals had been conspicuously absent from the first two performances of *Kohlhaas* and the post-expatriation reading of *Wintermärchen*. Marlis Helmschrott from the SED-*Bezirksleitung* distinguished between the reactions of those sitting in the cheaper seats at the back, away from the VIPs, and the rest of the audience:

Ungewöhnlich verhielt sich während der Vorstellung ein Teil des Publikums im letzten Drittel des Zuschauerraumes. Es klatschte frenetisch Beifall vor allem an Stellen, die politisch mehrdeutig waren. Es muß allerdings gesagt werden, daß Art und Weise des Spiels dazu provozierten. Der größte Teil des Publikums verhielt sich zurückhaltend und war offensichtlich mit der Inszenierung nicht einverstanden.[133]

A section of the audience in the back third of the auditorium behaved unusually during the performance. They clapped frenetically, especially at lines that were politically ambivalent. It must be said, though, that the manner of the performance provoked that reaction. The greater part of the audience behaved with restraint and obviously did not agree with the production.

Whilst this equation of restraint with disapproval sounds like wishful thinking, the Volksbühne's own records of audience response indicate that the text and the production did elicit mixed reactions. In April 1978, for example, an administrator from the district council had announced that she never watched plays like this; as she had two children and her housework, she did not know the meaning of the word boredom.[134]

[131] 'Aktennotiz betr.: Premiere *Leonce und Lena* von Georg Büchner in der Volksbühne am 5. September 1978', 6.9.1978, LAB C Rep. 902 4576.
[132] 'Information', 6.9.1978.
[133] 'Aktennotiz', 6.9.1978.
[134] Elke Tasche, '*Leonce und Lena*: Stückdiskussion am 20.4.1978 beim Rat des Stadtbezirkes Mitte', 21.4.1978, in VA 'Gesprächsprotokolle *Leonce und Lena*'.

144   *Part I. Theatre Censorship in East Berlin*

The Volksbühne had opened up some rehearsals to members of the public, and its dramaturge Elke Tasche produced transcripts of the discussions. Some spectators acknowledged Gosch's contemporary allusions, perhaps encouraged by the fact that discussions during rehearsals were less formal than those held after a performance. One worker argued that the action could be happening in a back yard in Berlin, and a young man commented:

Ich habe auf der Bühne den Prenzlauer Berg gesehen... Keine aufgesetzte Aktualität, Schauspielkunst in den Dienst der Konzeption gestellt... Was die Frage anbelangt, wie das mit unserer Jugend aussieht, Alkoholismus, darf man nicht sagen. Zahlen werden totgeschwiegen.[135]

I saw Prenzlauer Berg on stage... No forced topicality, acting placed in the service of the concept... As for the question of how things stand with our young people, alcoholism, we aren't allowed to say. The statistics are hushed up.

At the public dress rehearsal, the allusions to the GDR's travel restrictions attracted particular interest. Veronika thought that the characters might be going to West Berlin, and Werner related the characters' claustrophobia to the fact that people in the GDR could not visit Italy.[136]

Even so, the discussions after rehearsals and performances were not free from self-censorship or manipulation. The following extract indicates how a teacher steered a conversation with his well-trained students:

LEHRER Wir waren vor ein paar Tagen in der Volkskammer. Könnte sich jemand vorstellen, daß bei uns der Präsident diese Rolle spielt?

JUNGE Sowas könnte in unserer Gesellschaftsordnung gar nicht auftreten, daß ein paar Leute aus der Regierung so auftreten. Das gibt es nur noch im Kapitalismus und früher im Feudalismus.[137]

TEACHER We were in parliament a few days ago. Can anyone imagine our president playing this role?

BOY That sort of thing could not happen at all in our social order, I mean that people from the government would act like that. That only happens now under capitalism and before that it used to happen under feudalism.

---

[135] Elke Tasche, '*Leonce und Lena*: Besuch der 1. Hauptprobe am 30.5.1978', AdK ID 323a.

[136] Tasche, '*Leonce und Lena*: Öffentliche Generalprobe'.

[137] 'Diskussion mit Schülern aus 2 8. Klassen nach einem Probenbesuch am 31. März 1978', in VA 'Gesprächsprotokolle *Leonce und Lena*'.

Spectators claimed that the policewomen reminded them only of the Nazis, and just one girl drew a link with the Stasi:

Ich weiß nicht, ob meine Assoziationen richtig sind. Zum Beispiel, das Zwischenstück, wie die beiden aus der Tür wollen, das hat bei mir ein bißchen den Eindruck erweckt, na ja, ich weiß nicht. Vielleicht bezieht sich das auf die Westreisen, auf die Situation BRD/DDR? Das kann falsch sein. Die beiden Frauen in Uniform, ich vermute, die Staatssicherheit könnte gemeint sein?[138]

I don't know if my associations are right. For instance, the interlude when they both try to go through the door, that sort of gave me the impression that, well, I don't know. Perhaps it's a reference to travel to the West, to the situation of the FRG/GDR? That may be wrong. The two women in uniform, I suppose they might refer to the Stasi?

These topical references were expressed extremely cautiously: prefaced by the disclaimer 'I don't know', watered down by 'sort of' and 'perhaps', and hedged in by another 'I don't know' and 'that may be wrong'. Whilst some spectators were willing to explore the contemporary relevance of Gosch's criticisms, they discriminated clearly between those topics that could be discussed, like social problems, and those that it was safer to avoid, like the Stasi.

Unlike most spectators, GDR reviewers claimed that the production's contemporary relevance was unclear. Carl Schwant told the readers of *RFZ Frequenz* that he personally had not been able to construct any link between the performance and the present, and Günther Bellmann reached a similar verdict in the *BZ am Abend*.[139] Western reviewers were only too happy to enlighten their East German colleagues and explain why performances had sold out in advance. Jürgen Beckelmann wrote:

Man will's eben wohl gesehen haben: wie da eine Tür zerkracht im Ansturm der Sehnsucht nach der Fremde, nach südländischen Früchten und der großen weiten Welt; wie da ein närrischer König (in der Tat eine Beckett-Figur) einem Staatsrat von lauter Blinden vorsitzt; wie es denn heißt: 'Teufel! Wir sind schon wieder auf der Grenze'... Das hat, mit Büchner, heute in der DDR eine... 'natürliche' Brisanz.[140]

[138] Tasche, '*Leonce und Lena*: Öffentliche Generalprobe' and '*Leonce und Lena*: Öffentliches Foyergespräch' am Mittwoch, dem 8. November 1978', 9.11.1978, AdK ID 323a.

[139] Carl Schwant, 'Hilf, Rödel, hilf!', *RFZ Frequenz* (East Berlin), 27.9.1978; Günther Bellmann, 'In Streifen gerissen: *Leonce und Lena* in der Volksbühne', *BZ am Abend* (East Berlin), 8.9.1978.

[140] Jürgen Beckelmann, 'Fröhlich-Kritisches von gestern und heute', *Spandauer Volksblatt* (West Berlin), 7.1.1979.

People just want to have seen it for themselves: how [Leonce and Valerio] break down a door in their rush of longing for foreign places, for southern fruits, and the big, wide world; how a foolish King (really a Beckett character) presides over a Council of State full of blind people; how a character says: 'Damn! We've reached the border yet again'... That has a... 'natural' explosive force in the GDR today, along with Büchner himself.

Similarly, Sibylle Wirsing told readers of the *FAZ*:

Auf einmal ist einer da, auf den man nicht rechtzeitig aufgepaßt hat, und setzt sich in aller Öffentlichkeit mit Bedürftigkeiten auseinander, die es öffentlich gar nicht geben darf. Die Reaktion erfolgt prompt. Die Zeitungen protestieren im Namen des Publikums, und das Publikum steht Schlange.[141]

Suddenly someone appears who hasn't been noticed in time, and he grapples in full public view with needs that don't officially exist. The reaction is swift. The newspapers protest in the name of the audience, and the audience queues up.

In 2005, the theologian Friedrich Schorlemmer recalled that such liberating laughter was rare and that he could hardly believe that he was watching this kind of theatre in the GDR.[142]

Friedrich Dieckmann was the only GDR critic who spoke out unambiguously in favour of the production, albeit four months after the premiere. In the *Thüringische Landeszeitung*, published a safe distance from Berlin, Dieckmann praised Gosch for disregarding Büchner's custodians and bringing him up to date, arguing that he had taken the SED's rhetorical homage to Büchner at its word.[143] In contrast, Rolf-Dieter Eichler argued that Gosch had abused and robbed the cultural heritage.[144] In his view, contemporary social criticism belonged only in new plays:

Wer das ohne historische Distanz kritisch darstellen will, der möge das ganz konkret zeigen (in einem anderen Stück) und nicht dem Büchner seine Figuren stehlen, die uns in ihrem Urzustand viel Genaueres zu sagen hätten als hier.[145]

Anyone who wants to depict that critically without historical distance should do so quite explicitly (in a different play) and not steal Büchner's characters, who would have far more definite things to say to us in their original state than they do here.

[141] Sibylle Wirsing, 'Büchner erregt Anstoß', *FAZ*, 16.12.1978.
[142] Friedrich Schorlemmer, 'Was für ein Theater damals in Berlin', *Freitag* (Berlin), 18.11.2005.
[143] Friedrich Dieckmann, 'Phantastik in großen Bildern: Büchners *Leonce und Lena* in der Volksbühne', *Thüringische Landeszeitung* (Weimar), 27.1.1979.
[144] Eichler, 8.9.1978.
[145] Ibid.

Whilst writers and theatre directors had, during the past decade, been moving towards a more critical treatment of the GDR's cultural heritage, Eichler continued to use the language of ownership and theft.

Although *Leonce und Lena* was more explicitly subversive than *Wintermärchen* or *Kohlhaas*, the authorities still decided to manage the performance run rather than ban the production. The *Bezirksleitung* even refrained from making emergency cuts, arguing that Gosch's entire concept was wrong and cosmetic changes would not camouflage his criticism.[146] Officials recommended restricting the number of performances and dropping the production quietly in the near future.[147] Both the Theatre Department and the *Bezirksleitung* blamed the production on the failure of the Volksbühne's new manager, Fritz Rödel, to take preventative measures, such as those seen in 1975 in Schwerin.[148] Shortly after the premiere, the Deputy Culture Minister warned head dramaturges from the GDR's theatres not to follow the Volksbühne's lead. He told them that when people wanted to watch Büchner's plays, they did not mean adaptations by Gosch.[149]

The legend that *Leonce und Lena* was banned persists to this day,[150] but once the initial controversy had subsided, the production remained in repertoire until 25 November 1980 and was performed forty-nine times. Girod explained in June 1980 that a ban would have complicated the already difficult situation under the Volksbühne's new manager, and that the production had not yet been dropped because the Volksbühne had few performable plays in its repertoire.[151] Censorship decisions were becoming increasingly unpredictable, as pragmatic and strategic considerations led officials to desist from bans in some cases, only to impose them in others.

7. CONCLUSION

Although censorship is often described as a cat-and-mouse game in which artists seek to outwit the authorities, officials were well aware of

---

[146] 'Betr.: Inszenierung', BArch DY 30 IV B 2/9.06/66.
[147] Ibid.
[148] Ibid.
[149] 'Bericht vom Chefdramaturgenseminar in Berlin', 25.9.1978, BArch DY 30 IV B 2/9.06/67.
[150] <http://www.deutschestheater.de/ensemble/regie_detail.php?pid=277>, 12.6.2007.
[151] BStU BV Bln. Abt. XX 4109, i.i, fo. 120.

the contemporary resonances of these productions and analysed them in their reports. Their decision not to ban or alter the productions indicates a shift away from the strong-arm tactics of the 1960s towards more differentiated and less public strategies. This suggests that they had learned from the controversies of the 1960s, when press campaigns had stirred up more interest in provocative productions, when attempts to break theatres publicly had generated resentment, and when prominent cuts had encouraged audiences to read subversion into stagings. The SED's less overtly confrontational approach was particularly suited to productions of the classics: GDR reviewers could deny their contemporary relevance and theatres could maintain the charade by gesturing towards the texts' historical origins in their programmes. This meant that 'administrative measures' could be reserved mainly for new GDR plays, such as *Tinka*, *Che Guevara*, and *Flüsterparty*, all of which were banned before their respective premieres in East Berlin during this period. Censorship now prioritized cooperation over conflict, an approach that often worked because many theatre practitioners cooperated with officials when productions were at risk, and because most spectators moderated their reactions at times of heightened political tension. Where cooperation failed, usually in the case of contemporary drama, pre-premiere bans were the favoured alternative.

This new approach to censorship was supported by none other than Kurt Hager. At a discussion with Culture Secretaries from the GDR's *Bezirksleitungen* in 1972, he instructed officials to adopt a more understanding approach and to censor works of art more tactfully.[152] Hager chose the example of literature:

Für einen Schriftsteller, der ein Buch geschrieben hat, der mitunter drei bis fünf Jahre an diesem Buch gearbeitet hat, ist dieses Buch buchstäblich sein Herzblut... Und dann kommen irgendwelche Leute, die innerhalb einer halben Stunde die Arbeit von fünf Jahren zunichte machen... Er wird ... sagen, daß das Grobiane sind, wenn er nicht Verständnis fühlt, wenn es ihm nicht sehr geduldig und kameradschaftlich erläutert wird... Wenn wir es aber ruhig und kameradschaftlich sagen, dann ist er nach unseren Erfahrungen in den meisten Fällen auch bereit gewesen, Änderungen vorzunehmen.[153]

For a writer who has written a book, who has worked in some cases for three to five years on it, this book will literally mean everything to him... And then some strangers come along and destroy five years' work in half an hour. He'll

---

[152] 'Stenografische Niederschrift der Beratung', BArch DY 30 IV B 2/2.024/29.
[153] Ibid.

say... that they are philistines unless he feels their understanding, unless they explain their points in a very patient, comradely fashion... But if we speak calmly and in a comradely fashion, then our experience says that in most cases he'll be prepared to make changes.

Hager was not authorizing a softening of the Party line; he made it clear that he had no intention of compromising on artistic content or relinquishing the Party's leading role, and that bans would be imposed if necessary.[154] Rather, he had made a calculated decision that a less overtly confrontational approach would be more likely to secure the desired results from artists.

Even before Biermann's expatriation, Stasi infiltration and surveillance of the theatre scene increased significantly. So whilst post-premiere bans became less frequent and audiences were able to see more innovative and provocative productions on stage, the regime's capacity to monitor theatre was actually being strengthened. Controversial stagings still carried risks for those involved, particularly if they had not yet secured the kind of international reputation that afforded Dresen some protection. After *Leonce und Lena*, one of the Volksbühne's dramaturges lost his position and Gosch saw little chance of gaining work as a director in the GDR in the near future. Hayner regards the production as the start and abrupt end of a new approach, as Gosch was not given the opportunity to continue his experimentation.[155] Indeed, we might even argue that censorship was deferred from the production to its potential successors. Theatrical experimentation is of course vulnerable in any system, and Gosch was only a guest at the Volksbühne. But the conditions of production discouraged managers from employing a director with Gosch's track record. As a result, Gosch asked Hager for permission to work in the West, which Hager granted.[156]

The productions in this chapter point to significant differences between GDR theatre practitioners, including signatories of the protest. *Leonce und Lena* was the most subversive of the three productions, yet its director had not taken sides publicly over Biermann's expatriation. Whilst Esche and Dresen both signed the protest, they defended their

[154] Ibid. Cf. Hubertus Knabe, '"Weiche" Formen der Verfolgung in der DDR: Zum Wandel repressiver Strategien in der Ära Honecker', *Deutschland Archiv*, 30 (1997), 709–19.

[155] Birgid Gysi, 'Weiße Flecken (6): *Leonce und Lena* von Georg Büchner', *TdZ* 46/11 (Nov. 1991), 70–5 at 74.

[156] Gosch to Hager, 28.3.1979, LAB C Rep. 902 4576.

actions on different grounds: Esche presented his signature as a personal matter separate from his loyalty to the SED, and Dresen presented his protest as a point of principle, demanded his exclusion from the SED, but still identified with socialism and the GDR. Both Esche and Dresen made substantial efforts to mute the contemporary resonances of their productions in 1976–7, even though Dresen had added topical allusions to *Faust* in 1968 and Esche had exploited the resonances of *Winter-märchen* in 1974. They had both signed the protest against Biermann's expatriation, for different reasons, but did not want to hand further ammunition to the GDR's critics. Dresen emphasized this in a letter informing Wolfram of his departure from the GDR.[157]

The aesthetic contrasts between *Michael Kohlhaas* and *Leonce und Lena* reveal a new diversity in approaches towards the cultural heritage. Dresen may have spearheaded the reaction against traditional GDR interpretations of the classics, but Gosch took this approach in a more radical direction. His production included elements of the Theatre of the Absurd, and its emphasis on physical and sensory experience led the Central Committee's Culture Department to compare it with the work of Polish director Jerzy Grotowski.[158] In comparison, Dresen's production of *Kohlhaas* seems aesthetically conservative and shows how far self-censorship could impinge on performance. The production team may have retained controversial lines, but they were under pressure not to share their engagement of the text with the audience. The performance conditions discouraged audiences from reacting openly to the text, and thus theatrical communication was compromised at the first two performances. Events at the Deutsches Theater at this time were complex: members of the company had taken sides publicly in response to Biermann's expatriation, they had been engaged in often frank discussions in internal meetings, but then became complicit in confining this conflict behind the scenes.

The departures of Dresen and Gosch from the GDR were symptomatic of broader developments. In order to avoid public confrontations and export known troublemakers, the SED allowed leading theatre practitioners to direct in the West. These included directors and actors who had been instrumental in the successes of the 1960s and 1970s: Manfred Karge, Matthias Langhoff, Einar Schleef, Angelica Domröse, and Hilmar Thate. The nature of their break with the GDR varied from

---

[157] Dresen to Wolfram, 12.4.1977, BArch DR 1/7229.
[158] 'Betr.: Inszenierung'.

case to case: Domröse and Thate left entirely, whereas Karge and Gosch had visas which allowed them to work abroad while they retained apartments in East Berlin, a situation that continued into the early 1980s. Other established directors, such as Schroth and Wekwerth, continued to work in the GDR, and new directors like Alexander Lang and Frank Castorf came to the fore. But from the late 1970s, a significant number of leading theatre practitioners began to pursue their careers outside the GDR.

PART II

THEATRE CENSORSHIP
IN THE REGIONS

5

Political Patchwork? Regional
Experiences of Theatre Censorship

1. INTRODUCTION

In 1989, the theatre critic Christoph Funke launched a serious attack on regional inconsistencies in the regulation of GDR theatre:

Mitunter scheint mir sogar, die Kunde davon, wir lebten in einem territorial kleinen Land könne nicht stimmen. Denn es zeugt doch von Größe, wenn im Kreis Alpha eine ganz andere Kulturpolitik möglich ist als im Kreis Beta oder gar im Kreis Omega! Aber im Ernst: was in einem Territorium unserer Republik für möglich, nützlich, anregend und herausfordernd gehalten wird, stößt in einem anderen auf den Verdacht kulturpolitischer Falschmünzerei, ungerechtfertigter Kritik und versuchter Verunsicherung des Publikums.[1]

Sometimes it even seems to me that we can't be living in such a small country as people say. For surely it's a testament to the country's size if District Alpha can have a completely different cultural policy from District Beta, not to mention District Omega! But seriously: what is seen in one region of our Republic as possible, useful, stimulating, and challenging, is suspected in the next of defrauding cultural policy, making unjustified criticisms, and trying to unsettle the audience.

This attack echoed comments made two years earlier by the dramatist Rudi Strahl, who had argued that even after a play had finally been accepted for performance in one region, it could still encounter stiff resistance in the next. Strahl had claimed that opinions varied between regions as if the GDR consisted of different principalities.[2] In popular parlance, the regional First Secretaries were indeed known as *Bezirksfürsten*, provincial princes who dictated much of what went on in their

---

[1] Christoph Funke, 'Theater und neue Dramatik', in *Mitteilungen*, ed. Schriftsteller-verband der DDR, 3/4 (Mar./Apr. 1989), 3–9 at 7, SächsStA-L 21123 2405.

[2] 'Sitzungsprotokoll vom 30.6.1987', AdK Georg-Seidel-Archiv 507.

territories.[3] Linzer argues that their patronage or, alternatively, opposition could determine the success or failure of innovative theatre.[4] Arno Hochmuth, a former head of the Central Committee's Culture Department, agrees that differences in theatre censorship depended less on central cultural policy than on the personality of the First Secretaries; some were supportive of the arts and others were hostile. Perhaps mindful of the difficulties involved in working with these First Secretaries, Hochmuth adds that most had little understanding of the arts.[5]

But how are we to reconcile these references to a personalized, idiosyncratic form of regional rule with the overwhelming evidence of centralization in the GDR? Historians agree that the GDR was a heavily centralized state and that the replacement of the five *Länder* by fourteen *Bezirke*, or administrative regions, extended and consolidated the reach of the central administration. East Berlin was an additional *Bezirk* in its own right, and the *Bezirke* were subdivided into *Kreise*, or districts. Mary Fulbrook argues that these reforms rapidly demolished federal traditions, and Klaus Schroeder sees them as having provided for the creation of an *Einheitsstaat*, a centralized state in which one size fitted all.[6] Both the principle and practice of democratic centralism referred local officials back to the central authorities. Policy decisions were taken at the centre, and central state and Party authorities passed on resolutions to regional bodies elected from lists of candidates that they had already vetted.[7] Whilst regional bodies decided how to implement central directives, the central Party and state authorities could reject their proposals for implementation. So why did Ursula Ragwitz, one of Hochmuth's successors, nevertheless talk in 1984 of the difficulties of implementing a standardized theatre policy across the Republic?[8]

One reason is that the system envisaged a certain amount of local discretion in theatre censorship so that local needs and interests could be

[3] See Jay Rowell, 'Le Pouvoir périphérique et le "centralisme démocratique" en RDA', *Revue d'histoire moderne et contemporaine*, 49 (2002), 102–24 at 103.

[4] Linzer, '*Ich war immer . . .*', 51.

[5] Interview with Hochmuth, 7.10.2004.

[6] Mary Fulbrook, 'Democratic Centralism and Regionalism in the GDR', in Maiken Umbach (ed.), *German Federalism: Past, Present, Future* (Basingstoke: Palgrave, 2002), 146–71 at 147; Klaus Schroeder, *Der SED-Staat* (Munich: Carl Hanser, 1998).

[7] Friedrich-Ebert-Stiftung (ed.), *Der demokratische Zentralismus: Herrschaftsprinzip der DDR* (Bonn: Neue Gesellschaft, 1984), 13.

[8] 'Notizen zum Vortrag der Genossin Ursula Ragwitz . . . an der Akademie für Gesellschaftswissenschaften beim ZK der SED am 4.6.1984', SächsStA-D 11857 IV E-2/09/02/543.

taken into account.[9] In a detailed study of secretaries of the SED-*Bezirksleitungen*, Mario Niemann argues that they had room for manoeuvre when interpreting and implementing central Party decrees, although the central authorities could rein in regional secretaries at any time.[10] Whilst Fulbrook places less emphasis on room for manoeuvre, she writes that democratic centralism in the GDR included a 'very local experience of (restricted) debate and input into central decision-making processes', allowing for 'controlled and channelled incorporation of popular opinion'.[11] But she also stresses that this debate took place within the parameters set by central government, which were not open to question. We therefore need to establish in how much detail the central authorities set out theatre policy, how much discretion was left to local functionaries, and how (far) theatre censorship took account of local interests and priorities. This will help us gain a more differentiated understanding, in Jan Palmowski's terms, of how 'the exercise of power . . . was transmitted in local contexts'.[12]

In 1987–9 dramatists, theatre practitioners, and theatre critics began to complain publicly about regional inconsistencies in theatre censorship. At that time, censorship of the arts and media was being challenged in the GDR. The question is whether these complaints reflected only the breaking of the long-standing taboo on references to censorship, or whether they also point to qualitative and quantitative changes in regional variations in censorship, as debates about artistic control were played out in the localities. In Dresden, First Secretary Hans Modrow was relatively open to perestroika and gave cautious support to Gerhard Wolfram and Horst Schönemann at the Staatsschauspiel, as we shall see in Chapter 7. Modrow also allowed theatre practitioners in Bautzen to stage a perestroika play by Jürgen Groß, *Revisor oder Katze aus dem Sack* (The Government Inspector or The Cat's Out of the Bag). In contrast, Modrow's counterpart in Potsdam, Günther Jahn, intervened to halt performances of the selfsame play soon after its

---

[9] 'Probleme der staatlichen Leitungstätigkeit auf dem Gebiet der Kultur', 29.9.1966, BArch DY 30 IV A 2/9.06/51.

[10] Mario Niemann, *Die Sekretäre der SED-Bezirksleitungen 1952–1989* (Paderborn: Ferdinand Schöningh, 2007), 197.

[11] Fulbrook, 'Democratic Centralism', 156.

[12] Jan Palmowski, 'Regional Identities and the Limits of Democratic Centralism in the GDR', *Journal of Contemporary History*, 41 (2006), 503–26 at 525.

premiere at the city's Hans-Otto-Theater.[13] Andrew Coulson sees stark regional differences like this as symptomatic of government across the Eastern bloc in the late 1980s:

in their later stages the communist parties were characterized by shambolic power struggles and administrative chaos, which allowed a degree of local independence. The centralized Stalinist system gradually collapsed into something more akin to a network of baronial fiefs, consisting of party bosses each engaged in the pursuit of their own ends.[14]

This chapter will assess the extent of regional variations in theatre censorship, focusing on the 1960s and 1970s in order to provide a point of comparison with the case studies of censorship in the 1980s in Chapters 6 and 7.

In order to proceed, we need to identify potential sources of regional variations in censorship. Working practices lend themselves well to cross-regional comparison: the implementation of central regulations and procedures, the relationships between different theatres and sets of officials, and the ways in which these relationships affected the experience of censorship. This enables us to see censorship as a human system, not just as a set of bureaucratic procedures. Another possibility is to examine cases where the same new scripts and productions elicited contrasting responses from officials in different *Bezirke*. But we need to be cautious here: the fact that a play was banned in one *Bezirk* but staged in another does not prove that one set of officials was stricter than the other; the reasons may lie in differences between the theatres' textual interpretations, production concepts, or target audiences. An avant-garde production may work for a specialist audience in East Berlin but not for a small town such as Anklam. These factors feature in any theatre's decision-making, and functionaries had to consider them when deciding whether to approve productions. This is precisely why a degree of local discretion was built into the system.

Section 2 of this chapter examines the institutional framework and bureaucratic procedures that governed decision-making. This provides an opportunity to evaluate developments in theatre censorship, as the

[13] Adrianus Schriel, 'The History of the Hans-Otto-Theater Potsdam and its Reflection of Cultural Politics in the German Democratic Republic' (Ph.D. diss., University of Georgia, 1998), 284–91; Baker, '"From Page to Stage"', 250–3.

[14] Andrew Coulson, 'From Democratic Centralism to Local Democracy', in Coulson (ed.), *Local Government in Eastern Europe: Establishing Democracy at the Grassroots* (Aldershot: Edward Elgar, 1995), 1–19 at 9.

central authorities moved to professionalize and streamline the system. Sections 3 and 4 then investigate how the system was implemented, focusing on the 1960s and 1970s. They explore different types of regional variations, the reasons for them, and the extent to which the Culture Department and Ministry tolerated them. The main theatrical examples are dramatizations of contemporary prose texts in the 1970s. The sensitivity of the representation of the GDR, coupled with the perennial problem of defining the difference between constructive criticism and subversion, means that these texts and productions are particularly suited to revealing regional variations in censorship. The theatrical examples also offer a counterpoint to Chapter 4 and its focus on the classics, providing further insights into developments in GDR drama and theatre in the 1970s.

2. THE BUREAUCRATIC FRAMEWORK

The Lines of Command

Theatre does not lend itself to central control, at least not on a day-to-day basis, as it is tied to its performance location and its productions are recreated live each evening before an audience. In the GDR, the Culture Department and Ministry recognized the need to delegate day-to-day control of theatre to local government, whose officials could supervise developments on the spot. Central officials kept a tighter control over literature and film, which generated fixed products with a much wider distribution and a potentially unlimited shelf-life. But the central authorities still set theatre policy, supervised local planning and management, and reserved the right to intervene. As we shall see in Chapter 6, the Ministry's Theatre Department sometimes became involved in the management of high-profile productions outside East Berlin, in this case Volker Braun's *Dmitri* in Schwerin. There were limits, though, to what it could realistically achieve. Its head, Heinz Schröder, complained in 1967 that understaffing prevented the Department from carrying out a whole series of important tasks.[15] Willi Schrader was reluctant to succeed Schröder, largely because he saw a grave mismatch between the Department's tasks and what it could actually accomplish.[16] In 1981,

---

[15] Schröder to Bork, 4.3.1967, BArch DR 1/8845.
[16] Willi [Schrader] to Kurt [Bork], 9.3.1967, BArch DR 1/8845.

departmental head Gisela Holan warned that she and her colleagues could not produce detailed assessments of theatres because they were familiar only with individual examples of their activity.[17]

The process of codifying theatre censorship accelerated in the 1970s, and further specialization in the Ministry went some way towards relieving the pressure on the Theatre Department. The Direktion für das Bühnenrepertoire (Office for the Management of the Stage Repertoire, henceforth Repertoire Management) was founded in Berlin on 17 December 1974, led by Schrader.[18] It was responsible to the Ministry and liaised with the regional state councils, the *Räte der Bezirke*. Its main task was to supervise the annual repertoire consultations with theatres, but it was also charged with improving long-term planning, analysing the repertoire, producing and circulating information, and promoting the development of new plays. The Repertoire Management was thus designed to improve central oversight of theatre and to provide greater central coordination. It continued in this form until 1986, when it merged with the Direktion für Theater und Orchester (Office for the Management of Theatres and Orchestras), an organization that assigned artists to ensembles and supervised their training.[19] The new organization retained the name Direktion für Theater und Orchester (DTO).

At regional level, the power centre of each *Bezirk* was the Secretariat of the SED-*Bezirksleitung*, the executive organ of the regional Party administration. Its head, the regional First Secretary, usually belonged to the Politbüro. Whilst the Central Committee supervised the *Bezirksleitung*, the *Bezirksleitung* was responsible both for the *Kreisleitungen* and *Stadtleitungen* and—in practice—for the regional, district, and municipal state councils, the *Rat des Bezirks, Räte der Kreise*, and *Räte der Städte*. These councils conducted the repertoire consultations and planned the development of theatre in their areas, in line with central directives.[20] However, the *Bezirksleitung* participated in these consultations and checked the draft programmes before the *Rat des Bezirks* confirmed them. Indeed, Dietmar Keller, who served as Culture Secretary of Leipzig's *Bezirksleitung* from 1977 to 1984, argues that the

---

[17] Holan to Hoffmann, 9.3.1981, SächsStA-D 11857 IV D-2/09/02/577.
[18] 'Protokoll der konstituierenden Zusammenkunft der Kommission für das Bühnenrepertoire beim Ministerium für Kultur am 17. Dezember 1975 [*sic*]', Jan. 1975, SächsStA-L 20237 8034.
[19] Sprink to theatre managers, received 26.5.1986, LHAS 7.11-1 Z36/1993 5.
[20] 'Versuch zur Entwicklung', BArch DR 1/8846.

Culture Department of the *Rat des Bezirks* essentially carried out decisions reached in the Culture Department of the *Bezirksleitung*.[21] Officially, though, the *Rat des Bezirks* was responsible to the Ministry, which retained the authority—for example—to approve the supply of Western literature to theatres.[22] The state administration in the regions thus illustrates the principle of dual subordination, on the one hand to parallel Party organs, and on the other to the central state authorities.

Even though the lines of authority were clear, the number of institutions involved in theatre censorship made for a complicated system and increased the potential for confusion. Theatre managers had to negotiate with Party and state functionaries at both central and local levels; even if these functionaries were in agreement, the negotiations acted as a drain on time and resources. In 1989, the manager of the Theater Junge Garde Halle reportedly complained:

Die Duplierungen und Triplierungen von Leitungen, die für ein und dieselbe Einrichtung zuständig sind und sich in die Arbeit einbringen, ist ein arbeitsbehindernder, unhaltbarer Zustand. Sein Theater wird unterschiedlich direkt angeleitet durch die Bezirksleitung, die Stadtleitung und die Stadtbezirksleitung, ebenso die Gewerkschaft Kunst, den Bezirksvorstand des FDGB [Freie Deutsche Gewerkschaftsbund] und den Stadtvorstand des FDGB.[23]

Work is impeded by the duplication and triplication of the authorities that are responsible for one and the same institution and contribute to its activity; this situation is untenable. His theatre is supervised directly, in different ways, by the *Bezirksleitung*, the *Stadtleitung*, and the *Stadtbezirksleitung*, and also by the Trade Union for the Arts, the Regional Executive of the FDGB [Federation of Free German Trade Unions], and the Town Executive of the FDGB.

Interestingly, the manager omitted to mention central or local state bodies and organizations. This suggests that the *Bezirksleitung* and *Stadtleitung* may have played a more direct role in theatre than the *Rat des Bezirks* in Halle at this time. It also implies that the Ministry may not have paid much attention to the Theater Junge Garde, which was not Halle's principal theatre.

Censorship was only one of the responsibilities of local officials dealing with theatre. They also provided more general administrative

---

[21] Dietmar Keller, 'Die Machthierarchie der SED', *ND*, 1.3.1993.

[22] Rackwitz to Wolf, 12.1.1977, SächsStA-L 20237 28583.

[23] 'Aktennotiz über eine Intendantenberatung des Genossen Günther Kuhbach am 7.11.1989', 9.11.1989, LHASA Abt. MER, SED-BL Halle IV/F-2/9.02/341.

and logistical support, for example in allocating resources, supervising renovation work, sorting out transport, and finding accommodation for theatre practitioners. The competing demands on local officials led some to prioritize resource management over artistic controls. In 1973, the Theatre Department complained that it was not rare for officials to judge theatres only on how they measured up to their financial forecasts, or how they marked particular anniversaries, rather than on their artistic results.[24] But the variety of functions devolved to local functionaries also meant that they had patronage at their disposal, at least within the constraints of the GDR's economy. In 1989, for instance, the chair of Halle's *Rat des Bezirks* reported having promised to help bring forward the delivery of a Wartburg car for the manager of the Landestheater Halle and to put in a good word so that a telephone could be installed in the manager's work apartment.[25] Such encounters did not necessarily involve a direct trade-off, but they have implications for our understanding of the working relationships between theatre practitioners and functionaries: they had contact over a whole range of issues, not just the control of artistic interpretation.

Training and Supervision

Training events helped the central authorities to maintain their overall control of local officials, and the Culture Ministry increased the frequency of these events in the 1970s, as it strove to professionalize theatre management. From the 1970s, managers could undertake a long-distance course in theatre management at the Hans Otto Theatre University in Leipzig.[26] The Ministry also offered week-long courses for all GDR theatre managers, which focused primarily on organizational, political, and ideological issues, rather than artistic practice. In 1976, the course covered topics such as economics, planning, and employment law in theatre; the career of the dramaturge; and crime prevention.[27]

---

[24] 'Zur Theatersituation', BArch DY 30/IV B 2/9.06/67.
[25] 'Aktennotiz über ein Gespräch des Vorsitzenden des Rates des Bezirkes mit dem Generalintendanten des Landestheaters Halle', LHASA Abt. MER, SED-BL Halle IV/F-2/9.02/341.
[26] 'Lt. Maßnahme 002 des Theaterbeschlusses vom 21.3.1979', 5.6.1979, LHAS 7.21-1 Z106/1991 18729.
[27] 'Intendantenseminar des Ministeriums für Kultur, Schildow, 5.–9. Januar 1976', SächsStA-L 20237 8031.

In addition, the Ministry provided training and guidance for directors of planning and resources, dramaturges, and state functionaries such as the theatre advisers from the *Räte der Bezirke.*[28] Meanwhile, the Central Committee's Culture Department trained Party officials, such as Party Secretaries from individual theatres and Culture Secretaries from the *Bezirksleitungen.*

The advice given at these events in the 1970s confirms that the Culture Department and Ministry were increasingly concerned to avoid production bans, as we saw in Chapter 4. But the Culture Department was also keen to dampen expectations of liberalization after Honecker's 'no taboos' speech in 1971. The following year, the Department's representative Klaus Pfützner told theatre Party Secretaries that the GDR had not entered a phase of liberalization and that the decisions of the Eleventh Plenary remained in force.[29] In 1973, Ragwitz made it clear that the authorities were concerned to avoid the political damage caused by production bans, while still retaining ideological control. She told theatre managers and Party Secretaries that no one had the right to resort to 'administration' instead of trying to convince artists, but that the Ministry and the *Räte der Bezirke* needed to strengthen central management of theatre.[30] Representing the Repertoire Management, Schrader adopted the same line in 1975, when he told local officials to improve consultations with theatres and hold theatre practitioners to their plans, but to avoid 'administration' wherever possible.[31]

The central authorities maintained this broad line after Biermann's expatriation, while reserving the right to make striking exceptions. On 22 May 1979, a court imposed a fine of 9,000 marks on the writer Stefan Heym for publishing his novel *Collin* in the Federal Republic without permission. Sixteen days later, a meeting of the Berlin branch of the Writers' Union voted to exclude Heym and eight other writers, some of whom had sent a letter of protest at Heym's treatment to

[28] 'Informationsbericht über die Zusammenkunft der Theaterreferenten am 28/2/73 in Berlin', 5.3.1973, LHASA Abt. MER, RdB Halle 4. Abl. 6607.
[29] 'Information über die Anleitung der Parteisekretäre der Bedeutungsgruppen B und C im Zentralkomitee, Abteilung Kultur, am 28. August 1972', 30.8.1972, LHASA Abt. MER, SED-BL Halle IV/C-2/9.02/0517.
[30] 'Information über die Beratung...am 2.7.73', LHASA Abt. MER IV/C-2/9.02/ 0517.
[31] 'Information über eine Beratung mit den Theaterreferenten beim Ministerium für Kultur am 17.12.1975', LHASA Abt. MER, RdB Halle 4. Abl. 6607.

Honecker and the Western media.[32] But on the very same day, 7 June, Hager told Culture Secretaries from the *Bezirksleitungen* that they should remain firm in such a way that oppositional individuals could not present themselves as martyrs.[33] Given that Hager's officials—particularly Ragwitz—had been involved in the decision to seek the writers' exclusion from the Union, it is unlikely that Hager's comments point to a difference in policy. On the contrary, they suggest that the exclusions were part of a differentiated strategic approach to censorship. These exclusions had sent a powerful signal that the regime would not tolerate transgression, warning other artists to exercise greater self-censorship.

Controls on the Repertoire

In the 1960s, the central authorities betrayed occasional concerns that their control over the theatre repertoire was not guaranteed. In Chapter 2, we saw how the controversy over *Die Umsiedlerin* prompted Hans Bentzien to call on the *Räte der Bezirke* to strengthen their checks on new plays.[34] After the Eleventh Plenary, the controversy over new plays such as *Der Bau* and *Moritz Tassow* led Hager to tell the Culture Department that all new plays needed to be discussed thoroughly before rehearsals could start.[35] The fact that Hager felt the need to say this suggests that it may not have been standard practice.

The Culture Ministry organized 'consultations' where the theatres' draft programmes were discussed and vetted until December 1974, when this task was delegated to the newly created Repertoire Management. After 1974, the Ministry continued to provide guidelines for these discussions; in 1976, for example, Culture Minister Hoffmann sent a set of instructions to the *Rat des Bezirks* in Leipzig. The instructions included details of anniversaries that theatres should celebrate, along with a list of GDR plays that officials could use to make suggestions to theatres.[36] Theatres were required to consult local 'social

[32] See Joachim Walther and others (eds.), *Protokoll eines Tribunals: Die Ausschlüsse aus dem DDR-Schriftstellerverband 1979* (Hamburg: Rowohlt, 1991).
[33] 'Vertraulich! Niederschrift über eine Beratung bei Genossen Hager... am 7. Juni 1979', SächsStA-D 11857 IV D-2/09/02/556.
[34] Bentzien to Sieber, 25.11.1961, SächsStA-D 11430 6539.
[35] 'Aktennotiz über die Anleitung beim Genossen Hager am 21.12.1965', BArch DY 30 IV A 2/9.06/34.
[36] Hoffmann to Wolf, 20.12.1976, SächsStA-L 20237 8035.

partners' about their draft programmes, and in 1975 the Landestheater Altenburg discussed its plans with spectators and deputies from the district assembly, as well as its own trade union and Party representatives.[37] This requirement potentially allowed some local input into theatre programming within the parameters set by the central authorities.

Both before and after 1974, repertoire consultations involved officials from central and local bodies: the Theatre Department, Union of Theatre Practitioners, Trade Union for the Arts (Gewerkschaft Kunst), and *Räte der Bezirke*. They examined theatres' draft programmes and accompanying production concepts, although the Theatre Department complained in 1973 that some *Räte der Bezirke* had failed to assess these concepts in detail, while others had not submitted even a cursory assessment. The *Bezirksleitungen* discussed the draft programmes before the *Räte der Bezirke* confirmed them.[38] In December 1976, Hoffmann informed a functionary in Leipzig that the Repertoire Management had to approve the plans of the GDR's leading theatres and world or GDR premieres before these plans were passed at local level.[39] By vetting plans in advance, the Repertoire Management and *Bezirksleitungen* avoided the appearance of disagreement with the *Räte der Bezirke* while maintaining the fiction that locally elected state councils had the final say. When Hoffmann codified these arrangements in a directive that took effect on 1 January 1978, the directive stated only that the Culture Minister took note of these plans and premieres, and that his approval was needed for changes in planned world and GDR premieres.[40] However, the phrase 'take note' ('zur Kenntnis nehmen') appears to have been euphemistic, as Schrader subsequently wrote that the directive required the plans of leading theatres and world or GDR premieres to be approved by the Minister.[41]

A brief look at repertoire consultations in Neubrandenburg in the first half of the 1980s suggests that their impact varied from case to case. The rejection of a draft programme would not necessarily lead to substantive changes, unless the authorities insisted. In 1982, Alfred

[37] 'Spielplanvorhaben des Landestheaters Altenburg in der Spielzeit 1975/76', 5.3.1975, SächsStA-L 20237 28583.
[38] 'Entwicklung der Theaterarbeit im Bezirk Leipzig im Jahre 1973', 30.1.1973, SächsStA-L 20237 28583.
[39] Hoffmann to Wolf, 20.12.1976.
[40] *Dokumente zur Kunst-, Literatur- und Kulturpolitik der SED 1975–1980*, ed. Peter Lübbe (Stuttgart: Seewald, 1984), 473.
[41] Schrader to Hafranke, 17.5.1979, BArch DY 30 IV B 2/9.06/68.

Netik, the member of the *Rat des Bezirks* responsible for culture,
complained that the programme submitted by the Friedrich-Wolf-
Theater in Neustrelitz was insufficiently detailed and contained significant omissions, including Soviet drama, finished contemporary plays
from the GDR, and productions marking forthcoming anniversaries.[42]
Whilst the revised version was significantly more detailed, it contained
no substantive changes in response to Netik's demands.[43] In contrast,
the *Rat des Bezirks* had reportedly secured significant revisions to a script
of Uwe Saeger's play *Glashaus* (Glass House) earlier on in the year, to
the extent that it sounded almost like a different play. According to
Netik, Saeger had changed the title and ending, added a new scene,
and altered several passages.[44] On other occasions, the *Rat des
Bezirks* rejected plays entirely. In 1985, it refused to confirm Mikhail
Sostschenko's play *Geehrter Genosse* (Respected Comrade) and Georg
Seidel's *Jochen Schanotta* and *Kondensmilchpanorama* (Condensed Milk
Panorama) in Anklam.[45] These examples indicate that officials had
substantial powers over local theatre programmes, but that they did
not always use them. In Neubrandenburg in the 1980s, officials seem to
have prioritized the ideological control of contemporary drama over
other aspects of the Ministry's guidelines.

Attempts to subject theatre to the logic—or otherwise—of the
planned economy made no allowances for experimentation during
rehearsals. The system assumed that dramaturges could supply a definitive production concept long before rehearsals had begun, and yet few
directors would be content to limit their actors to a pre-planned
concept. This caused the authorities considerable frustration; in 1979
Hoffmann warned Modrow about the director Horst Schönemann,
saying that his production concepts were generally correct, but that
the finished stagings rarely corresponded to the concepts.[46] The records
show that theatres' programmes frequently changed: in 1979, there
were thirty-six examples of managers changing their production
plans before the start of rehearsals. Not for the first time, exasperated
functionaries reminded managers that the confirmed plan was legally

---

[42] Netik to Weindich, 15.3.1982, LHAS 7.21-1 Z106/1991 27302.

[43] 'Spielplanvorhaben 1983', 12.4.1982, LHAS 7.21-1 Z106/1991 27302.

[44] 'Uwe Saeger *Glashaus*', LHAS 7.21-1 Z106/1991 27302.

[45] 'Protokoll Spielplankonsultation 16.10.1985', LHAS 7.21-1 Z106/1991.

[46] 'Streng vertraulich! Information des Ministers für Kultur, Genossen Hans-Joachim
Hoffmann, an Genossen Modrow in der Beratung am 18.1.1979 in Dresden', 1.2.1979,
SächsStA-D 11857 IV D-2/09/02/575.

binding, just as in any other workplace.[47] Matters were potentially more serious when theatres changed their plans before or shortly after a premiere, usually for political reasons. This occurred twice in the Halle region in 1979. Central officials warned that such actions wasted resources, damaged the working atmosphere within theatres, and created negative publicity at home and abroad.[48] Concern for the regime's international and domestic image was an important factor in central cultural policy in this period, but did not necessarily prevent local officials from banning productions.

3. VARIATIONS IN PRACTICE

Relationships between Theatre Practitioners and Officials

Theatres may have been subject to the same bureaucratic framework in the GDR, but policy implementation allowed room for variation. Differences in working practices and decision-making were related to theatre managers and directors, not just officials. I focus first on two politically powerful director-managers: Hanns Anselm Perten and Karl Kayser. Both were regarded as ideologically sound and entrusted with premieres of new GDR plays and, particularly in Perten's case, Western drama. The actor Hans-Peter Minetti—himself a former member of the Central Committee and President of the Theatre Union—calls them two veritable high priests: the theatrical equivalent of the *Bezirksfürsten*.[49]

Perten managed the Volkstheater Rostock from 1958 to 1970 and 1972 to 1985, interrupted only by his brief, ill-fated tenure at the Deutsches Theater. At a meeting with local theatre advisers in 1975, Schrader praised the Volkstheater, saying that a series of authors felt at home there and that everyone was prepared to share the risks.[50] This referred to the risks of staging new contemporary plays, and the support of a trusted director such as Perten did enable the theatre to pursue a more innovative programme. Yet Perten and the functionaries in Rostock's *Rat des Bezirks* resented central involvement in theatre and

[47] 'Ausführungen zur Intendantenberatung am 31.10.79', LHASA Abt. MER, RdB Halle 4. Abl. 6629.
[48] Ibid.
[49] Hans-Peter Minetti, *Erinnerungen* (Berlin: Ullstein, 1997), 225.
[50] 'Tagung der Theaterreferenten 5.6.–6.6.75', SächsStA-L 20237 8034.

argued that politically reliable theatres should be allowed to supervise their own programmes. The strength of their resentment became clear at the repertoire consultations in 1979, which were led by the member of the *Rat des Bezirks* responsible for culture and attended by representatives from the Repertoire Management, *Bezirksleitung, Rat des Kreises, Rat der Stadt,* theatre managers, and head dramaturges.

The consultations in Rostock got off to an awkward start in 1979. The member of the *Rat des Bezirks* had reportedly failed to attend the pre-consultation meeting and to submit an analysis of the past season and the theatre's plans for the coming year, evidence enough for the Repertoire Management that he was not taking the consultations seriously. The tone of the meeting grew increasingly angry, as first the representative of the *Rat des Bezirks* and then Perten reportedly complained of the increasing bureaucratization of theatre. According to the Repertoire Management, Perten referred to his past achievements and his track record of political responsibility, and complained that institutions in Berlin were obstructing his work. His main target was the Repertoire Management, whereas at the consultations in 1978 he had distinguished between it and the Theatre Department, speaking less favourably of the latter. Perten even compared the Repertoire Management with the 'Zentraldramaturgie unseligen Angedenkens' (Central Dramaturgy of infernal memory)—a euphemistic but nonetheless transparent reference to Nazi theatre censorship. He looked down on state officials in Berlin, reportedly arguing that he had nine dramaturges in Rostock, including one professor and three dramaturges with doctorates; the representative of the *Rat des Bezirks* also had a doctorate. Perten found it inconceivable that there were more intelligent individuals in Berlin who were entitled to monitor his programme.[51] Significantly, neither Perten nor the member of the *Rat des Bezirks* questioned the need for ideological control over the repertoire. Instead, they used their unblemished record and academic status to argue that Rostock should be exempt from external checks. We see a clear alliance and identity of views between Perten and the representative of the *Rat des Bezirks,* against central state functionaries.

According to Schrader, such outspoken rebellion was the exception; it contrasted sharply both with the behaviour of officials in Rostock in

---

[51] 'Bericht über Vorbereitung und Durchführung von Vorgespräch und Bezirkskonsultation zur Erarbeitung der Theaterspielpläne im Bezirk Rostock', 25.4.1979, BArch DY 30 IV B 2/9.06/68.

previous years and with that of officials elsewhere.[52] He explained that the catalyst was the new requirement that the Culture Minister should approve the programmes of all leading GDR theatres and all world and GDR premieres.[53] The issue was not that Perten wanted to stage plays that the Ministry was likely to reject on ideological or aesthetic grounds, but that he did not want Rostock's interests to be subordinated to those of other GDR theatres. As this case indicates, agreement with SED ideology did not preclude resistance to the central coordination of GDR theatre.

There are some similarities between Perten and Karl Kayser, who managed the Theater Leipzig, an industrial-style conglomerate that included theatre, opera, musical comedy, and youth theatre. It almost seems surprising that Kayser had time to direct operations and productions in Leipzig, given that he was also a deputy in the GDR's parliament (Volkskammer); a member of the Central Committee, Central Executive of the Trade Union for the Arts, and Committee of the Cultural League (Kulturbund); and, from 1966, Vice President of the Union of Theatre Practitioners. Local theatre historian Manfred Pauli notes that Kayser was virtually unassailable as a theatre manager, not least because of these political offices.[54] The Ministry had little reason to challenge Kayser on ideological grounds, as he prided himself on defending ideological and aesthetic orthodoxy in GDR theatre and disapproved of experimentation at theatres such as the BE, even in the 1960s. In fact, the real source of tension in the 1960s and 1970s was that Ministry officials considered Kayser too conservative, and he complained that officials in Berlin occasionally treated him and his production team as 'grausame Sektierer' (terrible sectarians).[55] Kayser resisted external interference in his production plans but directed his aversion primarily towards local controls, unlike Perten. He used his power to internalize censorship within the theatre, allowing the *Rat der Stadt* to

---

[52] Schrader to Hafranke, 17.5.1979.
[53] See 'Anweisung zur Erarbeitung', SächsStA-L 20237 8035.
[54] Manfred Pauli, *Ein Theaterimperium an der Pleiße: Leipziger Theater zu DDR-Zeiten* (Schkeuditz: Schkeuditzer Buchverlag, 2004), 32.
[55] Kayser to Wagner, 5.1.1965, BArch DY 30 IV A 2/9.06/117. Kayser allowed the Schauspiel Leipzig to stage more innovative plays in the 1980s, although the theatre was never in the vanguard of artistic experimentation. See Thomas Irmer, 'Ein letzter Kayser', in Wolfgang Engel and Erika Stephan (eds.), *Theater in der Übergangsgesellschaft: Schauspiel Leipzig 1957–2007* (Berlin: TdZ, 2007), 76–83 at 76.

rubber-stamp his plans but not to attend meetings or rehearsals.[56] Kayser also side-stepped the SED-*Stadtleitung*, preferring to direct Party operations within the theatre himself.[57] Whilst the SED-*Bezirksleitung* discussed developments in his theatre two or three times a year, these sporadic contacts did not impinge significantly on Kayser's authority.[58]

The case of Leipzig highlights the disparity between the theory and practice of theatre censorship in the regions. The *Rat des Bezirks* drew up a statement of practice that bore little resemblance to reality:

Der Rat der Stadt Leipzig und die Räte der Kreise Altenburg und Döbeln übergeben den von ihnen geleiteten Theatern auf der Grundlage der Aufgaben-stellung des Rates des Bezirkes jährlich Vorgaben für die Spielplangestaltung und üben eine straffe Kontrolle über deren Erfüllung durch die Theater aus.[59]

Leipzig City Council and the District Councils of Altenburg and Döbeln give the theatres under their supervision annual guidelines for drawing up the repertoire, based on the tasks set by the Regional Council, and exercise tight control over their implementation by the theatres.

In practice, there was no evidence of any such 'tight control' over Kayser's theatre, and pre-performance state censorship seems to have been virtually non-existent. Revealingly, the *Rat des Bezirks* argued that the *Rat der Stadt* should discuss productions before they were pre-miered, not just afterwards.[60] This would clearly be difficult if its members were excluded from rehearsals.

One reason for the disparity between theory and practice was that the *Rat der Stadt* was hopelessly understaffed. In 1972, it had only one unqualified official responsible for music and theatre, in a city that had four theatres, an opera house, a musical comedy theatre, and an inter-nationally renowned orchestra and choir. In contrast, Dresden's *Rat der Stadt* had two university-educated officials responsible for music and theatre respectively.[61] Leipzig's sole official seems to have been no

---

[56] 'Probleme zur prognostischen und perspektivischen Entwicklung der Leipziger Theater', [*c.*1970], SächsStA-L IV/B/2/9/2/606.
[57] 'Bericht über den Einsatz der Arbeitsgruppe zum Studium der Führungstätigkeit der Stadtleitung der Partei in Vorbereitung der 13. Arbeiterfestspiele der DDR in Leipzig', 20.5.1971, SächsStA-L IV/B/2/9/2/598.
[58] Ibid.
[59] 'Die langfristige Entwicklung des sozialistischen Theaters im Bezirk Leipzig', 13.10.1972, SächsStA-L 20237 5504.
[60] 'Probleme zur prognostischen und perspektivischen Entwicklung'.
[61] 'Analyse der gegenwärtigen Situation beim Gewandhausorchester und den Theatern der Stadt Leipzig', SächsStA-L 20237 8019.

match for Kayser; the *Rat des Bezirks* reported that Kayser dealt exclusively with his equals and tolerated only sporadic contacts with local officials. Members of the *Rat des Bezirks* looked with some envy at Dresden, where the official responsible for theatre participated in weekly management meetings at the Staatsschauspiel and where the *Rat der Stadt* could actually influence the repertoire.[62] In Leipzig, the *Rat des Bezirks* assumed direct responsibility for the Schauspiel in 1972.[63] The member responsible for culture resolved to assert his authority, asking to see the scripts of proposed plays rather than relying simply on Kayser's interpretation. He added that the *Rat des Bezirks* could not always approve Kayser's decisions retrospectively.[64] Even so, these intentions do not seem to have made any real difference to the balance of power between Kayser and local officials.

The limits of state control in Leipzig owed much, but not everything, to Kayser's management style. Other reports criticized the activity of the *Rat des Bezirks*. Whilst Peter Posdzech—the manager of the Landestheater Altenburg—praised the activity of the *Bezirksleitung* and *Kreisleitung* in 1978, he claimed that in the past thirteen years he had never seen any serious evidence of management activity on the part of the *Rat des Bezirks*, except in its demands for reports and analyses.[65] Little seems to have changed by 1982, when the Theatre Department declared that the *Rat des Bezirks* in Leipzig was one of the councils whose guidance of theatre was the least pronounced.[66] At least where the Schauspiel Leipzig was concerned, the *Rat des Bezirks* seems to have done little more than fulfil the letter of the system's requirements. Although Pauli attributes its limited activity to the fact that the key decisions were all taken in Berlin, this does not explain the reported discrepancies between Leipzig and other regions.[67] Kayser's determination to assume sole responsibility for censorship in the Schauspiel was clearly important here.

A very different set of relationships prevailed in Halle in the late 1960s and in Dresden in the 1980s, interestingly involving the same

---

[62] Ibid.
[63] Ibid.
[64] 'Probleme für die Aussprache mit Prof. K. Kayser', 19.2.1973, SächsStA-L 20237 24316.
[65] Posdzech to Nebe, 26.12.1978, BArch DY 30/vorl. SED/34866.
[66] 'Information der Abt. Theater an den Minister für Kultur', 12.1.1982, LHASA Abt. MER, RdB Halle 4. Abl. 6656.
[67] Pauli, *Ein Theaterimperium an der Pleiße*, 32.

theatre practitioners in each case, Wolfram and Schönemann. In Halle, they developed a relatively close partnership with First Secretary Horst Sindermann, who sought to use theatre to raise the profile of his industrial region. In November 1969, for example, they solicited the cooperation of the *Bezirksleitung* on a planned production of *Faust*, probably to avoid the controversy unleashed by Dresen's recent staging at the Deutsches Theater. Schönemann wrote to Culture Secretary Edith Brandt:

Wir möchten natürlich auch bei diesem Unternehmen, zumal es kulturpolitisch von besonderer Bedeutung ist, unsere Vorstellungen mit Euch beraten, alle Eure Hinweise und Gedanken erfahren und so auch in Sachen FAUST einen produktiven Kontakt aufnehmen. Wir würden uns freuen, wenn ein erstes Gespräch Ende November mit Dir und Deinen Genossen zu ermöglichen wäre.[68]

We would naturally like to discuss our ideas about this project with you too, especially as it is of particular significance in terms of cultural politics, to find out all your advice and thoughts, and thereby establish a productive working relationship on FAUST too. We would be glad if we could have an initial conversation with you and your comrades at the end of November.

At least one member of Schwerin's theatre regarded this cooperation with a certain amount of envy, writing in 1971 that in Halle theatre practitioners and officials did not just come into contact when the cat was already among the pigeons ('wenn das Kind im Brunnen liegt').[69]

Theatrically Challenged Officials

Compared to the 1950s, staff provision and expertise in local government had undoubtedly improved significantly by the mid-1960s. As Niemann points out, in 1952 70 per cent of secretaries in the *Bezirksleitungen* had received only eight years of schooling, and just three secretaries had an *Abitur*, the school certificate needed for entry into higher education.[70] Initially, the drive to educate officials in Marxism-Leninism took priority over subject-specific training, but from the end

---

[68] Schönemann to Edith [Brandt], 3.11.1969, LHASA Abt. MER, SED-BL Halle IV/B-2/9.02/707.

[69] Schmidt to Quandt, 16.2.1971, LHAS 10.34-3 2197.

[70] Niemann, *Die Sekretäre der SED-Bezirksleitungen*, 72.

of the 1950s both aspects were equally important.[71] This new approach soon achieved results, and between 1962 and 1965 the proportion of officials in the *Bezirksleitungen* and *Kreisleitungen* with degrees rose from 30.7 per cent to 47.9 per cent.[72] Some officials responsible for culture even had higher degrees, such as Roland Bauer in East Berlin. But the theatrical expertise of local officials still varied across the regions, despite central training events. In 1973, the Theatre Department discerned strong differences in the quality of local management, related to staff provision.[73] Esther von Richthofen argues that a lack of time and inclination led many cultural functionaries to avoid professional development courses, a problem that was compounded by the high rate of staff turnover.[74]

In the 1960s and 1970s, the number of officials and their qualifications and experience varied from one region to the next. In 1964, Schwerin's *Rat der Stadt* noted that its Culture Department was understaffed and essentially restricted its supervision of the Staatstheater to checking its fiscal plans, indicating that such problems were not confined to Leipzig.[75] Complaints about the administration in the towns and *Kreise* were particularly common; as late as 1972, Potsdam's SED Culture Secretary reported that the *Kreisleitungen* had hardly a single comrade with a specialist qualification.[76] However, this may well reflect the fact that a *Bezirksleitung* or *Rat des Bezirks* was more likely to criticize its subordinate organizations than its own officials. Central reports criticized the *Räte der Bezirke* too; in 1975, for example, the Ministry noted that problems attracting suitably qualified theatre advisers to work in the *Räte der Bezirke* made state management more difficult.[77] As late as 1981, Ministry officials reported that it was evident from local officials' reports that many of them lacked sufficient specialist knowledge.[78] The reports confirm that this was the case; an official in Leipzig's

---

[71] Ibid. 126, 136, 149.   [72] Ibid. 141.
[73] 'Zur Theatersituation'.
[74] Esther von Richthofen, *Bringing Culture to the Masses: Control, Compromise and Participation in the GDR*, Monographs in German History, 24 (New York and Oxford: Berghahn, 2009), 61.
[75] 'Untersuchungen über die Krise des Mecklenburgischen Staatstheaters und Empfehlungen zu ihrer Überwindung', 1.7.1964, LHAS 7.11-1 Z31/1981 19112.
[76] 'Stenografische Niederschrift der Beratung', BArch DY 30 IV B 2/2.024/29.
[77] 'Tagung der Theaterreferenten'.
[78] 'Aktennotiz über eine Beratung des Ministeriums für Kultur mit den Informationsbeauftragten der Räte der Bezirke', 21.4.1981, LHASA Abt. MER, RdB Halle 4. Abl. 6659.

Rat des Bezirks recommended that the Landestheater Altenburg should perform *Franziska Lesser* by Heiner Müller in 1976–7.[79] This was going to be difficult, as the play was actually by Armin Müller. It seems more than likely that the official had not read the play that he was recommending, given that he attributed it to the wrong author.

Whilst members of the Ministry's Theatre Department had often studied or worked in theatre, local officials were rarely specialists and were not necessarily particularly interested in performance. Writing of officials in the *Kreisleitungen* and of local trade union leaders, the First Secretary of Halle's *Bezirksleitung* noted in 1962:

[Sie] sind selbst wenig Vorbild in ihrer Einstellung zum Theater und zum regelmäßigen Theaterbesuch... Die Kreisleitung Quedlinburg hat z. B. in dieser Spielzeit überhaupt keine Anrechte abgeschlossen... Deshalb ist in den Köpfen der Genossen... gründliche Klarheit darüber zu schaffen, daß ein Theaterbesuch nicht schlechthin Freizeitgestaltung ist und jedem Genossen nach Gutdünken überlassen bleibt, ob er sich kulturell bildet oder nicht.[80]

[They] themselves do not set a particularly good example in their attitude to theatre and regular theatre attendance... The *Kreisleitung* in Quedlinburg, for example, has not taken out any subscriptions at all this season... For this reason,... it needs to be made absolutely clear to our comrades that going to the theatre is not simply a leisure activity and that it is not left to the discretion of individual comrades to decide whether or not to educate themselves in cultural matters.

By 1972, Edith Brandt was able to report that roughly twenty-five secretaries from Halle's thirty *Kreisleitungen* now attended the theatre regularly.[81] However, there was still some way to go: Brandt stated that officials did not always find it easy to form opinions on productions and were often reluctant to do so.[82]

It was not just in the districts that officials were sometimes unsure how to judge productions. In 1968, after the premiere of Josef Topol's *Fastnacht* (Carnival) in Schwerin, the Party organization of the Mecklenburgisches Staatstheater complained that regional Party and state

[79] 'Stellungnahme zu den Spielplanentwürfen der Theater des Bezirkes Leipzig für die Spielzeit 76/77', SächsStA-L 20237 28583.
    [80] Koenen to the First Secretary of the *Kreisleitung*, 20.2.1962, LHASA Abt. MER, SED-BL Halle IV/2/3/549.
    [81] 'Stenografische Niederschrift der Beratung', BArch DY 30 IV B 2/2.024/29.
    [82] Ibid.

officials had neither helped to prepare the production nor shown what they thought of it:

Auf den Mienen der Genossen der Bezirksleitung, die in der Mittelloge saßen, war auch nicht die Spur einer Anerkennung,—na das muß ja auch nicht sein, —aber Gefallen oder Mißfallen in einer so bedeutsamen Angelegenheit sollte zwischen diesen Genossen und uns nicht unausgesprochen bleiben! Vor allem nicht so lange!![83]

There was not even a trace of appreciation on the faces of the comrades from the *Bezirksleitung* sitting in the central box—well, that isn't strictly necessary—but in such an important matter these comrades should not keep their approval or disapproval from us! Above all not for such a long time!!

Christoph Schroth, Schwerin's leading theatre director from 1974 to 1989, argues that this uncertainty was typical, that officials found it difficult to reach verdicts, and that they preferred to consult experts.[84] When the Mecklenburgisches Staatstheater planned to stage *Faust* in 1979, the *Bezirksleitung* asked a committee of academics to assess the theatre's interpretation. The success of this production, and the continuous work of Schroth and his dramaturge Bärbel Jaksch with the *Bezirksleitung* and *Rat des Bezirks*, helped to create a viable working relationship. But the theatre manager Fritz Wendrich argues that this relationship of trust developed only after a four-year-long battle.[85]

In 1982, a Theatre Department report made some revealing comparisons between working practices in the regions. The Department claimed that local state officials' knowledge of theatres and their managements differed significantly due to the quality and turnover of officials responsible for theatre in the *Räte der Bezirke*. The Department praised officials in Dresden, Rostock, Suhl, Magdeburg, and Gera, but criticized activity in Leipzig and Frankfurt/Oder, arguing that officials continually postponed decisions on improvements urgently needed in theatre.[86] Whilst the Theatre Department was broadly positive about theatre administration in Schwerin, it was now more critical of officials in Halle, claiming that they were able to make general comments on managers but were reluctant to make thorough assessments of their

---

[83] 'Rechenschaftsbericht (ENTWURF)', 26.8.1968, LHAS IV/7/242/004.

[84] Irmer and Schmidt, *Die Bühnenrepublik*, 116.

[85] Martin Linzer and others (eds.), *Wo ich bin, ist keine Provinz: Der Regisseur Christoph Schroth* (Berlin: TheaterArbeit, 2003), 79.

[86] 'Information der Abt. Theater an den Minister für Kultur', 12.1.1982, LHASA Abt. MER, RdB Halle 4. Abl. 6656.

professional and artistic abilities.[87] This suggests that although a clear framework and training programme were in place, by the early 1980s they had not succeeded in eradicating unevenness of provision between different *Bezirke*.

Inconsistency and Confusion

Inconsistencies in theatre censorship occurred particularly in the late 1940s and early 1950s, when the apparatus and procedures were first being developed. In 1949, for example, three theatres in Thuringia—Erfurt, Gera, and Meiningen—were planning to stage Goethe's *Egmont*. Several days before the new season started, the Thuringian Education Ministry instructed Erfurt to cancel its staging, due to fears that Goethe's treatment of the Dutch revolt against Spanish occupying forces might incite resentment against Soviet troops stationed in the eastern zone. Although Erfurt's theatre manager disagreed with the Ministry, he complied with its instruction. This news came as a surprise to his counterpart in Gera, Hans-Georg Rudolph, as the Ministry had not objected to his own plans to open the season with *Egmont*. After some discussion, Rudolph agreed to drop his production and use the illness of the lead actress as a pretext.[88] These were precisely the kinds of confusions that the establishment of the Office for Theatre Affairs had been intended to alleviate in 1948.

Although a clear framework for theatre censorship was in place, and indeed in the process of being refined, occasional inconsistencies persisted in the 1960s and 1970s, usually across rather than within regions. The overriding impression, as in Thuringia in 1949, is that theatre managers were prepared to follow official policy but received contradictory instructions and advice. In 1966, Rudi Kostka—Wendrich's predecessor as manager of the Mecklenburgisches Staatstheater—complained of a lack of central coordination of the repertoire:

Es geht nicht an, daß wir monatelang über ein Stück diskutieren, . . . wo man empfiehlt, es lieber nicht zu spielen, und eines Tages spielt es jemand, und dann heißt es: Jetzt ist es möglich, jetzt geht es. Solche Fälle gab es eine ganze Reihe.[89]

---

[87] 'Information der Abt Theater'.
[88] 'Aufführung Goethe *Egmont*', BArch DY 30 IV 2/9.06/186.
[89] 'Abschrift aus dem Protokoll der Zentralvorstandssitzung der Gewerkschaft Kunst am 3.2.1966', BArch DY 30 IV A 2/9.06/118.

It is not acceptable for us to spend months discussing a play . . . and be advised
not to perform it, only for someone else to stage it one day and for us then to be
told: it is possible now, it is OK now. There have been a whole series of cases
like this.

As central guidelines were not always sufficiently clear, theatre practitioners and local functionaries sometimes struggled to interpret or even
second-guess the central authorities' intentions. In 1969, a production
of Hermann Kant's *Die Aula* (The Auditorium) was dropped in Stralsund but was still being performed by twenty-two professional GDR
theatres. An official from Erfurt's SED-*Bezirksleitung* asked if the
cancellation of the Stralsund production was a signal to perform the
play less frequently, let the run peter out, or drop the production
entirely, a question echoed by officials in Neustrelitz.[90] The confusion
returned in 1971, when a negative review of a student production in
Rostock appeared in *Neues Deutschland*, which had previously praised
the dramatization. The publishing house Henschel was promptly in-
undated with queries as to whether productions of *Die Aula* could
continue, and its representative Karl Heinz Schmidt reminded the
Central Committee's Culture Department that a negative review in
Neues Deutschland was bound to have an effect.[91] Schmidt called on
the Culture Department to tell him if the central authorities had
changed their assessment of the play.[92]

Later on in the 1970s, the Repertoire Management and central
training seminars helped to improve communication between central
and local officials. A functionary in Halle recorded Hoffmann's instruction at a meeting in 1978:

Das Stück *Flüsterparty* von Rudi Strahl, das sich mit Problemen der Erziehung
der Jugend beschäftigt, ist *nicht* aufführbar.

Hier wird das Rowdytum dargestellt, ohne den Kampf gegen das Rowdytum
zu führen, und das wird verbunden mit den Intershops. Dieses Stück kann
nicht zur Aufführung kommen, was nicht heißt, daß die anderen Stücke
von Rudi Strahl nicht gezeigt werden. Natürlich darf alles andere von ihm
gespielt werden.[93]

---

[90] 'Information', BArch DY 30 A 2/9.06/116.
[91] Schmidt to Hentschel, 24.11.1969, BArch DY 30 A 2/9.06/116.
[92] Ibid.
[93] 'Vertraulich: Notiz zu politisch-ideologischen Fragen—Darlegungen des Ministers
für Kultur der DDR auf der Dienstberatung am 12.10.1978', LHASA Abt. MER, RdB
Halle 4. Abl. 6628.

The play *Secret Party* by Rudi Strahl, which deals with problems in the upbringing of the young, *cannot* be staged.

It depicts hooliganism without combating hooliganism, and it links the problem to the Intershops. This play cannot be staged, which does not mean that Rudi Strahl's other plays cannot be put on. Of course all his other works can be performed.

These instructions provided the clarity that had been so clearly absent in the cases of *Egmont* and *Die Aula*. Even so, an official from Leipzig's *Rat des Bezirks* mistakenly recorded that Hoffmann had instructed theatres not to stage *Flüchtlingsgespräche* (Conversations among Refugees) by Rudi Strahl.[94] This was unlikely to be a problem, given that *Flüchtlingsgespräche* was by Brecht.

Nimbyism

'Not in my back yard' syndrome may be an Anglo-American term, but it describes an attitude that was alive and well in the GDR's localities. Indeed, Thomas Irmer and Matthias Schmidt see regional First Secretaries as the fiercest guards of theatre and argue that they were responsible for some of the harshest attacks on it.[95] In 1971, Kostka claimed that regional officials had repeatedly told him that the fact that a play had been performed abroad or in other parts of the GDR did not necessarily mean that it could be staged in Schwerin, their area of responsibility.[96] On the record, officials in Schwerin professed their commitment to democratic centralism, saying that they were not following their own line in cultural policy.[97] However, they had little interest in handling the dramatic equivalent of a hot potato. In 1983, Schwerin's Culture Secretary Heide Hinz resisted suggestions from Schroth and Jaksch that Heiner Müller's *Germania Tod in Berlin* (Germania Death in Berlin) should be staged in Schwerin. She told First Secretary Heinz Ziegner that the *Bezirksleitung* had no interest in transferring the 'Müller

[94] 'Im Nachgang zu meiner Information vom 16.10.78 . . .', 20.10.1978, SächsStA-L 20237 25563.
[95] Irmer and Schmidt, *Die Bühnenrepublik*, 113.
[96] 'Information an die Genossen Quandt und Wandt', 10.2.1971, LHAS 10.34-3 2197.
[97] Ibid.

problem' from Berlin to Schwerin.[98] Hinz did not argue that *Germania* should not be staged in the GDR, rather that the Mecklenburgisches Staatstheater was already the focus of unwelcome attention due to its existing productions, including *Faust*.[99] Without support from the *Bezirksleitung*, there was no chance of *Germania* being staged in Schwerin. It was not performed in the GDR until January 1989, at the Berliner Ensemble.

Whilst Irmer and Schmidt attribute such attitudes to the *Bezirksleitungen*, theatre managers were not immune to attacks of Nimbyism. In Leipzig, Kayser informed the *Bezirksleitung* that he had no intention of inviting Ruth Berghaus to stage a production in his theatre:

Wenn schon in der Staatsoper ästhetische und damit ideologische Fragen bei den Inszenierungen eine Rolle spielen, so sehe ich keinen Grund, Ruth Berghaus für Leipzig als Gast zu verpflichten. Wüßte gar nicht, was ich ihr anbieten sollte.[100]

If aesthetic and therefore ideological questions play a role even in productions in the Staatsoper, then I see no reason to engage Ruth Berghaus as a guest in Leipzig. Wouldn't have a clue what to offer her.

Kayser had a point here: Berghaus did not fit the profile of his theatre, which had resisted precisely the kinds of avant-garde experimentation that she had pursued, both as the BE's director-manager from 1971 to 1977 and as an opera director. But the central authorities were not always sympathetic to such considerations, as they were concerned to find employment for the GDR's leading theatre practitioners. Ragwitz alluded to these problems in 1980, when she noted that idiosyncratic decisions in individual regions or theatres were preventing some directors from finding work in the GDR.[101] Ragwitz was not known for her liberal views, but even she subsequently argued that GDR theatres needed to take greater risks, saying that the climate in many regions was not conducive to contemporary drama.[102]

[98] Hinz to Ziegner, 1.2.1983, LHAS 10.34-3 4007.
[99] Ibid.
[100] Kayser to Keller, 21.1.1981, SächsStA-L 21123 2502.
[101] 'Niederschrift über die Information...über die Beratung von Gen. Prof. Kurt Hager mit den Leitungen der Künstlerverbände und der Akademie am 17.11.1980', SächsStA-D 11857 IV D-2/09/02/556.
[102] 'Aktennotiz zu einer Beratung bei Genossin Ursula Ragwitz am 12.1.1983', SächsStA-D 11857 IV E-2/09/02/544.

Contemporary Drama: *Franziska Linkerhand* (1978–1979)

The problems of local officials' uncertainty and aversion to risk converged in the censorship of contemporary East German drama, the most politically sensitive genre in GDR theatre. In 1978, Klaus Pfützner—now First Secretary of the Union of Theatre Practitioners—highlighted the problems facing contemporary drama in the localities:

[Es] entstehen immer wieder Meinungsverschiedenheiten zu Genossen in den politischen Leitungen besonders der Territorien über das Recht und die Pflicht des Theaters, zu wichtigen gesellschaftlichen Problemen . . . Stellung zu nehmen und Widersprüche parteilich und konstruktiv zu benennen, auch dort, wo eine Lösung nicht sofort parat ist. Zum Teil werden solche Meinungsverschiedenheiten durch administrative Eingriffe in die Theaterarbeit beendet, ohne daß die Probleme gründlich geklärt werden.[103]

Differences of opinion keep on arising [between theatre practitioners] and their comrades in the political authorities, particularly in the regions, concerning the right and duty of theatre to take a stand on important social problems . . . and to point out contradictions in a partisan and constructive manner, even in instances where a solution is not immediately to hand. In some cases, administrative interventions in theatre productions are used to put an end to such differences of opinion, without the problems being thoroughly discussed and resolved.

This uncertainty grew as it became more common for dramatists to leave social conflicts unresolved in their plays and to present the GDR as engaged in a longer and more contradictory process of change. In such cases, local officials were sorely tempted to err on the side of caution.

In order to investigate different attitudes towards contemporary drama, I shall examine the reception of a dramatization of Brigitte Reimann's novel *Franziska Linkerhand*. The dramatization was premiered in Schwerin on 21 April 1978 and performed on tour in Leipzig during the First GDR Drama Workshop, which ran from 4 to 8 May. It was subsequently performed in Meiningen during the Seventeenth Workers' Festival, which ran from 30 June to 2 July, and in East Berlin on 15 October. Theatre practitioners in Wittenberg and Halle also considered staging the play. *Franziska Linkerhand* thus offers an opportunity to compare the reactions of theatre practitioners and officials in Schwerin with those of their counterparts elsewhere.

---

[103] 'Text I', sent by Pfützner to Ragwitz, 11.10.1978, BArch DY 30 IV B 2/9.06/70.

Fig. 5.1. *Franziska Linkerhand*: 'the town is the most precious invention of civilization'. Set designed by Lothar Scharsich (Sigrid Meixner, Stiftung Archiv Akademie der Künste)

Brigitte Reimann began writing *Franziska Linkerhand* in 1963, and the unfinished novel was published posthumously in 1974, during the cultural thaw after the Eighth Party Conference. The novel's eponymous heroine, an idealistic young architect, moves to the provinces in order to help construct a new socialist town, 'Neustadt' (Fig. 5.1). Yet as soon as she arrives, her mentor—Schafheutlin—tells her to lower her aspirations.[104] Franziska is merciless in her criticism of Schafheutlin's seemingly mediocre ambitions and the pathology of urban life in Neustadt, where violence and suicide are endemic. But a later temporal strand, narrated in the first and third person, raises the possibility of a synthesis between Franziska's idealism and Schafheutlin's pragmatism. In this strand, we learn that Franziska has left Neustadt but is exploring the idea of returning. Schafheutlin has progress to report: a new department store is being built, work may begin on the town centre in a year or two, and twelve million marks have been granted—or as good as

[104] Brigitte Reimann, *Franziska Linkerhand* (East Berlin: Neues Leben, 1974), 139–40.

granted—for a theatre.[105] Yet when Bärbel Jaksch and Heiner Maaß adapted the novel for performance in Schwerin, they cut the later strand. In their dramatization, Schafheutlin's announcements are made during Franziska's time in Schwerin, and they turn out to be empty promises. Jaksch and Maaß also removed Franziska's provocative judgements from the context in which they had been carefully embedded in the novel, using them as powerful punchlines at the end of certain scenes.

In Schwerin, Christoph Schroth's highly imaginative staging continued this process of radicalization. The production opened with a short, sharp succession of scenes, presenting episodes from Franziska's childhood, youth, and early adulthood. At the end of the sequence, Franziska sat on a chair, with strings attached to her limbs as if she were a marionette. After her tormentors had pulled her in different directions, she crawled forward and reached for a large pair of scissors, threatening to slit her left wrist.[106] The staging thus made explicit what had been toned down in the publication process: in the manuscript of Reimann's novel, the third-person narrator reveals that Franziska offers conflicting explanations for her scarred wrists, yet in the GDR edition, the scars are attributed simply to a teenage accident.[107] In another scene of Schroth's staging, the residents of Neustadt queued up before Franziska, who pulled a plastic sack over each resident's head before pulling one over her own head too (see Fig. 5.2). The suicide motif thus returned in an image of suffocation, linked to the industrial assembly line—itself an indictment of the GDR's unimaginative approach towards town planning. These examples show how Schroth used non-realistic stage sequences to comment on psychological and social processes, heightening the text's visual and emotional impact.

When Schroth's production was premiered in Schwerin, Ministry officials lobbied journalists for support, and the overall response was positive.[108] Christoph Funke called the production extraordinary, exciting, and pugnacious, and he argued that it would significantly

---

[105] Reimann, *Franziska Linkerhand* (East Berlin: Neues Leben, 1974), 505.

[106] Unless otherwise indicated, comments on the staging are based on a video recording of a performance on 23.5.1979, AdK AVM 33.8349.

[107] See Withold Bonner, 'Franziska Linkerhand: Vom Typoskript zur Druckfassung', in Brigitte Reimann, *Franziska Linkerhand*, 6th rev. edn. (Berlin: Aufbau, 2003), 605–31 at 620.

[108] Email from Josef Budek, 21.10.2008.

Fig. 5.2. *Franziska Linkerhand*: life on the conveyor belt (Sigrid Meixner, Stiftung Archiv Akademie der Künste)

advance the debate on the depiction of everyday GDR life on stage.[109] There were hints, though, of the controversy that the production would subsequently unleash: Christine Ullrich complained that the adaptation did not establish enough historical distance from the problems that it depicted, and that it was hard for spectators to view Franziska critically.[110] Ullrich was writing for the *Schweriner Volkszeitung*, the organ of the SED-*Bezirksleitung*, and her views corresponded to doubts that one of its functionaries expressed in an internal report. The functionary warned Schroth and his colleagues not to get carried away by their apparent success. In his view, the fact that the production was to open the Drama Workshop in Leipzig should not lead the ensemble to

[109] Christoph Funke, 'Vom Abenteuer des Sich-Findens', *Der Morgen* (East Berlin), 25.4.1978; cf. Rainer Rossner, '*Franziska Linkerhand* in Schwerin uraufgeführt', *Freie Erde* (Neustrelitz), 26.4.1978.
[110] Christine Ullrich, 'Franziska Linkerhand: Anmerkungen zur Uraufführung des gleichnamigen Stücks am Schweriner Theater', *Schweriner Volkszeitung*, 29.4.1978.

conclude that it was a masterpiece, simply because other theatres had
nothing better to offer.[111]

The reception of the premiere did little to prepare Schroth for the
controversy that his production caused in Leipzig, where it was subjected to the scrutiny of theatre practitioners from across the GDR. The
informer 'Sumatic' submitted a detailed report to the Stasi, claiming
that a leading theatre manager had called the production counter-
revolutionary and that Schwerin's theatre practitioners had been
shunned at the post-show reception—a point that Schroth confirmed
when I interviewed him.[112] The next day, the discussion of the performance lasted for two hours, and the room was packed with nearly a
hundred theatre practitioners, who were sitting on chairs and tables, and
even standing in the aisles.[113] The objections did not differ in content
from those already raised in Schwerin; theatre practitioners criticized
the production's subjective viewpoint, pessimism, and lack of *joie de
vivre*.[114] What had changed was the tenor of the discussion. The
production had sparked a heated debate within the theatre community
about the 'responsibilities' of theatre practitioners when depicting the
GDR on stage.[115]

After the Workshop, representatives of the Ministry and Union of
Theatre Practitioners tried to prevent any public escalation of the
debate. Favourable reviews appeared in *Der Demokrat* and the *Liberal-
demokratische Zeitung*, and Funke defended the production again in *Der
Morgen*.[116] A fortnight after the Workshop, Rainer Kerndl published a
critical review in *Neues Deutschland*, singling out the production for

---

[111] 'Zur Inszenierung von *Franziska Linkerhand* am Meckl. Staatstheater Schwerin
am 21.4.78', LHAS 10.34-3 3472.
[112] BStU BV Bln. XV 2194-71, ii, fo. 277; personal telephone interview with
Christoph Schroth, 1.10.2009.
[113] VdT, *Werkstatt DDR-Schauspiel, Leipzig 4.–8. Mai 1978, 1. Tag*, 4; VdT,
Werkstatt DDR-Schauspiel, Leipzig 4.–8. Mai 1978, 2. Tag, 1. Both in AdK ID 838.
For a photograph of the discussion, see Linzer, *Wo ich bin*, 45.
[114] 'Stenografische Niederschrift des Auswertungsgesprächs des Verbandes der
Theaterschaffenden der DDR zu den Werkstatt-Tagen des DDR-Schauspiels am
8. Mai 1978 in Leipzig', AdK VdT 984.
[115] For further details of the debate and the staging itself, see Laura Bradley,
'Censorship and Opinion Formation: *Franziska Linkerhand* on the GDR Stage', *GLL*
63 (2010), 234–49.
[116] Anon. 'Zwingende theatralische Bilder', *Der Demokrat* (Schwerin), 12.5.1978;
M. Frede, 'Uraufführung nach einem Gegenwartsroman: *Franziska Linkerhand*', *Liber-
al-demokratische Zeitung* (Halle), 11.5.1978; Christoph Funke, 'Tage streitbaren Nach-
denkens', *Der Morgen* (East Berlin), 10.5.1978.

heightened scrutiny. But Kerndl's review was less a denunciation than a balancing act: he said that the production was a courageous undertaking and that many of Schroth's solutions had impressed him. The scheduled performance went ahead in Meiningen without incident. In September, Deputy Culture Minister Klaus Höpcke—who had approved the publication of Reimann's novel—criticized those who had opposed the production in Leipzig, even saying that they had been foaming at the mouth.[117]

Just over a month later, *Franziska Linkerhand* was performed at the Volksbühne during East Berlin's annual theatre festival. Tickets had sold out far in advance, and crowds waited outside the Volksbühne into the interval in the hope of gaining admission.[118] But just five days before the performance, Konrad Naumann had intervened in the debate on contemporary drama. In one section of a longer speech, Naumann had criticized those who thought that the Party had reneged on its ideals and was attempting to construct a consumer society. This was a covert reference to Strahl's *Flüsterparty*, which was built around the fact that scarce goods were available in the Intershops in return for Western currency. Naumann added that contemporary drama should interpret and reflect on reality, filtering it through the writer's artistic and political education and clear class position.[119] Schroth remembers how Naumann vented his fury and indignation during the interval of *Franziska Linkerhand*, and how the festival director frantically disclaimed responsibility for the staging.[120] Afterwards, Josef Budek—a member of the Theatre Department—received a telephone call informing him that a 'castastrophe' had occurred. Kurt Hager and Culture Minister Hans-Joachim Hoffmann had not applauded.[121]

The next morning, the Deputy Culture Minister in charge of theatre was summoned to Hoffmann and, according to Budek, returned subdued. The Deputy Minister reportedly informed a meeting of the fully assembled Theatre Department that, after speaking to Hoffmann, he

[117] 'Bericht vom Chefdramaturgenseminar in Berlin', BArch DY 30 IV B 2/9.06/67.
[118] Fritz Wendrich, 'Im Streit der Meinungen reifer geworden', *Schweriner Volkszeitung*, 17.10.1978; Marianne Eichholz, 'Unberechenbare Frauen: Reimann *Franziska Linkerhand* in Schwerin', *Theater heute*, 19/12 (Dec. 1978), 52.
[119] Anon. 'Revolutionäre Aktivität aus revolutionärer Überzeugung', *Berliner Zeitung*, 10.10.1978. Productions of *Flüsterparty* in East Berlin and Leipzig had been cancelled on 25.9.1978.
[120] Interview with Schroth, 1.10.2009.
[121] Email from Budek, 21.10.2008.

now realized that his earlier opinion of the production had not been properly thought through. Budek says that he interrupted the Deputy Minister, asking him how he could allow himself to be humiliated in this fashion, reminding him that they had always agreed on the production's importance, and saying how pleased they had been at having won back some intellectual freedom. Refusing to retract his positive assessment of the production, Budek announced his resignation and slammed the door shut on his way out. He was subsequently deemed 'unsuitable' for work in any cultural institution, and most of his former friends and colleagues avoided him. Theatre managers who considered employing Budek as a dramaturge were warned off by the Culture Department, his contracts as an author were cancelled, and he was even unable to work in an amusement park.[122]

The reception of *Linkerhand* in Berlin also had reverberations in Schwerin. On the morning after the performance, an official from East Berlin's *Bezirksleitung* rang his counterparts in Schwerin, calling on them to ban the production and punish those responsible.[123] Fritz Wendrich remembers being summoned to the Central Committee and Culture Ministry, along with the member of the *Rat des Bezirks* responsible for culture. According to Wendrich, the Minister for Construction had felt personally offended by the production.[124] As a result of the opposition in East Berlin, Jaksch notes that the production was surreptitiously dropped: it was performed only a few more times and was not included in the programme for the following season.[125] Although Wendrich claims that the run continued for two years, it actually finished on 23 May 1979, little over a year after its premiere.[126]

Plans were meanwhile under way to stage the play at the Elbe-Elster-Theater in Wittenberg, which belonged to the Halle region. Werner Süß, the member of the *Rat des Bezirks* responsible for culture, decided that the planned production was not unproblematic. In the run-up to a meeting held in September, he argued that the Schwerin adaptation was a positive experiment, but one that was ideologically flawed, as it failed to locate the action in a particular historical phase of the GDR's development.[127] These comments suggest an awareness of the criticisms

[122] Email from Budek, 21.10.2008.   [123] Linzer, *Wo ich bin*, 45.
[124] Ibid. 77.   [125] Ibid. 45.
[126] Ibid. 77. I am grateful to Ilka Hermann (Mecklenburgisches Staatstheater) for providing the final performance date.
[127] 'Einschätzung der endgültigen Spielpläne der Theater des Bezirks', LHASA Abt. MER, RdB Halle 4. Abl. 6629.

made in Kerndl's review. Süß instructed officials in Wittenberg to check the plans thoroughly and establish which version should be used, or who should produce a new script.[128] In November, the manager of the Landestheater Halle rejected his dramaturges' suggestion that they should stage *Franziska Linkerhand*, instructing them to replace it and another unnamed play with texts by Jewgeni Schwarz and Rudi Strahl.[129] Plans for the Wittenberg production were finally abandoned at the start of February 1979, officially due to problems with casting.[130]

Whilst these events reveal differences between the decisions made in Schwerin and other parts of the GDR, these differences were closely related to changes in the central policy on contemporary drama. In September 1978, when Süß was considering whether to allow *Linkerhand* in Wittenberg, the Ministry's representatives were still defending the production. But by mid-October, advocates of a more conservative line had won, and Hoffmann imposed the new line on Ministry officials, with his deputy's support. In January 1979, Hoffmann informed Modrow of the change in policy:

Es ist bekannt, daß die Aufführung *Linkerhand* [in] Schwerin ausläuft [und] daß die *Flüsterparty* untersagt wurde . . .
Das Ministerium für Kultur setzt diese Linie nicht fort.[131]

As you know, the performance run of *Linkerhand* in Schwerin is coming to an end [and] *Secret Party* has been forbidden . . .
The Culture Ministry will not be continuing this line.

The production's reception in East Berlin acted as a catalyst for its demise in Schwerin, strengthening and legitimizing the doubts that the *Bezirksleitung* had always harboured. When the manager of the Landestheater Halle decided not to stage the play, he was acting in full knowledge of the controversy that it had provoked in Leipzig and East Berlin. Given Hoffmann's comments, it is likely that casting issues were not the only reason for the abandonment of plans to stage *Linkerhand* in Wittenberg. Officials in Schwerin did stop short of the intervention demanded by East Berlin's *Bezirksleitung*, as they allowed performances

---

[128] Ibid.
[129] 'Information über ein Gespräch mit Gen. Schröder, Intendant LTH Halle, am 9.11.1978', LHASA Abt. MER 4. Abl. 6629.
[130] 'Information über die Aufführung *Jutta oder Die Kinder von Damutz*', 15.5.1979, BArch DY 30 IV B 2/9.06/70.
[131] 'Streng vertraulich!'

to continue until the end of the season, but they were not actively and intentionally pursuing a more liberal line than their colleagues in Wittenberg and Halle. The Schwerin production had fitted into a window in theatre policy that was closed soon after the premiere.

4. PRESCRIBED BOUNDARIES

There were clear limits to local room for manoeuvre: no local official could secure a performance of a play if the Central Committee or Culture Ministry completely opposed it. The Ministry used meetings with local officials to issue directives concerning new contemporary dramas that were not to be performed. This move towards greater central direction, matched by the insistence that the Ministry should approve the premieres of new plays, went some way towards countering the uncertainty that Kostka had complained of in the 1960s. There is no indication that officials resisted central directives, or that they wanted to overstep these boundaries. The limits of local room for manoeuvre are exemplified by discussions of plans to stage *Die Parteibraut* (The Party Bride) by Jürgen Groß at Dresden's Staatsschauspiel.

If anything, it seems surprising that Dresden's officials even entertained the idea of staging *Die Parteibraut*, as it was based on Volker Braun's *Unvollendete Geschichte* (Unfinished Story). This had been published in *Sinn und Form* in 1975 but was not released for wider circulation until 1988. Like Braun's text, Groß's adaptation depicts a love affair between two young people, Frank and Karin, which is almost ruined by the suspicions of a paranoid state and Party. These suspicions are based solely on the fact that Frank has received a letter from a friend who had escaped to the West, not on any actual criminal behaviour on his part. The extreme pressure causes the relationship briefly to break up, and Frank makes a failed suicide attempt. When Karin becomes pregnant, Braun contrasts the warmth and understanding she receives from Frank's supposedly dysfunctional family with the rejection she experiences from her own parents, model SED members, and with the domestic violence that her sister suffers in her marriage. The text traces Karin's journey from unquestioning obedience to self-knowledge and self-assertion, ending on a note of fragile optimism as she accompanies Frank out of hospital. These were extremely sensitive issues in the GDR, and so Hans Modrow sent a copy of *Die Parteibraut* to Ragwitz in July

1978, seeking her advice.[132] The Culture Department rejected the script, and officials in Dresden informed the Staatsschauspiel that the current version could not be staged.[133]

By November, Groß had revised the script, and local officials expressed the opinion that it could be performed if further changes were made.[134] But when they finally asked the Culture Ministry to confirm the plans for the production, Hoffmann took a different view. He became personally involved in the case and travelled to Dresden with his deputy Werner Rackwitz to discuss the text with the *Bezirksleitung*— a sign of the importance accorded to the staging. Hoffmann was critical of the theatre for publicizing the production before sending the material to the Ministry; he warned that this approach was inadmissible and could only be interpreted as an attempt to exert pressure on the state authorities.[135] The Minister was clearly concerned that theatre practitioners in Dresden were trying to exploit the regime's desire to avoid censorship becoming public. If this was their strategy, it failed. The report of the discussions stated:

Es wurde Übereinstimmung darüber festgestellt, daß dieses Stück in der vorgelegten Fassung unter keinen Umständen zur Aufführung gelangen darf. Die politischen Einwände sind so prinzipiell, daß eine 'Reparatur' nicht gegeben ist.[136]

It was agreed that this play can under no circumstances be performed in the version submitted. The political objections are so fundamental that the play cannot be 'repaired'.

It was agreed that Rackwitz would talk to Schönemann, who had planned to direct the play, that the *Bezirksleitung* would talk to the theatre manager Fred Larondelle and also to the *Rat der Stadt* and *Rat des Bezirks*, and that there would be further talks with Groß and Dresden's head dramaturge.[137] It is worth noting that Hoffmann worked through the *Bezirksleitung*, rather than the *Rat des Bezirks*, on this case. This suggests not only that the *Rat des Bezirks* was the junior

---

[132] 'Chronologie der Gespräche und Absprachen . . . zur Vorbereitung einer Inszenierung am Staatsschauspiel Dresden', 19.2.1979, SächsStA-D 11857 IV D-2/09/02/575.
[133] Ibid.
[134] Ibid.
[135] 'Protokoll der Beratung mit der Bezirksleitung der SED Dresden am 18.1.1979', SächsStA-D 11857 IV D-2/09/02/556.
[136] Ibid.
[137] 'Ergebnis-Protokoll der Arbeitsberatung in der Bezirksleitung der SED Dresden am 18. Januar 1979', SächsStA-D 11857 IV D-2/09/02/556.

partner in theatre censorship, but also that the Central Committee delegated supervision of the *Bezirksleitung* to the Culture Minister in this instance. For his part, Hoffmann made it clear that the text allowed no room for negotiation, saying that the current version could not be staged, even by the best director in the GDR. In the unlikely event that any doubt remained, he added that it was the worst thing that had hitherto been presented to the Ministry.[138]

5. CONCLUSION

During the 1970s, the Culture Ministry refined the bureaucratic procedures for censorship and provided for regular contact with key officials, managers, and dramaturges. The creation of the Repertoire Management may not have been universally welcomed, but it guaranteed regular central involvement in, and supervision of, discussions concerning theatre programmes. It thus helped to relieve the pressure on the overburdened Theatre Department. The Ministry and Central Committee continued to set the limits of what would be tolerated in contemporary drama; they were involved in major decisions on new plays and potentially controversial high-profile projects. Most local authorities welcomed the reassurance of central approval and checked decisions when they were unsure, at least in the 1960s and 1970s. When Perten did challenge central supervision of his theatre, this was because he regarded it as an unnecessary interference, given his political track record. Variations in decision-making occurred when the parameters of official tolerance were contested centrally, and inconsistencies usually arose when the central guidelines were insufficiently clear.

In the 1960s and 1970s, regional variations in decision-making were often caused by the reluctance of local officials and theatre practitioners to move freely within the parameters set by the central authorities, rather than by attempts to overstep these parameters. When Naumann opposed productions of critical contemporary drama, he was arguing for tighter controls than those imposed by the Ministry. The Repertoire Management explicitly praised Perten for his willingness to take on risky texts that were close to the boundaries of what was tolerated, and at the 1978 Workshop in Leipzig, Schönemann expressed his concern that

---

[138] 'Streng vertraulich!'

precisely those theatres that were committed to the risky business of staging contemporary drama would leave worried.[139] Tolerance of risk could vary from one case to the next, even in local officials' treatment of the same theatre: in Schwerin, officials reluctantly backed *Franziska Linkerhand* in 1978, yet Hinz lobbied against Schroth's plans to stage *Germania* in 1983. Conversely, a First Secretary of a *Bezirksleitung* had the power to choose to take risks, provided the central authorities sanctioned them. In Dresden, Modrow agreed to take on Schönemann, despite the health warning that Hoffmann had attached to his support for the director. These kinds of decisions are where the boundaries between censorship and theatre management are fluid. In the reunified Germany, theatres develop their own profiles and reject plays that other companies stage. But in the GDR, artistic considerations intersected with political and ideological concerns, and with the authorities' real or perceived expectations.

In fact, the late 1960s and particularly the 1970s saw far more variety in theatres and their profiles than in decisions about productions that had already been accepted into the repertoire. Theatres emerged with distinct profiles in the regions; Leipzig and Rostock developed reputations as theatres that premiered new drama, and Schroth won acclaim for his concept of popular theatre in Schwerin. In the 1970s, the Theatre Department encouraged local authorities to develop theatrical concepts that worked for their specific audiences and to see variety as a sign of vitality. In 1982, an official in Dresden argued that theatre lived from the fact that *Faust* in Schwerin was different from *Faust* in Leipzig, or from the *Faust* that Dresden had seen in the 1920s.[140] This contrasted with the attempts to impose Stanislavskian acting techniques in the early 1950s and to enforce the *Bitterfelder Weg* and a standardized model of Socialist Realism in the 1950s and early 1960s. As both officials and theatre practitioners reacted against the idea of a homogeneous theatre, variations in the repertoire, stage interpretations, and performance aesthetics multiplied.

We also see significant regional variations in the ways in which theatre censorship was practised in the 1960s and 1970s, even though officials operated within the same regulatory framework. These differences related primarily to interpersonal factors, provision, and expertise.

---

[139] 'Stenografische Niederschrift des Auswertungsgesprächs', 51.
[140] 'Diskussionsbeitrag Gen. Forker zur Konzeption Staatstheater', 12.3.1982, SächsStA-D 11857 IV E-2/09/02/572.

Whilst the Ministry made considerable efforts to professionalize theatre censorship, provision across the GDR was still uneven. The city of Dresden was better staffed than Leipzig at the end of the 1970s, and some officials—particularly in the districts—were reluctant to pronounce opinions on productions. In some cases, regional officials had little input into theatres' production concepts and repertoires, particularly if premieres of new contemporary plays were not involved. Working relationships also varied according to theatre managers and directors: Perten resented central state interference, whilst Kayser effectively sidestepped local officials in Leipzig. So whilst there was a strong bureaucratic framework that pointed towards the centre, it was personalized by the officials and theatre practitioners who operated within it.

Theatre censorship may, of necessity, have been devolved to local authorities, but the centre always had the final say, if it so chose. Compared to the Central Committee, the Culture Ministry was potentially the weaker central partner, but it was far more heavily involved in the business of theatre censorship. Some local officials and theatre practitioners operated according to stricter criteria than the Ministry, preferring to steer clear of experimental work. Their attitudes already point to the source of the regional variations that theatre practitioners would complain of in the late 1980s, during the power struggles over Gorbachev's policies of glasnost and perestroika. It was then that the parameters of central policy and the very existence of censorship were being questioned, and groups within the regional and central authorities responded differently to these challenges. During this period, the zone of contention encompassed far more than just new contemporary drama.

6

Schwerin and Anklam in the Early 1980s: Cooperation and Conflict

1. INTRODUCTION

In the 1980s, central cultural policy was characterized not by new public initiatives, but by their absence. There was no equivalent of Ulbricht's programmatic speeches on the *Bitterfelder Weg*, the denunciation of plays and films at the Eleventh Plenary Session, or Honecker's promises of 'no taboos'. Whilst Honecker and Hager continued to address cultural matters in their speeches, they did so through the old familiar clichés, usually without targeting individual artists or works. When the FDJ leadership started a campaign against the Volksbühne's production of Müller's *Macbeth* in 1982, other sections of the administration did not join in the chorus of disapproval. The central authorities were proceeding case by case, relying increasingly on the Stasi to monitor and influence cultural developments, in an attempt to avoid a repeat of the damaging protests of 1976 and 1979.[1] Whilst the overall room for manoeuvre had narrowed, the reduction in central orientation meant that local circumstances had become more important than ever before.

This chapter examines synchronic differences in censorship, focusing on productions whose premieres were scheduled for April 1984 in neighbouring rural regions, Schwerin and Neubrandenburg. When Christoph Schroth staged Schiller's *Demetrius* and Volker Braun's *Dmitri* in Schwerin, pre-performance censorship functioned broadly as intended. The premiere and ensuing performances passed without incident, surprising some experts. In Anklam, however, Frank Castorf became embroiled in a bitter and protracted conflict with local officials, who were seeking his removal. His staging of Brecht's *Trommeln in der*

---

[1] See Jäger, *Kultur und Politik*, 163–208.

Nacht (Drums in the Night) was banned before its premiere, even though representatives of the Union of Theatre Practitioners had raised no objections at the run-through. My investigation focuses on the working relationships between theatre practitioners and officials, and between the central and local authorities. The intention is not to reinstate a false binary division between loyal and oppositional artists, but to probe the sources, nature, and extent of cooperation and conflict in these contrasting examples of censorship.

There are significant differences between the directors, theatres, and plays involved in these case studies, and they affected the censorship process. Whilst Schroth was committed to practising explicitly political theatre, political considerations were not central to Castorf's work. As Castorf explains, it was his total rejection of the principle of fidelity to the original work that led him to be perceived as politically subversive in the GDR.[2] Schroth and Castorf occupied significantly different positions within the GDR's cultural field in 1984. Schroth had established himself as a leading director, whose work was recognized internationally. He was working with one of the GDR's most celebrated writers, Volker Braun, and the central authorities had a keen interest in securing a 'safe' GDR premiere of *Dmitri*, which had previously been staged only in Karlsruhe, in the Federal Republic. In contrast, Castorf was in the early stages of his career and was just beginning to make his mark on the East German theatre scene. As *Trommeln in der Nacht* had received its belated GDR premiere two years earlier, Castorf's production commanded less attention from the central authorities than *Dmitri*. But the key difference concerns the way in which Schroth and Castorf operated within the system: how far they were willing and able to negotiate with officials, and whether a basis for negotiation was even present.

This chapter investigates both productions in their broader context, but the balance between contextual and performance analysis differs in each case. As the censorship process in Schwerin focused on specific aspects of Braun's text and Schroth's staging, my case study includes some close analysis of the production concept and its theatrical realization. In Anklam, officials never engaged in any serious discussion of *Trommeln in der Nacht*, even though the play's hero turns his back on the Spartacist uprising—a point that had caused Brecht considerable

---

[2] Hans-Dieter Schütt, *Die Erotik des Verrats: Gespräche mit Frank Castorf* (Berlin: Dietz, 1996), 118.

embarrassment in the 1950s.[3] We can only understand the production ban as a culmination of the long-standing differences that local officials had with Castorf and his theatrical aesthetic. Accordingly, my case study investigates these differences as they developed between 1982 and 1984.

2. *DEMETRIUS* AND *DMITRI* IN SCHWERIN

Strategic Concessions and Repressive Patronage

Studies of theatre censorship usually focus on controversial or banned stagings, but censorship was designed to avoid or at least suppress conflict, and the vast majority of GDR productions survived a full performance run. This was certainly the case when Schroth staged Schiller's *Demetrius* and Volker Braun's *Dmitri* in Schwerin, even though officials had seen the twin staging as a high-risk project. This section examines how the pre-performance controls worked, how and how far they influenced the staging, and what the political and theatrical implications were of performing Braun's play alongside Schiller's. It offers an opportunity to revisit working relationships in Schwerin, six years after the controversy over *Franziska Linkerhand*.

Whilst the emphasis in this case is on cooperation, it is important to stress the difficulties that Volker Braun faced in the GDR. He was subjected to intense surveillance from the Stasi, which opened the OV 'Erbe' (Heritage) against him in 1975. Officers collected 3,285 pages of reports in eleven files before closing the investigation in December 1983, and they continued to collect information on Braun in the ensuing years.[4] He faced long delays in securing the publication and performance of his works, waiting ten years for a production of his first play *Kipper Paul Bauch* (Digger Paul Bauch) and eighteen for a staging of *Lenins Tod* (Lenin's Death). Four months after the premiere of *Dmitri*, Braun complained that none of his works seemed publishable, not even his poetry. It was an unbearable contradiction, he explained, supporting and representing a cultural policy that he regarded as important, while being treated as a thorn in its side.[5]

---

[3] See Bertolt Brecht, 'Bei Durchsicht meiner ersten Stücke', *BFA*, xxiii (1993), 239–45.
[4] BStU AOP 15582/83.
[5] Volker Braun, '21., 22. August 1984', in *Verheerende Folgen mangelnden Anscheins innerbetrieblicher Demokratie* (Leipzig: Reclam, 1988), 124–34 at 126–7.

Strategic concessions were an integral part of leading cultural officials' method of dealing with Braun, as they sought to counter both his
sense of alienation and Western claims that he was an oppositional
writer. In their view, these concessions were worthwhile because Braun
had established himself as one of the GDR's leading literary figures. So
officials offset production bans with offers of support. When a planned
production of *Dmitri* was banned at the BE in 1982, Karl-Heinz
Hafranke from the Central Committee's Culture Department reportedly promised to help Braun overcome the difficulties that might arise if
a theatre wanted to stage one of his plays.[6] When the election of Braun
and Müller to the Academy of Arts was being discussed in 1982, a Stasi
officer noted that this would serve the Stasi's political and operational
goals, as it would enable other members of the Academy to engage with
both writers, influence them, and allow them to vent their frustrations.[7]
Such concessions amounted to a form of repressive patronage: they
served the goals of containment and surveillance, and they were accompanied by obstruction and restriction.

The Mecklenburgisches Staatstheater, Schwerin

Schwerin was the former seat of the Duchy of Mecklenburg, and in the
GDR it was the capital of a predominantly agricultural region. In
addition to drama, the Mecklenburgisches Staatstheater staged opera,
ballet, marionette theatre, concerts, and performances in Low German
dialect. Whilst the company was classed as a Category B theatre, i.e. of
national but not international significance, its size and variety gave it the
potential for development at a time when the GDR's economic planners
intended to transform Schwerin into an 'agrarian-industrial' region.
This was to be achieved partly through an influx of skilled workers
and members of the technical intelligentsia. Between 1971 and 1983,
the number of inhabitants rose by 27,000, the numbers employed in
food processing and the manufacturing industries rose to 66,000, and the
average age of residents fell to 34.[8] In theory, these demographic changes

---

[6] BStU AOP 15582/83, v, fo. 299.
[7] Ibid. 327. The report is dated 13.10.1982, approximately six months before
Honecker agreed that Braun and Müller could become members of the Academy.
[8] Renate Ullrich, *Schweriner Entdeckungen: Ein Theater im Gespräch* (East Berlin:
Dietz, 1986), 22.

increased Schwerin's capacity to support innovative and challenging theatre.

When Christoph Schroth moved to Schwerin in 1974, he already had fourteen years' experience in professional theatre. He had worked at the Maxim Gorki Theater from 1960 to 1965, assisted on Besson's production of *Moritz Tassow* at the Volksbühne, and directed in Halle alongside Schönemann from 1966 to 1971, before returning to the Volksbühne to work with Besson, Karge, and Langhoff. Two of Schroth's own productions were banned in Halle, and he initially struggled with the ensemble and the authorities in Schwerin. Matters came to a head in 1975, when Schroth's attempt to classify actors according to their abilities provoked protests and several stagings had to be dropped because of falling audience numbers.[9] Local officials blamed Schroth for not taking action sooner against Jürgen Gosch, and the incoming manager initially refused to work with Schroth.[10]

Schroth's response to these challenges pointed to his long-term strategy of working within the Party and its institutions. By creating the *Parteigruppe Schauspiel*, a group of Party members directly involved in staging drama, he gave himself and his colleagues a political voice within the company.[11] But in the short term, it was a high-risk theatrical project that won him the ensemble's respect. Schroth proposed an ambitious programme of *Entdeckungen* (Discoveries), modelled on theatre festivals in Halle and at the Volksbühne. The theatre staged nine productions on one evening, allowing spectators to choose between parallel stagings in different parts of the building.[12] The event was designed to attract new spectators, to involve them in the theatrical process, and make them feel at home in the theatre. Food, music, and even a disco were available, and those who lasted until the next morning were rewarded with breakfast. The challenge of mounting such an ambitious programme mobilized the company, allaying some actors' fears of being sidelined. The event's success proved that contemporary socialist theatre could work as popular entertainment in Schwerin.

---

[9] Ibid. 154; 'Information über die gegenwärtige Situation am Mecklenburgischen Staatstheater', 8.4.1976, LHAS 10.34-3 2809.

[10] 'Information', 8.4.1976; Wendrich to Schroth, 26.3.1976, LHAS 10.34-3 2809.

[11] Jens P. Rosbach and Stefan Baerens, 'dafür, daß sich die menschen mehr suchen: gespräch mit christoph schroth', in Jens P. Rosbach and Stefan Baerens (eds.), *Das Land. Die Zeit. Der Mensch. Gespräche in Mecklenburg und Vorpommern* (Rostock: Norddeutscher Hochschulschriftenverlag, 1995), 53–71 at 55–6.

[12] Ullrich, *Schweriner Entdeckungen*, 56.

Schroth's key theatrical partner was the dramaturge Bärbel Jaksch, who also joined the Mecklenburgisches Staatstheater in 1974 and worked with Schroth until 1992. She seems to have functioned partly as a political guarantor, at least until the mid-1980s. After a series of contact meetings with the Stasi, Jaksch reportedly agreed on 13 June 1975 to serve as an informer under the codename 'Jutta'.[13] The file contains reports of a further forty-four meetings, plus over two hundred and fifty reports that Stasi officers produced using information that they said 'Jutta' had provided at these meetings.[14] 'Jutta' ceased her collaboration in December 1983 after being elected the theatre's Party Secretary and becoming a candidate for membership of the *Bezirksleitung*.[15] Although the break in her activity was deemed temporary, there is no evidence that she subsequently resumed her collaboration. The files suggest that she was motivated primarily by political conviction and the desire to have a discussion partner outside the theatre, at a time when the *Bezirksleitung* was not sympathetic to Schroth's aims.[16]

It took Schroth time to establish a political track record with the regional authorities and to win their support. In 1979, the success of *Faust* marked a turning point: the production attracted spectators from far afield, enhancing the profile of the theatre and its region, and rewarding the *Bezirksleitung* for taking a calculated risk. *Faust* was still sold out at the eighty-fifth performance in November 1985,[17] and this success strengthened Schroth's negotiating position and established the basis for cooperation with the authorities. But some differences and mutual suspicions remained; as late as 1983, 'Jutta' questioned whether officials in Schwerin actually wanted Schroth's form of theatre, or whether the rise in the profile of drama had been accidental.[18] Despite its public image of success, the Staatstheater faced management difficulties after the departure of Fritz Wendrich. In November 1983, Schroth reportedly claimed that the theatre had never been in such a wretched state and that there was no longer any discipline. He is said to

---

[13] BStU BV Schwerin AIM 364/84, i, fos. 31, 33, 44–6. The report of Jaksch's recruitment states that officers did not require her to declare in writing that she would work for the Stasi, in order not to push her too far (fo. 46). Officers intended to require her to sign a declaration later (fo. 46), but the file does not contain one.

[14] BStU BV Schwerin AIM 364/84, ii.

[15] BStU BV Schwerin AIM 364/84, i, fos. 154–5.

[16] Ibid. 151; BStU BV Schwerin AIM 364/84, ii.i, fo. 119.

[17] Report dated 14.2.1986, LHAS 7.11-1 Z36/1993 1.

[18] BStU BV Schwerin AIM 364/84, ii.i, fo. 483–4.

have given the acting manager two months to turn matters around; the implication was that he might otherwise leave.[19]

Demetrius and *Dmitri*: the Plot

Demetrius and *Dmitri* are based on the same historical events. Demetrius, the heir to the Russian throne, was reported killed in 1591. But rumours of his survival spread, and in 1603 a pretender emerged in Poland. He gathered military support from the Polish nobility, invaded Moscow, and took power in 1605. Both Schiller and Braun present Demetrius/Dmitri as an unwitting impostor, who discovers on the eve of his coronation that he has no hereditary claim to the throne. Ironically, this is the moment when he begins to conform to the despotic model associated with the Tsar he thought was his father: Ivan the Terrible. Demetrius abandons his planned reforms and rules through terror. His support base crumbles and he is assassinated, whereupon a new pretender emerges.

Demetrius was Schiller's last play and is far from complete. He drafted two acts in 1804–5 and left notes for a further three. In 1980, Braun drew extensively on this material while introducing a clear Marxist perspective, showing that Dmitri's reforms, including the liberation of Russia's serfs, could never be achieved through the existing feudal power structures. There are important dramaturgical differences between the texts: Braun abandoned Schiller's planned five acts in favour of an open structure with multiple historical layers. In one interlude, three Bolsheviks survey the historical action and reflect on the challenges they face in setting up a socialist state.[20] Another interlude provides a metatheatrical commentary: a speaker analyses the reactions of an imaginary audience in the future, reminding us of the play's real-life audience.[21] So a key question was whether a production would separate out Braun's historical and theatrical layers: whether it would present 1917 as a caesura and suggest that there were fundamental differences between the nature of power under Tsarism and socialism, or whether it would allow the layers to resonate with each other, so that spectators

[19] Report dated 17.11.1983, LHAS BPA IV/7/242/007.

[20] Volker Braun, *Texte in zeitlicher Folge*, 10 vols. (Halle and Leipzig: Mitteldeutscher Verlag, 1990–3), vi (1991), 184–7.

[21] Ibid. 206–10.

might draw parallels between Tsarist rule in Russia and the democratic deficit in the GDR and USSR, or question how much had been achieved since 1917. The authorities' initial fear was that spectators would compare the antagonism between Russia and Poland in the seventeenth century with recent tensions over the Solidarity movement in Poland. This was the principal reason why the BE had had to abandon its production in 1982, just one year after Jaruzelski had imposed martial law in Poland, with Soviet support.

Forging an Alliance

New plays needed strong backers in the GDR, and this was particularly true of those by politically challenging writers. The cooperation of six sets of people was crucial in securing the premiere of *Dmitri* in Schwerin, and it is difficult to see how the production could have gone ahead if even one group had withdrawn its support. Schroth and Jaksch had initially responded critically to *Dmitri* in a conversation about the planned BE production. According to Braun, Schroth had said that the play presented an oppressive portrait of a world that could not be mastered; staging it would amount to a slap in the face to his own work as a director.[22] Despite their initial misgivings, Schroth and Jaksch lobbied in 1983 for permission to stage *Dmitri* in Schwerin. Hoffmann noted their argument that the production would follow on from Schroth's 1978 staging of Pushkin's *Boris Godunow*, which dealt with the same historical material.[23] Schroth assured officials that he was aware of the responsibility involved in staging *Dmitri* and would proceed in consultation with the *Bezirksleitung* and researchers at the Academy of Social Sciences.[24]

Schroth and Jaksch would have got nowhere without the support of local Party officials. Culture Secretary Heide Hinz was proud of the theatre's success under Schroth and was concerned that Schwerin might now be too small for him. Fearing that Schroth wanted to move to Leipzig, she believed that she needed to take calculated risks to keep him

---

[22] Quoted in Renate Ullrich, 'Demetrius und Dmitri', in *Mecklenburgisches Staatstheater Schwerin: Demetrius/Dmitri*, ed. Martin Linzer, Theaterarbeit in der DDR, 10 (East Berlin: VdT, 1985), 155–62 at 156.
[23] Hoffmann to Hager, 23.11.1983, LHAS 10.34-3 4007.
[24] 'Demetrius-Dmitri-Projekt', LHAS 10.34-3 4007.

in Schwerin and maintain the theatre's reputation.[25] But she was only prepared to take these risks because Kurt Hager and officials in the Ministry and Central Committee's Culture Department shared the responsibility, participating in preparations for the production.

The final partner was Volker Braun, who noted that Schroth and Jaksch had been visibly reassured by his protests against their initial reactions to *Dmitri*.[26] Braun lobbied Hoffmann for permission to stage the play, telling him:

Wir haben nicht zu bitten, wenn es um die Rechte der Künstler geht; ich fordere Sie auf, verehrter Genosse Minister, uns die Möglichkeit zur künstlerischen Arbeit zu geben.[27]

We are under no obligation to make polite requests, not when the rights of artists are at stake. I call on you, esteemed Comrade Minister, to give us the opportunity to carry out our artistic work.

Braun's opening statement was forceful, even if it was mitigated by the respectful address that followed. Just as Hinz wanted to keep Schroth on board, the Minister was keen to offset Braun's earlier disappointments over production and publication bans. He wrote to Hager, reminding him that Braun had accepted the cancellation of the BE's production, but that it had impeded his work and damaged his relationship with the theatre and the authorities.[28] Hoffmann advised Hager to let work on *Dmitri* proceed—a sign that Hager had the final say, even though Hoffmann was officially responsible for approving GDR premieres. All would now depend on Hager's reaction.

Censorship Negotiations

The main censorship discussions took place before rehearsals started: officials highlighted problems in the text and discussed the proposed staging. Hinz raised her concerns with Schroth and Jaksch on 21 November 1983, and her deputy, Hans-Jürgen Audehm, assessed the play on 15 December. Jaksch delivered the team's production concept

[25] Hinz to Hager, 1.12.1983, LHAS 10.34-3 4007; 'Aktennotiz über ein Gespräch mit Genossen Christoph Schroth... am 27. Oktober 1981', BArch DY 30/vorl. SED 32803.
[26] Volker Braun, 'Notate zu *Dmitri* (2)', in *Mecklenburgisches Staatstheater Schwerin: Demetrius/Dmitri*, ed. Martin Linzer, 52–5 at 53.
[27] Braun to Hoffmann, 2.10.1983, LHAS 10.34-3 4007.
[28] Hoffmann to Hager, 23.11.1983.

to the Ministry on 28 December and asked Hinz to check the text before it was forwarded to Hager—another indication that his verdict would be decisive. The director's script contains four pages of notes in Schroth's handwriting, headed with the name 'Hager' and a colon.[29] When I interviewed him, Schroth confirmed that he had made these notes during a meeting with Hager in Berlin.[30] The phrasing, arguments, and structure of Schroth's notes correspond to more detailed, undated documents in the Landeshauptarchiv Schwerin, which also record Schroth's interjections during the meeting.[31]

The production concept was designed to allay the authorities' concerns about the play's topical relevance and the risk that it might—as Audehm put it—turn Schwerin into a 'pilgrimage site' for advocates of democratic socialism.[32] Schroth and Jaksch presented themselves as Braun's strongest critics, citing their initial rejection of his play. But they attributed this reaction partly to misunderstandings, implying that some of the authorities' doubts were similarly unwarranted, and they claimed that Braun had agreed to changes that would clarify the play's political thrust. After stressing their critical distance towards Braun, Schroth and Jaksch explained that their staging would foreground the historical distance between the action and the present. *Dmitri* would now start with a scene in which modern-day spectators looked down on the historical action, so that what Braun had envisaged as a metatheatrical interlude within *Dmitri* would now function as a hinge between the two plays. Schroth and Jaksch argued that this change, together with their presentation of 1917 as a caesura, would prevent the play from functioning as a parable. Instead, the historical action would form a productive contrast to the socialist present, in which spectators were in the process of breaking the vicious circle shown in the play. Accordingly, the actors would retain a critical distance towards their roles.[33]

It was only after this sustained attempt at reassurance that Schroth and Jaksch tested out the scope for a critical evaluation of socialist government. Here too, they began by indicating their distance from Braun's text: they admitted that they had initially considered cutting the

---

[29] Regiebuch (Dmitri), [n.p.], AdK CSA 23.
[30] Interview with Schroth, 1.10.2009.
[31] 'Demetrius-Dmitri-Projekt'.
[32] 'Gedanken zum Stück *Dmitri* von Volker Braun', LHAS 10.34-3 4007.
[33] 'Thesen zu einem Theater-Abend', LHAS 10.34-3 4007.

Schwerin and Anklam in the Early 1980s   203

Bolshevik scene, in which the third Bolshevik warns about the danger of a gulf opening up between the Party and the masses:

(Sehr leise) ABER WENN, SCHREIE ICH, WENN DIE MASSEN SICH VON DEN SPITZEN ENTFERNEN, WENN SICH EIN ABSTAND, EINE KLUFT AUFTUT, WENN DIE MASSE SICH ERREGT, WENN SIE DENKT, KRITISIERT, WENN SIE HARTNÄCKIG GEGEN IHRE GELIEBTEN FÜHRER STIMMT, DANN WIRD ES ERNST. DANN IST ES AUFGABE DER PARTEI, SICH ERNSTHAFT IN DIE FRAGE HINEINZUDENKEN, WAS DIE MASSE WILL![34]

(Very quietly) BUT IF, I SCREAM, IF THE MASSES MOVE AWAY FROM THOSE AT THE TOP, IF A DISTANCE—AN ABYSS—OPENS UP, IF THE MASSES GROW AGITATED, IF THEY THINK, CRITICIZE, IF THEY PERSISTENTLY VOTE AGAINST THEIR BELOVED LEADERS, THEN MATTERS WILL BECOME SERIOUS. THEN IT IS THE PARTY'S DUTY TO THINK SERIOUSLY ABOUT WHAT THE MASSES WANT!

This was controversial stuff: a quotation from Alexandra Kollontai, one of the leaders of the Workers' Opposition in post-revolutionary Russia and an early critic of undemocratic tendencies in Leninism.[35] Schroth and Jaksch argued that they now viewed the Bolshevik scene as essential, as events in Poland had demonstrated the need to renew socialist democracy. They proceeded to spell out the dangers that Braun saw in socialist government, such as careerism, a lack of independent thinking amongst officials, and a separation of the leaders and the masses. Schroth and Jaksch explained that they accepted Braun's views, provided the production did not make any cheap, anachronistic analogies.[36] This section employed the same rhetorical strategy as the overall production concept, progressing from an initial rejection of Braun's text to cautious, critical support.

Schroth and Jaksch had done enough to convince Audehm that they were acting responsibly. He told Hinz that they were not trying to stage the play in opposition to socialism or its functionaries, citing their critical distance as evidence that Braun was being 'forced' in the

---

[34] Braun, *Texte*, vi. 187. Braun uses capitals here to denote an unattributed quotation.

[35] See Heinz-Bernhard Wohlfahrth, 'Utopisches Schreiben: Untersuchungen und Überlegungen zum Werk Volker Brauns' (Ph.D. thesis, Freie Universität Berlin, 2005), 198; Volker Braun, *Werktage 1: Arbeitsbuch 1977–1989* (Frankfurt/M.: Suhrkamp, 2009), 486, 517.

[36] 'Thesen zu einem Theater-Abend'.

'right' direction [quotation marks in the original].[37] Whilst Audehm still had some concerns, he accepted that the development of socialist democracy was a dialectical process, requiring responsible action from both the leadership and the people. Hager, however, took a different view. Judging by the punctuation in the surviving reports, he seems to have had an apoplectic fit at the sight of the third Bolshevik's speech. The records in Schwerin call the speech '*eine zutiefst falsche Stelle im Stück*' (a profoundly wrong point in the play), with 'keine historische Berechtigung!!' (no historical justification!!).[38] Schroth noted the main thrust of Hager's objections: 'Das Volk ist legitim—die Herrschaft nicht!!!' (The people are legitimate—the rulers are not!!!)[39] Hager argued that the masses were not to be trusted, citing German support for Hitler and Polish support for the recent 'counter-revolution'. In his view, the masses would act correctly only under the Party's leadership.[40]

Even so, Hager agreed that the staging could go ahead, if Braun agreed to cuts. He stressed that the staging, costumes, and acting must present the action as historical:

Es darf nicht herauskommen, daß irgendeiner im Zuschauerraum [die Hand-lung] auf die Gegenwart bezieht—auf jetzigen Haß von Polen gegen die Sowjetunion, auf Verhältnisse in der Sowjetunion, auf Beziehungen zwischen der SU und Polen.[41]

The result must not lead anyone in the auditorium to relate [the action] to the present—to Poland's current hatred of the Soviet Union, to conditions in the Soviet Union, to relations between the USSR and Poland.

Hager also stipulated that the play should not be staged elsewhere in the GDR.[42] Censorship involved placing plays with trusted practitioners, and Hager was concerned to secure the propaganda value of a GDR premiere, not to enable *Dmitri* to be staged by other theatres.

The authorities had no direct input into the day-to-day business of rehearsals, relying during this second phase on the theatre's internal controls. But officials checked the results three times, at run-throughs on 4 and 24 April and at the dress rehearsal on 26 April. Maud

[37] Audehm to Hinz, 4.1.1984, LHAS 10.34-3 4007.
[38] 'Demetrius-Dmitri-Projekt'.
[39] Regiebuch (Dmitri), [n.p.].
[40] 'Demetrius-Dmitri-Projekt'.
[41] Ibid. The first reference to 'Polen' can also be translated as 'Poles'.
[42] Regiebuch (Dmitri), [n.p.].

Klevenow attended both run-throughs on behalf of the Theatre Department; at the first, Christoph Funke and a representative of the Union of Theatre Practitioners, Rüdiger Volkmer, accompanied her.[43] But it was the second run-through that attracted a whole host of prominent guests: Hans-Peter Minetti from the Central Committee, Karl-Heinz Hafranke from the Culture Department, Klaus Pfützner and Rolf Rohmer from the Union of Theatre Practitioners, and members of the Academy of Social Sciences.[44] This broad base of external support was crucial: it involved officials in the search for solutions, avoided unwelcome surprises at the premiere, and ensured that central and local officials would judge the production against the initial range of possible interpretations.

As promised, Schroth's staging foregrounded the breaks between Tsarism and socialism. In the Bolshevik scene, he followed Braun's stage direction stipulating that the melody played by the bells of the Kremlin should change from 'God save the Tsar' to the 'Internationale'.[45] Schroth also adopted Jaksch's idea that the three Bolsheviks should be played by actors who had appeared earlier on as starving peasants, showing their progression from passive victims to revolutionary leaders.[46] The West German critic Andreas Roßmann argued that the production team had put Braun's text through the dramaturgical mangle; in Braun's original text, the starving peasants have been forbidden to leave the land, whereas in the Schwerin version they have been forbidden to leave the terrain.[47] But of the lines that Hager had identified as problematic, many survived intact. The changes that were made toned down the text, rather than expunging controversial material entirely. In the opening scene, lines pointing to differences between the political culture in Poland and Russia were cut:

HIER IST NICHT MOSKAU NICHT DESPOTENFURCHT
SCHNÜRT HIER DIE FREIE SEELE ZU HIER DARF
DIE WAHRHEIT WANDELN MIT ERHABNEM HAUPT[48]

---

[43] Untitled document, AdK CSA 24.

[44] Hinz to Ziegner, 25.4.1984, LHAS 10.34-3 4007.

[45] 'Thesen zu einem Theater-Abend'.

[46] 'Protokoll: Gespräch mit Volker Braun über *Dmitri*', 25.–26.11.1983, AdK CSA 21.

[47] Andreas Roßmann, 'Volker Brauns *Guevara* und *Dmitri* als DDR-Erstaufführungen in Leipzig und Schwerin', *Deutschland Archiv*, 17 (1984), 1238–9 at 1239. Braun had already noted in his journal on 25.6.1982 that this change would be required for the published version. See Braun, *Werktage 1*, 467.

[48] Regiebuch (Dmitri), 7. The capitals denote text that the characters have learned by heart; there is no punctuation in the original.

THIS IS NOT MOSCOW FEAR OF DESPOTS DOES NOT
STRANGLE OUR FREE SOULS HERE TRUTH
CAN WALK HERE WITH ITS HEAD HELD HIGH

But these lines were cut only in the metatheatrical frame, in which the
actors rehearse their roles and slip between lines from Schiller's *Demetrius* and their own commentary. Given that they were part of a larger
block of text cut from the frame, political considerations may well have
coincided with the practical need to accelerate the move from the
extended frame to the dramatic action. The controversial lines were
cut when they were isolated from their dramatic context and presented
as a quotation, but retained when embedded in a longer speech, in both
Demetrius and *Dmitri*.[49] Their subsequent survival indicates that Schiller's authorship probably protected some of Braun's text.

It was the Bolshevik scene that most preoccupied the authorities, to
the extent that it would define the production's success or failure. On
Hager's advice, Hinz consulted the Central Committee's Institute for
Marxism-Leninism, whose Lenin department duly produced two papers
on the scene. These argued that the third Bolshevik's comments had no
historical justification and were reminiscent of the doom-laden proph-
ecies of the Workers' Opposition.[50] One member of the production
team objected strongly to this interpretation:

das ist keine Arbeiteropposition, das sind reale Schwierigkeiten, und dafür gibt es
mittlerweile hieb- und stichfeste Beweise (Polen)/ ich [*sic*] verstehe die Haltung in
dieser Frage nicht, wie kann man sich so in die eigene Tasche lügen.[51]

this is not the Workers' Opposition, these are real difficulties, and we now have
cast-iron proof (Poland). I do not understand the [authorities'] attitude on this
question: how can people delude themselves with such lies?

The authorities persisted with their objections at the first run-through,
and the production team decided that the Bolsheviks should hover over
the stage, looking down on the historical action.[52] Braun was highly
critical of this change; he argued in his work journal that the Bolsheviks

---

[49] Regiebuch (Dmitri), 9; Friedrich Schiller, 'Demetrius' (Regiebuch), 10, AdK ID
846.
[50] Diehl to Hinz, 28.3.1984, LHAS 10.34-3 4007.
[51] Unsigned, undated letter to Schroth, AdK CSA 30.
[52] Anon., 'Friedrich Schillers *Demetrius* und Volker Brauns *Dmitri* in der Praxis des
Mecklenburgischen Staatstheaters Schwerin', AdK CSA 31.

now seemed to have all the answers, so that the spectators' opinions did not matter and the play no longer concerned them.[53] Whilst Minetti and Hafranke approved the new version at the second run-through, the production team changed the scene again at the dress rehearsal.[54] An indignant Hinz warned Schroth that any deviation from the approved version would be seen as a breach of trust and would have consequences for the theatre.[55] At the premiere, the team reverted to the agreed version, and Klaus Höpcke reportedly deemed the scene acceptable.[56]

Braun as Schiller, Schiller as Braun

Throughout the censorship process, the authorities focused on *Dmitri*. They had a blindspot as far as *Demetrius* was concerned: Hager had declared that Schiller's play was not problematic, that there were no grounds for a topical interpretation, and that Schiller was simply concerned with the discrepancy between appearance and reality.[57] This was a fatal underestimation: the discourse on freedom and the legitimacy of government is already central to Schiller's fragment, reflecting the political aftermath of the French Revolution and Reign of Terror.

The contrast between the two halves of Schroth's production demonstrates again how much more freedom GDR directors usually had when staging the classics. Schroth read Schiller's *Demetrius* through the lens of twentieth-century European history, effectively superimposing the additional layers of Braun's play onto Schiller's. In an initial discussion about the production, Schroth voiced his intention of staging Braun as Schiller and Schiller as Braun.[58] Schiller's play depicts the former Tsarina, mother of the real Demetrius, in a nunnery in a barren wintry region. Schroth abandoned the nunnery and set the scene in a Siberian wasteland, and the white landscape, rocks, railway tracks, and cart invited comparison with the gulags.[59] In contrast, he set the corresponding scene in Braun's version in a crypt. The authorities did not object to

[53] Braun, *Werktage 1*, 595.
[54] 'Auswertung, 24.4', AdK CSA 26.
[55] Hinz to Ziegner, 30.4.1984, LHAS 10.34-3 4007.
[56] Ibid. It is unclear whether Schroth had also cut some or all of the third Bolshevik's lines; Roßmann indicates only that Lenin—not the third Bolshevik—had the final word. See Roßmann, 'Volker Brauns *Guevara* und *Dmitri*', 1239.
[57] 'Demetrius-Dmitri-Projekt'.
[58] 'Protokoll: Gespräch'.
[59] *Mecklenburgisches Staatstheater*, ed. Linzer, 71–5.

Fig. 6.1. The Polish parliament in *Demetrius* (Sigrid Meixner, Stiftung Archiv Akademie der Künste)

Demetrius at the premiere, partly because Schroth was working within an established GDR tradition of using the classics to comment obliquely on recent history. But it was also because Schroth drew on a broader range of twentieth-century reference points than just Stalinism, setting up the Polish parliament to suggest the Bundestag, with a circular structure, microphones, and an eagle in the background (Fig. 6.1).[60] Given that the parliament scene shows the Polish nobility searching for a pretext for war against Russia, the setting recalled the Bundestag's recent decision to allow Pershing missiles to be stationed in the Federal Republic. A rehearsal note actually likened Braun's Dmitri to the Pershing missile, saying that he—like it—was about to be deployed.[61] The final scene of *Demetrius* showed refugees fleeing the war, reminding spectators of the massed forced migrations in 1945. This reference to the Second World War allowed Helmut Ullrich to interpret the icy labour camp as a Nazi concentration camp.[62]

---

[60] *Mecklenburgisches Staatstheater*, ed. Linzer, 67; 'Bühnenbildgespräch am 16.12.83', AdK CSA 27.
[61] Ibid.
[62] Helmut Ullrich, 'Von Demetrius zu Dmitri', *Neue Zeit* (East Berlin), 9.5.1984.

Fig. 6.2. Dmitri and his advisers (Sigrid Meixner, Stiftung Archiv Akademie der Künste)

Schroth's approach towards Schiller undermined the distinctions between the three historical periods represented or alluded to in Braun's *Dmitri*: the seventeenth century, the Russian Revolution, and the GDR. The staging of *Demetrius* encouraged spectators to look for topical and recent historical resonances in *Dmitri*, and the symbolism in the set facilitated this task. In *Dmitri*, an outsize throne accentuated the distance between the Tsar and his subjects (Fig. 6.2), and the lack of period detail ensured that the point was historically transferable. Braun's statement on a publicity leaflet supported this interpretation:

ich sehe was ich sehe, aber ich weiß eine Menge mehr, ich weiß eine neue Zeit, die aus der alten gekommen ist, Meinedamenundherrn, die Schluß gemacht hat / die noch kämpft / die sich noch elend lange auseinandersetzt mit den alten Regeln und Mechanismen. Und das Bild der puren Vergangenheit leuchtet, eine furchtbare Fackel, uns heim in die Zukunft.[63]

I see what I see, but I know a great deal more, I know of a new age which has come forth from the old times, ladies and gentlemen, which has drawn a line

---

[63] Publicity leaflet for *Demetrius/Dmitri*, AdK ID 846.

under the past / which is still fighting / which is still waging a wretchedly long battle against the old rules and mechanisms. And the unrelenting image of the past—a terrible torch—is the light guiding us home to the future.

This statement encapsulates Braun's faith and his ambivalence: he depicts the period since 1917 as a new era, but not as a clean break with the past; he presents a forward trajectory towards a utopian goal, but sees society as dogged by the ingrained habits of the past. He presents the past as a terrible warning, but as one that will spur us on towards a better future. Like the staging of *Demetrius*, the programme undermined the clear-cut distinctions of the production concept.

There were three main reasons why this premiere was able to go ahead: the theatre's willingness to collaborate and compromise with the authorities, the involvement and support of officials from a broad range of central and local institutions, and the fact that memories of Solidarity were less fresh than in 1982. The premiere passed without incident, and in that sense the production was a textbook case of censorship. But the censorship process did not neutralize the texts or the staging: lines survived that had initially been seen as major problems, and officials paid little attention to Schiller's *Demetrius*. The initial talks and final run-throughs functioned as the external frame of censorship, while the work of changing the text and finding performance solutions was internalized within the theatre and subsumed into the rehearsal process—a way of reducing bilateral conflict and leaving the work to trusted professionals.

In some ways, the twin production was a clever compromise: Schroth used Schiller's *Demetrius* to achieve the kinds of associations envisaged in his production concept for *Dmitri*. Jaksch is said to have told her colleagues that it was a major achievement to have staged the play, given the uncertainty in GDR theatre and the management situation at the Staatstheater.[64] But the compromise was also uneasy: Schiller's *Demetrius* stood undecided between two different political readings; Braun's *Dmitri* was split between the insistence on historical breaks and continuities, an ambiguity present in the original. The material for a dialogue between the plays was certainly there, but it was asking a lot to expect the audience to manufacture this dialogue. The theatre's own assessment conceded that the production was unusually challenging for spectators in

---

[64] 'Diskussion, Parteileitungssitzung', 10.5.1984, LHAS BPA IV/7/242/008.

Schwerin.[65] These uneasy compromises reflect not only the theatrical and political constraints of the system, but also the ambivalence of Schroth and Jaksch in 1984: the two theatre practitioners were committed to the SED but were flirting with ideas of reform, from a safer distance than Braun.

3. *TROMMELN IN DER NACHT* IN ANKLAM

In the early 1980s, production bans became a regular occurrence in Anklam. Local officials stopped performances of *Othello* after its premiere in November 1982, cancelled *Woyzeck* at the planning stage in spring 1983, and banned *Trommeln in der Nacht* before its premiere, scheduled for 7 April 1984. An official from the *Rat des Bezirks* tried to press criminal charges against Castorf, and the theatre manager applied for Castorf's dismissal. This increasingly vitriolic conflict indicates a fundamentally different working relationship from the one prevailing in Schwerin.

Whilst this case might initially seem to exemplify a binary conflict between censors and artists, closer inspection reveals a more complex set of relationships. From 1983, the theatre was split between Castorf's allies, the manager's supporters, and those caught in the middle. Whilst Castorf was universally unpopular with officials in Anklam and Neubrandenburg, he did have influential contacts in Berlin. The former Culture Minister, Klaus Gysi, came to Anklam to watch his daughter, Gabi, act in Castorf's premieres. Gabi Gysi was Castorf's partner at the time, and her brother Gregor provided him with legal advice. Given that regional and district officials were driving the campaign against Castorf's stagings, this case offers an opportunity to gauge the extent of their censorship powers.

This study draws on extensive interviews that Claudia Sieling carried out with theatre practitioners in Anklam in 1990–1, published interviews with Castorf, and my own interviews with Peter Ullrich and Siegfried Wilzopolski. Ullrich represented the Union of Theatre Practitioners at the official run-through of *Trommeln*, together with Volkmer, and Wilzopolski acted as the production's dramaturge. Whilst few other sources were available to Sieling in 1991, this situation has since

---

[65] 'Auswertung Demetrius/Dmitri', AdK CSA 31.

changed fundamentally. This investigation uses the Stasi files and the records of the Union of Theatre Practitioners and the *Rat des Bezirks* and SED-*Bezirksleitung* in Neubrandenburg.

Although Sieling attributes the conflict in Anklam to a clash between the SED's centralistic attitudes and Castorf's theatre practice,[66] the archive material shows that objections to Castorf's work originated locally. The SED was not a unitary actor, and regional and district officials had a significantly narrower view of what should be tolerated in Anklam than their counterparts in the Ministry and Union of Theatre Practitioners. Sales of theatre tickets in Anklam did fall dramatically from 80,000 in 1980 to 30,000 in 1983, and theatre subscriptions dropped from 1,977 to 194 during the same period.[67] Even if a proportion of the fall can be attributed to production bans and an alleged lack of advertising for Castorf's productions, the statistics support local officials' claims that the repertoire no longer appealed to its traditional audience. The censorship conflicts in Anklam involved a clash of cultural expectations, and local officials believed that they were defending the interests of their community against those of avant-garde practitioners from East Berlin.

Anklam and Castorf

Anklam was situated near the GDR's north-east coast in Neubrandenburg, now part of Mecklenburg-Vorpommern. Martin Linzer refers to it as 'nowhere north-east', Matthias Matussek calls it 'a penal colony at the end of the world', and Castorf declares that the whole town consisted of just one street.[68] These colourful claims are something of an exaggeration: Anklam is an old Hanseatic town, which lies on a main railway line to Berlin. In the GDR, it was the administrative centre of a district with thirty-six surrounding communities, mainly small villages.

---

[66] Claudia Sieling, '"Aber sagen Sie nichts gegen Anklam!": Eine Analyse des Provinztheaters Anklam von 1981 bis 1985 im Tätigkeitszeitraum des Regisseurs Frank Castorf als Fallbeispiel für das Verständnis von Theaterkunst in der DDR' (Diplomarbeit, Universität Hildesheim, 1991), 47.

[67] Holan, 'Notiz über die Konsultation in der Abteilung Kultur bei der SED-Bezirksleitung Neubrandenburg', 10.2.1984, AdK VdT 936.

[68] Linzer, '*Ich war immer...*', 215; Matthias Matussek, 'Rodeo im Wilden Osten: Das Provinztheater in Anklam, DDR, Mai 1990', in Rudolf Augstein (ed.), *Ein deutsches Jahrzehnt: Reportagen 1985–1995* (Hamburg: Spiegel, 1995), 191–203 at 192; Irmer and Schmidt, *Die Bühnenrepublik*, 252.

The Theater Anklam was far smaller than the Mecklenburgisches Staatstheater, with a much shorter tradition. It had been established in 1950 in a community hall and was classed as a Category C theatre, of only local significance; its productions were performed on fifteen stages in the surrounding villages. Neubrandenburg had just two other theatres, the Friedrich-Wolf-Theater in Neustrelitz and a marionette theatre in the regional capital, although Greifswald was relatively near. Anklam had difficulty retaining actors, and 90 per cent of the actors moved on approximately every three years.[69] The town was small and provincial, with no tradition of avant-garde theatre.

Anklam's theatre faced an uphill task attracting audiences even before Castorf's arrival. It served an agricultural region with an older demographic structure than Schwerin. Manager Wolfgang Bonness reported in 1979 that the local population included few people aged between 25 and 30, and a disproportionately small number between 30 and 40. Hardly any of the over 65s went to the theatre, and only 15 per cent of the population was of school age and could therefore be made to attend.[70] Surveys indicated that local residents preferred to spend their leisure time with family and friends, attending football matches and discos, and visiting local pubs.[71] Those who did go to the theatre had conservative tastes. They wanted plays with a clear plot and genre, and they expected productions to confirm their experience of reality, to take sides for or against events and characters, and to end harmoniously.[72] In effect, Bonness had described exactly the kind of theatre that Castorf had always reacted against. From today's perspective, it is easy to see that Castorf was on a collision course with local spectators.

The question is whether this should have been clear to the officials who recommended his appointment. In 1982, Castorf was not yet an established director; as Peter Ullrich argues, he had yet to become the Castorf we know today.[73] After studying theatre at East Berlin's Humboldt University from 1972 to 1976, Castorf had worked in Senftenberg, Greifswald, and Brandenburg, where his production of *Golden fließt der Stahl*—co-directed by Manfred Rafeldt—had been banned. Castorf's two years in Brandenburg ended in an employment tribunal,

[69] 'Jahresanalyse 1982', 21.3.1983, LHAS 7.21-1 Z106/1991 27302.
[70] Bonness to the Culture Department of the RdB Neubrandenburg, 24.9.1979, LHAS 7.21-1 RdB Nbg. 27304.
[71] Sieling, '"Aber sagen Sie nichts gegen Anklam!"', 27–8.
[72] Bonness, 24.9.1979.
[73] Interview with Ullrich, 26.7.2007.

and Siegfried Wilzopolski sees his subsequent transfer to Anklam as a punishment.[74] Yet Ullrich actually views the appointment as a promotion, given that Castorf was made *Oberspielleiter* and was thus placed in charge of the repertoire.[75] The surviving correspondence indicates that the head of the DTO worked hard to convince Bonness to employ Castorf, arguing that the dispute in Brandenburg had not been his fault.[76] The DTO was probably simply trying to solve two problems at once: to find somewhere for Castorf to work and to provide Anklam with a new *Oberspielleiter*, not least because one director had already turned down the post.[77] There is no evidence of any attempt to ensure a good match between Castorf and his target audience; this reflects the low status of the theatre and the fact that Castorf was in the early stages of his career.

Anklam's attraction for Castorf was its potential as a space for experimentation. He assembled a group of young actors, who surprised their lecturers at East Berlin's Acting School by suddenly announcing their desire to go to Anklam. They turned down offers of appointments elsewhere, saying that Anklam itself was 'the pits' ('das Letzte') but that it offered them a chance to develop and prove themselves as a group.[78] In rehearsals, Castorf used plays as a starting point for improvisation, breaking up the text, searching for the underlying processes, and relating them to GDR reality, other texts and cultures, and rock music. Whilst this experimentation was bound to trigger allergic reactions in conservatives, Linzer never felt that Castorf was violating the authors' intentions or their plays. Instead, he saw Castorf's methods as a search for other means of describing situations and for ways of viewing characters from new perspectives.[79] In April 1982, Castorf's production of Heiner Müller's *Die Schlacht* (The Battle) actually won a prize at the Hans Otto Competition for the best staging in Neubrandenburg.[80] Whilst officials may not have had many productions to choose from, the award surely also reflects the expectations they brought to a play by Müller, which differed from those that they would subsequently bring to works by Shakespeare and Brecht.

---

[74] Interview with Siegfried Wilzopolski, 11.7.2007.
[75] Interview with Ullrich, 26.7.2007.
[76] Sprink to Bonness, 4.8.1980, LHAS 7.21-1 Z106/1991 18729.
[77] Ibid.
[78] BStU BV Bln. AIM 6210/91, iii, fo. 153–4.
[79] Irmer and Schmidt, *Die Bühnenrepublik*, 230.
[80] Sieling, '"Aber sagen Sie nichts gegen Anklam!"', 46.

Soon after Castorf's arrival in Anklam, the theatre became a talking point in and beyond the GDR theatre scene, partly due to Herbert König's avant-garde stagings. Officials warned that 'the enemy' was very interested in Anklam's theatre and might be steering developments there; these claims were probably based on an article in *Theater heute* and a radio broadcast on *Deutschlandfunk*.[81] Castorf's own productions attracted like-minded spectators from across the GDR, including members of the rock group City and the actor Henry Hübchen. But local officials complained that Castorf was attracting the wrong kind of spectators, with long hair and jeans.[82] Officials inaccurately lumped the visitors together as 'the Berliners', and one functionary claimed that they sometimes seemed to dominate the show, so that local residents were guests in their own theatre.[83] Gregor Gysi suggests that local officials did have a point; the local population had been deprived of its theatre—albeit a theatre that only a minority seems to have wanted in the first place.[84]

The Campaign Takes Shape

On 1 November 1982, Bonness sent a letter of resignation to the DTO. He subsequently told the DTO that he felt out of touch with his young colleagues and their new ideas on theatre.[85] Five days later, Castorf's production of *Othello* was premiered, only then to be banned. The Stasi informer 'Zumpe', the cultural editor of the *Freie Erde* Neubrandenburg, provided a catalogue of objections to the production. These included the fact that the small amount of surviving text was muttered in English, a pianist used a person as a piano stool, and the actors splashed each other with water from a tap in the wall. 'Zumpe' added that the production hinted at a homosexual relationship between Othello and Iago, some scenes had lesbian overtones, and the costumes were

[81] Andreas Roßmann, 'Bilder ferner Hoffnung', *Theater heute*, 24/1 (Jan. 1983), 9–11; 'Information (Beratung beim Gen. Dr. Tremper am 3.2.1983)', 9.2.1983, LHAS 7.21-1 Z106/1991 27303.

[82] BStU BV Nbg. AIM 648/8889, ii, fo. 27.

[83] 'Zur gegenwärtigen Lage im Theater Anklam', 7.12.1982, LHAS 7.21-1 Z106/1991 27301.

[84] Irmer and Schmidt, *Die Bühnenrepublik*, 272.

[85] 'Gespräch mit Genossen Wolfgang Bonness', 2.12.1982, LHAS 7.21-1 Z106/1991 27301.

made from PVC.[86] What 'Zumpe' did not point out is that Castorf's version of *Othello* used the situation in Anklam as a source of productive tension. It opened with a conversation between two prompters, who simultaneously represented members of the provinces in Cyprus and local residents of Anklam. They discussed how they used to enjoy going to the theatre but preferred the circus and sports matches; one remembered having to queue up for theatre tickets, and the other replied that this was no longer necessary.[87] Castorf may not have conformed to local expectations, but he did not ignore the situation in Anklam.

After *Othello*, the local authorities' long-term aim was to secure Castorf's departure, unless he agreed to change.[88] The immediate priority, however, was to force out König—an easier task, as he was employed on a temporary basis. Officials decided to fix the ticket sales for König's next production—*Man spielt nicht mit der Liebe* (Don't Play with Love) by Alfred de Musset—so that only local residents could attend. Orders from Berlin for 160 tickets were to be turned down on the grounds that the premiere was sold out, and König was not to stage any further productions.[89] In February 1983, the *Rat des Bezirks* decided that Castorf should be told to abandon his plans to stage *Woyzeck*, as it would not interest spectators.[90] According to the Stasi, the *Bezirkslei-tung* hoped that this intervention would provoke Castorf to resign.[91] Local officials were acting on their own initiative, and their central counterparts appear to have made a limited attempt to rein them in. On 11 February, the Stasi reported that the Central Committee had told the *Bezirksleitung* not to hold direct talks with 'negative forces' at the theatre.[92]

As local officials intensified their efforts to secure Castorf's departure, the Stasi stepped up its activity. In addition to 'Zumpe', officers could call on the theatre's technical director 'Wolke', who had been working unofficially for the Stasi since 1976.[93] On 16 February 1983, central

---

[86] BStU BV Nbg. AOPK 1580/85, i, fo. 54.
[87] Siegfried Wilzopolski, *Theater des Augenblicks: Die Theaterarbeit Frank Castorfs. Eine Dokumentation* (Berlin: Zentrum für Theaterdokumentation und -information, 1992), 33.
[88] 'Anlage zum Material vom 07.12.82', LHAS 7.21-1 Z106/1991 27301.
[89] 'Kurzprotokoll der Beratung am 27.12.1982 über Maßnahmen zur Stabilisierung der Lage am Theater Anklam', 29.12.1982, LHAS 7.21-1 Z106/1991 27303.
[90] 'Information (Beratung beim Gen. Dr. Tremper)'.
[91] BStU BV Nbg. Abt. XX 99, fo. 22.
[92] Ibid.
[93] BStU BV Nbg. III 1620/88, i, fo. 13.

Stasi officers undertook to ensure via the Culture Ministry that no more 'negative' actors would be sent to Anklam.[94] The Stasi opened the investigation 'Othello' against Castorf and set to work to recruit a new informer linked to the 'hard core' of the ensemble. Officers identified 'Dario Fo' as a potential informer on 2 June, and he signed up as an IM on 21 September.[95] 'Dario Fo' had worked as a prompter and technician, and was said to harbour ambitions of becoming an actor. His handwritten oath contains frequent spelling and grammatical errors, but he was attentive to details in rehearsals. 'Dario Fo' met Stasi officers once every two to three weeks, receiving 450 marks in 1984, a further 450 in 1985, and then 100 in 1986 and 1987.[96] The first payment was made on 11 April 1984, just days after *Trommeln in der Nacht* was cancelled.

The irony is that 'Dario Fo' was extremely impressed by Castorf—so much so that Castorf describes the informer as his greatest protector.[97] 'Dario Fo' filed glowing reports about the level of discipline at rehearsals, the strength of the collective, and the standard of acting:

Wenn Castorf Regie führt, dann besteht unter den Schauspielern eine hohe Disziplin. Keiner traut sich, etwas gegen seine Entscheidungen zu sagen. Auch die Schauspieler, die keine Rolle in seinen Stücken erhalten haben, verfolgen interessiert die Proben. Andere, die aufgetreten waren, kehren sofort in den Zuschauersaal zurück, um die Proben von dieser Seite aus weiter verfolgen zu können.[98]

When Castorf is directing, then there is a high level of discipline among the actors. No one dares to object to his decisions. Even the actors who do not have a part in his plays follow the rehearsals with interest. Others, who have finished their scenes, return immediately to the auditorium so that they can carry on following the rehearsals from there.

This positive attitude towards Castorf reflected the difficulty, from the Stasi's perspective, of recruiting informers from 'negative circles': such informers were prone to sympathize with those on whom they were informing. Officers noted that they needed to impress a firm image of the

---

[94] BStU BV Nbg. Abt. XX 99, fo. 20.
[95] BStU BV Nbg. III 1620/88, i, fos. 4, 13.
[96] Ibid. 10.
[97] Jürgen Balitzki, *Castorf, der Eisenhändler: Theater zwischen Kartoffelsalat und Stahlgewitter* (Berlin: Ch. Links, 1995), 42.
[98] BStU BV Nbg. III 1620/88, ii.i, fo. 9. The oral report was written up by Oltn. Hansen.

enemy on 'Dario Fo', but their apparent success brought new risks.[99] In March 1984, a report warned that 'Dario Fo' was in danger of outing himself as an informer by going on the offensive in public.[100]

The New Manager Arrives

By 23 February 1983, when Wolfgang Bordel met Ministry officials to discuss the possibility of succeeding Bonness as theatre manager, the Stasi's HA XX/7 had already cleared his appointment.[101] Bordel was a keen amateur who had managed a student theatre but lacked any experience of professional theatre. He was currently working at the Academy of Sciences, having trained as a physicist and written a doctoral thesis on philosophy. But he had discussed the situation in Anklam with local officials, and his letter of application corresponded exactly to their views:

Die Massenwirksamkeit des Theaters ist eine Grundbedingung künstlerischer Theaterarbeit. Das bedeutet in erster Linie Theater für die Zuschauer. Theater für das Territorium[,] in dem es sich befindet. Ein gutes Theater ist nicht deshalb gut, weil es in der Republik bei sogenannten Eingeweihten bekannt ist, sondern weil die Begeisterung und Beachtung[,] die das Theater bei der Bevölkerung im Kreis und Bezirk erfährt, über die Grenzen des Kreises und Bezirkes inaus [sic] Aufmerksamkeit erregt.[102]

Mass impact is a basic condition of artistic theatre practice. That primarily means theatre for the spectators. Theatre for the region in which it is based. A good theatre is not good because it is known throughout the Republic by so-called insiders, but because the enthusiasm and respect that it commands from the population of the district and region arouse attention beyond the boundaries of that district and region.

On 30 March, over a month after the Stasi and Ministry had unofficially approved Bordel's appointment, the *Rat des Bezirks* recommended Bordel as manager and asked Hoffmann to agree to the appointment.[103]

[99] BStU BV Nbg. III 1620/88, i, fo. 70.
[100] Ibid. 80.
[101] 'Gespräch in der Abt. Theater des MfK mit Gen. Dr. Bordel am 23.2.83', LHAS 7.21-1 Z106/1991 27303; BStU BV Nbg. Abt. XX 99, fo. 20.
[102] LHAS 7.21-1 Z106/1991 26996. The file contains only the second page of a copy of Bordel's letter. Bordel used this concept to secure the theatre's future and enable it to expand after reunification.
[103] Netik to Hoffmann, 30.3.1983, LHAS 7.21-1 Z106/1991 27303.

Bordel was sent to shadow Siegfried Böttger, the theatre manager in Stralsund, to gain experience.[104]

In hindsight, Bordel describes his appointment as a suicide mission.[105] The *Bezirksleitung* already wanted Castorf to resign, and the actors were wary of the new manager because he had been appointed to keep watch over them.[106] The actors' fears were fuelled when Bordel arrived with his own management team, reportedly on the local authorities' instructions.[107] As the authorities' representative, Bordel had little chance of mediating between the groups within the theatre and between the theatre and the authorities, particularly given his lack of professional theatre experience. In August 1983, when Bordel was directing rehearsals of a fairy tale by Joachim Knauth, the actors reportedly complained that they did not want to work at a level below Castorf's productions.[108] As the tensions increased, one actor allegedly called a colleague a strikebreaker and threatened to kick him in the shins so that he would have to be signed off work.[109] By late October, six of the production's seven actors had gone on sick leave, and rehearsals had become virtually impossible.[110]

This mutiny sealed the local authorities' determination to remove Castorf and his head dramaturge. On 17 October, officials in the *Rat des Bezirks* decided to inform them on 31 October that their contracts would be terminated on 31 July 1984, alleging that they were not suited to work at the Theater Anklam and had failed as state managers.[111] These were indeed grounds for dismissal under §54 of the employment code. However, to invoke this paragraph successfully, Bordel needed to seek the agreement of the two theatre practitioners and to offer them an alternative contract, either in the Theater Anklam or elsewhere. He also needed to prove that they were incapable of fulfilling their existing

[104] 'Gespräch in der Abt. Theater'.
[105] Sieling, '"Aber sagen Sie nichts gegen Anklam!"', 51.
[106] BStU BV Nbg. AOPK 1580/85, i, fo. 52.
[107] Sieling, '"Aber sagen Sie nichts gegen Anklam!"', 51.
[108] 'Kurzprotokoll der Beratung zu Problemen des Theaters Anklam am 31.8.1983', LHAS 7.21-1 Z106/1991 27303.
[109] 'Kurzprotokoll der Beratung zu Fragen des Theaters Anklam am 26.9.1983', LHAS 7.21-1 Z106/1991 27303.
[110] 'Protokoll der Beratung zu Problemen im Theater Anklam am 6.10.1983', LHAS 7.21-1 Z106/1991 27303.
[111] Ibid.

contracts or that they were unwilling to do so.[112] Article 24 of the 1968/
74 constitution guaranteed citizens the right to work, and it was difficult
to dismiss workers.

On 26 October, the Culture Department of the *Rat des Bezirks* noted
that an attempt to dismiss Castorf and his head dramaturge would
probably not succeed, and that it had no central or regional support.[113]
According to the Stasi, the Ministry now wanted Castorf to remain in
Anklam so that he could be persuaded to change his artistic views over a
longer period. Officers concluded that the Ministry had no interest in
transferring Castorf to another theatre, as similar problems were bound
to arise there.[114] They added that the *Rat des Bezirks* now planned to
place Castorf in a compromising legal position so that he could be
'extricated' from the theatre.[115]

It would be unfair to conclude that the Ministry and DTO had
abandoned the theatre to local officials. Albert Bußmann, a former
manager of the Theater Anklam, visited the town on behalf of the
DTO in October 1983 and February 1984. On the second occasion,
he argued that the Ministry and *Rat des Bezirks* urgently needed to agree
on an approach.[116] In February, Holan met officials in Neubrandenburg's SED-*Bezirksleitung*, and she accepted their concerns and their
claims that they had done everything possible to remedy the situation.[117] But her subsequent departure from the Ministry prevented
the development of any coordinated strategy, allowing local officials
to pursue their own agenda. The minimal demand in Anklam for
Castorf's productions meant that local opinion might actually favour
production bans. Whilst such bans would inevitably heighten tensions
within the ensemble, this suited the local strategy of forcing Castorf
out. Consequently, the usual pragmatic constraints on censorship did
not apply.

[112] See Stefan Middendorf, *Recht auf Arbeit in der DDR: Von den theoretischen
Grundlagen bis zu den Berufsverboten für Ausreisewillige* (Berlin and Baden-Baden: Berlin
Verlag and Nomo Verlagsgesellschaft, 2000), 201–12.
[113] 'Varianten der Kaderprobleme im Theater Anklam', 26.10.1983, LHAS 7.21-1
Z106/1991 27303.
[114] BStU BV Nbg. AOPK 1580/85, i, fo. 83.
[115] Ibid.
[116] Bußmann, 'Notizen über eine Informationsreise nach Anklam am 7. und
8.2.1984', 10.2.1984, LHAS 7.21-1 Z106/1991 27303.
[117] Holan, 10.2.1984.

Trommeln in der Nacht

Whilst some reports suggest that Castorf's relations with Bordel had improved by early 1984, Bordel reportedly warned that *Trommeln in der Nacht* would exacerbate the situation by setting the standard for future productions.[118] On 24 February, 'Zumpe' told the Stasi that if Castorf were appointed to a major theatre elsewhere, *Trommeln* would have a normal premiere; otherwise, guests from Berlin would be excluded. Either way, subsequent performances would be cancelled due to lack of demand.[119] The manager and local authorities took no interest in the content of the play or the production, reportedly arguing that Castorf would stage any play in a manner that would offend local audiences.[120]

The production team knew nothing of the authorities' plans. 'Dario Fo' filed a characteristically glowing report, saying that rehearsals would run like clockwork, the actors would be disciplined and punctual, and no one would complain about having to rehearse on Saturdays.[121] But the atmosphere changed two weeks before the premiere, when the actor playing Murk—Horst-Günter Marx—was arrested after lodging an application to leave the GDR. Siegfried Wilzopolski explains that he and his colleagues interpreted the arrest as a declaration of war on the theatre, and Stasi reports noted an immediate increase in suspicion and loss of trust amongst its members.[122]

The run-through on 6 April must surely count as one of the most notorious events in GDR theatre history. Bordel had cancelled the dress rehearsal, postponed the premiere, and announced that morning that the run-through would be held in private.[123] But Castorf had already invited a number of guests, and estimates indicate that between thirteen and forty turned up.[124] By this time, tensions were running high, as a video recording of the production had been forbidden.[125] As Castorf pointed out, the run-through would now be his friends' only

---

[118] Bußmann, 10.2.1984.
[119] BStU BV Nbg. AOPK 1580/85, i, fo. 94.
[120] 'Information über einen Besuch der beiden Sekretäre Rüdiger Volkmer und Dr. Peter Ullrich im Theater Anklam am 6. April 1984', 11.4.1984, AdK VdT 760.
[121] BStU BV Nbg. AOPK 1580/85, i, fo. 91.
[122] Interview with Wilzopolski, 11.7.2007; BStU BV Nbg. AOPK 1580/85, i, fo. 108. See also <http://www.vorwaerts.de/artikel/20-jahre-maverfall-1>, 15.7.2010.
[123] BStU BV Nbg. AOPK 1580/85, i, fo. 116.
[124] Ibid. 116, 122, 125, 174.
[125] Ibid. 114.

opportunity to see the production.[126] When they refused to leave, an increasingly heated exchange developed, involving representatives of the *Bezirksleitung, Rat des Bezirks, Kreisleitung,* and *Rat des Kreises.* An official from the *Rat des Bezirks* announced that he was far more interested in the audience in Anklam than in the audience from Berlin. Castorf countered that the theatre belonged to the GDR, not just Anklam.[127] He also reportedly said that theatre practitioners had been driven out of the theatre fifty years ago, a reference to censorship under National Socialism.[128] One guest tapped the official from the *Rat des Bezirks* on the shoulder, asking for his name so that he could complain about him.[129] Castorf, meanwhile, questioned whether state officials were even competent to judge theatre, allegedly advising one to buy a bottle of beer and sit down in front of the television instead.[130] Although his guests called on the representatives of the Union of Theatre Practitioners to offer their opinion, they said only that the manager had the right to decide who could attend.[131] When Bordel threatened to call the police, Castorf's guests finally left. They were prevented from re-entering the auditorium and from watching with the sound technicians.

It is hardly surprising that these events have eclipsed the production in the existing accounts and even in the memory of some of the participants. However, Stasi reports offer new insights into the staging. Both they and the programme indicate that local officials were wrong to accuse Castorf of disregarding the play's original context; the programme contains primary material from the period during and immediately after the First World War, including articles from the communist newspaper *Die Rote Fahne* and the contemporary medical literature.[132] The production presented Brecht's characters as individuals scarred by the psychological trauma of war. 'Dario Fo' found the staging exhausting to watch, as it amounted to an onslaught on spectators' nerves. The actors moved in slow motion, emitting long, drawn-out screams.[133] Castorf used erotic tension to unsettle the audience further, casting a young man and a much older woman as the parents of Anna, the returning soldier's unfaithful bride.[134] He also cast Silvia Rieger in the

126 BStU BV Nbg. AOPK 1580/85, i, fo. 117.   127 Ibid. 122.
128 Ibid. 121.   129 Ibid. 126.   130 Ibid. 125.
131 'Information über einen Besuch'.
132 See Wilzopolski, *Theater des Augenblicks,* 59–74.
133 BStU BV Nbg. AOPK 1580/85, i, fos. 109–10, 127.
134 Ibid. 100.

Fig. 6.3. Scene from *Trommeln in der Nacht* (Britta Jähnichen, Stiftung Archiv Akademie der Künste)

role of Anna's male lover Murk (Fig. 6.3), and she slipped in and out of character. As Ullrich and Volkmer explained in their report, the actors either alluded to their characters and then relinquished them, or took them satirically to extremes.[135]

---

[135] 'Information über einen Besuch'.

Stasi officer Hansen agreed with 'Dario Fo' that the acting was outstanding, and Ullrich and Volkmer considered it astonishing for a Category C theatre. Ullrich and Volkmer argued that the production did not set out to provoke politically incorrect reactions, even if the absence of a historically concrete reading allowed potential meanings to proliferate.[136] Even the Stasi were unable to construct a politically negative interpretation. 'Dario Fo' pointed out that Kragler stripped off his red armband and used it to wipe away some quark, and that newspapers were torn up on stage. But he too conceded that there was no proof of deliberate political subversion.[137] There was no serious discussion of the production after the run-through; instead, Bordel announced that he and the local authorities had decided to cancel the production. This announcement breached protocol, as the decision was officially Bordel's alone.[138]

Peter Ullrich remembers the run-through as one of the most unpleasant experiences in his career. He had assumed that the Union had been invited to provide advice, not to justify a predetermined ban.[139] Ullrich and Volkmer were caught between the expectations of the local authorities and those of the theatre practitioners. Both were disappointed: local officials complained that they had come unprepared, and Castorf's colleagues felt let down.[140] Siegfried Wilzopolski argues that Ullrich and Volkmer might have been able to achieve more, as they came from Berlin and had a certain status in the theatre hierarchy.[141] The dramaturge Gudrun Wilzopolski, who attended the post-show meeting, says that they raised no objections to the ban in her presence.[142] After their return to Berlin, Ullrich and Volkmer concluded that there were no convincing political or artistic grounds for a ban, even though the production was relatively far removed from realistic theatre. They added that they could not comment on whether the production was suitable for local spectators, but they did warn of the possible consequences of the ban and said that they did not support it.[143] Ullrich argues now that the only conceivable objection to the production could

---

[136] 'Information über einen Besuch'.
[137] BStU BV Nbg. AOPK 1580/85, i, fo. 127.
[138] 'Information über einen Besuch'.
[139] Interview with Ullrich, 26.7.2007.
[140] BStU BV Nbg. AOPK 1580/85, i, fo. 118.
[141] Interview with Wilzopolski, 11.7.2007.
[142] Sieling, '"Aber sagen Sie nichts gegen Anklam!"', 58.
[143] 'Information über einen Besuch'.

have come from Brecht's heirs, as it stood outside the norms that they had established for Brecht's work.[144] Yet far from objecting to the production, Barbara Brecht-Schall was rumoured to have complained to the Ministry about officials in Neubrandenburg, on the grounds that they were hostile to Brecht.[145]

Censorship vs the Law

Whilst local officials were able to ban Castorf's productions without any serious external scrutiny, they were to encounter far greater difficulty in their attempts to dismiss him. On 11 April, an official from the *Rat des Bezirks* filed charges against Castorf for his comments at the run-through, citing §220 of the criminal code. This paragraph covered attempts to disparage or slander representatives of the state and carried penalties ranging from a public rebuke to a two-year prison sentence.[146] But just two days later, Neubrandenburg's Criminal Police Department instructed the district police officer to stop working on the charge sheet for the time being.[147] Castorf attributes this instruction to an intervention from Hager's office.[148] Bordel suspended Castorf and opened disciplinary proceedings against him, reportedly acting on the orders of the *Rat des Bezirks*. Castorf stood accused of disregarding Bordel's instructions at the run-through, exceeding his own authority, and neglecting his responsibility for order and discipline at the theatre.[149]

Although theatre practitioners had no legal means of challenging censorship decisions, matters were different when it came to disciplinary charges and employment disputes. Castorf had the right to respond to Bordel's charges, and he issued a legalistic refutation. It reached a climax in his response to the charge that he had failed to support Bordel's demand for guests to leave the auditorium:

Eine von Ihnen ausgesprochene Weisung gegenüber dritten Personen verlangt nur dann zwingend mein Eingreifen, wenn Sie dies ebenfalls anweisen. Wenn Sie einer dritten Person eine Weisung erteilen, besteht ein Rechtsverhältnis nur

[144] Sieling, '"Aber sagen Sie nichts gegen Anklam!"', 59.
[145] BStU BV Nbg. AOPK 1580/85, i, fo. 183.
[146] Ibid. 120–1; Ministerium der Justiz, *Strafgesetzbuch der Deutschen Demokratischen Republik* (East Berlin: Staatsverlag der Deutschen Demokratischen Republik, 1968), 81.
[147] BStU BV Nbg. AOPK 1580/85, i, fo. 139.
[148] Irmer and Schmidt, *Die Bühnenrepublik*, 255.
[149] BStU BV Nbg. AOPK 1580/85, i, fo. 131.

zwischen Ihnen und der dritten Person. Ein Eingreifen meinerseits—auch in unterstützender Hinsicht—ist nicht erforderlich und könnte sogar eine Kompetenzüberschreitung sein.[150]

An order issued by you to a third party only requires my intervention if you order this too. If you give an order to a third party, a legal relationship exists only between you and that third party. Intervention on my part—even in support of you—is not required and might even exceed my authority.

The final point alluded to Bordel's claim that Castorf had indeed exceeded his authority, and it is easy to see why the regional authorities suspected Gregor Gysi of having had a hand in the letter. The refutation ended:

Im übrigen sehe ich meine Arbeitspflichten in erster Linie darin, Theater auf die Bühne zu bringen und Sie werden mir sicherlich zustimmen, daß die Schwierigkeiten mehr darin liegen, daß ich in der Erfüllung dieser Arbeitspflichten behindert werde und weniger darin, daß ich Arbeitspflichten verletze.[151]

Besides, I see my work duties as consisting primarily of staging theatre, and I am sure that you will agree that the difficulties have more to do with the fact that I am hindered in carrying out these duties, than with their neglect on my part.

Castorf signed the letter 'with socialist greetings', a formula which officials may well have seen as derisory under the circumstances.

Despite Castorf's refutation, Bordel applied on 18 May for him to be dismissed immediately.[152] When the matter came before the theatre's trade union representatives, three opposed the application and the remaining five abstained. Although the Stasi confidently assumed that the district committee of the FDGB would brush these objections aside, the regional employment court advised that a dismissal was not possible. The court official cited the worker's right to work, the impossibility of transferring the 'pedagogical process' elsewhere, and the fact that Castorf's file was clean. He advised Bordel to conclude the disciplinary proceedings with a severe reprimand (*Verweis*) and to offer Castorf a different contract in Anklam or a new one elsewhere. Neither option was realistic, as the local authorities wanted Castorf out of Anklam and the Ministry did not support a transfer. But Bordel could dismiss Castorf only if he refused alternative offers of employment, and even then he would have to give him notice.[153] The second attempt to

---

[150] BStU BV Nbg. AOPK 1580/85, i, fo. 135.
[151] Ibid.   [152] Ibid. 136.
[153] Ibid. 186–7. See Middendorf, *Recht auf Arbeit in der DDR*, 213–19.

dismiss Castorf had failed, the theatre was back where it had been in October 1983, and Bordel had suffered another blow to his authority.

GDR employment law ensured that the conflict in Anklam actually ended in compromise. In mid-August, Bordel offered Castorf the opportunity to stage a play with the actors of his choice, four guaranteed performances, and a video recording, if he applied to cancel his contract. Castorf would retain his job title and salary, but Bordel would carry out his duties.[154] Castorf accepted the deal, chose to stage Ibsen's *Nora*, and was offered three more performances in return for giving up his apartment in Anklam.[155] After *Nora* had been premiered on 23 February 1985, a local teacher told Siegfried Wilzopolski that he finally understood what Castorf was trying to achieve through theatre.[156] The Stasi, however, remained in the dark. On 15 April 1985, officers noted that they had not succeeded in establishing the reasons and aims behind Castorf's 'so-called' view of art, or the influences behind his actions.[157]

4. CONCLUSION

Writing in 1993 of his experiences as Culture Secretary in Leipzig's SED-*Bezirksleitung*, Dietmar Keller argues that the room for decision-making in the regions was relatively large, provided officials did not cross the authorities in East Berlin. He explains that regional secretaries had two options: writing letters to the central authorities and covering their backs, or getting on with their work independently.[158] In Schwerin, Heide Hinz and her colleagues took the first option, soliciting the advice and involvement of central officials from as many institutions as possible. Both she and her central counterparts had an incentive to invest time and energy in the staging of *Dmitri*, due to their respective desires to keep Schroth and Braun on board. In contrast, officials in Neubrandenburg seem to have made no serious or sustained attempt to win central support for their attempts to dismiss Castorf. Whilst meetings with central officials did take place, local functionaries and Stasi officers were suspicious of the Ministry and DTO, believing

---

[154] BStU BV Nbg. AOPK 1580/85, i, fo. 194.
[155] Balitzki, *Castorf, der Eisenhändler*, 55.
[156] Interview with Wilzopolski, 11.7.2007.
[157] BStU BV Nbg. AOPK 1580/85, i, fo. 229.
[158] Keller, *ND*, 1.3.1993.

that they were not taking Anklam's interests seriously. As Anklam was a Category C theatre with a set of relatively unknown directors, it was not a priority for the overburdened Theatre Department.

The two approaches identified by Keller applied to theatre practitioners, not just officials. Schroth sought central and local support for his production, helped to forge an alliance, and solicited Hager's advice. Even though Schroth's relationship with the acting theatre manager was tense, the confrontation did not affect his relationship with the authorities. Castorf, meanwhile, treated Anklam as a niche for experimentation and staged productions without making concessions to local expectations. Whilst there was never a realistic basis for cooperation between Castorf and officials in Anklam and Neubrandenburg, Castorf does not appear to have sought sustained support from officials outside the region. He did not solicit the support of the Union of Theatre Practitioners, an organization which he regarded with scepticism.[159] Ullrich contrasts Castorf's approach directly with that of Schroth and Jaksch, who kept the Union informed of developments so that its representatives could react.[160]

The advantage of cooperation was greater transparency. In Schwerin, officials shared their concerns about the text with Schroth and Jaksch, laid down the ground rules for the production, and agreed a coordinated response. There was no such transparency in Anklam: officials did not discuss Castorf's production concepts or stagings, Castorf and his actors did not know that the cancellation of *Trommeln* had been decided long before the scheduled premiere, and they were left to guess at the nature and extent of Stasi involvement and sabotage. But there was also only a limited amount of vertical and horizontal coordination within the bureaucracy: officials in Anklam and Neubrandenburg tried to second-guess the motives of the Culture Ministry and DTO, and the regional courts were not prepared to expedite Castorf's dismissal. Legal historians emphasize the primacy of politics in GDR law, and evidence of politically motivated dismissals in other cases—including that of Josef Budek—suggests that Castorf could have been dismissed if the political will had been there.[161]

---

[159] Sieling, '"Aber sagen Sie nichts gegen Anklam!"', 18; Schütt, *Die Erotik des Verrats*, 103.

[160] Interview with Ullrich, 26.7.2007.

[161] See e.g. Roger Engelmann and Clemens Vollnhals (eds.), *Justiz im Dienste der Parteiherrschaft: Rechtspraxis und Staatssicherheit in der DDR*, 2nd rev. edn. (Berlin: Ch. Links, 2000), 9; Middendorf, *Recht auf Arbeit in der DDR*, 376–80.

Whilst these case studies represent two poles in the practice of GDR theatre censorship, they do not exemplify 'pure' types of cooperation and conflict. It was partly the spectre of conflict that led Hoffmann to back *Dmitri* and encouraged Schroth and Jaksch to respond to the authorities' concerns. When local officials came up against the limits of their powers in Anklam, a reluctant compromise emerged as the only means of securing Castorf's removal from the theatre. But the contrast between these experiences of censorship was substantial, and frustration at regional differences in the treatment of theatre was mounting. When the Fifth Congress of the Union of Theatre Practitioners met in November 1985, directors complained that productions of new contemporary drama were blocked in some regions but not others, and they blamed regional officials.[162] Given that Hager had decreed that other theatres should not be allowed to stage *Dmitri*, these criticisms were probably not entirely fair. But theatre practitioners argued that the Ministry needed to take a clear stand on key issues and to force local officials to heed its views.[163] These calls for central intervention marked the prelude to a campaign for the reform of theatre censorship, as we shall see in Chapter 7.

---

[162] BStU HAA XX/AKG, i, fo. 183.
[163] Ibid. 184.

7

Dresden and Bautzen in the Late 1980s: Performing Perestroika

> Ich will weder das Verbot noch die Genehmigung als Geschenk haben. (I want neither bans nor permission as a gift.)
>
> Christoph Hein, 'Weder das Verbot noch die Genehmigung als Geschenk', 168

1. INTRODUCTION

In the spring and summer of 1987, the Culture Ministry came under mounting pressure to reform the 'approval procedures' for contemporary drama. It responded by backing productions of previously unstaged plays, leading to real changes in the repertoire in 1988–9. In East Berlin alone, spectators could choose among three 'new' plays by Heiner Müller, including the long-awaited *Germania Tod in Berlin*. This chapter investigates how the national debate about theatre censorship affected negotiations in Bautzen and Dresden, in the south-east of the GDR. It focuses on two world premieres: Jürgen Groß's *Revisor oder Katze aus dem Sack* (Government Inspector or the Cat's out of the Bag) and Christoph Hein's *Die Ritter der Tafelrunde* (The Knights of the Round Table). These productions were staged under the jurisdiction of the same regional authorities, the *Rat des Bezirks* and the SED-*Bezirksleitung* in Dresden. But Bautzen was some sixty kilometres east of Dresden, and the *Rat des Kreises* and SED-*Kreisleitung* served as the immediate points of contact for the town's theatre practitioners.

Since 1973, the Dresden region had been under the control of Hans Modrow, who was seen in the late 1980s as the First Secretary most open to Mikhail Gorbachev's policies of glasnost and perestroika. These policies raised tremendous hopes and expectations in the GDR, particularly as the USSR had been the main opponent of earlier attempts to reform socialism in Hungary and Czechoslovakia. Yet in spring 1987, the distance between Honecker and Gorbachev was becoming increasingly clear. Whilst Honecker professed his support for the GDR's traditional alliance with the USSR, he denied that Gorbachev's reforms were relevant to the GDR. Honecker even implied that the Soviet leadership needed to learn from the SED and its alleged economic achievements, not the other way round.[1] In an interview with the West German magazine *Stern*, Kurt Hager famously dismissed perestroika as a 'wallpaper change', arguing that the GDR had no need to redecorate just because the USSR had decided to do so.[2] Although Hager was only saying what Honecker had already implied, his forceful dismissal came as a slap in the face to those hoping for reform in the GDR. When the interview was reprinted in *Neues Deutschland*, complaints in theatres and other workplaces mounted, alongside criticisms of the media and shortages of consumer goods.

Whilst Hager's comments provoked numerous letters of complaint from individuals, a letter from the Staatsschauspiel Dresden stood out from the pile. The letter came from the theatre's entire Party organization, exposing the company to accusations of forming a 'platform' hostile to the SED leadership. Party members at the Staatsschauspiel had discussed Hager's interview fully and frankly in five meetings between 15 April and 2 June, attended by officials from the *Bezirksleitung* and/or *Stadtleitung*.[3] These officials had attempted to moderate the content of the letter, but they—like the manager Gerhard Wolfram— had failed to dilute its central charge: that Hager's characterization of perestroika was completely wrong and was bound to mislead his readers. Modrow had forwarded the letter to Hager, but without denouncing it.

Hager's initial reaction was relatively restrained: he wrote an eleven-page reply, dismissing the theatre's criticisms.[4] But when Egon Krenz— who was deputizing for Honecker during his summer holiday—saw the

[1] Peter Jochen Winters, 'Die Reformen Gorbachevs und die DDR-Bevölkerung', in Konrad Löw (ed.), *Beharrung und Wandel: Die DDR und die Reformen des Michail Gorbatschow*, Schriftenreihe der Gesellschaft für Deutschlandforschung, 28 (Berlin: Duncker & Humblot, 1990), 31–40 at 34–5.
[2] Peter Pragal and Ulrich Völklein, 'Jedes Land wählt seine Lösung', *Stern*, 40/16 (9.4.1987), 140–4. Reprinted as 'Kurt Hager beantwortete Fragen der Illustrierten *Stern*', *ND*, 10.4.1987.
[3] 'Zur Entstehung des Briefes an Genossen Kurt Hager', 24.7.1987, SächsStA-D 11857 A 13938. For a detailed account of the controversy, see Niemann, *Die Sekretäre der SED-Bezirksleitungen*, 299–325.
[4] Niemann, *Die Sekretäre der SED-Bezirksleitungen*, 305.

correspondence, he summoned an emergency meeting of the Central Committee's Secretariat. The reactions at this meeting show the substantial differences that had emerged between the Secretariat, reformers in the Staatsschauspiel, and officials in Dresden. The minutes are full of rhetorical questions, conveying horror and disbelief at Modrow's approach. Pointing out that Modrow had received advance warning of the letter, Hermann Axen asked if he had forgotten the most basic rules of politics.[5] Horst Dohlus asked what was going on in the *Bezirksleitung*, and whether Party organizations were being allowed to do exactly as they liked.[6] The Secretariat denounced Modrow's political negligence, and Krenz told the *Bezirksleitung* that he could not understand why it had allowed the matter to drag on for three months. After all, he added, the Central Committee had taken a clear stand after just fifteen hours.[7] Krenz launched an investigation of the *Bezirksleitung* and the Staatsschauspiel, which resulted in the departure of the theatre's Party Secretary, Lilian Floß.

This episode helps us to understand the nature and limits of Modrow's room for manoeuvre in Dresden. He and his officials had tolerated discussions that Krenz thought should have been stopped immediately. Members of the Staatsschauspiel recognized all along that they had more room for manoeuvre than theatre practitioners in other regions.[8] But Modrow's own room for manoeuvre was always contingent on the Party leadership, and his increasing marginalization in the Central Committee made reprisals more likely. When Krenz arrived in Dresden to discipline the *Bezirksleitung*, Modrow fell into line and apologized for his handling of the matter.[9] However, Modrow exercised discretion in the manner in which he conducted the ensuing disciplinary proceedings, telling the *Stadtleitung* to resolve the issue through political debate, not 'administration'.[10] He took the director Horst Schönemann into his confidence, even showing him the

[5] 'Mitschrift über die Aussprache der Sondersekretariatssitzung im ZK am 15.7.1987', SächsStA-D 11857 A 13208.
[6] Ibid.
[7] 'Mitschrift über die Auswertung der Sekretariatssitzung des Zentralkomitees... am 17.7.1987', SächsStA-D 11857 A 13208.
[8] 'Rechenschaftsbericht anläßlich der Parteiwahlen 1987', SächsStA-D 11857 A 13938.
[9] 'Genosse Egon Krenz hat uns parteilich...', SächsStA-D 11857 A 13208.
[10] 'Niederschrift über die Beratung... am 04.08.1987', SächsStA-D 11857 A 13938.

Central Committee's reports.[11] Wolfram reportedly commented that he had often found himself in the firing line, but never before with a First Secretary on his side.[12]

The shades of opinion within the SED apparatus were evidently far more varied than the official line on perestroika suggests. This variety is evident not only from the contrast between Modrow and Hager, but also from the difference between the instinctive reactions of Hager and Krenz. These differences extended to the Party administration in Dresden. According to Floß, officials in the *Stadtleitung* disregarded Modrow's instructions by forcing theatre practitioners to choose between remaining in the Party and supporting the letter to Hager.[13] The Central Committee's intervention may well have undermined Modrow's authority within his administration, encouraging officials to err on the side of caution.

2. CHALLENGES TO THEATRE CENSORSHIP

At the Tenth Writers' Congress in November 1987, Christoph Hein launched a scathing attack on GDR censorship. Disregarding the conventional euphemisms, he declared: 'die Zensur der Verlage und Bücher, der Verleger und Autoren ist überlebt, nutzlos, paradox, menschenfeindlich, volksfeindlich, ungesetzlich und strafbar.'[14] (The censorship of publishing houses and books, of publishers and authors, is outdated, useless, paradoxical, inhuman, against the public interest, illegal, and criminal.) This denunciation focused on pre-publication censorship, but Hein went on to address the conditions facing contemporary drama and theatre. Arguing that these conditions were more severe than those facing poetry or prose, he suggested devoting a minute's silence to GDR drama.[15] Hein added that drama had suffered from repeated disciplinary incursions, and he reminded his listeners of

---

[11] Uta Dittmann, 'Das große Jahrzehnt: Erinnerungen von Horst Schönemann und Wolfgang Engel', in Dittmann (ed.), *Sein oder Nichtsein? Theatergeschichten: Staatsschauspiel Dresden 1913 bis heute* (Dresden: Staatsschauspiel Dresden and Sächsische Zeitung, 1995), 93–111 at 109.

[12] Hans Modrow, with Hans-Dieter Schütt, *Ich wollte ein neues Deutschland* (Munich: Econ & List, 1999), 208–9.

[13] BStU BV Ddn. Abt. XX 9330, fos. 42–3.

[14] Hein, 'Literatur und Wirkung', 228.

[15] Ibid. 239.

Wolfgang Langhoff's humiliating public apology in 1963.[16] We have
already seen how this event lived on in the individual memory of
members of the Deutsches Theater, but Hein's speech shows how the
episode had entered into cultural memory, coming to epitomize the
injustice of political censorship in the GDR.

Hein's speech was the most thorough and explicit attack on censorship to date, and the novelist Günter de Bruyn echoed his comments at
the Congress. But these interventions had actually been preceded by a
campaign to reform theatre censorship earlier in 1987. Following discussions at a drama workshop in March, Irina Liebmann had proposed
the creation of a 'Theater der Autoren' (Authors' Theatre) that would
premiere plays, free from state control. She produced a paper criticizing
the so-called 'approval procedures', circulating the paper to other writers
and to Hager:

Ein neues Stück hat kaum Aussichten, nach seiner Fertigstellung auf der Bühne
ausprobiert zu werden, wird in der Regel jahrelang hin- und hergeschoben, bis
das Interesse von Theater und Autor erlahmt und die Sache als inzwischen
veraltet zugunsten neuerer Stücke, die dann auch nicht inszeniert werden, aus
der Diskussion verschwindet.[17]

A new play hardly has any prospect of being tried out on stage once finished, is
usually passed from pillar to post for years on end, until the interest of the
theatre and author has waned. The play then disappears from the discussion
board on the grounds that it is out of date, in favour of more recent plays, which
are not staged either.

A group of dramatists drew up a set of suggested measures designed to
'cure' the relationship between drama and theatre, breaking a long-
standing taboo by referring explicitly to censorship. But instead of
suggesting its abolition, the paper proposed its legalization: the creation
of a censorship bureau that would give explicit reasons for its decisions.[18]

A report in the Stasi files purports to present Peter Hacks's views
concerning the proposal. This report—dated 17 August 1987—was
based on information supplied by 'a reliable unofficial source', the
writer Dieter Noll (codenamed 'Romanze'). Noll was in close contact
with Hacks during the summer months, as their summer homes were

[16] Ibid. 241.
[17] Irina Liebmann, 'Diskussionsvorschlag zur Gründung eines Theaters der Autoren',
10.3.1987, AdK Rainer-Kirsch-Archiv 325.
[18] 'Maßnahmen zur Einleitung einer Genesung des Verhältnisses zwischen DDR-
Dramatik und DDR-Theater', BArch DY 30/vorl. SED/40143.

close together. In a letter written in honour of Hacks's seventy-fifth birthday, Noll recalls how they used to meet for an afternoon and evening once a fortnight during the summer. He even adds—ironically, in view of the Stasi report—that it was a shame that their conversations were not recorded.[19] Noll was thus in a strong position to comment on Hacks's views. However, as Major Pönig wrote up the final report, it does offer only a third-hand account of Hacks's position, filtered through Noll and Pönig.

According to Pönig, Hacks argued:

Das Wesentliche an dieser Eingabe sei, aus der unmöglichen Situation herauszukommen, daß ein Autor nie erfahre, warum sein Stück nicht uraufgeführt werde. Es gehe nicht darum, eine Aufführung gegen den Willen des Staates zu erzwingen, sondern es gehe um das Recht des Autors, durch das...Urteil eines 'Zensors' zu erfahren, *warum* man meine, ein Stück solle in der DDR besser nicht aufgeführt werden.[20]

The main aim of this proposal is to find a way out of the impossible situation whereby an author never finds out why his play is not premiered. The point is not to force a production against the will of the state, but rather that the author should have the right to find out through the...verdict of a 'censor' *why* it is thought that a play had better not be performed in the GDR.

The inverted commas gestured towards the fact that the SED did not acknowledge that censorship existed in the GDR, yet they do not necessarily constitute evidence of ideological manipulation by Pönig, or even by Noll. Given that Hacks was critical of calls for artistic freedom in the GDR,[21] it is entirely conceivable that he would have deployed the term 'censor' ironically—particularly in a conversation with Noll, who had consistently demonstrated his support for Party policy. Hacks reportedly argued that the Culture Ministry had only itself to blame for this campaign: officials had left drama to take care of itself, provoking dramatists and theatre practitioners into taking matters into their own hands.[22] He argued that dramatists were simply attempting to solve a domestic problem without attracting outside attention. Unless their efforts were heeded, they might go public at the Writers'

[19] Dieter Noll, 'Lieber, sehr verehrter Peter Hacks', in André Thiele (ed.), *In den Trümmern ohne Gnade: Festschrift für Peter Hacks* (Berlin: Eulenspiegel, 2003), 69–70 at 69.
[20] BStU HA XX 13578, fo. 9.
[21] Peter Hacks, *Verehrter Kollege: Briefe an Schriftsteller*, ed. Rainer Kirsch (Berlin: Eulenspiegel, 2006), 260.
[22] BStU HA XX 13578, fo. 7.

Congress.[23] Hein's comments at the Congress proved just how prescient Hacks's warning had been.

The Ministry made every effort to avoid a public confrontation over Liebmann's proposal. Deputy Minister Martin Meyer attempted to dampen her expectations in private, before attending a meeting of dramatists, theatre practitioners, and theatre critics in the Academy of Arts on 30 June. Meyer accepted the need for change, using the rhetoric of glasnost: 'Das Genehmigungsverfahren muß verändert werden. Die Diskussion zu den anstehenden Fragen muß offener stattfinden.'[24] (The approval procedures must be changed. The questions on the agenda need to be discussed more openly.) Whilst those present agreed on the difficulties facing contemporary drama, they disagreed on how to tackle them. Both Christoph Schroth and Dieter Mann, the manager of the Deutsches Theater, spoke out in support of an Authors' Theatre, but they were outnumbered.[25] It was not only the hardliners who objected to Liebmann's proposal: Wolfram argued that officials simply needed to apply the existing procedures correctly.[26] Others feared that an Authors' Theatre would distract from the need to provide a long-term solution. In March, Hacks had already warned Liebmann that they needed to fight against the trick of the 'alibi premiere', whereby a play was performed once and never again. He argued that an Authors' Theatre would be an ideal location for just that.[27]

Although the meeting deferred any decision on Liebmann's proposal, the project now had no realistic chance of success. Given that the Ministry had never intended to allow an Authors' Theatre, it had pulled off a clever coup by transferring the focus to the disagreements within the theatre community. Even Liebmann's closest ally, the dramatist Georg Seidel, wrote:

Ich glaube fast, daß man die Ministerien und das ZK umstimmen könnte, also die uns die Gelder und Räume für so ein Theater zur Verfügung stellen könnten, [aber] wir werden nicht klarkommen mit den Autoren. Da sind unterschiedliche Eitelkeiten und Konzepte, die niemals unter einen Hut zu bringen sind.[28]

[23] Ibid. 10.
[24] 'Sitzungsprotokoll vom 30.6.87', AdK Georg-Seidel-Archiv 507.
[25] Ibid.
[26] Ibid.
[27] Hacks, *Verehrter Kollege*, 253.
[28] Georg Seidel, undated draft letter to Irina Liebmann, AdK Georg-Seidel-Archiv 515.

I almost believe that we could win round the Ministries and the Central Committee, that they might give us the funds and premises for such a theatre, [but] we will not cope with the authors. There are too many different egos and ideas, which can never be brought under one umbrella.

When other members of the group failed to attend a meeting on 19 September, Liebmann and Seidel declared that they regarded it as having disbanded.[29]

Liebmann may not have achieved her key objective, and her attempt at an organized campaign was over. But the need to make it easier for new plays to be performed had entered the mainstream of cultural debate.[30] The Ministry was keen to be seen taking the initiative, and it created an Advisory Committee for Drama (Beirat für Dramatik), which would help to approve new plays and productions. The committee had approximately twenty-five members, including Müller, Strahl, Schroth, and representatives from bodies such as the Writers' Union, Union of Theatre Practitioners, and the Theatre Department.[31] By March 1988, the Committee had met twice. Even Hager did not rule out reform, telling Wekwerth that the Committee's work should show whether the approval procedures for premieres needed to be changed.[32]

Some scepticism about the Ministry's newfound commitment to 'democratic' decision-making is certainly in order. Hoffmann had been in office since 1973, helping to shape cultural policy and decide which plays would be premiered. He had ceded none of his powers to the new Advisory Committee, whose hand-picked members were able only to make recommendations. The Stasi informer 'Nowotny' suggested that the Ministry had actually made a shrewd tactical move by tying important dramatists to the regime.[33] Even Stasi officers now argued that the Ministry needed to review existing bans on new drama, promote contemporary GDR plays, and prevent regional inconsistencies.[34] This

---

[29] Copy of a letter from Georg Seidel to Buhss, Brasch, and Edelmann, 23.9.1987, AdK Georg-Seidel-Archiv 512. Hacks formally disbanded the group in May 1988 after Liebmann had left the GDR. See Hacks, *Verehrter Kollege*, 264 and 266.

[30] See e.g. Klaus Höpcke, 'Zum Drama des Dramas', *TdZ* 42/10 (Oct. 1987), 12–13; Hermann Kant, 'Zum Schriftstellerberuf gehört, stets auf Posten zu sein in den Kämpfen der Zeit', *ND*, 25.11.1987.

[31] Peter von Becker and Michael Merschmeier ' "Das Sicherste ist die Veränderung": THEATER HEUTE-Gespräch mit DDR-Kulturminister Hans Joachim [*sic*] Hoffmann', *Theater 1988: Jahrbuch der Zeitschrift Theater heute*, 29 (1988), 10–20 at 11.

[32] Hager to Wekwerth, 23.9.1987, BArch DY 30/vorl. SED/40143.

[33] BStU HA XX/AKG 852, i, fo. 163.

[34] BStU HA XX 4808, fo. 34.

strategy reflected the need to head off discontent and secure central control over cultural management. As Lennartz points out, it was convenient for the Ministry to shift the blame to the regions, just as it suited Höpcke—as the Deputy Minister in charge of publishing—to shift the blame onto Meyer, his colleague in charge of theatre and music.[35] Since the GDR's collapse, the former President of the Union of Theatre Practitioners has questioned the sincerity of Hoffmann's gestures towards cooperation. Hans-Peter Minetti claims that Hoffmann launched a tirade against the Union's theatre policy at a meeting in March 1988, accusing its leaders of undermining socialism and the GDR.[36] These accusations were made in Ragwitz's presence, perhaps partly for her benefit.

Even so, Hoffmann's subsequent actions and statements indicate that the Ministry became significantly more open to reform than the Central Committee's Culture Department and the Politbüro. After his own interview with *Stern*, Hager was bound to take it as a personal insult when the West German periodical *Theater heute* published an interview with Hoffmann entitled 'Das Sicherste ist die Veränderung' (The safest thing is change). Hoffmann presented himself here as the embodiment of glasnost, allowing his interviewers to depart from the agreed list of questions and waiving his right to check the interview before it went to press. Hoffmann called for greater cooperation between East and West and argued that Cold War clichés were out of date.[37] Although he adhered to the Party line that the GDR had no need to copy the USSR, he still claimed that Soviet developments were a source of inspiration.[38] An indignant Honecker scribbled the question 'Wozu haben wir diesen Kulturminister?' (What's the point of having this Culture Minister?) on his copy of the interview.[39]

When news of the interview broke in the Politbüro, Hoffmann was in Cuba. On his return to Berlin, he was informed at the airport that Hager was expecting him immediately. During the ensuing confrontation, Hoffmann collapsed and was rushed to hospital with a suspected stroke. Uwe Behnisch, who worked in the Theatre Department at the time, remembers how Siegfried Böttger—Meyer's successor—sent one of his colleagues to West Berlin to buy a copy of *Theater heute*, so that

[35] Lennartz, 'Klaus Höpcke', 13.
[36] Minetti, *Erinnerungen*, 296–9.
[37] von Becker and Merschmeier, '"Das Sicherste"', 15.
[38] Ibid. 18.
[39] Peter von Becker and Michael Merschmeier, 'Wir wollten Sozialismus und wurden Stalinisten', *Theater heute*, 31/7 (July 1990), 2–18 at 5.

officials could see what had caused the row.[40] News of Hoffmann's interview soon spread within the theatre community, and Hoffmann remembers being repeatedly asked if he had a spare copy.[41] After his recovery, he was instructed to explain his actions to the Central Committee, and only the intervention of a series of artists succeeded in persuading Honecker not to sack him.[42] Following this episode, Hoffmann reportedly started praising Honecker at meetings in the Ministry, assuming that the Stasi was monitoring his comments.[43] Once again, the Minister was tailoring his comments to his perceived audience.

Peter Hacks, a staunch opponent of perestroika, believed that Hoffmann and his colleagues had more than a tactical interest in Gorbachev's reforms. In February 1989, Hacks reportedly told André Müller sen. that Hoffmann and the Culture Ministry were the main supporters of liberalism in the GDR.[44] In his diary, Müller sen. recorded his own impression of functionaries from the Party and cultural apparatus, claiming that they all supported Gorbachev and wanted the GDR to be transformed in accordance with his views.[45] On 28 February, Strahl told representatives of the Writers' Union and Union of Theatre Practitioners that contemporary drama now seemed to have more committed, courageous partners in central institutions than in some districts and regions.[46] Even before Hoffmann's interview in *Theater heute*, Böttger had reportedly told local officials that no theatre could turn down GDR plays once the Ministry had approved them.[47] This had crucial implications for planned stagings of *Revisor* and *Die Ritter der Tafelrunde*, two of the titles on Liebmann's list of unperformed plays.

[40] Interview with Uwe Behnisch, 21.4.2009.
[41] von Becker and Merschmeier, 'Wir wollten Sozialismus', 3.
[42] Hermann-Ernst Schauer, 'Der verdächtigte Demokrat', in Gertraude Hoffmann and Klaus Höpcke (eds.), *'Das Sicherste ist die Veränderung': Hans-Joachim Hoffmann. Kulturminister der DDR und häufig verdächtigter Demokrat* (Berlin: Dietz, 2003), 10–24 at 20–1.
[43] Lothar Bisky, 'Nur scheinbar robust', in Hoffmann and Höpcke (eds.), *'Das Sicherste ist die Veränderung'*, 112–14 at 113–14.
[44] A. Müller sen., *Gespräche mit Hacks*, 333.
[45] Ibid. 334.
[46] Rudi Strahl, 'Zur Situation der Bühnenautoren', in *Mitteilungen*, ed. Schriftstellerverband der DDR, 3/4, 9–14 (11–12), SächsStA-L 21123 2405.
[47] 'Niederschrift wesentlicher Gesichtspunkte der Dienstberatung im Ministerium für Kultur am 2.3.1988', LHASA Abt. MER, RdB Halle 4. Abl. 6677.

3. *REVISOR ODER KATZE AUS DEM*
SACK IN BAUTZEN

The Theatre, the Manager, and the Play

Bautzen is probably one of the last places where anyone would expect to find a theatre staging perestroika plays. In the public imagination, the town remains firmly associated with the Stasi prisons, Bautzen I and II. Bautzen was also the centre of the GDR's minority Sorbian population, and the Deutsch-Sorbisches Volkstheater staged productions in both German and Sorbian. As a result of its unique bilingual status, the company was deemed nationally significant and classed in Category B. Its repertoire in 1987–9 included six GDR premieres, alongside stagings of Mikhail Schatrow's *Diktatur des Gewissens* (Dictatorship of Conscience), Heiner Müller's *Der Auftrag* (The Mission), and Ulrich Plenzdorf's *Zeit der Wölfe* (Era of Wolves). Even so, the theatre's role has been forgotten in local accounts of the end of the GDR, which foreground the roles of the church, the Stasi prison, and the Sorbs.[48] In 2005, this omission prompted the actor Michael Lorenz to interview the theatre's former manager Jörg Liljeberg and to deposit material on its productions in the town archive. In an accompanying statement, Lorenz argued that the Deutsch-Sorbisches Volkstheater was one of the starting points and sources of strength for the political changes in Bautzen, perhaps even the most active and effective one.[49]

In October and November 1989, Liljeberg played an active role in the political protests in Bautzen, chairing meetings of the citizens' forum. The Stasi files contain a highly critical report of his behaviour at a performance of *Diktatur des Gewissens* on 18 October, claiming that he invited spectators to challenge the local functionaries present. But in 1992, Liljeberg resigned from his new post as manager of the theatre in Chemnitz, when it emerged that he had worked as an unofficial Stasi informer. One 332-page Stasi file contains extensive evidence of his

---

[48] See e.g. Ronny Heidenreich, *Aufruhr hinter Gittern: Das 'Gelbe Elend' im Herbst 1989* (Leipzig: Leipziger Universitätsverlag, 2009); Martin Kasper (ed.), *Die Lausitzer Sorben in der Wende 1989/90: Ein Abriss mit Dokumenten und einer Chronik*, Schriften des Sorbischen Instituts, 28 (Bautzen: Domowina, 2000).

[49] Michael Lorenz, 'Das Deutsch-Sorbische Volkstheater als Keimzelle und Sprachrohr der Wende in Bautzen und Umgebung', 2005, Stadtarchiv Bautzen, Abgabe Michael Lorenz.

activity between 1966 and 1980, showing how he supplied information on theatre practitioners in Halle, Greifswald, Brandenburg, and East Berlin.[50] As the manager of the Deutsch-Sorbisches Volkstheater, Liljeberg would have been expected to have official contacts with the Stasi in Bautzen, but a question mark remains over the nature and extent of this contact. The surviving material does not allow us to reach any definitive judgements on Liljeberg's motives in the late 1980s, but he did facilitate perestroika productions in Bautzen, and he provided local political leadership in the autumn of 1989.

As in Dresden, it was Hager's dismissal of perestroika that provoked Bautzen's theatre practitioners to focus on new political drama. Their resolve was strengthened in November 1988, when the Politbüro discontinued the distribution of *Sputnik*, a Soviet German-language magazine that had become an important channel for communicating Gorbachev's reforms. Now that the GDR's international isolation seemed complete, members of the Deutsch-Sorbisches Volkstheater were all the more determined to initiate a direct dialogue about local problems with spectators. This explains the appeal of *Revisor*, a satire on the corrupt bureaucracy of a small GDR town, based on *The Government Inspector* by Nikolai Gogol. In Jürgen Groß's version, the central character—Wölf Revisor—has just been released from prison, having served an eighteen-month sentence for insulting officials. He encounters Patsch, a government chauffeur who has finished his final day's work and wants to make up for thirty years spent living by the rulebook. Patsch takes Revisor to the local Interhotel, which is reserved for visiting dignitaries and foreign tourists. When local officials spot the government limousine and hear that a *Revisor* (Inspector) is in town, they assume that he has come to carry out a surprise inspection. Panic-stricken, they each attempt to save their skin by denouncing their colleagues in confidential dossiers, which they deliver to Revisor. This results in a comedy of mistaken identity and intent: Revisor interprets the welcome visit of the public prosecutor and judge as a threat, and they interpret his oblique references to re-education in prison as evidence that he has come fresh from ideological training in Moscow.

Revisor is not a sophisticated comedy; it lacks psychological depth and relies heavily on one-liners and comic catchphrases. But its lack of subtlety was what guaranteed it an impact in 1989: the play publicly

---

[50] BStU BV Bln. AIM 7282/91, ii.i.

ridiculed the entire establishment of a provincial town, including the Party, FDGB, FDJ, army, police, judiciary, school inspector, and theatre manager. The Party Secretary, for example, reports that he has rung his colleagues in the capital twelve times in a bid to discover what is going on in his own town.[51] Even the mayor, who decides to use Revisor to expose his subordinates' shortcomings, has no claim to moral authority. He has a string of affairs and instigates a cover-up at the end of the play: after Revisor and Patsch have made a hasty escape, the mayor dispatches cleaners to remove every trace of the confidential dossiers. As the play ends with the restoration of the old order, it suggests that rebellion is possible only through a temporary period of misrule. This conservative twist is mitigated to some extent by an earlier episode, in which the suicide of a local factory director is announced. In his suicide letter, the factory director explains that he has borrowed money from 'the devil' on the world market, and that the devil is demanding repayment.[52] The intended parallel with the GDR's economic situation was clear: Honecker's government had financed a rise in living standards through Western loans, which would eventually have to be repaid.

The Approval Procedures

The Staatsschauspiel Dresden had originally planned to stage *Revisor* in 1982–3, when Liljeberg was its deputy manager. The plans were reportedly 'withdrawn' in consultation with Klaus Schumann, who headed the Culture Department in the *Rat des Bezirks*.[53] On 3 March 1988, Liljeberg applied for permission to perform the play in Bautzen, in a production devised by the guest director Hella Müller. In 2005, Liljeberg told Lorenz that he had bypassed the *Rat des Bezirks*, knowing that it would oppose the production, and got approval from the Deputy Culture Minister.[54] The records do confirm that the Ministry approved the production, in conjunction with Hager. However, they indicate that the main opposition came from the *Rat des Kreises*. On 11 April 1988,

---

[51] Jürgen Groß, 'Revisor oder Katze aus dem Sack', *TdZ* 44/3 (Mar. 1989), 52–64 at 54.
[52] Ibid. 63.
[53] BStU BV Ddn. AKG PI 18/89, fo. 101.
[54] Michael Lorenz, interview with Jörg Liljeberg, 5.1.2005, Stadtarchiv Bautzen, Abgabe Michael Lorenz.

Monika Pohl—the local official responsible for culture—informed Schumann that she could not support the production on dramatic or political grounds. She argued that the situations were artificial and unrealistic, the dialogue was poor, and the social criticism was unacceptable.[55] Schumann forwarded the application and script to the Ministry on 22 April, saying that he found it hard to envisage the play being performed. Even so, he asked Hoffmann to see if the play was stageable and—if appropriate—to allow the theatre to start rehearsals.[56] So whilst Liljeberg is right about Schumann's reservations, he seems to have overestimated the strength of his opposition.

On 5 September, Schumann informed Pohl that Hoffmann had agreed to the premiere, provided officials checked the revised script.[57] A representative of the *Rat des Kreises* attended the run-through on 13 January, together with Maud Klevenow, who now headed the Ministry's Theatre Department. Whilst Klevenow objected to the use of police and army uniforms, the theatre succeeded in convincing her that they were necessary.[58] Klevenow agreed that the premiere could go ahead, and Böttger subsequently presented this decision as a response to Hein's criticisms of censorship at the Writers' Congress.[59] *Revisor* thus owed its premiere to central decision-making and the absence of active opposition from the regional authorities. No officials from the *Rat des Bezirks* or *Bezirksleitung* attended the run-through, suggesting that they did not regard the production as a priority and were prepared to defer to the Ministry's judgement. This may in turn explain why Hoffmann did not invite the Advisory Committee to the run-through. There is no evidence that Modrow intervened at this stage.

The Programme: from Mimicry to Plagiarism

The dramaturge Eveline Günther designed a controversial programme for the production, which was first distributed at the premiere. The front cover was stamped 'streng vertraulich' (highly confidential) and 'nur für den Dienstgebrauch' (only for internal use), likening the

[55] BStU BV Ddn. AKG PI 18/89, fo. 100.
[56] Ibid. 101.
[57] Ibid. 105.
[58] BStU BV Ddn. Abt. XX 9426, fo. 39.
[59] BStU BV Ddn. AKG PI 18/89, fo. 56.

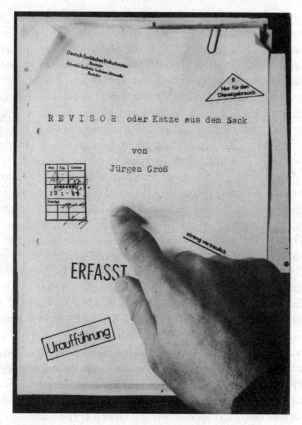

Fig. 7.1. Programme cover for *Revisor* (Eveline Günther and Miroslaw Nowotny, Stiftung Archiv Akademie der Künste)

programme to the confidential dossiers in the play and presenting the production as illicit (Fig. 7.1).[60] The highlight of the programme was a fictitious response by an outraged spectator called Karl Mager, whose name was easily decoded as an amalgamation of Kurt Hager and Karl Marx. This response mimicked the conventional patterns of protest:

Ich frage mich nun ernstlich: Was bezweckt das Theater bzw. seine Leitung mit der Auswahl dieses Werkes? Man bedenke: das ausgerechnet im 40.

---

[60] The following comments are based on the unpaginated programme, AdK ID 710.

Gründungsjahr der Republik! Haben die Kollegen Dramaturgen wirklich nichts besseres [*sic*] gefunden?

I ask myself in all seriousness: what did the theatre or its management intend by choosing this play? Let us remember: it is being staged in the year of the fortieth anniversary of the foundation of the Republic, of all times! Were the theatre's dramaturges really unable to find anything better?

The mimicry was so successful that Colonel Jankowski, head of the Stasi in Bautzen, would subsequently incorporate some of Mager's criticisms into his own report of the production, without acknowledging his source. Jankowski borrowed isolated phrases, such as claims that the mayor lived in a moral quagmire ('in einem moralischen Sumpf') and that officials denounced their colleagues in order to escape scot-free ('um selbst ungeschoren davonzukommen').[61] But he also borrowed a far lengthier criticism of Groß's characterization of officials:

> es [handelt] sich nicht um Leute, die mit ihrer Arbeit etwas zum Wohl der Bürger bewirken wollen, sondern die sich den ganzen Tag und mit aller Kraft und Initiative nur an ihrem Stuhl festklammern.[62]

> we are not dealing with people who are striving to benefit the public through their work, but who instead spend the entire day and all their energy and initiative clinging on to their position.

In the programme, Günther added to the humour by simulating censorship, blacking out individual phrases from the report and thus subjecting 'Karl Mager' to a taste of his own medicine.

Günther also courted controversy in the programme by addressing conditions in Bautzen explicitly. Using material that had already been published in the press, she referred to shortages in consumer goods, quoted public prosecutor Jürgen Schär on the social causes of rowdy behaviour, and even cited Modrow on the need to improve state leadership in the localities. She also included photographs of Bautzen, depicting the dilapidated old town, modern high-rise flats, and queues outside shops. The Minister of the Interior was sufficiently concerned to send for the programme by courier, and the Stasi and *Bezirksleitung* also placed copies on file. Even so, the theatre was able to continue selling the programme throughout the performance run.[63]

---

[61] BStU BV Ddn. AKG PI 18/89, fo. 62.
[62] Ibid. 62.
[63] Interview with Eveline Günther and Michael Lorenz, 23.4.2009.

Calls for Post-performance Censorship

Revisor was premiered on 20 January 1989, to a rapturous reception. A local Sorbian actor announced gleefully that glasnost had finally arrived in Bautzen, and tickets quickly sold out for performances until the end of April.[64] This corresponded to the interest that the play had attracted within the theatre during rehearsals, when actors and technicians had snapped up spare copies of the script.[65] Predictably, the production unleashed protests from outraged Party members. Helmut Mieth, the First Secretary of the SED-*Kreisleitung*, wrote to Modrow on 22 January, objecting to Groß's 'malicious' attacks on Party policy and functionaries, and reporting that many Party members could not understand why the staging had ever been allowed.[66] Mieth asked for a meeting between the *Kreisleitung* and those members of the Ministry and *Rat des Bezirks* who had approved the theatre's repertoire.[67] On 30 January, he then sent a telegram to Hoffmann, demanding to know why the production had been allowed.[68] This flurry of activity seems to have been designed to demonstrate that responsibility for the production lay elsewhere; Mieth never actually demanded a ban. Günther believes that officials in Bautzen were never entirely sure what to make of Liljeberg's connections in Berlin, and that this uncertainty made them reluctant to intervene directly.[69]

The production also provoked an early objection from Bautzen's police department. Lieutenant-Colonel F. wrote to his superior in Dresden, complaining that the production was defamatory. He objected particularly to a scene outside the prison gates, where functionaries march in a circle as if they are taking exercise in a prison yard (Fig. 7.2).[70] But there is more to this complaint than initially meets the eye. According to Liljeberg, Lieutenant-Colonel F. had lent the theatre his uniform on the understanding that he and his wife would be allowed a free choice of carnival outfits from the theatre's costume department.[71] By 29 January,

[64] BStU BV Ddn. KD Bautzen 8622, fos. 75–6.
[65] BStU BV Ddn. AKG PI 18/89, fo. 114.
[66] Ibid. 20.
[67] Ibid. 20.
[68] Ibid. 22.
[69] Interview with Günther, 23.4.2009.
[70] BStU BV Ddn. AKG PI 18/89, fo. 110.
[71] Lorenz, interview with Liljeberg.

Fig. 7.2. Scene from *Revisor oder Katze aus dem Sack* (Miroslaw Nowotny, Stadtarchiv Bautzen)

the theatre had replaced the police uniform with a grey suit, encouraging spectators to identify the character as a Stasi officer rather than as a policeman.[72] The theatre did manage to retain the army uniform that it had borrowed, reportedly in return for free theatre tickets.[73] Liljeberg informed the indignant owner—a major at the flying school—that the new head of the school's political department, a recent graduate from Moscow, actually thought that the production let the army off too lightly.[74]

The controversy over *Revisor* quickly came to the attention of Horst Böhm, the head of the Stasi in Dresden. By 23 January, Böhm had already reported the matter to Rudi Mittig, the Deputy Minister for State Security.[75] Böhm had also asked the head of HA XX to get the Ministry to review its decision to allow the production.[76] On 29 January, three representatives of the SED-*Bezirksleitung* finally arrived in Bautzen to view the production. According to the Stasi, Culture

---

[72] BStU BV Ddn. AKG PI 18/89, fo. 97.
[73] Ibid. 21.
[74] Lorenz, interview with Liljeberg.
[75] BStU BV Ddn. AKG PI 18/89, fo. 113.
[76] Ibid. 113.

Secretary Gabriele Fink reported that a series of passages were unacceptable.[77] However, she—like Mieth—seems to have been more concerned to apportion blame than to push for a ban. Fink reportedly argued that the *Rat des Bezirks* and *Rat des Kreises* had failed to work with the theatre during rehearsals, conveniently ignoring the fact that no one from her own department had attended the run-through.[78] When Modrow and Fink advised the Ministry not to ban the production, Mittig instructed Stasi officers in Dresden to accept this decision.[79] Officers used five informers to monitor audience reactions, and Captain Asche reported on 22 March that interest in the production was declining, compared to the premiere.[80]

Even so, the controversy was revived in May and June, when two spectators complained separately to the SED's Central Control Commission.[81] One of these spectators, H. P., had never actually intended to see *Revisor*. He had bought tickets to see *Das Bad auf der Tenne* (The Bath on the Threshing-Floor), a risqué comedy in which villagers spy on a woman having a bath in her lover's barn. However, the theatre substituted *Revisor* for the scheduled performance on 6 May, the eve of the local elections. Whilst the number of performances of *Revisor* had been agreed in advance, the theatre did have the discretion to schedule additional performances if actors in other productions fell ill. According to Liljeberg, the Chairman of the *Rat des Kreises* had once hinted that this might offer a way round the regulations.[82] The fact that *Revisor* was performed on 6 May certainly indicates that Mieth had failed to limit the political damage caused by the play in the run-up to the local elections, as he had originally intended.[83]

After seeing *Revisor*, a horrified H. P. turned to the Control Commission, expecting it to call the Ministry to account for having approved the production. He suggested that the Commission should send its representatives disguised as ordinary spectators, even offering to buy tickets for them.[84] But a theatre production in Bautzen was not high on the Commission's agenda in May 1989, and it referred the complaint to

[77] Ibid. 56.
[78] Ibid. 56–7.
[79] Ibid. 58.
[80] BStU BV Ddn. Abt. XX 9426, fo. 60.
[81] See SächsStA-D 11857 A 13939.
[82] Lorenz, interview with Liljeberg.
[83] BStU BV Ddn. AKG PI 18/89, fo. 20.
[84] H. P. to Mückenberger, 18.5.1989, SächsStA-D 11857 A 13939.

Modrow. On 9 and 13 June, H. P. met officials from the *Kreisleitung*, who explained how the production had come about.[85] Despite their advice, H. P. continued to insist that the production should be cancelled immediately. It was only at a third meeting, on 19 July, that he finally accepted that Bautzen could not afford the scandal of a production ban.[86]

Although the Commission did not investigate H. P.'s complaint directly, its deputy chairman Werner Müller asked Modrow to formulate a response. The files of the *Bezirksleitung* contain a draft letter to Müller, justifying the decision to allow performances of *Revisor* to continue. The writer—Modrow or a functionary working on his behalf—claimed that the *Bezirksleitung* had tried to influence the production from the start, through the *Kreisleitung* and the *Rat des Bezirks*.[87] The writer added that the production had not added any superficial local references. This was demonstrably untrue: the prison walls were painted yellow in a reference to the Stasi prison Bautzen I, known locally as 'the Yellow Misery' (*das Gelbe Elend*), and a picture presented to Revisor as a gift showed Bautzen's old town on one side and its House of Fashion—a notorious local eyesore—on the other.[88] The writer noted that although officials had suggested changes, they could only have enforced them 'administratively' by overruling Liljeberg, a solution that would have caused a scandal beyond Bautzen itself.[89] The performance run would end after a further three performances, and none would be held in the month of the GDR's fortieth anniversary.[90] In actual fact, a further five performances took place between 22 September and 3 December, followed by guest performances in West Berlin in March 1990.[91]

The significance of Modrow's restraint becomes clear in comparison with a subsequent production in Potsdam, which Adrianus Schriel and Barrie Baker have examined.[92] The Hans-Otto-Theater premiered

---

[85] 'Aktennotiz', 9.6.1989; unsigned draft letter from the First Secretary to Werner Müller, 3.8.1989. Both in SächsStA-D 11857 A 13939.

[86] Stremlow to R. Hoffmann, 20.7.1989, SächsStA-D 11857 A 13939.

[87] First Secretary to Müller, 3.8.1989.

[88] Amateur audiovisual recording of the dress rehearsal, Stadtarchiv Bautzen; interview with Günther and Lorenz, 23.4.2009.

[89] First Secretary to Müller, 3.8.1989.

[90] Ibid.

[91] Lorenz confirmed this using his diaries for 1989 and 1990.

[92] See Schriel, 'The History of the Hans-Otto-Theater', 284–91; Baker, '"From Page to Stage"', 239–58.

Revisor on 21 May, to a tumultuous response from the audience. The manager Gero Hammer had tried to tone down the production before the premiere, removing an article by Gorbachev from the programme. The audience's response prompted him to make further changes, and he cut the gift of a framed picture of Potsdam's ruined Garrison Church, which had been razed by the SED. Even so, when First Secretary Günther Jahn saw the third performance on 24 May, he was horrified. According to Schriel, Jahn declared that the production was the worst thing that he had experienced in Potsdam in fifteen years, warning that the SED members involved in the production would answer for their actions. Following Jahn's intervention, the *Bezirksleitung* ordered Hammer to withdraw the production, organized written protests from the functionaries insulted in the play, and arranged for these functionaries to invite the actors playing their fictional counterparts to shadow them at work. On 27 June, Jahn wrote to Honecker, demanding that the Culture Ministry desist from recommending plays like *Revisor*.[93] The fact that the production in Bautzen survived the ban in Potsdam highlights synchronic differences in censorship, directly related to what the SED's First Secretaries were prepared to tolerate in their regions.

4. *DIE RITTER DER TAFELRUNDE* IN DRESDEN

The Theatre and its Manager

As the historic seat of the Electors of Saxony, Dresden is steeped in cultural tradition, with the Semper opera house, the Zwinger palace, and Grünes Gewölbe art collection. The Staatsschauspiel was classed as one of the GDR's Category A theatres, and it enjoyed a renaissance in the 1980s under Gerhard Wolfram, who became its manager in 1983. Wolfram succeeded in bringing together directors with very different styles and methods: Wolfgang Engel, Horst Schönemann, Klaus Dieter Kirst, and Irmgard Lange. Engel's iconoclastic productions of the classics raised the theatre's international profile, and a highly successful Western tour in 1986 helped to increase Wolfram's bargaining power at home. Wolfram did not shy away from high-risk projects, inviting Tragelehn to restage *Die Umsiedlerin* in 1985 and encouraging Engel

---

[93] I am indebted to Schriel, 'The History of the Hans-Otto-Theater', 287–90, for this account.

to direct the long-overdue GDR premiere of *Waiting for Godot* in 1987. The function of theatre as a substitute for the official media was particularly significant in Dresden and the surrounding area, the only part of the GDR where it was impossible to receive Western television. In Bautzen there were just a few places where people could sometimes receive a television signal from the West.[94]

Wolfram's success in Dresden owed a great deal to his collaboration with Hans Modrow. In the summer of 1984, Wolfram had discussed his plans with Modrow in detail. The two men had agreed that theatre should engage with topical social problems, and they seem to have become friends. The files include letters from Wolfram addressed to 'Lieber Hans' (Dear Hans), referring to evening conversations in a local pub, and Modrow read theatre scripts and vouched for productions.[95] This working relationship would have been unthinkable with Konrad Naumann in Berlin. The basis for Wolfram's collaboration with Modrow was a shared sympathy for the reforms that became associated with Gorbachev, and achieving these reforms through the GDR's existing structures. Wolfram never set out to work against the regime; he was a member of the *Bezirksleitung* in Dresden, had official contacts with the Stasi in his capacity as theatre manager, and had also served as an unofficial Stasi informer between 1963 and 1972.[96] It is worth noting that Wolfram's relationship with the Stasi had been tense during his time at the Deutsches Theater; Girod seems never to have forgiven him for complaining of excessive interference from Stasi officers in Berlin.[97] There is also evidence of early tensions in Wolfram's relationship with the *Rat des Bezirks* in Dresden. Culture Secretary Klaus Schumann was critical of both Wolfram and Schönemann, claiming that they lacked the basic ability to manage a theatre.[98] Even so, Wolfram had encountered serious difficulties with only two productions by 1987: *Die Umsiedlerin* and a programme of 1920s cabaret songs. In both cases, he was able to negotiate a compromise and avoid a ban.

From 1987 onwards, these local relationships came under increasing strain. After Wolfram had signed the letter to Hager, he was placed under Stasi surveillance: his post was intercepted and his telephone was

---

[94] Email from Eveline Günther, 23.3.2010.
[95] See e.g. SächsStA-D 11857 IV E-2/9.02/573.
[96] BStU AIM 2268/77. File ii.i contains nineteen reports on developments in theatre.
[97] BStU AP 3743/89, i, fos. 5, 21.
[98] 'Zum Staatsschauspiel' [*c.*1984], SächsStA-D 11857 IV E-2/9/02/573.

bugged.[99] He was presiding over an increasingly critical repertoire, and in 1988 Irmgard Lange even incorporated a protest against the ban on *Sputnik* into her production of Volker Braun's play *Die Übergangsgesellschaft* at the Staatsschauspiel. At the start of the production, copies of *Sputnik* were lying around on stage. A lorry driver entered and collected them without comment. The local authorities tolerated this theatrical protest, asking Wolfram to intervene only when the actor—Lars Jung—announced that this was all that remained of censorship.[100] The fact that Jung was stopped only when he named censorship, not when he acted it out, points to the widening loopholes in theatre controls in Dresden.

The Play and the Production Concept

Die Ritter der Tafelrunde is the play that came to symbolize the collapse of Honecker's regime: it would eventually be performed at twelve GDR theatres, running in Dresden until July 1998. It deals above all with the threatened loss of ideals: how King Artus (Arthur) and his ageing knights respond to their failure to find the Holy Grail, and how they react to the scepticism and hostility of the younger generation. As such, the play seems tailor-made for the situation in 1989, but it was actually the product of a much longer period of gestation. Christoph Hein had begun engaging with the legend of King Arthur in 1978 and had finished an initial draft in 1985–6. After Klaus Dieter Kirst had directed the world premiere of his play *Passage* at the Staatsschauspiel in 1987, Hein had promised to offer him his next dramatic text. On returning home from an evening performance on 30 October 1988, Kirst found the script of *Die Ritter der Tafelrunde* waiting for him at last. As Wolfram was unavailable until 1 November, Kirst had thirty-six hours in which to read and reflect on the play. He knew that it would not be enough to hand Wolfram the script; he also needed to present his views on how to stage it.[101]

[99] BStU BV Ddn. Abt. XX 9330, fo. 6.
[100] 'Information zur Aufführung der *Übergangsgesellschaft* von Volker Braun am 27.11.1988', 28.11.1988, SächsStA-D 11857 A 13937.
[101] 'Endspiel DDR: 20 Jahre *Ritter der Tafelrunde*', MDR FIGARO Radiocafé, broadcast on 12.4.2009. Presented by Thomas Bille, with Christoph Hein and Klaus Dieter Kirst. Staatsschauspiel Dresden Archive.

Hein's play differs substantially in mood, tone, and content from *Revisor*.[102] Hein takes his characters and their ideals seriously, offering a differentiated portrait of the knights' ideological positions and their reactions to failure. Keie is the most doctrinaire, calling for a ruthless crackdown on dissenters, whereas Orilus combines his conservatism with a naive enthusiasm, fuelled by alcohol. Parzival is busy producing an oppositional newspaper, read chiefly by the regime. Mordret, the heir to Artus's kingdom, rejects Parzival's efforts and the knights' quest, yet he is unable to offer any constructive alternative. Artus himself shies away from uncomfortable facts, spending the first act refusing to read a letter from the absent knight Gawain. When he does finally read the letter, he learns that Gawain has abandoned his search for the Grail. This letter, and the devastating testimony that Lancelot subsequently delivers on his return to the court, help Artus to realize that he must hand over his kingdom to Mordret, despite the risks. The play ends with a managed transition to an entirely uncertain future. There is no overthrow or palace coup, let alone a revolution. The people are excluded from the entire process; their views enter the play only through mediated reports.

Staging *Die Ritter der Tafelrunde* as a political satire was not a feasible option in 1988–9, and Kirst chose instead to present the play as a study of mankind. He emphasizes that his decision was not based on tactical considerations, even though it did make his task easier.[103] Hein's play functions as a parable, encouraging spectators to make their own comparisons with the GDR—or, indeed, whichever state in which the play is staged. By respecting the mythical setting of the action, Kirst sought to enable spectators to step back from the political situation in the GDR and to regard failure as a historical phenomenon. He was treating the play as an example of Brechtian historicization,[104] an approach that enabled spectators to spot the differences as well as the obvious similarities between Hein's characters and their own politicians. As Kirst points out, the irony was that the heated debates among Hein's knights were conspicuously absent from the Politbüro,

---

[102] Christoph Hein, *Die Stücke* (Frankfurt/M.: Suhrkamp, 2005), 355–407.

[103] 'Endspiel DDR'.

[104] For Brecht, historicization (*Historisierung*) is a means of showing that the status quo is not an eternal given: things were different in the past, and they will be different again in the future. See Brecht, *BFA*, xxxii.ii. 701–2 at 701.

which was steadfastly refusing to acknowledge evidence of stagnation in the GDR.[105]

The Approval Procedures

Since the *Wende*, individuals involved in the negotiations on *Die Ritter der Tafelrunde* have published contradictory accounts of the approval process. In 1990, Wolfram stated that the Ministry supported the production and that the main opponent was in Dresden's state apparatus, not the *Bezirksleitung*.[106] In contrast, Minetti has argued that the *Bezirksleitung* was the main opponent.[107] He claims in his autobiography that Modrow had taken too many political liberties and was not prepared to incite the central authorities' rage by performing a play reputed to represent the Politbüro.[108] Minetti attributes the premiere to the efforts of the Union of Theatre Practitioners, which he headed at the time, and argues that the Union forced the production through despite the Ministry's reluctance.[109] The theatre's Party Secretary Christine Ostrowski offers a different version again, in which she gives the impression that the theatre stood alone, united in opposition to the regime. She does not mention any support from the Union or Ministry, and she says that local dignitaries boycotted the premiere.[110] Whilst Ostrowski attributes the production 'ban' to Hager, the dramaturge Karla Kochta actually claims that Hager was responsible for granting approval for the production.[111]

Like Hein's play, Kirst's production has attracted significant scholarly interest. In 1993, Ralph Hammerthaler published an illuminating account based mainly on interviews conducted in 1990 and 1992, before Minetti and Ostrowski published their testimony.[112] Barrie Baker has since analysed some of the archive material available on the production and the ensuing disciplinary proceedings against Wolfram, and I am indebted to him for the documents published in the appendix

---

[105] Ibid.
[106] Gerhard Wolfram, 'Wir waren alle auf der Suche...', in Lennartz (ed.), *Vom Aufbruch zur Wende*, 82–9 at 89.
[107] Irmer and Schmidt, *Die Bühnenrepublik*, 116.
[108] Minetti, *Erinnerungen*, 315.
[109] Irmer and Schmidt, *Die Bühnenrepublik*, 116.
[110] Christine Ostrowski, *Im Streit*, ed. Joachim Jahns (Querfurt: Dingsda, 1993), 11–12.
[111] Ibid. 11; Baker, '"From Page to Stage"', 326.
[112] Hammerthaler, 'Die Position des Theaters in der DDR', 226–45.

to his thesis.[113] My own investigation focuses on the pre-performance negotiations, which represented the greatest challenge for Ministry officials since Liebmann's campaign for an Authors' Theatre. I use new interviews and material from the Stasi files and Dresden's state archive, in addition to evidence from the Federal Archive, Academy of Arts, and Staatsschauspiel.

This evidence indicates that the Ministry supported the staging in principle but was wary of its potential to cause controversy, perhaps explaining why Minetti accuses its officials of timidity. The Ministry allowed Hein to introduce his play to GDR dramaturges at a meeting on 14 November 1988, two weeks after he had sent the script to Kirst. Ministry officials considered that the Staatsschauspiel offered the best chance of performing the play, given its track record of staging contemporary drama.[114] Rehearsals began on 10 January, and the official cast list carried the proviso that the production depended on the Minister's agreement.[115] Schumann had made his opposition to the production clear, agreeing only that the play could be rehearsed for a workshop. He reportedly returned after a period of illness to discover that plans for a public premiere were in place, and the *Rat des Bezirks* subsequently launched disciplinary proceedings against Wolfram.[116] This explains why Wolfram claimed that the main enemy was in Dresden's state apparatus.

Material from Dresden's state archive and the Stasi files sheds new light on Modrow's role in the negotiations. On 16 February 1989, Modrow informed Rudi Mittig that he had received strictly confidential information on *Die Ritter der Tafelrunde* from Stasi officers in Dresden. Significantly, he compared the reports on Hein's play with those on *Revisor*, which had been premiered just three weeks earlier:

Da bereits vor kurzem ein Stück von Jürgen Groß *Der* [sic] *Revisor—oder die* [sic] *Katze aus dem Sack* zu einer ähnlichen Information führte und darin geäußerte politische Bedenken nicht ohne Berechtigung waren, möchte ich zu diesem Vorgang gern Deinen Rat und evtl. eine Konsultation mit einem Genossen.[117]

---

[113] Baker, '"From Page to Stage"', 213–38, D1–25.

[114] BStU BV Ddn. Abt. XX 9427, fo. 12.

[115] 'Uraufführung *Die Ritter der Tafelrunde* von Christoph Hein', Staatsschauspiel Dresden Archive, file 388.

[116] BStU BV Ddn. Abt. XX 9427, fos. 42–5.

[117] Modrow to Mittig, 16.2.1989, SächsStA-D 11857 A 13207.

As a play by Jürgen Groß— *The* [*sic*] *Government Inspector—or the Cat's out of the Bag*—recently led to a similar report, and as the political reservations expressed in this report were not without justification, I would appreciate your advice and possibly the opportunity to discuss the matter with a comrade.

This letter was written approximately two weeks after Modrow had been summoned to the Politbüro over a critical report that he had submitted on the economic situation in Dresden. The Politbüro had deflected the charges by arguing that any problems must be due to Modrow's own shortcomings. On 7 February, the Politbüro had passed a resolution instructing Günter Mittag to investigate Dresden, and Modrow claims that over a hundred officials were sent to take the region to task.[118] Modrow's letter to Mittig falls directly in the phase of the inspection, six days before Mittag submitted his report to the Politbüro. The fact that Modrow reported the production to the Deputy Minister for State Security lends credence to Minetti's claim that the First Secretary had taken too many risks and was now being cautious, not actively supporting or opposing the production at this stage.

The main encouragement in this phase came from the Culture Ministry. Wolfram was in close contact with the Theatre Department, as he belonged to a working party that had been appointed to draft a new regulatory framework for theatre. When he subsequently had to defend his decision to prepare the premiere, Wolfram claimed that Hoffmann had indicated that he was inclined to approve it.[119] A Stasi note of a conversation with Hoffmann on 22 February 1989 confirms that the Minister was indeed reluctant to ban the production, in view of Hein's outspoken opposition to censorship:

Da Hein auf dem letzten Schriftstellerkongreß am massivsten die Abschaffung einer angeblichen Zensur in der DDR gefordert hatte und nach Meinung des Genossen Hoffmann am Umgang mit seinen eigenen Stücken in der DDR prüfen wolle, wie sich die staatlichen Organe zu diesem Problem verhalten, müsse man alle Möglichkeiten erhalten, dieses Stück spielbar zu machen.[120]

As Hein was the most outspoken advocate at the last Writers' Congress of the abolition of an alleged censorship in the GDR, and as Comrade Hoffmann believes that he wants to use the way in which his own plays are dealt with in the

---

[118] Modrow, *Ich wollte ein neues Deutschland*, 246–8; Niemann, *Die Sekretäre der SED-Bezirksleitungen*, 325–36.
[119] Gerhard Wolfram, 'Stellungnahme zur Begründung des gegen mich am 22. März eröffneten Disziplinarverfahrens', in Baker, '"From Page to Stage"', D4–D7 at D4.
[120] BStU HA XX 10282, fo. 5.

GDR to test the state authorities' attitudes towards this problem, we need to keep alive every chance of making this play performable.

In fact, the Ministry had just awarded Hein the Lessing Prize for Drama as a sign that the GDR could accommodate his constructive criticism. According to the Stasi, Hoffmann believed that the authorities had always drawn the short straw when it had rejected controversial plays, as the bans had subsequently had to be revoked or modified.[121] The element of *Realpolitik* was unmistakeable: Hoffmann was aware that the cost of banning plays had risen dangerously high. He planned to invite the Advisory Committee to a run-through on 15 March and consult its advice. The Stasi noted that if the verdict were to be negative, Hein would not be able to object to the democratic means used to arrive at the decision.[122]

Meanwhile, Stasi officers were keeping track of rehearsals through their informers. 'Stein' opposed the production, telling officers that it would open the floodgates for similar plays.[123] 'Günter' took a different view, arguing that the play was optimistic and of great philosophical importance, although he conceded that critics of the state would interpret the play as supporting their views.[124] 'Engler', meanwhile, reported that Kirst was trying hard not to produce any obvious contemporary references.[125] Although the Stasi suggested that the SED-*Stadtleitung*, the theatre's *Parteileitung*, and the theatre management should try to influence rehearsals, Kirst says that he and the actors were left completely to their own devices. He argues that the authorities and the theatre's *Parteileitung* probably stayed away out of fear: no one wanted to have to make a decision for or against the production.[126]

Kirst's staging did indeed avoid overt parallels with the GDR. The set confronted spectators with a dark, hermetic space, which looked more like a crypt than a festive hall.[127] The stage was dominated by a round table, surrounded by chairs (Fig. 7.3). One chair was covered in plastic, reserved for the finder of the elusive Grail. Orilus and Keie were dressed

---

[121] BStU HA XX 10282, fo. 7.
[122] Ibid. 6.
[123] BStU BV Ddn. Abt. XX 9427, fo. 5.
[124] Ibid. 3.
[125] Ibid. 9.
[126] Interview with Kirst, 24.4.2009.
[127] Dieter Zumpe, 'Artus—mit nathanischer Weisheit', *Sächsisches Tageblatt* (Dresden), 21.4.1989. My comments on the staging are based on an audiovisual recording made by ZDF and ORF, first broadcast in 1990 and held in AdK AVM 33.8026.

Fig. 7.3. Scene from *Die Ritter der Tafelrunde* (H.-L. Böhme, Staatsschauspiel Dresden)

as old warriors, covered in dust. Kirst did not attempt to suggest parallels between Artus and Honecker, or even between Artus and Gorbachev. Instead, Hein and Kirst agree that the characterization of Artus turned into a covert study of Wolfram: a friendly elderly man, understanding but somewhat helpless, who was striving towards reconciliation and trying to find a way out of a hopeless situation, never letting his despair show.[128] The main sources of energy and activity came from Mordret's violent gestures of frustration, when he threw himself on the floor or knocked over chairs. Kirst also allowed the audience to glimpse Mordret's underlying despair; Mordret rested his head on Parzival's chest while saying quietly that he did not want to watch himself wasting his life in this place.

Whilst the limited stage business subsequently led some theatre critics to call the production unimaginative, Hein argues that Kirst

---

[128] Christoph Hein, 'In illoyaler Verantwortung', in Staatsschauspiel Dresden, *Passage 1987, Die Ritter der Tafelrunde 1989, Randow 1994: Christoph Hein Uraufführungen* [1995], 22–3 at 22, AdK ID 2308; interview with Kirst, 24.4.2009.

supplied the staging that the situation demanded.[129] Any attempt to underline the play's topical relevance would have prompted a ban, and there was no need to add to the associations that the audience would inevitably perceive in the play.[130] In any case, self-censorship was not the only reason for the company's restraint. In spring 1989, most members of the Staatsschauspiel wanted the GDR to participate in Gorbachev's reforms so that socialism could be improved, not abolished. Whilst the ending of the production expressed the conviction that change must come, it also conveyed a reluctance to break entirely with the past. When Mordret piled the knights' chairs on top of the once-sacred round table, he stopped short of seizing the chair reserved for the finder of the Grail. He refused to break that final taboo and to consign the chair to the scrap heap of history. The production ended with Mordret standing in front of Artus, leaving the audience to wonder whether he would leave his father seated or add his chair to the pile.[131]

The guest list for the run-through indicates just how much importance the authorities attached to this production, particularly in comparison with *Revisor* in Bautzen. This time, Deputy Culture Minister Siegfried Böttger accompanied Maud Klevenow. Uwe Behnisch remembers how closely Böttger cooperated with Hoffmann and Klevenow during the negotiations over *Die Ritter der Tafelrunde*:

Dr. Hans-Joachim Hoffmann und Siegfried Böttger haben sich täglich mehrmals zu diesem Thema verständigt. Das Büro des Ministers befand sich in der Beletage des Schweriner Palais am Molkenmarkt. Siegfried Böttger... saß genau über ihn. Böttger brauchte nur eine Treppe runter, um Argumente für die Aufführungsgenehmigung zu liefern. Die hatte Dr. Hoffmann nicht, er war kein Theatermann, er vertraute auf die fachliche Kompetenz von Böttger. Maud Klevenow, eine studierte Theaterwissenschaftlerin, war ständig bei ihm, und Böttger ständig bei Hoffmann. So war es![132]

Dr Hans-Joachim Hoffmann and Siegfried Böttger discussed the matter several times a day. The Minister's office was on the first floor of the Schweriner Palais

[129] Ingeborg Pietzsch, 'Suche nach dem Gral: *Die Ritter der Tafelrunde* von Christoph Hein am Dresdner Staatsschauspiel uraufgeführt', *TdZ* 44/7 (July 1989), 53–4; Reinhard Wengierek, 'Zur Aufführung', *Die Union* (Dresden), 28.4.1989; Susanne Burkhardt, 'In Dresden wird *Die Ritter der Tafelrunde* uraufgeführt', 12.4.2004, Deutschland Radio Berlin, <http://www.dradio.de/dlr/sendungen/kalender/254105>, 6.6.2007.
[130] Burkhardt, 12.4.2004.
[131] 'Endspiel DDR'.
[132] Email from Uwe Behnisch, 23.11.2009.

on Molkenmarkt. Siegfried Böttger...had the office directly above. Böttger only had to go down one flight of stairs to supply the arguments for the production permit. Hoffmann didn't have the arguments, as he wasn't a theatre practitioner; he relied on Böttger's professional expertise. Maud Klevenow, who had studied theatre, was always in Böttger's office, and Böttger was always in Hoffmann's. That's exactly how it was!

Böttger and Klevenow were accompanied by numerous representatives of the Writers' Union, Union of Theatre Practitioners, *Bezirksleitung*, *Rat des Bezirks, Stadtleitung,* and *Parteileitung.* So even though Wolfram had put up a notice in the theatre asking those not involved to stay away from the run-through, Kirst estimates that approximately two hundred people saw the performance.[133] A far smaller group attended the discussion afterwards. Its members included Strahl, Funke, Pfützner, Hans-Rainer John (the editor-in-chief of *Theater der Zeit*), and Wolfgang Schuch (representing the publisher Henschel).[134]

After the performance, Schumann made his opposition clear by refusing to take part in the discussion.[135] He left the theatre, and so the meeting went ahead without the production's key opponent. Members of the Advisory Committee spoke first, using the discourse of responsibility. Wolfgang Hauswald (the deputy manager of the Schauspiel Leipzig) paid tribute to Hein's responsibility, and Pfützner, Funke, Schuch, and John stressed the responsibility of the theatre and production team.[136] Schuch congratulated them particularly on their depiction of Artus, implying relief that he had not been reduced to a caricature of Honecker.[137] Funke even compared Artus to Lessing's Nathan the Wise, perhaps explaining why the literary critic Peter Reichel thought that Artus might have been portrayed too positively.[138]

As the theatre had acted 'responsibly', the discussion shifted to the question of the audience's 'responsibility' and 'maturity'. Kirst explains that different interpretations of 'maturity' were in play: for some,

---

[133] Notice dated 8.3.1989, Staatsschauspiel Dresden 388; interview with Kirst, 24.4.2009.

[134] BStU BV Ddn. Abt. XX 9427, fo. 29.

[135] Interview with Kirst, 24.4.2009; letter signed by nineteen members of the Staatsschauspiel, 1.2.1991, Staatsschauspiel Dresden Archive.

[136] Karla Kochta, 'Beratung des Dramatikerbeirates...über die Entscheidungsfindung zum Genehmigungsverfahren *Die Ritter der Tafelrunde* von Christoph Hein am 15. März 1989', in Baker, '"From Page to Stage"', D19–D26.

[137] Ibid. D21.

[138] Ibid. D20–1.

'maturity' meant that spectators would understand the political need for them to react with restraint; for others, it meant that spectators would understand that the Arthurian legend had only limited relevance to the GDR.[139] Whilst Strahl argued that spectators deserved to be treated as adults, the representative of the *Bezirksleitung* was unconvinced.[140] He insisted that the local political situation could not take any more strain and that the play might well have a devastating effect.[141] So even though Hammerthaler and Wolfram claim that the *Bezirksleitung* did not oppose the production, its representative actually sided with Schumann and against the production. He failed to convince Klevenow, who argued that spectators would understand their 'responsibility'.[142] She reportedly added that if spectators caused a riot, the authorities would simply have to review their decision.[143] Kirst says that he could never have anticipated that the delegation would offer such solid support for the production.[144]

It was only when the discussion touched directly on questions of censorship that differences emerged between Hein and the Ministry's representatives. Whilst Hein objected to any form of censorship, Böttger argued against a ban on the pragmatic grounds that it would cause all sorts of difficulties.[145] Yet despite this important difference, for most of the meeting Hein, Böttger, and Klevenow were arguing on the same side. Just as Hein warned that bans or cuts only led theatres to deal with issues other than those uppermost in spectators' minds, Klevenow declared that it was ludicrous to pretend that problems did not exist when spectators had to deal with them on a daily basis.[146] Like Hein, Böttger used the term 'verboten' rather than the conventional euphemisms for production bans. Whilst he did not go as far as to refer to 'censorship' instead of 'approval procedures', he did argue that the latter term should be reinvested with its original meaning. Böttger reminded those present that the approval procedures existed so that plays could be approved, not banned.[147]

---

[139] Interview with Kirst, 24.4.2009.
[140] Kochta, D25.
[141] Ibid. D23; see also BStU BV Ddn. Abt. XX 9427, fo. 29.
[142] Kochta, D26.
[143] 'Zur politisch-ideologischen Situation an den Theatern des Bezirkes', 11.5.1989, SächsStA-D 11857 A 13936.
[144] Interview with Kirst, 24.4.2009.
[145] Kochta, D25.   [146] Ibid. D26.   [147] Ibid. D25.

All twelve Committee members present voted for the production, arguing that democratic bodies could not be created only for their opinions to be ignored.[148] After Böttger had visited Hoffmann and secured his approval, the Ministry informed Modrow on 17 March that the production could go ahead.[149] But Schumann attempted to block this decision, securing a meeting with Major Salomo, the head of the Stasi department responsible for culture in Dresden. According to Salomo, Schumann had written to Hoffmann, saying that he would accept only an explicit order to stage the play.[150] On 20 March, Modrow reportedly said that he wanted the production to go ahead but was unwilling to overrule Schumann.[151] The contrast between Modrow's cautious expression of support and the outspoken opposition of his representative at the run-through points to splits within the *Bezirksleitung*, not just between Modrow and the *Rat des Bezirks*. Events since the end of January had constrained Modrow's room for manoeuvre, and he now referred the decision to the central authorities. He arranged for Stasi officers to consult Mittig, who would talk to Hoffmann and inform Hager.[152]

The archival evidence suggests that no one individual bore responsibility for the final decision to allow the production. A memorandum addressed to Hager indicates that Modrow telephoned Ragwitz's office and expressed his gratitude for Hager's advice. According to the memorandum, Modrow reported that a decision had been reached as a result of thorough discussions with everyone involved ('mit allen Beteiligten'): two previews would take place in March, the premiere would follow on 12 April—not on 24 March as originally planned—and a further performance would take place on 24 April if the premiere went well.[153] On 23 March, notices were published in the local press indicating that the premiere had indeed been postponed until 12 April and that four—not two—previews would take place beforehand.[154]

According to Kirst, permission for the production was conditional on two cuts to the text and one cut to the programme. Whilst he had always regarded cuts as inevitable, he had seen no reason to pre-empt the

---

[148] VdT, 'Information', 16.3.1989, AdK VdT 794.
[149] BStU BV Ddn. Abt. XX 9427, fos. 32, 56.
[150] Ibid. 43.
[151] Ibid. 32.
[152] Ibid. 32.
[153] 'Theater in Dresden', 21.3.1989, BArch DY 30 vorl. SED 42322/2.
[154] e.g. 'Premiere verschoben', *Sächsische Zeitung* (Dresden), 23.3.1989.

authorities by making them himself.[155] Kochta's notes indicate that Klevenow and two members of the Advisory Committee had suggested limited cuts after the run-through, and two of the actual cuts corresponded to Klevenow's suggestions.[156] The first concerned a section inviting comparison with Stalin's Purges. Mordret subjects Parzival to a relentless inquisition, asking why he has not written about the death of the red knight Ither. Parzival looks away, swallows, and resorts to a formulaic excuse that reveals the limits of his critical enquiry: the knights had to make necessary but painful decisions, parting with some of their number. Whilst the theatre was allowed to retain this dialogue, Mordret's retort was deleted: that they had deemed it necessary to cut off the knights' heads.[157] The second cut concerned Lancelot's report that the public has lost its traditional respect and affection for the knights, treating them only with derision. Lancelot reveals that people spat at him when he spoke of the Grail, and that they cursed and threw stones at him when he tried to speak of Artus's kingdom. Even so, the authorities insisted only that the brutal conclusion of the speech should be cut: 'Für das Volk sind die Ritter der Tafelrunde ein Haufen von Narren, Idioten und Verbrechern.'[158] (As far as the people are concerned, the knights of the round table are a collection of fools, idiots, and criminals.) The theatre was also instructed to cut a poem by Walther von der Vogelweide on the decline of Artus's court, including a description of the hall's rotten roof and crumbling walls.[159] These changes did nothing to alter the overall thrust of the production.

The reactions to the previews were critical, as any disturbances would have provided local opponents with a pretext to ban the production. Modrow had assured Hager that measures would be taken to influence the composition of the audience, and Kochta feared that Stasi officers might have bought up tickets with the aim of creating disruption.[160] These fears proved unfounded, and spectators intuitively grasped the need for restraint. Indeed, the lack of audience reaction turned the first preview into an even greater ordeal for Kirst and his actors, as they had no way of gauging how the production was being received—or, presumably, who their audience was.[161] It was only at the very end that

---

[155] Interview with Kirst, 24.4.2009.
[156] Kochta, D19, D22, D26.
[157] Staatsschauspiel Dresden, *Passage 1987*, 14.
[158] Ibid. 14.   [159] Ibid.
[160] 'Theater in Dresden'; Baker, '"From Page to Stage"', 328.
[161] 'Endspiel DDR'.

spectators joined in a ten-minute ovation. The remaining previews passed without disruption, and the Stasi monitored audience reactions. Colonel Tzscheutschler described most spectators at a performance on 20 April as 'betroffen und nachdenklich' (moved and thoughtful), prompting one of his colleagues to scribble underneath: 'ich nicht!' (I wasn't!).[162]

Covert Declarations of Solidarity

After the official premiere on 12 April, reviews were published in the GDR press. In the *Sächsische Zeitung* and *Der Morgen*, reviewers gave the production a clean bill of health by stressing the lack of obvious topical references.[163] Whilst Heinz Klunker criticized GDR theatre critics for this deliberate oversight,[164] the reviews were almost certainly designed to protect the theatre. After all, Funke had written the review in *Der Morgen*, and he had argued hard on behalf of the production behind the scenes, both at a meeting of the Writers' Union in February and at the run-through in March.

On 26 April, Hein complained that the production had not been reviewed in the 'better papers', a reference to *Neues Deutschland*.[165] According to Hammerthaler, the newspaper's review was doing the rounds of the central authorities, ending up in the Central Committee's Culture Department.[166] The publication of the review in May came as a surprise, particularly as it was positive. Gerhard Ebert used the characterization of Artus to reclaim the play for the SED, arguing that Artus was an enlightened monarch, that spectators could identify with him, and that his decision to hand over power showed that the apparent endgame was actually a new beginning. Ebert also argued that there was more democracy at Artus's court than Mordret recognized, and he presented the production as a warning against carelessly relinquishing

[162] BStU BV Ddn. Abt. XX 9427, fo. 62.
[163] Lothar Ehrlich, 'Um die Unsterblichkeit der Gralsidee wissend', *Sächsische Zeitung* (Dresden), 20.4.1989; Christoph Funke, 'Artus in der Nachfolge Lessings', *Der Morgen* (East Berlin), 17.4.1989.
[164] Heinz Klunker, 'Angst vorm Gral: Zur Nicht-Kritik der Hein-Uraufführung in den Zeitungen der DDR', *Theater heute*, 30/7 (July 1989), 24.
[165] Ibid.
[166] Hammerthaler, 'Die Position des Theaters in der DDR', 243.

hard-won achievements.[167] By concluding that the production was an
optimistic piece of theatre, he made his review an easy target for
Western critics like Klunker. The Culture Department of Dresden's
SED-*Bezirksleitung* was similarly unimpressed, arguing that the reviews
in *Neues Deutschland* and the *Sächsische Zeitung* had backfired, as they
were simply not credible.[168] Even so, Hoffmann, Kochta, and Hein all
state that Ebert's review benefited the theatre significantly.[169] Indeed,
Hein agrees with Dieter Kranz that the article was less a review than a
covert declaration of solidarity with the theatre and the playwright.[170]

Local Repercussions

The Ministry's determination to override local opposition aroused
considerable resentment amongst officials in Dresden, provoking the
Rat des Bezirks to launch disciplinary proceedings against Wolfram.
Hammerthaler sees these proceedings as a rearguard action,[171] and the
main impetus certainly came from state officials in Dresden. But the
summary of Modrow's telephone call to Ragwitz's office, revealing
the terms and conditions for the premiere, states: 'Der Intendant
wurde bestraft' (the theatre manager was punished).[172] The use of the
past tense is odd, because the authorities had only just reached their
verdict and the *Rat des Bezirks* launched the sole recorded disciplinary
action two days later, on 23 March. It may even be an error, given that
the functionary writing the memorandum had not attended the negotiations. However, the memorandum does point to a compromise
whereby Wolfram was punished, probably to placate officials in
Dresden, but the premiere was allowed to proceed.

The key charge against Wolfram was that he had allowed rehearsals to
go ahead on the basis of verbal agreements with the Ministry, even

[167] Gerhard Ebert, 'Parabel auf das Streben nach menschlicher Vervollkommnung',
ND, 3.5.1989.
[168] 'Zum Stand der Diskussion um die Spielpläne 1990', 9.5.1989, SächsStA-D
11857 A 13936.
[169] Hammerthaler, 'Die Position des Theaters in der DDR', 242; Baker, '"From Page to
Stage"', 329; anon., 'Wende in der DDR-Theaterkritik: Zum Training des aufrechten Gangs',
Theater heute, 31/1 (Jan. 1990), 2.
[170] Anon., 'Wende in der DDR-Theaterkritik'.
[171] Hammerthaler, 'Die Position des Theaters in der DDR', 237; see also Baker,
'"From Page to Stage"', 215–19.
[172] 'Theater in Dresden'.

though he knew that Schumann was against a public premiere. Officials were additionally annoyed that a West German student had attended rehearsals. Wolfram refuted the charges point by point, copying the correspondence to Modrow, Hoffmann, and the Presidents of the Writers' Union and Union of Theatre Practitioners. Once again, this indicates how theatre practitioners had to mobilize central alliances in order to counter local opposition. Unlike Castorf, Wolfram was prepared to pull all the strings that he could.

Whilst the Chairman of the *Rat des Bezirks* subsequently agreed to halt proceedings, he continued to object to the Ministry's encroachment on the council's power. He informed Wolfram:

[Es] kann nicht übersehen werden, daß durch Ihre direkten Verhandlungen mit dem Ministerium für Kultur und daraus resultierende Entscheidungen eine Situation entstanden ist, die die Entscheidungsmöglichkeit und Handlungsfähigkeit des Mitglieds des Rates des Bezirkes für Kultur eingeengt hat.[173]

[It] is impossible to overlook the fact that your direct negotiations with the Culture Ministry, and the decisions that have resulted from these negotiations, have given rise to a situation that has restricted the councillor for culture's scope for decision-making and capacity for action.

On 28 March, Wolfram reminded members of the Staatsschauspiel to adhere strictly to the regulations. He stipulated that the script for a planned Hölderlin matinee must be submitted to the *Rat des Bezirks* and that no dates could be agreed until the production had been approved, and he also ordered the withdrawal of the cast list for a production called *Frauenbilder* (Images of Women).[174] 'Stein' informed the Stasi that the regional authorities' attack on Wolfram had prompted some theatre practitioners to resign from the SED, and that some had argued that Schumann—not Wolfram—should be dismissed.[175] The failure of the disciplinary proceedings represented another major blow for the *Rat des Bezirks*, and Wolfram's correspondence indicates that his relationship with Schumann had broken down completely by the summer.[176]

---

[173] Witteck to Wolfram, no date, in Baker, '"From Page to Stage"', D17–D18 at D17.
[174] 'Festlegungen zu den [*sic*] Genehmigungsverfahren', 28.3.1989, SächsStA-D 12992 (Staatsschauspiel Dresden) 172.
[175] BStU BV Ddn. Abt. XX 9427, fo. 65.
[176] See Staatsschauspiel Dresden 388.

Opponents of reform in Dresden continued to lay the main blame for developments in theatre at the Culture Ministry's door. On 9 May 1989, the Culture Department of the *Bezirksleitung* complained that the Ministry had caused major problems by agreeing to everything.[177] On 11 May, officials in the Culture Department accused the Ministry of encouraging theatres to perform politically provocative plays and of questioning the approval procedures. Klevenow had even announced that these procedures would probably be stopped entirely soon so that theatre managers alone would decide what was performed.[178] Dresden's Culture Department objected that the Ministry showed no restraint and accepted no limit to the region's capacity to tolerate controversial plays. Officials claimed that *Die Ritter der Tafelrunde* had a huge resonance among young spectators, and they expressed their anxiety about performances continuing in the autumn. In their view, the Staatsschauspiel had deliberately misrepresented the production's impact by claiming that it was of purely philosophical interest. Officials added that in private many theatre practitioners did not attempt to conceal what they really thought, quoting a member of staff at the opera house as saying: 'Das Regime muß weg' (the regime has to go).[179]

5. CONCLUSION

The fact that *Revisor* and *Die Ritter der Tafelrunde* were premiered at all indicates that real changes were under way in the theatre repertoire. Even though it undoubtedly suited Hoffmann after the *Wende* to present himself as a proponent of perestroika, the Ministry made increasingly significant gestures towards reform in 1987–9. These gestures were evident first in the statements made by Meyer at the Academy of Arts, and then in comments made by Hoffmann, Böttger, and Klevenow. Behnisch stresses that Meyer, Böttger, and Klevenow would not have been able to use the language of glasnost without Hoffmann's backing.[180] From today's perspective, the Ministry's actions resemble a last-ditch offensive or *Flucht nach vorne*, as officials tried to mitigate criticisms of censorship by crossing off titles on

---

[177] 'Zum Stand der Diskussion'.
[178] 'Zur politisch-ideologischen Situation'.
[179] Ibid.
[180] Interview with Behnisch, 21.4.2009.

Liebmann's list of unperformed plays. The ambivalence of officials' motives should come as no surprise. Ministry officials were compromised and constrained by their position in the system; they were aware of the audiences to which they were speaking; and they presented their arguments accordingly. But their support was instrumental to the premieres of both *Revisor* and *Die Ritter der Tafelrunde* in 1989.

The Ministry's support for new productions of critical contemporary drama meant that the main censorship battles would be fought in the regions. Even though the Staatsschauspiel and the Deutsch-Sorbisches Volkstheater were both operating in the same region, with the support of the Ministry and a relatively sympathetic First Secretary, their experiences of censorship in 1989 differed substantially. The pre-performance negotiations on *Revisor* in Bautzen were relatively unproblematic. Bautzen was a safe distance away from the regional capital, and officials in the *Rat des Bezirks* did not lend their weight to local opposition from the *Rat des Kreises*. Regional Party and state officials did not attend the run-through, and Klevenow's verdict was enough to secure the premiere. The *Rat des Kreises* did not attempt to block the production, probably because Klevenow had taken responsibility for the decision. The real problems occurred only after the premiere, and even then the objections were limited to isolated protests. The decision whether performances should continue was left to Modrow and the Ministry, and they resisted calls for a ban. Modrow's actions absolved officials in the *Kreisleitung* from personal responsibility, and the local conflict did not escalate. This case underlines the importance of the Ministry in pre-performance negotiations, and that of the regional First Secretary in post-performance censorship. In Potsdam, Jahn intervened personally to ban *Revisor* after its premiere.

The Ministry again played a crucial role in the pre-performance negotiations on *Die Ritter der Tafelrunde* in Dresden. But these negotiations were considerably more complex, explaining why the Ministry enlisted the support of advisers from the theatre community. There was clearly more at stake than there had been in Bautzen. *Revisor* focuses on the corruption and moral weakness of individual provincial officials, and the play ends with the restoration of the old order. In contrast, *Die Ritter der Tafelrunde* indicates that the leaders of the realm have failed despite their noble intentions, and that radical change is inevitable. Officials in the *Rat des Bezirks* and *Bezirksleitung* were determined to block the production; their opposition was fuelled by panic at growing unrest in the population and by frustration at the Ministry's perceived lack of understanding for the situation in Dresden. So even though Modrow, Hoffmann, Böttger, and Klevenow all supported the production, neither Modrow nor Hoffmann could afford to take the main responsibility for it. Both men had to negotiate with Hager and the Stasi, invoking the opinions of the Advisory Committee, in order to achieve a compromise. Whilst Ostrowski presented the Staatsschauspiel as standing alone in the case of *Die Ritter der Tafelrunde*, Wolfram acknowledged the broad alliance that had made the production possible. He explained that the theatre's achievements were down to a great many people, including people in Ministries, in the administration, and in the Party apparatus.[181]

Both productions demonstrate the extent to which censorship remained contingent on individual circumstances. The Advisory Committee had no independent authority, and it was not invited to the run-through of *Revisor* in Bautzen. Its role in Dresden was remarkably similar to that of the experts invited to the run-through of *Dmitri* in Schwerin in 1984. As approval remained officially in the gift of the Ministry, its functionaries had the discretion over whether to mobilize alliances in support of high-risk productions. It was not until October 1989 that Erich Mielke, the Minister for State Security, finally agreed to the long-awaited theatre regulations, which granted managers full responsibility for what went on in their ensembles. Managers no longer needed to obtain the Ministry's approval for world and GDR premieres, or the approval of the *Rat des Bezirks* for the theatre repertoire.[182] The Ministry finally seemed to be offering the structural change that Hein had demanded. But the GDR's demise meant that the new regulations were never put to the test.

---

[181] Wolfram, 'Wir waren alle', 89.
[182] Lennartz, *Vom Aufbruch*, 102.

8

Conclusion

1. DRAMA AND THEATRE IN THE GDR

In 1972, the writer Horst Kleineidam complained that GDR dramatists needed three times as much energy to stage a play as they had needed to write it in the first place.[1] In some cases, no amount of energy or effort could secure a staging. The vehement clashes over *Die Umsiedlerin*, *Die Sorgen und die Macht*, and *Moritz Tassow* had discouraged theatre managers from taking risks, and theatres relied increasingly on plays by Bertolt Brecht and Friedrich Wolf to fill their quota of 'contemporary' drama. In Dresden, SED officials reported in 1969 that a number of authors had decided to stick to safe topics that would guarantee professional success.[2] Censorship discouraged experimentation, and it delayed the reception and creative uptake of innovative drama. Many of Heiner Müller's cutting-edge plays were premiered in the Federal Republic, and Adolf Dresen and Jürgen Gosch joined the exodus of theatre practitioners to the West. In the 1980s, observers could even have quipped that GDR theatre was alive and well in the Federal Republic.

In the immediate post-war years, stagings of the classics were also subject to stringent controls. Officials stopped theatres in Thuringia from staging Goethe's *Egmont*, and they cut the famous call for intellectual freedom from Schiller's *Don Carlos* in Meiningen.[3] But the propaganda war with the Federal Republic led to the first relaxations in censorship, as the SED leadership strove to present the GDR as a democracy and as the true home of German culture. After the construction of the Berlin Wall, officials decided to allow the Deutsches Theater

---

[1]   Kleineidam to Hoffmann, 14.11.1972, BArch DY 30 IV B 2/9.06/66.
[2]   'Zur Vorlage des Rates des Bezirkes', 13.2.1969, SächsStA-D 11857 IV B-2/9.02/ 487.
[3]   Interview with Kirst, 24.4.2009.

to stage Schiller's *Wilhelm Tell*, without cutting the famous line 'Wir sind *ein* Volk, und einig wollen wir handeln' (We are *one* nation, and we want to act as one). Siegfried Wagner subsequently cited the production as evidence of the 'trust' between officials and theatre practitioners, saying that the staging would go down in history.[4] Whilst officials still reserved the right to block productions that offended their notion of fidelity to the original text, the political damage of banning *Faust I* at the Deutsches Theater was too great for the Ministry to contemplate in 1968. Directors increasingly used classic and classical texts to comment critically on conditions in the GDR and the Eastern bloc, whether through the guise of Japanese aesthetics in *Sieben gegen Theben*, or through allusions to borders and transgression in *Leonce und Lena*. Officials recognized these allusions and highlighted them in internal reports, yet in the 1970s and 1980s they tended to refrain from intervention. As long as productions relied on allegory and allusion, Honecker's officials could choose to accept theatre practitioners' assurances that the texts were purely of historical interest. It is unthinkable that Gosch's production of *Leonce und Lena* would have been left in the repertoire a decade earlier.

Whilst the room for manoeuvre in contemporary drama narrowed immediately after the Eleventh Plenary Session, the 1970s saw new attempts to increase the space for stagings of texts that engaged explicitly with East German experiences. But the productions that shifted boundaries were usually adaptations of prose texts. As the originals had already been tested on the reading public and literary critics, adaptations offered a means of reducing the risks associated with new drama. After the Landestheater Halle had premiered *Die neuen Leiden des jungen W.* successfully in 1972, numerous theatres across the GDR followed suit. But there were still false starts: the fortunes of *Franziska Linkerhand* show how the Mecklenburgisches Staatstheater, Ministry officials, and theatre critics thought that they had widened the scope of what could be shown on stage, only for the restrictions to be reinforced months later. Where new drama was concerned, the regime was increasingly resorting

---

[4] Bork, notes on a meeting at the DT, 11.1.1963, BArch DR 1/8850. This 'trust' reflected the fact that the actors had, as Moray McGowan writes, reduced the 'ringing pathos' of the Rütli oath to 'a secretive mutter'. See McGowan, '"Der aktuelle Kabarettist zur Lage der Nation"? *Wilhelm Tell*, Staatstheater Schwerin, February 1989', in Florian Krobb and Hans-Walter Schmidt-Hannisa (eds.), *Schiller—On the Threshold of Modernity* (= *Germanistik in Ireland*, 1 (2006)), 67–74 at 69.

to the 'alibi' premiere: granting a showcase production as a one-off event. Officials hoped that the premiere of *Dmitri* in Schwerin would strengthen Volker Braun's links to the GDR, but Hager made it clear that the play was not to be staged elsewhere in the Republic. Dramatists were at a major disadvantage if they had not had an opportunity to accumulate symbolic capital, as the authorities had little incentive to make strategic concessions to them. Linzer comments that the GDR had the oldest 'young' dramatists in the world, citing the examples of Georg Seidel and Lothar Trolle.[5] It was not until 1988 that a rush of 'new' GDR plays were approved for performance, as the central authorities came under sustained pressure to ease the troubled relationship between drama and theatre. The theatre repertoires of 1988 and 1989 turned into an exhibition of GDR plays from the last two decades, and the content of *Revisor* and *Die Ritter der Tafelrunde* shows just how far the scope for contemporary drama had widened.

The richness and ambiguity of the theatrical medium enabled directors to exploit the public demand for the kinds of social and political observations that were absent in the GDR press, on radio, or on television. Ulf Reiher, who managed theatres in Senftenberg and Halle, even argues that theatre was an important source of information.[6] But the productions in this study did not tell spectators anything that they did not already know. Instead, they drew attention to experiences, attitudes, and modes of behaviour that usually went unacknowledged in public discourse. Spectators commented on the similarity between the characters in *Die Sorgen und die Macht* and their own colleagues, or felt that they had recognized Prenzlauer Berg in *Leonce und Lena*. Whilst Western television functioned as the main substitute for the official media, theatre could offer domestic perspectives on current events and communicate live with its audience. In the anonymity of the auditorium, spectators could share in a sense of collective recognition and response. When the authorities' representatives walked out of the premiere of *Faust I* at the Deutsches Theater, they presented the rest of the

---

[5] Martin Linzer, 'Anmerkungen zu Georg Seidels Werk und Wirken', in Georg Seidel, *Villa Jugend: Das dramatische Werk in einem Band*, ed. Andreas Leusink (Berlin and Frankfurt/M.: henschel SCHAUSPIEL and Verlag der Autoren, 1992), 381–9 at 381.

[6] Anon. 'Die Weitergabe des Feuers: Das Interview mit dem scheidenden Landestheater-Intendanten Ulf Reiher', <http://www.landestheater-detmold.de/upload/Aktuell_Landeszeitung_Interview_Reiher02.html>, 12.7.2004.

audience with choices: whether to stay or walk out, whether to applaud or remain silent. By choosing to stay and applaud, the majority rejected the authorities' verdict and expressed their solidarity with the performers. The politicization of performance enabled spectators to express political dissent legitimately through the theatrical code.

At the same time, GDR theatres faced challenges that would have been only too familiar to their contemporary counterparts in the Federal Republic, UK, or USA: adjusting to falling demand after the advent of television, sustaining the attention of parties of school pupils through productions of the classics, and catering for groups of spectators interested only in light entertainment. In 1979, the manager of the Friedrich-Wolf-Theater in Neustrelitz claimed that most spectators were simply not prepared to engage actively with his theatre and its productions.[7] Whilst efforts to attract non-traditional audiences met with some success, workers often chose not to use the tickets allocated to them through workplace subscriptions. Even in cities like Leipzig and Dresden, it was common for performances to be sold out on paper, only for significant numbers of seats to remain empty on the night—a phenomenon known as the *Tote-Seelen-Quote* (dead souls' quota). These difficulties in attracting spectators serve as a timely corrective to the post-reunification tendency to romanticize the relationship between GDR theatres and their audiences.

2. COOPERATION AND CONFLICT

On paper, the chain of responsibility for theatre was clear and simple. Managers had to submit their plans to the regional state authorities, which forwarded them to the Culture Ministry; managers remained personally accountable for the productions themselves. But there were multiple other lines of responsibility that the regulations never mentioned. Managers were expected to meet regularly with Stasi officers, and district and regional councils had to agree their actions with the parallel Party authorities. Theatre practitioners who belonged to the SED were accountable to their theatre's *Parteileitung*, which reported to the district or regional Party authorities. Unofficial informers answered to their supervising officers in the Stasi. This extensive network rooted

[7] Weindich to Netik, 14.3.1979, LHAS 7.21-1 Z106/1991 18729.

censorship in theatres themselves, enabling the authorities to rely on internal controls during rehearsals. Once the conditions for a production had been agreed, the work of changing the text and finding performance solutions was subsumed into the rehearsal process. The authorities expected Party members and Stasi informers to supply reports and signal concerns, but they only checked productions at formal run-throughs—unless, of course, theatre practitioners solicited their views at an earlier stage. Transparency was the first casualty of the diversification of controls. Even directors with good contacts in the Ministry and regional authorities could not be sure who was passing information to whom, or whose mind they needed to change. At the Tenth Writers' Congress, Peter Abraham reported that he had often heard people say that they would prefer to have an official bureau for censorship, so that they would know exactly where to turn.[8] But the diversification of controls did enable managers and directors to use their personal contacts to bypass the official line of command. Helene Weigel charmed Alfred Kurella into vouching for *Sieben gegen Theben*, and Albert Hetterle persuaded Margot Honecker to intercede with the Ministry on his behalf, after officials had told him to stop rehearsals of Mikhail Schatrow's play *Das Ende* (The End) at the Maxim Gorki Theater.[9] Personal intervention could also work against theatre practitioners: when productions were banned after their premieres, it was sometimes because individuals not privy to the pre-performance negotiations had taken offence.

Experiences of theatre censorship varied substantially, as so much depended on the working relationships between theatre practitioners and officials in the localities. According to the Stasi informer 'Sumatic', Gerhard Wolfram drew a contrast between his productive partnership with SED officials in Halle and the prescriptive approach meted out to him by their counterparts in Berlin:

Besonders beklagt er sich darüber, daß er in den Genossen der Bezirksleitung keine Partner finde. In Halle konnte er mit offenen Fragen zur Bezirksleitung gehen. In Streitgesprächen wurde dann um eine Lösung gerungen... Hier in Berlin versuche man nur immer fertige Rezepte zu verteilen. Eine Diskussion sei völlig unproduktiv.[10]

---

[8] Peter Abraham, 'Arbeitsgruppe IV: Literatur und Wirkung', in *X. Schriftstellerkongreß*, ed. Schriftstellerverband der DDR, i. 212–19 at 214.
[9] Memorandum from Margot Honecker, 3.3.1975, BArch DY 30 IV B 2/9.06/65.
[10] BStU MfS ZA AP 3743/83, i, fo. 12.

He particularly complains that he has not found any partners amongst his comrades in the regional Party authorities. In Halle he could go to the regional Party authorities with frank questions. They would then struggle to reach a solution through debate . . . He says that [the authorities] here in Berlin only ever try to prescribe fixed solutions. Any attempt at discussion is completely unproductive.

Experiences varied significantly even between East Berlin's theatres: Wolfram's difficulties contrasted with the working relationship that Wekwerth had established with the same officials a few years earlier. In Schwerin, Schroth slowly established a *modus vivendi* with local officials, enabling him to tackle politically challenging projects like *Franziska Linkerhand* and *Dmitri*. In other contexts, a basis for cooperation was not even present, particularly when officials conceived of their relationship with theatre practitioners solely in terms of subordination. This attitude was evident in the local authorities' reactions to Castorf's productions in Anklam, and in Jahn's opposition to *Revisor* in Potsdam. In Leipzig, meanwhile, Kayser used his political capital to exclude local officials from decision-making processes in the theatre, resulting in persistent low-level resentment. Even though the central authorities repeatedly encouraged officials to develop productive partnerships with theatres, they were unable to impose these working relationships in the regions.

Over time, theatre practitioners developed rituals of cooperation as a way of defusing conflicts. The contrasting cases of *Die Sorgen und die Macht* and *Faust I* show how theatre practitioners at the Deutsches Theater began to comply with the rhetoric of pedagogy. Whereas members of the theatre had held out for weeks over *Die Sorgen und die Macht*, accusing officials of hypocrisy, they were relatively quick to negotiate over *Faust* and even thanked the authorities for their 'help'. This performance of cooperation was designed to save the production and limit the damage to the theatre's long-term relationship with the authorities. It corresponds to a phenomenon that Jay Rowell has identified among state and business functionaries: Rowell argues that these functionaries gradually mastered the discursive forms that marked their rhetorical submission to the wisdom of the Party.[11] Dramaturges turned production concepts into exercises in the art of persuasion. The most successful concepts engaged with the authorities' fears: in Schwerin,

---

[11] Rowell, 'Le Pouvoir périphérique', 108.

Schroth and Jaksch presented themselves as responsible mediators, explaining how they intended to overcome the political risks allegedly posed by *Dmitri*.

Until 1987, theatre practitioners also performed their cooperation by adhering to the official line that they were not subject to censorship. In his reflections on the censorship of *Faust I*, Hamburger highlighted the unspoken 'gentleman's agreement' that the production team would not refer to the deleted Walpurgis Night's Dream in public.[12] Behind the scenes, theatre practitioners did occasionally withhold their cooperation over the regime's attempt to camouflage censorship. Weigel refused to cover for the Ministry's decision to ban *Johann Faustus* in 1968, and Dieter Klein told his colleagues at the Volksbühne in 1977 that local officials had warned him not to stage two plays by Heiner Müller. The *Bezirksleitung* reprimanded Klein for his candour, telling him that his politically irresponsible comments would strengthen the aversion that some of his colleagues already felt towards the authorities.[13] In some cases, theatre practitioners even tried to turn the regime's denial of censorship to their advantage. In 1979, Hoffmann took the Staatsschauspiel Dresden to task for publicizing its plans to stage *Die Parteibraut* before the Ministry had decided whether or not to approve it. He warned the company that its actions constituted an unlawful attempt to put pressure on the state authorities.[14] In this case, the attempt backfired: the theatre was not allowed to stage *Die Parteibraut*, and the incident damaged the 'trust' vested in the theatre.

As the authorities were already involved in overseeing theatre, it was only logical for dramatists and theatre practitioners to call on officials as allies in professional disputes. In 1964, after the Volksbühne had stopped rehearsals of her play *Ein Amerikaner in Berlin* (An American in Berlin), Hedda Zinner appealed to the Central Committee's Culture Department to reverse the decision, albeit without success.[15] Later that year, Kurt Barthel (KuBa) sought to block attempts by the Deutsches Theater to revise his play *Terra incognita*. He reportedly cited his collaboration with leading Party officials in Rostock as an argument against any changes:

[12] Hamburger, '*Faust* im DT', fo. 2, AdK D 52 c.
[13] 'Rechenschaftslegung in der Volksbühne am 15.7.1977', LAB C Rep. 902 4576.
[14] 'Protokoll der Beratung...am 18.1.1979', SächsStA-D 11857 IV D-2/9/02/556.
[15] Zinner to Schröder, 26.1.1964, BArch DY 30 IV A 2/2.024/33.

Das Stück sei ohne die bis ins einzelne gehende, grundlegende Mitarbeit des 1. Sekretärs sowie des Vorsitzenden der Ideologischen Kommission und anderer Genossen der Bezirksleitung Rostock der SED nicht denkbar. Deshalb fühle er sich auch als einzelner ans Endresultat gebunden.[16]

He says that it would be impossible to imagine the play without the detailed and fundamental contributions of the First Secretary, along with the Chairman of the Ideological Commission and other comrades from the regional SED authorities in Rostock. That is why he feels personally committed to the final result.

Theatre censorship also became caught up in larger management disputes. At the BE, Wekwerth and Berghaus were convinced that *Sieben gegen Theben* should not be allowed to go ahead for political reasons, but they also presented the production as proof of the alleged deficiencies in Weigel's management. As tensions escalated, members of the BE asked Ulbricht and the Council of State to intervene.[17]

The complexity of these patterns of cooperation and conflict defies any attempt to reduce GDR theatre to a 'socialist opposition' to the regime.[18] The term 'socialist opposition' does fit the activities of some theatre practitioners and ensembles at particular points in time: such as Karge and Langhoff's original plans for *Sieben gegen Theben* in 1968, Dresen's work at the Deutsches Theater in the 1970s, or productions at the Staatsschauspiel Dresden in the late 1980s. It certainly corresponds to the activities of GDR theatres in autumn 1989, when they campaigned for fundamental political changes designed to preserve socialism. But as soon as the term is applied to GDR theatre more generally, it obscures the multiple shades of opinion within the theatre profession, and the multiple conflicts and allegiances within individual biographies. One of the stumbling blocks to an understanding of GDR theatre has always been the way in which the East German authorities and Western critics seized on political allusions, jokes, and criticisms as evidence of intentional opposition—leading to individuals like Peter Hacks and Eberhard Esche being treated as suspected dissidents, even though they never identified with oppositional positions even within socialism. In the 1980s, Freya Klier was the only director who was actively and systematically involved in the opposition, primarily through her work

[16] 'Aktennotiz über ein Gespräch mit Genossen Dr. Kurt Barthel (KUBA) am 30.10.64', BArch DY 30 IV A 2/2.024/32.
[17] Gotsche to Hager, 5.11.1969, BArch DY 30 IV A 2/9.06/113.
[18] See Hammerthaler, 'Die Position des Theaters in der DDR', 156.

with the peace movement. She was unable to work in theatre after 1985, and she was imprisoned in January 1988 and expelled from the GDR soon afterwards.[19] It is important not to conflate the differences between her consistent political opposition and performances that tested the boundaries of tolerated dissent on the GDR stage.

3. DEVELOPMENTS IN THEATRE CENSORSHIP

In the 1960s, attempts to disguise theatre censorship often created more problems than they solved. By mounting press campaigns against *Die Sorgen und die Macht*, *Moritz Tassow*, and *Faust I*, the authorities inadvertently encouraged the public to watch the productions and search for subversion. Few people were convinced by the excuses used to camouflage production bans; spectators laughed when the Deutsches Theater used these excuses to explain why Müller and Hacks were unable to attend the Walpurgis Night's Dream in *Faust I*. As the authorities habitually tried to camouflage censorship, even real cases of illness generated rumours of production bans. When the Deutsch-Sorbisches Volkstheater had to cancel performances of *Revisor* because one of the actors was ill, a local Stasi officer arranged for informers to check if the production had actually been banned.[20] Similarly, when performances of *Die Ritter der Tafelrunde* had to be suspended because two actors needed operations, a Stasi informer warned that rumours of censorship would inevitably ensue.[21]

In the 1970s, the central authorities began to advocate a policy of damage limitation, partly to limit the domestic impact of unwelcome productions, and partly to avoid negative international publicity. After the Central Committee had discussed Hacks's *Der Frieden* in 1971, a functionary told officials in Schwerin that it would be politically inadvisable to take action against the play, as it was popular abroad.[22] Officials sought to soften the impact of potentially controversial productions by limiting ticket sales or performances, recognizing that overt cuts would attract unwelcome attention. After Müller's *Leben Gundlings*

---

[19] See Hubertus Knabe (ed.), *Gefangen in Hohenschönhausen: Stasi-Häftlinge berichten* (Berlin: List, 2007), 334–47, 369.
[20] BStU BV Ddn. AKG PI 18/89, fo. 22.
[21] BStU BV Ddn. Abt. XX 9427, fo. 61.
[22] 'Information an die Genossen Quandt und Wandt', LHAS 10.34-3 2197.

Friedrich von Preußen (Gundling's Life Frederick of Prussia) had been premiered at the Volksbühne in 1988, East Berlin's Culture Secretary reportedly warned that making changes would be the quickest way of increasing the play's popularity.[23]

This shift towards damage limitation was accompanied by a rise in covert repression and Stasi surveillance. Whereas *Faust I* had caught Stasi officers off guard, informers filed reports on *Michael Kohlhaas*, *Trommeln in der Nacht*, *Revisor*, and *Die Ritter der Tafelrunde* in advance. Stasi officers in Berlin engineered Volker Braun's move from the Deutsches Theater to the BE, and their counterparts in Dresden kept the Deputy Minister for State Security up to date with developments at the Staatsschauspiel in 1989. Officers in Dresden argued that the SED-*Stadtleitung*, *Parteileitung*, and theatre management should assess *Die Ritter der Tafelrunde* during rehearsals, and recommended that the *Rat des Bezirks* should investigate why the premiere had been announced before the production had officially been approved.[24] But there is no evidence that Stasi officers in Dresden took sides during the final showdown, and Böhm assured Modrow that he would go along with whatever the central authorities decided.[25]

Not everyone in the Party and state authorities subscribed to the policy of damage limitation. In the 1980s, the main variations in censorship practice occurred because local officials were resisting change and pursuing their own agendas independently of the authorities in Berlin. Officials in Anklam argued that they were defending the interests of local audiences against those of avant-garde theatre practitioners from the capital. In this case, the conflict arose from a clash of cultural expectations. Officials found it difficult to mount a political case against Castorf, and they argued—with considerable reason—that his stagings did not correspond to the tastes of local audiences. Matters were different in Dresden: in 1989, local officials were concerned that *Die Ritter der Tafelrunde* might act as a focal point for political discontent. Regional officials did sometimes challenge the central state authorities in earlier decades: in the mid-1970s, officials in Rostock questioned the right of the Ministry and Repertoire Management to intervene in local theatre planning. But in the 1980s, this mistrust of the Ministry was linked to perceptions that its officials were making decisions that were

[23] 'Aktennotiz', 8.12.1988, LAB C Rep. 902 6811.
[24] BStU BV Ddn. Abt. XX 9437, fo. 11.
[25] Ibid. 32.

too liberal, whether with regard to performance aesthetics or politics. Peter Ullrich dates this phenomenon to the protest against Biermann's expatriation, arguing that some provincial functionaries saw the protest as a sign that they needed to take control of cultural matters themselves—an attitude that the lack of central orientation in cultural policy encouraged.[26]

The greatest local variations in theatre censorship occurred in 1988–9, when the Ministry responded to pressure from dramatists and theatre practitioners by progressively lifting restrictions on the performance of new drama. In both Potsdam and Dresden, there were officials who strongly opposed the Ministry's actions; the main difference was their position in the hierarchy of power. In Potsdam, First Secretary Günther Jahn had the power to ban *Revisor*; in Dresden, the support of the Culture Minister and Modrow helped to overcome stiff local opposition to *Die Ritter der Tafelrunde*. Conservative officials seem to have felt that they were the last defenders of socialism: Jahn reportedly declared that there was no room for perestroika in Potsdam, whatever might be happening in other countries and in other regions of the GDR.[27] In Bautzen, however, officials seem to have been motivated by the desire to conform to their superiors' expectations, as soon as they had worked out what they were. The First Secretary of the *Kreisleitung* denounced *Revisor* and disclaimed responsibility for it, only for his officials to pacify similarly outraged spectators on the grounds that Bautzen could not afford the scandal of a production ban.

As GDR theatre censorship acquired its own history, the long-term cost of production bans was becoming clear. At leading theatres, the slow rate of staff turnover meant that censorship disputes continued to rankle in subsequent decades. After Biermann's expatriation, technicians at the Deutsches Theater referred to the censorship of *Die Sorgen und die Macht* fourteen years earlier, and Dresen revived the question of *Faust*. Past censorship decisions returned to haunt the authorities when *Die Umsiedlerin*, *Moritz Tassow*, and *Johann Faustus* were finally restaged. Given that these texts had been labelled 'wrong' and 'full of flaws' in the 1960s, their performance in the 1970s and 1980s highlighted the fallibility and in-built obsolescence of censorship. In 1987, Culture Secretary Ellen Brombacher asked Berlin's First Secretary

---

[26] Interview with Ullrich, 26.7.2007.
[27] Baker, '"From Page to Stage"', 249.

Günter Schabowski to consider whether the Maxim Gorki Theater should be allowed to stage *Diktatur des Gewissens*, telling him:

Das Stück wird auf die Dauer nicht zu umgehen sein, auch wenn heute eine Entscheidung nicht leicht ist. Also machen wir doch daraus lieber heute einen Sieg als morgen eine sichere Niederlage.[28]

We will not be able to avoid this play in the long run, even if it is not easy to reach a decision today. So let's make a victory of it today, rather than a certain defeat tomorrow.

The same pragmatic considerations influenced the Ministry's decision to release a succession of 'new' plays for performance in 1987–9, causing the pace of change in censorship to accelerate.

4. FROM PERFORMANCE TO PROTEST

Until the GDR's fortieth anniversary, the vast majority of theatre practitioners confined direct expressions of opposition to the rehearsal room, Party meetings, or discussions with the authorities. The main exception was the protest against Biermann's expatriation; yet even in this case, protesters did not solicit support from theatre audiences, and they disagreed over the decision to send the resolution to the Western press. The political dissent expressed through *Leonce und Lena, Die Ritter der Tafelrunde*, and even *Revisor* was qualitatively different from the opposition that theatres practised openly in October and November 1989. I shall conclude by examining the roles that theatres played in these protests, which marked a failure of belief in the controls that had hitherto regulated political and artistic discourse in the GDR.

In Chapter 7, we left officials in Dresden in May 1989, planning the repertoire for the next season. By the time performances started in September, the political situation had worsened substantially. The Hungarian borders had been opened on 10 September, allowing East German refugees to escape to the West. Theatres were affected too: thirty-one members of the Landestheater Halle left the GDR illegally in the summer and autumn of 1989.[29] On 12 September, members of the Maxim Gorki Theater produced a whole catalogue of complaints,

[28] Brombacher to Schabowski, 12.1.1987, LAB C Rep. 902 6767.
[29] Förster to Bernhardt, 8.11.1989, LHASA Abt. MER, SED-BL Halle IV/F-2/9.02/341.

criticizing the news coverage in *Neues Deutschland*, the lack of initiative from the SED leadership, and the damage that recent events had caused to the GDR's international image.[30] Similar reports prompted Hoffmann and Ragwitz to visit the Deutsches Theater to meet actors involved in the New Forum, an oppositional movement that had been founded on 9 September. Whereas central officials had previously cracked down on any sign of organized opposition, Hoffmann and Ragwitz now attempted to show that they were prepared to engage in dialogue.[31] On 2 October, the Central Committee's Culture Department noted that it would not be possible to return to the working practices of just three months earlier.[32] Power had begun to shift.

All this occurred just as the GDR was set to celebrate its fortieth anniversary. In an attempt to prevent disturbances, local officials and theatre managers imposed temporary production bans. In Schwerin, the manager of the Mecklenburgisches Staatstheater informed Schroth that his planned programme of FDJ and folk songs could not be staged in September or October.[33] A number of theatre practitioners boycotted the anniversary celebrations: in Dresden, Wolfgang Engel refused to accept a National Prize, and in Halle, Peer-Uwe Teska refused to recite a poem by Johannes R. Becher, saying that he could not identify with its sentiments.[34] There was soon no shortage of counter-texts to the regime's declarations of success. On 18 September, a group of musicians and entertainers produced a resolution expressing concern at the state of the GDR, the exodus of refugees, and the 'intolerable ignorance' of the Party and state leadership. The resolution called for reforms that would safeguard the continued existence of socialism in the GDR.[35] On 3 October, the authorities in Berlin reported that several cultural institutions had used the text as a basis for their own resolutions. The

---

[30] 'Information über die Mitgliederversammlung im Maxim Gorki Theater', 13.9.1989, LAB C Rep. 902 6772.

[31] 'Aktennotiz über eine Beratung in der Abteilung Kultur des ZK der SED', 2.10.1989, LHASA Abt. MER, SED-BL Halle IV/F-2/9.02/333.

[32] Ibid.

[33] 'Parteiinformation', LHAS 10.34-3 4706. On the production, see Moray McGowan, 'Staging the "Wende": Some 1989 East German Productions and the Flux of History', in Edward Batley and David Bradby (eds.), *Morality and Justice: The Challenge of European Theatre* (= *European Studies*, 17 (2000)), 73–90 at 84–9.

[34] 'Zur aktuellen politisch-ideologischen Situation . . .', SächsStA-D 11857 A 13304; Bernhardt to Böhme, 29.9.1989, LHASA Abt. MER, SED-BL Halle IV/F-2/5/259.

[35] *Wir treten aus unseren Rollen heraus: Dokumente des Aufbruchs Herbst '89*, ed. Angela Kuberski, Theaterarbeit in der DDR, 19 (Berlin: Zentrum für Theaterdokumentation und -information, 1990), 14–15.

following day, actors read out a resolution at a performance at the Staatsschauspiel in Dresden, to a standing ovation from the audience.[36] Tensions in Dresden escalated on 4 and 5 October, when trains full of East German refugees from Prague passed through the city en route to the Federal Republic. Violent clashes between security forces and protesters prompted actors at the Staatsschauspiel to produce a new resolution, which was read out for the first time on 6 October:

Wir treten aus unseren Rollen heraus.

Die Situation in unserem Land zwingt uns dazu.

Ein Land, das seine Jugend nicht halten kann, gefährdet seine Zukunft.

Eine Parteiführung, die ihre Prinzipien nicht mehr auf Brauchbarkeit untersucht, ist zum Untergang verurteilt.

Ein Volk, das zur Sprachlosigkeit gezwungen wurde, fängt an, gewalttätig zu werden.

Die Wahrheit muß an den Tag.

Unsere Arbeit steckt in dem Land. Wir lassen uns das Land nicht kaputtmachen.[37]

We are stepping out of our roles.

The situation in our country compels us to do so.

A country that cannot hold on to its young people endangers its future.

A Party leadership that has ceased to examine the practicability of its principles is condemned to decline.

A nation that was forced to remain silent is beginning to grow violent.

The truth must come to light.

We have invested our work in this country. We will not let our country be destroyed.

The opening line announced the shift from theatrical dissent to political opposition; as Loren Kruger argues, it functioned both as 'exhortation and performative utterance', calling on spectators to abandon the roles prescribed for them by the state.[38] When officials banned the resolution

---

[36] The theatre's own report states that the actors read out the musicians' resolution, and members of the ensemble confirmed this in interviews for a radio programme in 1999. However, Kuberski's volume includes a new resolution that was designed to be read out on 4.10.1989. See 'Bericht über die Vorstellung "Nina, Nina..." am 4. Oktober 1989 um 19 Uhr', SächsStA-D 12992 Vorstellungsberichte 89/90, 65/29; 'Wir treten aus unseren Rollen heraus: Die Ereignisse am Staatsschauspiel Dresden im Herbst '89', MDR, 1999. Presented by Thomas Stecher, Staatsschauspiel Dresden Archive. See also *Wir treten aus unseren Rollen heraus*, ed. Kuberski, 29.

[37] *Wir treten aus unseren Rollen heraus*, ed. Kuberski, 39.

[38] Loren Kruger, '*Wir treten aus unseren Rollen heraus*: Theater Intellectuals and Public Spheres', in Michael Geyer (ed.), *The Power of Intellectuals in Contemporary Germany* (Chicago: University of Chicago Press, 2001), 183–211 at 183.

the following day, members of the Staatsschauspiel decided to stand in silence on stage after the performance, complying with the letter of the ban but defying its spirit.[39] The resolution soon spread to other theatres: it was read out in Leipzig on 11 October, and even small theatres such as Parchim produced statements.[40] On 13 October, an official in Halle warned that since Hermann Kant and Manfred Wekwerth had published statements calling for change, other prominent artists were worried that they might be the last people to take a stand, unless they acted immediately.[41]

In the crucial days and weeks when events hung in the balance, theatre was in a position to substitute for the GDR media and to fulfil the informative function that Reiher claimed for it. At the Deutsches Theater and Mecklenburgisches Staatstheater, spectators crowded round the information posted in the foyer, copying down the texts of resolutions. Theatres provided a space for public dialogue; at the Staatsschauspiel, wardrobe staff were asked to stay for two hours after performances so that spectators could collect their coats after long post-show discussions.[42] Theatre practitioners used their professional network to exchange information. After members of East Berlin's theatres had decided on 15 October to plan a mass demonstration for the following month, they circulated the information to other theatres via the Union of Theatre Practitioners.[43] In Bautzen, meanwhile, the Deutsch-Sorbisches Volkstheater supplied platforms and sound equipment for the Monday night demonstrations.[44] On 4 November, the Theater Junge Garde in Halle hosted a forum on education. It was the theatre, not the local education department, which had invited local teachers and education professionals, and approximately a thousand people attended.[45] As political institutions failed, theatre was one of the institutions that stepped temporarily into the breach.

Individual managers and officials reacted differently to this unprecedented political activity. In East Berlin, Böttger signed a resolution

[39] 'Deutschlandfunk vom 9.10.1989', SächsStA-D 11857 A 13218.
[40] SächsStA-L SED-BL Leipzig 850; LHAS 7.11 A36/1993 8.
[41] Bernhardt to Böhme, 13.10.1989, LHASA Abt. MER, SED-BL Halle IV/F-2/9.02/333.
[42] See SächsStA-D 12992 A 151.
[43] 'Resolution', LHASA Abt. MER, SED-BL Halle IV/F-7/827/13.
[44] Lorenz, 'Das Deutsch-Sorbische Volkstheater...', Stadtarchiv Bautzen, Abgabe Michael Lorenz.
[45] Karin Fukowski, 'Halle: Forum in Sachen Volksbildung', *Mitteldeutsche Neueste Nachrichten* (Halle), 6.11.1989.

produced by the Deutsches Theater, protesting against the excesses of the security forces.[46] In Schwerin, however, the regional authorities launched disciplinary proceedings against theatre practitioners who had sent a letter of protest to Hager and Hoffmann.[47] At one theatre in the Dresden region, it was the manager who attempted to nip the protest in the bud: he reportedly threatened to shut the theatre if actors read out the resolution produced by the Staatsschauspiel.[48] Even after 18 October, when Egon Krenz—Honecker's successor—had authorized a limited public debate, pockets of local resistance to political discussions remained. This was partly because officials were unable to deal with the public hostility that they encountered: in Zeitz, local Party and state representatives attended the first public meeting but banned subsequent events. On 7 November, the theatre manager in Zeitz complained that the *Kreisleitung* was still treating theatre practitioners as criminals for opening the way for dialogue.[49] This was three days after East Berlin had seen the largest mass demonstration in the GDR's history, initiated by the city's theatre practitioners.

Theatres began to lose their *ersatz* function as the GDR media started to report the public debate. From 23 October, the size of audiences at the Staatsschauspiel Dresden fluctuated; numbers were significantly lower on nights when there were mass demonstrations on the streets.[50] On 11 November, Schönemann asked if the Staatsschauspiel had been overtaken by the public debate, and on 28 November, he worried that the opening of *Nina, Nina* now seemed naive.[51] Yet *Die Ritter der Tafelrunde* still packed in the crowds, and people queued up outside the theatre on 24 November, hoping for tickets.[52] Like other GDR theatres, the Staatsschauspiel quickly scheduled readings of previously banned texts, such as Walter Janka's *Schwierigkeiten mit der Wahrheit* (Difficulties with the Truth), an account of his imprisonment in Bautzen. But the intense phase of political dialogue in theatres was relatively short-lived. As the reform process gathered pace, the differences between

[46] DT, 'Chronik', 27.12.1989, AdK Schriften-DK 61.
[47] 'Protokoll der 23. Sitzung des Sekretariats der BL Schwerin der SED', LHAS 10.34-3 4306.
[48] 'Demo 19.11.89: . . . Sprechergruppe', AdK Schriften-DK 61.
[49] 'Aktennotiz über eine Intendantenberatung des Genossen Günther Kuhbach am 7.11.1989', 9.11.1989, LHASA Abt. MER, SED-BL Halle IV/F-2/9.02/341.
[50] SächsStA-D 12992 Vorstellungsberichte 89/90, 65/29.
[51] Ibid.
[52] Ibid.

the political views of the intellectual elite and the majority of the population were becoming clear. Right through November, theatre practitioners' resolutions continued to express their commitment to the GDR as a socialist state, yet protesters on the streets were already calling for reunification. As political censorship ended, new challenges for theatres were coming into view: in April 1990, the management of the Staatsschauspiel warned that economic uncertainty was leading many spectators to stay away.[53] It appeared increasingly likely that some of the GDR's smaller theatres would be forced to close.

It is ironic now to read the documents in which the Culture Ministry and regional authorities set out their plans for GDR theatre in the 1990s and beyond. An incredible amount of time and energy was devoted to planning and prognosis in the GDR, yet the process of pioneering new plays and approaches always involved trial and error. Even Ministry officials could only try to gauge the 'risks' associated with new plays like *Die Sorgen und die Macht*, or dramatizations like *Franziska Linkerhand*. When productions were banned after their premiere, it was rarely because they had slipped through the censors' net. Instead, post-premiere bans point to differences of opinion within the administration and the theatre community: to the dynamic and often unpredictable nature of censorship debates. In some regions and theatres, officials and managers chose to avoid this grey zone of uncertainty, imposing greater restrictions than the Ministry or Culture Department. When high-risk productions did go ahead, it was often because theatre practitioners and officials had managed to forge alliances and share responsibility. The system penalized innovative directors and dramatists who were reluctant to negotiate; in order to win and preserve space for experimentation, they needed to find managers, dramaturges, or officials willing to negotiate on their behalf. These processes of negotiation and cooperation—however willing or reluctant—are as central to the history of GDR theatre censorship as the more famous conflicts.

---

[53] 'Information zur aktuellen Zuschauersituation', 9.4.1990, SächsStA-D 12992 109.

Bibliography

For reasons of space, this list does not include entries for archival sources, newspaper articles (except interviews), theatre reviews, or internet resources. Full bibliographic details for these sources are provided in the footnotes.

1. ARCHIVES CONSULTED

Federal and regional state archives
BStU, Berlin
Bundesarchiv, Berlin
Kreisarchiv Anklam
Landesarchiv Berlin
Landeshauptarchiv Sachsen-Anhalt, Abt. Merseburg
Landeshauptarchiv Schwerin
Sächsisches Hauptstaatsarchiv Dresden
Sächsisches Staatsarchiv Leipzig
Stadtarchiv Bautzen
Stadtarchiv Schwerin
Stiftung Archiv der Akademie der Künste, Berlin

Theatre archives
Berliner Ensemble
Deutsches Theater
Deutsch-Sorbisches Volkstheater Bautzen
Staatsschauspiel Dresden
Volksbühne

2. INTERVIEWS CONDUCTED
Antoni, Carmen-Maja, 17.11.2006
Behnisch, Uwe, 21.4.2009
Günther, Eveline, and Michael Lorenz, 23.4.2009
Hinckel, Erika, 12.10.2004
Hochmuth, Arno, 7.10.2004
Jaksch, Bärbel, 18.7.2007
Karge, Manfred, 19.3.2004

Kirst, Klaus Dieter, 24.4.2009
Schroth, Christoph, 1.10.2009
Schumacher, Ernst, 19.7.2007
Ullrich, Peter, 26.7.2007
Wilzopolski, Siegfried, 11.7.2007

3. LITERATURE

Abraham, Peter, 'Arbeitsgruppe IV: Literatur und Wirkung', in *X. Schriftstellerkongreß*, ed. Schriftstellerverband der DDR, 2 vols. (East Berlin: Aufbau, 1988), i. 212–19.

Agde, Günter (ed.), *Kahlschlag: Das 11. Plenum des ZK der SED 1965: Studien und Dokumente* (Berlin: Aufbau, 1991).

Arlt, Herbert, and Bischof, Ulrike (eds.), ... *mir ist in den 80er Jahren kein DDR-Theater bekannt ... Dokumentationsgespräche, Materialien, Anmerkungen* (Frankfurt/M.: Peter Lang, 1993).

Baker, Barrie, '"From Page to Stage": The State and the Theatre in the German Democratic Republic in the 1980s' (Ph.D. thesis, University of Reading, 2005).

——— *Theatre Censorship in Honecker's Germany: From Volker Braun to Samuel Beckett*, German Linguistic and Cultural Studies, 23 (Bern: Peter Lang, 2007).

Balitzki, Jürgen, *Castorf, der Eisenhändler: Theater zwischen Kartoffelsalat und Stahlgewitter* (Berlin: Ch. Links, 1995).

Becker, Peter von, and Merschmeier, Michael, '"Das Sicherste ist die Veränderung": THEATER HEUTE-Gespräch mit DDR-Kulturminister Hans Joachim [*sic*] Hoffmann', *Theater 1988: Jahrbuch der Zeitschrift Theater heute*, 29 (1988), 10–20.

——— 'Wir wollten Sozialismus und wurden Stalinisten', *Theater heute*, 31/7 (July 1990), 2–18.

Bentzien, Hans, *Meine Sekretäre und ich* (Berlin: Neues Leben, 1995).

Biermann und kein Ende: Eine Dokumentation zur DDR-Kulturpolitik, ed. Dietmar Keller and Matthias Kirchner (Berlin: Dietz, 1991).

Biermann, Wolf, *Deutschland: Ein Wintermärchen* (West Berlin: Klaus Wagenbach, 1972).

Bisky, Lothar, 'Nur scheinbar robust', in Gertraude Hoffmann and Klaus Höpcke (eds.), *'Das Sicherste ist die Veränderung': Hans-Joachim Hoffmann. Kulturminister der DDR und häufig verdächtigter Demokrat* (Berlin: Dietz, 2003), 112–14.

Boldt, Hans, 'Heine im Zusammenhang der politischen Ideen seiner Zeit', in Wilhelm Gössmann and Manfred Windfuhr (eds.), *Heinrich Heine im*

Spannungsfeld von Literatur und Wissenschaft: Symposium anläßlich der Benennung der Universität Düsseldorf nach Heinrich Heine, Kultur und Erkenntnis, 7 (Bonn: Reimar Hobbing, 1990), 65–80.

Bonner, Withold, 'Franziska Linkerhand: Vom Typoskript zur Druckfassung', in Brigitte Reimann, *Franziska Linkerhand,* 6th rev. edn. (Berlin: Aufbau, 2003), 605–31.

Bourdieu, Pierre, 'Censorship and the Imposition of Form', in *Language and Symbolic Power,* ed. and introduced by John B. Thompson, trans. Gino Raymond and Matthew Adamson (London: Polity, 1991), 137–59.

—— 'The Field of Cultural Production, or: The Economic World Reversed', in *The Field of Cultural Production: Essays on Art and Literature,* ed. Randal Johnson (Cambridge: Polity, 1993), 29–73.

—— 'The Production of Belief: Contribution to an Economy of Symbolic Goods', in *The Field of Cultural Production,* 74–111.

—— *The Rules of Art: Genesis and Structure of the Literary Field,* trans. Susan Emmanuel (London: Polity, 1996).

Bradley, Laura, 'Censorship and Opinion Formation: *Franziska Linkerhand* on the GDR Stage', *GLL* 63 (2010), 234–49.

—— 'A Different Political Forum: East German Theatre and the Construction of the Berlin Wall', *Journal of European Studies,* 36 (2006), 139–56.

—— 'GDR Theatre Censorship: A System in Denial', *GLL* 59 (2006), 151–62.

—— '*Prager Luft* at the Berliner Ensemble: The Censorship of *Sieben gegen Theben,* 1968–9', *GLL* 58 (2005), 41–54.

—— 'Stealing Büchner's Characters? *Leonce und Lena* in East Berlin', *Oxford German Studies,* 35 (2006), 66–78.

Bräuer, Siegfried, and Vollnhals, Clemens (eds.), '*In der DDR gibt es keine Zensur': Die Evangelische Verlagsanstalt und die Praxis der Druckgenehmigung 1954–1989* (Leipzig: Evangelische Verlagsanstalt, 1995).

Braun, Matthias, '*Che Guevara—oder der Sonnenstaat*—Bedenken hatten nicht nur die kubanischen Genossen', in Frank Hörnigk (ed.), *Volker Braun,* TdZ Arbeitsbuch (Berlin: TdZ, 1999), 123–7.

—— *Drama um eine Komödie: Das Ensemble von SED und Staatssicherheit, FDJ und Ministerium für Kultur gegen Heiner Müllers 'Die Umsiedlerin auf dem Lande' im Oktober 1961* (Berlin: Ch. Links, 1995).

Braun, Volker, '21., 22. August 1984', in *Verheerende Folgen mangelnden Anscheins innerbetrieblicher Demokratie* (Leipzig: Reclam, 1988), 124–34.

—— 'Die ausgelassenen Antworten', in *Es genügt nicht die einfache Wahrheit* (Leipzig: Reclam, 1975), 108–10.

—— 'Büchners Briefe', in *Verheerende Folgen mangelnden Anscheins innerbetrieblicher Demokratie* (Leipzig: Reclam, 1988), 83–94. First published in *Connaissance de la RDA,* 7 (1978), 8–17.

Braun, Volker, 'Notate zu *Dmitri* (2)', in *Mecklenburgisches Staatstheater Schwerin*, ed. Linzer, 52–5.
—— *Texte in zeitlicher Folge*, 10 vols. (Halle and Leipzig: Mitteldeutscher Verlag, 1990–3), vi (1991).
—— *Werktage 1: Arbeitsbuch 1977–1989* (Frankfurt/M.: Suhrkamp, 2009).
Brecht, Bertolt, *Große kommentierte Berliner und Frankfurter Ausgabe* (cited as *BFA*), ed. Werner Hecht and others, 30 vols. (Frankfurt/M. and Berlin: Suhrkamp and Aufbau, 1988–2000).
Büchner, Georg, *Dantons Tod* (Stuttgart: Reclam, 1973).
Burt, Richard, *Licensed by Authority: Ben Jonson and the Discourses of Censorship* (Ithaca and London: Cornell University Press, 1993).
—— 'The "New" Censorship', in Burt (ed.), *The Administration of Aesthetics: Censorship, Political Criticism, and the Public Sphere*, Cultural Politics, 7 (Minneapolis and London: University of Minnesota Press, 1994), pp. xi–xxix.
Butler, Judith, 'Ruled Out: Vocabularies of the Censor', in Robert C. Post (ed.), *Censorship and Silencing: Practices of Cultural Regulation*, Issues and Debates, 4 (Los Angeles: Getty Research Institute, 1998), 247–59.
Coulson, Andrew, 'From Democratic Centralism to Local Democracy', in Coulson (ed.), *Local Government in Eastern Europe: Establishing Democracy at the Grassroots* (Aldershot: Edward Elgar, 1995), 1–19.
Darnton, Robert, 'Censorship, A Comparative View: France, 1789—East Germany, 1989', in Olwen Hufton (ed.), *Historical Change and Human Rights: The Amnesty Lectures 1994* (New York: Basic Books, 1995), 102–30.
Die DDR-Verfassungen, ed. Herwig Roggemann, 3rd rev. edn. (West Berlin: Berlin, 1980).
Die Debatte um Hanns Eislers Johann Faustus: Eine Dokumentation, ed. Hans Bunge (Berlin: BasisDruck, 1991).
Deutsche Verfassungen: Dokumente zu Vergangenheit und Gegenwart, ed. Hermann-Josef Blanke (Paderborn: F. Schöningh, 2003).
Dieckmann, Friedrich, and others, 'Das pazifistische Programm ist abgestürzt —25 Jahre, '68', *TdZ* 49/3 (Mar. 1994), 60–5.
Dittmann, Uta, 'Das große Jahrzehnt: Erinnerungen von Horst Schönemann und Wolfgang Engel', in Dittmann (ed.), *Sein oder Nichtsein? Theatergeschichten: Staatsschauspiel Dresden 1913 bis heute* (Dresden: Staatsschauspiel Dresden and Sächsische Zeitung, [1995]), 93–111.
Dokumente zur deutschen Verfassungsgeschichte, ed. Ernst Rudolf Huber, 3 vols. (Stuttgart: W. Kohlhammer, 1961), i.
Dokumente zur Kunst-, Literatur- und Kulturpolitik der SED, ed. Elimar Schubbe (Stuttgart: Seewald, 1972).

Dokumente zur Kunst-, Literatur- und Kulturpolitik der SED 1971–1974, ed. Gisela Rüß (Stuttgart: Seewald, 1976).

Dokumente zur Kunst-, Literatur- und Kulturpolitik der SED 1975–1980, ed. Peter Lübbe (Stuttgart: Seewald, 1984).

Domröse, Angelica, *Ich fang mich selbst ein: Mein Leben* (Bergisch Gladbach: Lübbe, 2003).

Dramaturgen des Berliner Ensemble, 'Theater zur Zeit der Mauer: Ein Gespräch mit dem Schauspieler Manfred Karge', *Berliner Zeitung*, 27.12.2002.

Dramaturgie in der DDR (1945–1990), ed. Helmut Kreuzer and Karl-Wilhelm Schmidt, 2 vols. (Heidelberg: Universitätsverlag Winter, 1998).

Dresen, Adolf, 'Opposition mit Klassikern: Meine Arbeiten am Deutschen Theater', in Henning Rischbieter (ed.), *Theater im geteilten Deutschland 1945 bis 1990* (Berlin: Propyläen, 1999), 98–104.

——*Siegfrieds Vergessen: Kultur zwischen Konsens und Konflikt* (Berlin: Ch. Links, 1992).

——*Wieviel Freiheit braucht die Kunst? Reden Briefe Verse Spiele 1964 bis 1999*, ed. Maik Hamburger, TdZ Recherchen, 3 (Eggersdorf: TdZ and Literaturforum im Brecht-Haus, 2000).

——'Zensur oder nicht Zensur?', *TdZ* 45/6 (June 1990), 5–8.

Du tust mir wirklich fehlen: Der Briefwechsel zwischen Peter Hacks und Heinar Kipphardt, ed. Uwe Naumann (Berlin: Eulenspiegel, 2004).

Ehrlich, Lothar, '*Faust* im DDR-Sozialismus', in Frank Möbus, Friederike Schmidt-Möbus, and Gerd Unverfehrt (eds.), *Faust: Annäherung an einen Mythos* (Göttingen: Wallstein, 1995), 332–42.

Eicher, Thomas, Panse, Barbara, and Rischbieter, Henning, in *Theater im 'Dritten Reich': Theaterpolitik, Spielplanstruktur, NS-Dramatik*, ed. Henning Rischbieter (Seelze-Velber: Kallmeyer, 2000).

Engelmann, Roger, and Vollnhals, Clemens (eds.), *Justiz im Dienste der Parteiherrschaft: Rechtspraxis und Staatssicherheit in der DDR*, 2nd rev. edn. (Berlin: Ch. Links, 2000).

Esche, Eberhard, *Der Hase im Rausch* (Berlin: Eulenspiegel, 2000).

Fischer, Ernst, 'Doktor Faustus und der deutsche Bauernkrieg: Auszüge aus dem Essay zu Hanns Eislers Faust-Dichtung', *Sinn und Form*, 4 (1952), 59–73.

Fischer, Heinz-Dietrich (ed.), *Pressekonzentration und Zensurpraxis im Ersten Weltkrieg* (West Berlin: V. Spieß, 1973).

Franke, Konrad, '"Deine Darstellung ist uns wesensfremd": Romane der 60er Jahre in den Mühlen der DDR-Zensur', in Ernest Wichner and Herbert Wiesner (eds.), '*Literaturentwicklungsprozesse': Die Zensur der Literatur in der DDR* (Frankfurt/M.: Suhrkamp, 1993), 101–26.

294 Bibliography

Freshwater, Helen, 'The Allure of the Archive', in *Poetics Today*, 24 (2003), 729–58.

Friedrich-Ebert-Stiftung (ed.), *Der demokratische Zentralismus: Herrschaftsprinzip der DDR* (Bonn: Neue Gesellschaft, 1984).

Fulbrook, Mary, 'Democratic Centralism and Regionalism in the GDR', in Maiken Umbach (ed.), *German Federalism: Past, Present, Future* (Basingstoke: Palgrave, 2002), 146–71.

—— *The People's State: East German Society from Hitler to Honecker* (New Haven and London: Yale University Press, 2005).

Funke, Christoph, 'Theater und neue Dramatik', in *Mitteilungen*, ed. Schriftstellerverband der DDR, 3/4 (Mar./Apr. 1989), 3–9.

Gendries, Klaus, 'Konterrevolutionäre Plattformbildung', in Sewan Latchinian and Harald Müller (eds.), *Glück auf! 60 Jahre Theater Senftenberg* (Berlin: TdZ, 2006), 40–2.

Goethe, Johann Wolfgang von, *Faust*, trans. Walter Arndt, ed. Cyrus Hamlin, 2nd edn. (New York and London: Norton, 2001).

Grieder, Peter, *The East German Leadership 1946–73: Conflict and Crisis* (Manchester and New York: Manchester University Press, 1999).

Groß, Jürgen, 'Revisor oder Katze aus dem Sack', *TdZ* 44/3 (Mar. 1989), 52–64.

Guntner, J. Lawrence, and McLean, Andrew M. (eds.), *Redefining Shakespeare: Literary Theory and Theatre Practice in the German Democratic Republic* (London: Associated University Presses, 1998).

Gysi, Birgid, '*Moritz Tassow* von Peter Hacks an der Volksbühne Berlin: Eine Dokumentation', in Christa Neubert-Herwig (ed.), *Benno Besson: Theater spielen in acht Ländern: Texte, Dokumente, Gespräche* (Berlin: Alexander, 1998), 275–86.

—— 'Weiße Flecken (3): *Moritz Tassow* von Peter Hacks an der Volksbühne Berlin, 1965', *TdZ* 45/10 (Oct. 1990), 31–6.

—— 'Weiße Flecken (6): *Leonce und Lena* von Georg Büchner', *TdZ* 46/11 (Nov. 1991), 70–5.

Habemma, Cox, *Mein Koffer in Berlin oder das Märchen von der Wende*, trans. Ira Wilhelm (Leipzig: Militzke, 2004).

Hacks, Peter, *Verehrter Kollege: Briefe an Schriftsteller*, ed. Rainer Kirsch (Berlin: Eulenspiegel, 2006).

Hager, Kurt, *Zu Fragen der Kulturpolitik der SED* (East Berlin: Dietz, 1972).

Hammerthaler, Ralph, 'Die Position des Theaters in der DDR', in Christa Hasche, Traute Schölling, and Joachim Fiebach, *Theater in der DDR: Chronik und Positionen. Mit einem Essay von Ralph Hammerthaler* (Berlin: Henschel, 1994), 151–273.

Heidenreich, Ronny, *Aufruhr hinter Gittern: Das 'Gelbe Elend' im Herbst 1989* (Leipzig: Leipziger Universitätsverlag, 2009).

Hein, Christoph, 'Literatur und Wirkung', in *X. Schriftstellerkongreß der Deutschen Demokratischen Republik*, ed. Schriftstellerverband der DDR, 2 vols. (East Berlin: Aufbau, 1988), ii. 225–47.

——*Die Stücke* (Frankfurt/M.: Suhrkamp, 2005).

——'Weder das Verbot noch die Genehmigung als Geschenk', in *Als Kind habe ich Stalin gesehen: Essais und Reden* (Frankfurt/M.: Suhrkamp, 2004), 168–73.

Heine, Heinrich, *Deutschland: A Winter's Tale*, trans. and introduced by T. J. Reed, 2nd edn. (London: Angel, 1997).

Hermand, Jost, *Streitobjekt Heine: Ein Forschungsbericht 1945–1975* (Frankfurt/M.: Athenäum Fischer, 1975).

Holtz, Corinne, *Ruth Berghaus: Ein Porträt* (Hamburg: Europäische Verlagsanstalt, 2005).

Höpcke, Klaus, 'Zum Drama des Dramas', *TdZ* 42/10 (Oct. 1987), 12–13.

Irmer, Thomas, 'Ein letzter Kayser', in Wolfgang Engel and Erika Stephan (eds.), *Theater in der Übergangsgesellschaft: Schauspiel Leipzig 1957–2007* (Berlin: TdZ, 2007), 76–83.

——and Schmidt, Matthias, *Die Bühnenrepublik: Theater in der DDR*, ed. Wolfgang Bergmann (Berlin: Alexander Verlag, 2003).

Jäger, Manfred, *Kultur und Politik in der DDR 1945–1990* (Cologne: Nottbeck, 1995).

——'Das Wechselspiel von Selbstzensur und Literaturlenkung in der DDR', in Ernest Wichner and Herbert Wiesner (eds.), *'Literaturentwicklungsprozesse': Die Zensur der Literatur in der DDR* (Frankfurt/M.: Suhrkamp, 1993), 18–49.

Kaiser, Monika, *Machtwechsel von Ulbricht zu Honecker: Funktionsmechanismen der SED-Diktatur in Konfliktsituationen 1962 bis 1972*, Zeithistorische Studien, 10 (Berlin: Akademie, 1997).

Kasper, Martin (ed.), *Die Lausitzer Sorben in der Wende 1989/90: Ein Abriss mit Dokumenten und einer Chronik*, Schriften des Sorbischen Instituts, 28 (Bautzen: Domowina, 2000).

Kaufmann, Hans, 'Zehn Anmerkungen über das Erbe, die Kunst und die Kunst des Erbens', *Weimarer Beiträge*, 19/10 (Oct. 1973), 34–53.

Knabe, Hubertus, '"Weiche" Formen der Verfolgung in der DDR: Zum Wandel repressiver Strategien in der Ära Honecker', *Deutschland Archiv*, 30 (1997), 709–19.

——(ed.), *Gefangen in Hohenschönhausen: Stasi-Häftlinge berichten* (Berlin: List, 2007).

Kochta, Karla, 'Beratung des Dramatikerbeirates... über die Entscheidungs-findung zum Genehmigungsverfahren *Die Ritter der Tafelrunde* von Christoph Hein am 15. März 1989', in Baker, '"From Page to Stage"', D19–D26.

Krug, Manfred, *Abgehauen: Ein Mitschnitt und ein Tagebuch* (Munich: Ullstein, 2003).

Kruger, Loren, '*Wir treten aus unseren Rollen heraus*: Theater Intellectuals and Public Spheres', in Michael Geyer (ed.), *The Power of Intellectuals in Contemporary Germany* (Chicago: University of Chicago Press, 2001), 183–211.

Lamport, Frank, 'Goethe's *Faust*: A Cautionary Tale?', *Forum for Modern Language Studies*, 35 (1999), 193–206.

Langermann, Martina, '"Faust oder Gregor Samsa?" Kulturelle Tradierung im Zeichen der Sieger', in Birgit Dahlke, Martina Langermann, and Thomas Taterka (eds.), *LiteraturGesellschaft DDR: Kanonenkämpfe und ihre Geschichte(n)* (Stuttgart and Weimar: J. B. Metzler, 2000), 173–213.

Lennartz, Knut, 'Klaus Höpcke und das Drama von Drama', *Deutschland Archiv*, 21 (1988), 12–14.

——(ed.), *Vom Aufbruch zur Wende: Theater in der DDR* (Velber: Erhard Friedrich, 1992).

Linzer, Martin, 'Anmerkungen zu Georg Seidels Werk und Wirken', in Georg Seidel, *Villa Jugend: Das dramatische Werk in einem Band*, ed. Andreas Leusink (Berlin and Frankfurt/M.: henschel SCHAUSPIEL and Verlag der Autoren, 1992), 381–9.

——'*Ich war immer ein Opportunist...*': *12 Gespräche über Theater und das Leben in der DDR, über geliebte und ungeliebte Zeitgenossen*, ed. Nikolaus Merck, TdZ Recherchen, 7 (Eggersdorf: TdZ and Literaturforum im Brecht-Haus, 2001).

——'Volksbühne Berlin: *Leonce und Lena*', *TdZ* 33/11 (Nov. 1978), 2.

——'Weiße Flecken (2): *Fräulein Julie* von Strindberg', *TdZ* 45/7 (July 1990), 28–33.

——'Weiße Flecken (4): *Faust* von Goethe, Deutsches Theater, 1968', *TdZ* 46/1 (Jan. 1991), 18–23.

——and others (eds.), *Wo ich bin, ist keine Provinz: Der Regisseur Christoph Schroth* (Berlin: TheaterArbeit, 2003).

Lokatis, Siegfried, *Der rote Faden: Kommunistische Parteigeschichte und Zensur unter Walter Ulbricht*, Zeithistorische Studien, 25 (Cologne: Böhlau, 2003).

Lukács, Georg, *Faust und Faustus: Vom Drama der Menschengattung zur Tragödie der modernen Kunst* (Reinbek bei Hamburg: Rowohlt, 1967).

——'Die Tragödie Kleists', in *Heinrich von Kleists Nachruhm: Eine Wirkungsgeschichte in Dokumenten*, ed. Helmut Sembdner (Munich: dtv, 1977), 459–60.

Mahl, Bernd, *Goethes 'Faust' auf der Bühne (1806–1998): Fragment—Ideologiestück—Spieltext* (Stuttgart and Weimar: Metzler, 1998).

Matussek, Matthias, 'Rodeo im Wilden Osten: Das Provinztheater in Anklam, DDR, Mai 1990', in Rudolf Augstein (ed.), *Ein deutsches Jahrzehnt: Reportagen 1985–1995* (Hamburg: Spiegel, 1995), 191–203.

McGowan, Moray, ' "Der aktuelle Kabarettist zur Lage der Nation"? *Wilhelm Tell*, Staatstheater Schwerin, February 1989', in Florian Krobb and Hans-Walter Schmidt-Hannisa (eds.), *Schiller—On the Threshold of Modernity* (= *Germanistik in Ireland*, 1 (2006)), 67–74.

—— 'Staging the "Wende": Some 1989 East German Productions and the Flux of History', in Edward Batley and David Bradby (eds.), *Morality and Justice: The Challenge of European Theatre* (= *European Studies*, 17 (2000)), 73–90.

Mecklenburgisches Staatstheater Schwerin: Demetrius/Dmitri, ed. Martin Linzer, Theaterarbeit in der DDR, 10 (East Berlin: VdT, 1985).

Michaelis, Rolf, 'Theater heute—in Ostberlin', *Theater heute*, 9/12 (Dec. 1968), 30–6.

Middendorf, Stefan, *Recht auf Arbeit in der DDR: Von den theoretischen Grundlagen bis zu den Berufsverboten für Ausreisewillige* (Berlin and Baden-Baden: Berlin Verlag and Nomo Verlagsgesellschaft, 2000).

Minetti, Hans-Peter, *Erinnerungen* (Berlin: Ullstein, 1997).

Ministerium der Justiz, *Strafgesetzbuch der Deutschen Demokratischen Republik* (East Berlin: Staatsverlag der Deutschen Demokratischen Republik, 1968).

Misterek, Susanne, *Polnische Dramatik in Bühnen- und Buchverlagen der Bundesrepublik Deutschland und der DDR* (Wiesbaden: Harrassowitz, 2002).

Mittenzwei, Werner, *Die Intellektuellen: Literatur und Politik in Ostdeutschland von 1945 bis 2000* (Leipzig: Faber & Faber, 2001).

Modrow, Hans, with Hans-Dieter Schütt, *Ich wollte ein neues Deutschland* (Munich: Econ & List, 1999).

Müller sen., André, *Gespräche mit Hacks 1963–2003* (Berlin: Eulenspiegel, 2008).

Müller, Beate, 'Censorship and Cultural Regulation: Mapping the Territory', in Müller (ed.), *Censorship and Cultural Regulation in the Modern Age*, Critical Studies, 22 (Amsterdam and New York: Rodopi, 2004), 1–31.

Müller, Christoph, 'Adolf Dresen: "Meine Situation ist experimentell" ', *Theater heute*, 19/6 (June 1978), 27–9.

Müller, Heiner, *Geschichten aus der Produktion 1* (Berlin: Rotbuch, 1988).

—— *Krieg ohne Schlacht: Leben in zwei Diktaturen*, rev. edn. (Cologne: Kiepenheuer & Witsch, 1994).

—— *Werke*, ed. Frank Hörnigk, 12 vols. (Frankfurt/M.: Suhrkamp, 1998–2008).

298   *Bibliography*

Müller-Enbergs, Helmut, Wielgohs, Jan, and Hoffmann, Dieter (eds.), *Wer war wer in der DDR? Ein biographisches Lexikon* (Berlin: Ch. Links, 2000).

Nabrotzky, Ronald H. D., 'Die DDR: Heinrich Heines verwirklichter Lebenstraum', *MLN* 92 (1977), 535–48.

Nicholson, Steve, *The Censorship of British Drama: 1900–1968*, 4 vols. (Exeter: University of Exeter Press, 2003–), i (2003): *1900–1932*.

Niemann, Mario, *Die Sekretäre der SED-Bezirksleitungen 1952–1989* (Paderborn: Ferdinand Schöningh, 2007).

Noll, Dieter, 'Lieber, sehr verehrter Peter Hacks', in André Thiele (ed.), *In den Trümmern ohne Gnade: Festschrift für Peter Hacks* (Berlin: Eulenspiegel, 2003), 69–70.

Ostrowski, Christine, *Im Streit*, ed. Joachim Jahns (Querfurt: Dingsda, 1993).

Palmowski, Jan, 'Regional Identities and the Limits of Democratic Centralism in the GDR', *Journal of Contemporary History*, 41 (2006), 503–26.

Pauli, Manfred, *Ein Theaterimperium an der Pleiße: Leipziger Theater zu DDR-Zeiten* (Schkeuditz: Schkeuditzer Buchverlag, 2004).

Pike, David, 'Censorship in Soviet-Occupied Germany', in Norman Naimark and Leonid Gibianskii (eds.), *The Establishment of Communist Regimes in Eastern Europe, 1944–1949* (Oxford: Westview, 1997), 217–41.

Post, Robert C., 'Introduction', in Post (ed.), *Censorship and Silencing: Practices of Cultural Regulation*, Issues and Debates, 4 (Los Angeles: Getty Research Institute, 1998), 1–12.

Pragal, Peter, and Völklein, Ulrich, 'Jedes Land wählt seine Lösung', *Stern*, 40/16 (9.4.1987), 140–4.

Prieß, Lutz, Kural, Václav, and Wilke, Manfred, *Die SED und der 'Prager Frühling' 1968: Politik gegen 'Sozialismus mit menschlichem Antlitz'* (Berlin: Akademie, 1996).

Profitlich, Ulrich, *Dramatik der DDR* (Frankfurt/M.: Suhrkamp, 1987).

Protokoll eines Tribunals: Die Ausschlüsse aus dem DDR-Schriftstellerverband 1979, ed. Joachim Walther and others (Hamburg: Rowohlt, 1991).

Reimann, Brigitte, *Franziska Linkerhand* (East Berlin: Neues Leben, 1974).

Richthofen, Esther von, *Bringing Culture to the Masses: Control, Compromise and Participation in the GDR*, Monographs in German History, 24 (New York and Oxford: Berghahn, 2009).

Riewoldt, Otto F., ' "… der Größten einer als Politiker und Poet, Dichter und Revolutionär": Der beiseitegelobte Georg Büchner in der DDR', in Heinz Ludwig Arnold (ed.), *Georg Büchner III* (Munich: text + kritik, 1981), 218–35.

Rosbach, Jens P., and Baerens, Stefan, 'dafür, daß sich die menschen mehr suchen: gespräch mit christoph schroth', in Jens P. Rosbach and Stefan Baerens (eds.), *Das Land. Die Zeit. Der Mensch. Gespräche in Mecklenburg und Vorpommern* (Rostock: Norddeutscher Hochschulschriftenverlag, 1995), 53–71.

Rosenfeld, Sophia, 'Writing the History of Censorship in the Age of Enlightenment', in Daniel Gordon (ed.), *Postmodernism and the Enlightenment: New Perspectives in Eighteenth-Century French Intellectual History* (London and New York: Routledge, 2001), 117–45.

Roßmann, Andreas, 'Volker Brauns *Guevara* und *Dmitri* als DDR-Erstaufführungen in Leipzig und Schwerin', *Deutschland Archiv*, 17 (1984), 1238–9.

Rowell, Jay, 'Le Pouvoir périphérique et le "centralisme démocratique" en RDA', *Revue d'histoire moderne et contemporaine*, 49 (2002), 102–24.

Salomon, Gottfried (ed.), *Saint-Simon und der Sozialismus*, trans. Hanna Hertz (Berlin: Paul Cassirer, 1919).

Schauer, Hermann-Ernst, 'Der verdächtigte Demokrat', in Gertraude Hoffmann and Klaus Höpcke (eds.), *'Das Sicherste ist die Veränderung': Hans-Joachim Hoffmann. Kulturminister der DDR und häufig verdächtigter Demokrat* (Berlin: Dietz, 2003), 10–24.

Schiller, Andrea, *Die Theaterentwicklung in der sowjetischen Besatzungszone (SBZ) 1945 bis 1949* (Frankfurt/M.: Peter Lang, 1998).

Schiller, Friedrich, 'Was kann eine gute stehende Schaubühne eigentlich wirken?', in *Sämtliche Werke*, 2nd rev. edn., 5 vols. (Munich: Carl Hanser, 1960), v (1960), 818–31.

Schmidt, Jürgen, 'Beilage', *Blätter des Deutschen Theaters*, 19 (1991).

——*Ich möchte Ich bleiben: Lebenslauf eines mittleren Kultur-Kaders geschrieben nach 40 Jahren DDR (gekürzte Fassung)* (Schkeuditz: GNN, 1996).

Schriel, Adrianus, 'The History of the Hans-Otto-Theater Potsdam and its Reflection of Cultural Politics in the German Democratic Republic' (Ph.D. diss., University of Georgia, 1998).

Schroeder, Klaus, *Der SED-Staat* (Munich: Carl Hanser, 1998).

Schumacher, Ernst, 'DDR-Dramatik und 11. Plenum', in Agde (ed.), *Kahlschlag*, 93–105.

Schütt, Hans-Dieter, *Die Erotik des Verrats: Gespräche mit Frank Castorf* (Berlin: Dietz, 1996).

——*Spielzeit Lebenszeit: Thomas Langhoff* (Berlin: Das Neue Berlin, 2008).

Schwarzkopf, Oliver, and Rusch, Beate (eds.), *Wolf Biermann: Ausgebürgert. Fotografien von Roger Melis* (Berlin: Schwarzkopf & Schwarzkopf, [1996?]).

Sieling, Claudia, '"Aber sagen Sie nichts gegen Anklam!": Eine Analyse des Provinztheaters Anklam von 1981 bis 1985 im Tätigkeitszeitraum des Regisseurs Frank Castorf als Fallbeispiel für das Verständnis von Theaterkunst in der DDR' (Diplomarbeit, Universität Hildesheim, 1991).

Šmejkalová-Strickland, Jiřina, 'Censoring Canons: Transitions and Prospects of Literary Institutions in Czechoslovakia', in Richard Burt (ed.), *The*

Administration of Aesthetics: Censorship, Political Criticism, and the Public Sphere, Cultural Politics, 7 (Minneapolis and London: University of Minnesota Press, 1994), 195–215.

Stark, Gary, *Banned in Berlin: Literary Censorship in Imperial Germany, 1871–1918*, Monographs in German History, 25 (New York and Oxford: Berghahn, 2009).

Stephan, Erika, 'Himmel, strahlender Azur? Eine Unterhaltung mit Wolfgang Pampel', in Wolfgang Engel and Erika Stephan (eds.), *Theater in der Übergangsgesellschaft: Schauspiel Leipzig 1957–2007* (Berlin: TdZ, 2007), 98–100.

Stuber, Petra, *Spielräume und Grenzen: Studien zum DDR-Theater* (Berlin: Ch. Links, 1998).

Ulbricht, Walter, *Zum neuen ökonomischen System der Planung und Leitung* (East Berlin: Dietz, 1966).

Ullrich, Renate, 'Demetrius und Dmitri', in *Mecklenburgisches Staatstheater Schwerin*, ed. Linzer, 155–62.

——*Schweriner Entdeckungen: Ein Theater im Gespräch* (East Berlin: Dietz, 1986).

Vaget, Hans Rudolf, 'Act IV Revisited: A "Post-Wall" Reading of Goethe's Faust', in Jane K. Brown, Meredith Lee, and Thomas P. Saine (eds.), *Interpreting Goethe's Faust Today* (Columbia, SC: Camden House, 1994), 43–58.

Das Verhör in der Oper: Die Debatte um die Aufführung 'Das Verhör von Lukullus' von Bertolt Brecht und Paul Dessau, ed. Joachim Lucchesi (Berlin: BasisDruck, 1993).

Vietor-Engländer, Deborah, *Faust in der DDR* (Frankfurt/M.: Peter Lang, 1987).

Walther, Joachim, *Sicherungsbereich Literatur: Schriftsteller und Staatssicherheit in der Deutschen Demokratischen Republik*, rev. edn. (Berlin: Ullstein, 1999).

Weigel, Alexander (ed.), 'Der Fall *Die Sorgen und die Macht* 1962/63: Dokumente', *Blätter des Deutschen Theaters*, 19 (1991), 609–52.

Wekwerth, Manfred, *Erinnern ist Leben: Eine dramatische Autobiographie* (Leipzig: Faber & Faber, 2000).

Wenzke, Rüdiger, *Die NVA und der Prager Frühling 1968: Die Rolle Ulbrichts und der DDR-Streitkräfte bei der Niederschlagung der tschechoslowakischen Reformbewegung*, Forschungen zur DDR-Geschichte, 5 (Berlin: Ch. Links, 1995).

Wilzopolski, Siegfried, *Theater des Augenblicks: Die Theaterarbeit Frank Castorfs. Eine Dokumentation* (Berlin: Zentrum für Theaterdokumentation und -information, 1992).

Winters, Peter Jochen, 'Die Reformen Gorbachevs und die DDR-Bevölkerung', in Konrad Löw (ed.), *Beharrung und Wandel: Die DDR und die Reformen des Michail Gorbatschow*, Schriftenreihe der Gesellschaft für Deutschlandforschung, 28 (Berlin: Duncker & Humblot, 1990), 31–40.

Wir treten aus unseren Rollen heraus: Dokumente des Aufbruchs Herbst '89, ed. Angela Kuberski, Theaterarbeit in der DDR, 19 (Berlin: Zentrum für Theaterdokumentation und -information, 1990).

Witteck, Günter, undated letter to Gerhard Wolfram, in Baker, '"From Page to Stage"', D17–D18.

Wohlfarth, Heinz-Bernhard, 'Utopisches Schreiben: Untersuchungen und Überlegungen zum Werk Volker Brauns' (Ph.D. thesis, Freie Universität Berlin, 2005).

Wolf, Christa, *Kein Ort. Nirgends* (East Berlin and Weimar: Aufbau, 1979).

Wolfram, Gerhard, 'Stellungnahme zur Begründung des gegen mich am 22. März eröffneten Disziplinarverfahrens', in Baker, '"From Page to Stage"', D4–D7.

——'Wir waren alle auf der Suche...', in Lennartz (ed.), *Vom Aufbruch zur Wende*, 82–9.

Index

Note: names in quotation marks denote Stasi codenames.